7x 11/12 LT 5/12

D0464889

WITHDRAWN

BLACK OPS

BLACK OPS

THE RISE OF
SPECIAL FORCES IN THE C.I.A.,
THE S.A.S., AND MOSSAD

TONY GERAGHTY

PEGASUS BOOKS
NEW YORK

BLACK OPS

Pegasus Books LLC
80 Broad Street, 5th Floor
New York, NY 10004

Copyright © 2010 by Tony Geraghty

First Pegasus Books cloth edition 2010

Interior design by Maria Fernandez

All rights reserved. No part of this book may be reproduced in whole or in part
without written permission from the publisher, except by reviewers who may
quote brief excerpts in connection with a review in a newspaper, magazine, or
electronic publication; nor may any part of this book be reproduced, stored in a
retrieval system, or transmitted in any form or by any means electronic,
mechanical, photocopying, recording, or other, without written permission
from the publisher.

Library of Congress Cataloging-in-Publication Data is available.

ISBN: 978-1-60598-097-3

10 9 8 7 8 6 5 4 3 2 1

Printed in the United States of America
Distributed by W. W. Norton & Company, Inc.

This book is dedicated to all those who practice honorably the profession of arms and those of whatever profession who choose to live one day as a lion, rather than spend a humdrum lifetime as a lamb. An increasingly conformist world needs people who do not allow others to do their thinking for them.
"What God abandoned, these defended . . ."

CONTENTS

PREFACE

The structure of this history of Special Operations Forces reflects an attempt to impose coherence on an idiosyncratic culture. A historical overview in the Introduction describes the various origins of modern Special Forces, notably the British influence on America's emerging SF teams during and after the Second World War. The major part of the narrative that follows is largely an American story. If it were a fairy tale, it would be Cinderella as told by the Brothers Grimm, with black edges, explaining how Cinderella became the Princess in response to the changing face of armed conflict. The role of the British SAS and Israel's multifarious SF teams including Isayeret Matkal, Zionism's SAS, round off the story toward the end of the book.

In practice, the chapters may be read in some other order, to suit the reader's taste, for describing Special Forces operations in any context is like trying to herd cats. Differing themes—raids, rescues, rearguard actions, psyops, spectacular failures, and occasional victories—coil around one another with little regard for a clearly defined chronology that begins "Once upon a time. . . ." Nevertheless, I have tried.

Who dares, writes.

—Tony Geraghty, Herefordshire, England, 2010

INTRODUCTION

At around 1600 hrs on 24 March 1985, Major Arthur D. ("Nick") Nicholson, Jr., a U.S. Army intelligence officer, became the last professional, regular soldier to die in the "bloodless" conflict known as the Cold War, an affair that was anything but bloodless on surrogate battlegrounds around much of Africa and Asia. What made Nicholson's case unique was that his death occurred on the well-prepared battlefield of postwar Germany, where massive tank and artillery divisions confronted one another for forty years, preparing for a nuclear Armageddon.

The manner of Nicholson's death and its political consequences are a textbook illustration of the inherent instability of Special Forces operations as well as their intrinsic importance. Uncertainty about the outcome, indeed, is a staple element of SF warfare, in which the most important decisions are usually taken on the hoof, without a fallback position if the worst happens.

Nicholson was no cowboy. Aged 37, happily married with a nine-year-old daughter, he held a degree in philosophy and a master's in Soviet studies. He spoke fluent Russian. After service in Korea he had worked in military intelligence on friendly territory in Frankfurt and Munich. At the time of his death he had made more than a hundred trips into hostile Communist East Germany.

He was one of a 14-strong espionage team implausibly identified—perhaps "moustached" or "barbouzed" would be more appropriate—as a military liaison mission to the Group of Soviet Forces, Germany. The organization, following an earlier, larger U.K. group known as Brixmis, emerged from the ashes of 1945. Its ostensible purpose in life was diplomatic, representing the wartime allies at commemorations of what the Russians styled "The Great Patriotic War" in spite of their earlier alliance with Hitler and shared invasion of Poland in 1939. There were also mundane, bread-and-butter matters such as the treatment of deserters from East to West or sometimes in the other direction.

In practice, both British and U.S. missions, often traveling off-road in specially equipped vehicles, stalked the Red Army on maneuvers, logged the movement of Soviet supplies, and, occasionally, pulled off an espionage coup. On May Day 1981, for example, Captain Hugh McLeod, a British officer, insinuated himself into Russia's latest tank (a T-64) using a forged turret key and spent an hour photographing and drawing diagrams of the interior. (The key was the work of British intelligence based on a photograph of the tank turret taken at a Red Army Day parade in Moscow.) The Soviet regiment that owned this beast was preoccupied with serious drinking on this, its public holiday. At one point in his exploration, McLeod dropped his distinctive British army flashlight. It clattered deep into the tank's interior. Haunted by the thought that the flashlight would be discovered during a routine maintenance check in Omsk, he spent another nightmarish half-hour recovering the device as his sergeant impatiently kept watch. As McLeod emerged, the sergeant wiped his boot marks from the hull of the T-64.

Some of the missions' research methods were not for the squeamish. As each phase of an exercise ended, the Russians, being provident, peasant folk, converted secret instructions into toilet

paper. The missions, suitably protected, came along afterward, dug up the debris, and carried it back to West Berlin, where one wing of their headquarters (formerly part of the 1936 Hitler Olympics building, memorable for Jesse Owens's victories) was used to sanitize the documents. The system, known to the British as Tamarisk operations, yielded vital intelligence.[1] The trick was later reinvented by the Vietcong.

Neither the Russians nor their East German clients accepted that the West was playing within the rules of cricket, or baseball, or Ivan's equivalent code of ethics. Mission vehicles, identified by U.S. and U.K. symbols "accidentally" camouflaged by good German mud, were regularly driven off the road by heavy Soviet trucks causing injury and death, events that were officially designated as accidents. The Russians often declared a formerly open exercise area out of bounds, regardless of their own published advice, and arrested mission teams for 24 hours or more. Mission vehicles, unless they were locked, were ransacked. At other times they were pursued at breakneck speed by the East German secret police, the Stasi. Some Western crews, in turn, took steps to ensure that Stasi vehicles crashed during such encounters, particularly after dark. One of the mission's favorite tricks was to disconnect brakestop lights on their vehicles, enhancing the likelihood of a Stasi road crash. If this was not a hot war, it got uncomfortably warm at times. In the surreal world of diplomacy, the mission crews, nursing their bruises, were sometimes hosted by their Russian adversaries at parties where the toasts were to Churchill, Roosevelt, and Stalin, and the same film— *The Sound of Music*—was screened yet again.

Four years after Hugh McLeod's illegal entry into a T-64, Nicholson went hunting the next generation of Moscow's armor, the 46-ton T-80. A classified official U.S. Army report makes the unlikely claim that Nicholson, with his driver, Staff Sergeant Jesse Schatz, was merely following fresh tank tracks in a training area known as Ludwigslust 475 without anything special in mind. The team approached the target—a shed where tanks were laagered—cautiously. Satisfied that all was well, Nicholson moved stealthily forward on foot, avoiding dried twigs or any other trap, to take photographs of training aids posted on a board alongside the shed. It was now late afternoon in the woods of Ludwigslust, but the light was good enough for Nicholson's Nikon L35 autofocus camera . . . and for the iron gunsight on an AK-47 brought to bear on the Americans by a young Soviet sergeant identified as Aleksandr Ryabtsev in a watch tower a mere 75 meters away.

Schatz, Nicholson's lookout, standing on the driver's seat, head and shoulders above the open sun roof, spotted Ryabtsev and shouted to his officer, "Sir! Get in the car!" Too late. The first round missed Schatz's head by inches. He "felt the whizzing of a bullet passing close to his head." Nicholson ran toward their jeep, a Mercedes Geländewagen. Schatz, back in the driver's seat, revved the engine and reversed toward Nicholson, unlocking the passenger door as he did so for the officer to make a getaway. Again, too late. A second shot brought Nicholson down. "As Schatz rolled his window down, Major Nicholson looked up at him and said, 'Jesse, I've been shot'." Another bullet hit Nicholson. "He then dropped his head into the dirt and twitched convulsively."

What followed was a sinister reminder of the lingering deaths of East Germans who were unwise enough to try to escape to West Berlin across the shooting gallery that separated the two parts of the city at that time. Schatz, carrying a first aid bag, exited the vehicle to aid his stricken officer. By now, Ryabtsev had closed to within a few feet and waved Schatz away. As Schatz hesitated, Ryabtsev brought his rifle up to his shoulder, pointed it at Schatz's head and curled his finger round the trigger. Schatz retreated. Nicholson died some time later from multiple abdominal wounds.

A diplomatic rumpus ensued, but there were larger stakes involved for Washington and Moscow than the killing—described by the Pentagon as murder—of a single Special Forces officer. A new Soviet leader, Mikhail Gorbachev, was steering his country toward a rapprochement with the West. A few months after Nicholson's death, Gorbachev and President Ronald Reagan met in Geneva and established a working relationship. One commentator suggested: "The Reagan administration's response to this crime has been to treat it like a traffic accident covered by no-fault insurance." When Reagan himself was baited by a reporter about the incident, he replied: "Lack of outrage? You can't print what I am thinking."

Yet Nicholson's death was not an empty sacrifice in a boys' own game of cowboys and Indians. Special Forces operations are supremely about strategic impact achieved by a small elite, or they are nothing. As the Cold War finally spluttered to its close, a veteran of the U.K.'s Brixmis mission revealed: "Preserving the peace in Europe in the 20th century was sometimes a damned close-run thing. It happened sometimes that all our nine Indicators of Hostilities"—intelligence measures by which the West would predict a pre-emptive Soviet attack—"read positive. We checked the situation on the ground, looked down their gun barrels, made sure there could be no surprise attack, no war by accident. That was our major contribution."[2] It was, essentially, a victory so low-profile, so discreet as to be invisible, but nonetheless real. In that, it resembled many successful non-violent Green Beret operations in Vietnam. It prevented Armageddon more than once, thanks to the magical substance provided by SF teams known to the intelligence community as "ground truth."

This is one key to understanding the Special Forces phenomenon. Another is the unusual chain-of-command, from the grunt on the ground, via satellite in modern times or by Morse before then, to a strategic headquarters perhaps thousands of miles away, rather than a local commander. Not surprisingly, local commanders—outside the information loop but caught up in the nausea if things go wrong—do not like that arrangement. It is the curse of the cuckold: responsibility without power. They also do not care for the seemingly ragged rank structure of SF soldiers, to say nothing of their necessary lack of personal hygiene. "You can't be British soldiers," a returning SAS desert patrol was told during the Second World War. "You have beards!" The modern SAS carefully bags up its own ordure to be carried away, so as to leave no trace of its presence. Yet another protocol problem is the delicate matter of links between the Special Forces teams in the field and intelligence agencies of various sorts, some of which—running deniable operations—are themselves cut-outs for departments of state.

Another difference lies in the psychology of the self-selecting minority of soldiers who volunteer for special operations, an instrument worth more than any secret weapon or new gizmo. Most soldiers—particularly conscripts—do not shoot to kill. Special Forces soldiers do. Most soldiers do not expect to die young. SF soldiers are agnostic about personal survival. They live with a contract poetically expressed by Alan Seeger, a young American who served with the French Foreign Legion until his slow, painful end on the Western Front in 1916: "I have a rendezvous with death." Many, having survived the battle, take their own lives.

The British SAS dispenses with the pathos, though not the mysticism. One of its regimental jokes suggests: "Death is just nature's way of telling you that you failed Selection," that is, their endurance test. In February 1979 one of the regiment's heroes, Major Mike Kealy DSO, did indeed die of exposure in the moonscape wilderness of the Welsh Brecon Beacons in an attempt to prove that he could still pass the test of selection. It is no coincidence that the SAS has adopted

James Elroy Flecker's lines from "The Golden Journey to Samarkand" as its mantra:

> *We are the Pilglrims, master; we shall go*
> *Always a little further: it may be*
> *Beyond that last blue mountain barred with snow,*
> *Across that angry or that glimmering sea.*

Sir Fitzroy Maclean, one of the regiment's most talented pirates, quoted an American scientist-philosopher, Rossiter Worthington Raymond, at a memorial service for the SAS founder, David Stirling: "Death is only a horizon; and a horizon is nothing save the limit of our sight." From Orde Wingate, the fundamentalist Christian-Zionist who created the jungle Chindits, to Spencer Chapman, whose mantra "the jungle is neutral" barely explained his extraordinary survival, many of the most successful Special Forces operators were personalities imbued with a mysticism that usually resulted from adventures alone in remote parts of the world long before they became warriors.

At such times, unsurprisingly, most of them came to terms with their own mortality and remained curiously untouched—perhaps unawakened is a better word—by the mundane concerns of normal life, including job security and marriage. They could never be your average soldier-ant and rarely good husbands. They are, by nature, *ubermensch*, willful beings not cut out to be part of the lumpenproletariat. Today, in a world governed by insurance, litigation, and risk avoidance, such men and women are an anachronism. They are, as one put it, "a bunch of misfits who happen to fit together." They are also increasingly hard to find, yet more than ever in demand by Western governments.

An American authority points out: "It has often been argued that any good infantryman will make a good Special Forces soldier. This

is simply not true. . . . Not everyone is suited to operations in hostile areas, or prepared for long periods of duty with predominantly indigenous forces and without artillery, helicopter or fighter air support. Not every good infantryman can perform well in a counterterrorist unit."[3]

There is another crucial difference between the Anglo-American Special Forces community and their more numerous comrades in regular, orthodox formations. Conventional armies serving democratic governments fastidiously stand aside from the political process. Special forces, by contrast, are profoundly political, a fact reflected by the emerging U.S. doctrine of Unconventional Warfare which suggests that in some targeted states, SF teams, working through surrogates, should take over the political process behind the scenes, combining Machiavellian velvet revolution with firepower. The SAS has had much experience of manipulating tribal politics around the world—for example, in Oman's "War of the Families" (1970–1976). So, too, did American Special Forces operators playing puppetmasters to the Hmong tribes in Laos and the Montagnards in Vietnam (1961–1975).

Finally, there is the similarity between terrorists, who occupy the territory of the mind rather than geographical space until final victory is won on the ground, and Special Forces, whose agenda is pretty well the same. Both practice what is described at the beginning of the 21st century as "asymmetric warfare," or, more simply, flea v. elephant. By the time President Obama took office, military elephants were becoming intolerably costly, even for America, as well as irrelevant. The change was no better illustrated than through the innovation of unmanned drones, striking targets in Pakistan but "flown" by pilots sitting in Nevada, while Air Force chiefs clung to the image of Biggles (or even Snoopy) in his latest toy, the F-22 fighter. The unit cost of the F-22, at $350 million, was twelve times the price of the humble but effective drone, the Raptor.

The genesis of Special Forces is long and complex, often rooted in guerrilla warfare and terrorism. It is a world of moral and ethical ambiguity. It is also, in many respects, an Anglo-American story. In spite of differences of scale—Uncle Sam's resources vastly outweigh John Bull's—British innovation has consistently provided a template that the U.S. refined and developed. The first U.S. Army Ranger battalion was activated in Northern Ireland in June 1942[4] and trained by British Commandos in Scotland.[5]

The modern history of SF warfare has its origins in the Irish War of Independence, a war the British lost but from which they learned a useful lesson. Between 1916, when Irish patriots were executed by firing squads in squalid circumstances, and the Anglo-Irish Treaty of 1921, native resistance was led by Michael Collins, a postal worker and a born guerrilla. From 1919 to 1921 his killers, known as The Squad and dressed as civilians, emasculated the British intelligence apparatus thanks to a program of selective assassination. The victims included Catholics serving with the Royal Irish Constabulary (1,087 killed and wounded), the cream of Dublin Special Branch, the head of police intelligence and Resident Magistrate Bell, travelling by tram in the Irish capital when his killers tapped his shoulder and ordered him off, with the words: "Your time has come." Collins's most potent weapon was the leakage of information to the IRA from spies within the British apparatus such as Edward Broy, a double agent who smuggled out carbons of his colleagues' Special Branch reports (as did Zionists working for the British Mandate in Palestine). One by one, the lights went out in rural police stations and the IRA took over civil administration to outgovern the British.

The pattern was to be followed in many places, notably Vietnam and Afghanistan. During the first half of 1961, Vietminh terrorists and guerrillas assassinated more than 500 local government officials, kidnapped more than 1,000 and killed almost 1,500 of the local armed forces.[6] In Afghanistan in 2009, the Taliban intimidated thousands and replaced government institutions with its own, to out-govern Kabul.

In Ireland, the British responded with their own assassination squads and militas known as the Black And Tans to carry out random atrocities, striking out blindly against much of the civilian population in a reprisal campaign. A previously equivocal population, often agnostic about Irish republicanism, responded as do most people to the experience of collective punishment. They fought back. They became the political and cultural sea within which the piranhas of the IRA could swim with impunity. As a result, in 1921 Collins went to London to sign the treaty that recognized his republic (twenty-six counties out of thirty-two) as an independent country.

It was the first time in modern history that an indigenous guerrilla army had defeated a major occupying power. The war of the flea was back, inspiring Indian and Zionist resistance to British rule. For example, Robert Briscoe, the only Jew to serve with the Irish Volunteers in 1916 and subsequently Lord Mayor of Dublin, assisted pioneers of the Zionist terrorist movement Irgun Zvai Leumi, triggering a process that finally levered the British out of Palestine. Yitzhak Shamir, Israel's seventh prime minister, used the nom de guerre "Michael" in honour of the Irish rebel leader, Michael Collins. Of a later generation, Chaim Herzog, a Belfast-born, Dublin-educated barrister and British intelligence officer, became a Haganah leader when Britain withdrew from Palestine. Later he was President Herzog, his country's head of state.

The Irish techniques of resistance had very deep roots. Since the defeat of King James II on the Boyne in 1690, irregular warfare was the Irish way, brutal and up-close, in which farm implements were used as tools of decapitation. The process is deodorized by nationalist historians as "the physical force tradition." Collins's historic success in liberating Ireland did not inhibit some of his own warriors from assassinating him when he failed to secure the six northern counties of Ireland, regardless of the fact that Ulster was a hornets' nest of embattled Orangemen who had settled in that country before, for example, the state of Massachusetts was formally established. The Irish War resumed in Northern Ireland in 1969 and splutters on still.

Two British officers serving in Dublin took a dispassionately professional interest in Collins's campaign and latched onto its possible application elsewhere, for Britain still had an empire to defend. There was J. F. C. (Joe) Holland DFC, a former Royal Flying Corps pilot who flew Lawrence of Arabia and raided Sofia in his stringbag flying machine during the First World War. Holland was a brilliant, irascible man whose impatience was reflected by his habits of chain smoking and book-throwing. Another veteran of the Irish War was Colin McVean Gubbins, artilleryman and Western Front survivor who served with the British mission in Russia in 1919—learning from the Bolshevik revolution—followed by three years in Ireland. Gubbins was a small, dark, intense man. Those who knew him sensed a coiled, concentrated energy beneath the soft, courteous voice. His deadly courtesy reminded some of Churchill's declaration of war on Japan in 1941. This concluded: "I have the honour to be, with high consideration, Sir, Your obedient servant." Challenged to justify such fulsome language, Churchill replied: "When you have to kill a man, it costs nothing to be polite."[7]

In 1938—the year Hitler seized part of Czechoslovakia with the boast, "Thus we begin our march into the great German future!"—Holland began another sort of quest. He was put in charge of a U.K. War Office research team studying guerrilla warfare, known as Military Intelligence (Research), or MI/R. A few months later, Gubbins joined him, from a quasi-diplomatic posting in the Sudetenland. Holland, says the SOE historian M. R. D. Foot, "thought that the army needed, to act in front of it and on its flanks in fluid battles, small teams of dedicated soldiers: extra-brave, extra-enterprising men, who could raid spots vital for the enemy and cause damage and dislocation quite out of proportion to their own small numbers."

The Czech crisis prompted the Chief of the Imperial General Staff, Lord Gort, to approve covert operations—including sabotage— against Nazis in that country months before Britain's formal declaration of war on Germany in September 1939. Gubbins was busy writing field service manuals entitled *The Art of Guerrilla Warfare, The Partisan Leader's Handbook,* and *How To Use High Explosives,* works for which there were no precedents in the gentlemanly English culture of war studies. These slender documents were basic statements of principle for guerrillas, later summarized by the Special Air Service in Borneo as a policy of "shoot-and-scoot."

In parallel, the British Secret Intelligence Service, in April 1938, set up its own guerrilla warfare department, known as Section D, headed by yet another chain-smoking military engineer, Laurence Grand, to consider the use of sabotage. The catalyst, again, seems to have been the Nazi occupation of Sudetenland (initially endorsed at Munich in 1936 by British appeasers of Hitler including Prime Minister Neville Chamberlain). It would be four years before members of the Czech resistance, trained by the U.K., retaliated with the ambush and assassination of Reinhard Heydrich, the Butcher of Prague, an event that provoked the Lidice atrocity.

The war triggered by Hitler's invasion of Poland in September 1939, Churchill's emergence as Prime Minister, and the Anglo-French defeat in France in 1940 put the planners of MI/R and Section D under enormous pressure to find a means to hit back, preferably by stirring up resistance in Occupied Europe. Thereby, Churchill hoped to reduce the chances of a successful German invasion of Britain. The result, in July 1940, was amalgamation of MI/R and Section D to create a hell-raising team known as Special Operations Executive, commanded by Gubbins. Hugh Dalton, Minister of Economic Warfare and SOE's political master, argued: "We have got to organize movements in enemy-occupied territory comparable to the Sinn Fein movement in Ireland, to the Chinese guerrillas now operating against Japan." Dalton did not mince his words about the methods to be employed: "Industrial and military sabotage, labor agitation and strikes, continuous propaganda, terrorist acts against traitors and German leaders, boycotts and riots."

In parallel with such notions, following Russia's invasion of Finland in November 1939, brave spirits from the Scots Guards and other British regiments took practical steps to go to another war. They learned to ski. But after Finland was overrun, they went instead to Norway to confront the Wehrmacht in a campaign that had little success. It produced one useful by-product: commando expertise and training in Scotland where many Special Forces, were trained.

Later historians did not agree about Britain's espousal of guerrilla warfare. John Keegan, for example, argued: "Our response to the scourge of terrorism is compromised by what we did through SOE. . . . Means besmirch ends. SOE besmirched Britain." M. R. D. Foot, the SOE historian, disagreed. He suggested: "The Irish [thanks to the example set by Collins and followed by SOE] can thus claim that their resistance provided an originating impulse for resistance to tyrannies worse than any they had to endure themselves. And Irish resistance, as Collins led it, showed the rest of the world an economical way to fight wars, the only sane way they can be fought in the age of the nuclear bomb." That still holds good. At the sunset of the nation state, asymmetric warfare is where it is at, though few conventional soldiers warm to that idea.

In June 1940, following the savage experience of the British retreat from Dunkirk after Hitler's invasion of France, yet another secret formation was raised to run an IRA-style campaign of resistance against a German army occupying Britain. The generic name for those involved was "stay-behind" forces and the concept they embodied was to have an impact on American involvement in European security long after the war ended. The British stay-behind cells were named, with deliberate official vagueness, "GHQ [for 'General Headquarters'] Auxiliary Units." These, in turn, were divided between Operational Patrols—murder squads in civilian clothes—and Special Duty operators who were to run intelligence and communications. The operational patrols were drawn from a cross-section of apparently average, peaceful citizens in largely rural areas. They included local worthies such as doctors and ministers of the church as well as gamekeepers and farmers. They accepted that if their resistance campaign were endangered by their neighbors, then they would be obliged to murder the neighbors to preserve operational security. The oath they took was confirmation of a basic human instinct, to kill another human being if the terms are right. The Special Duties operators included a number of women specially trained to use clandestine radios.

As well as an underground army to function in the event of Nazi occupation, Britain's battered morale needed a tonic, the healthy stimulus and satisfaction of striking back rather than cowering on a small island waiting for the worst to happen. Churchill gave it just that. An orchestra of Special Forces teams was invented to conduct what General Sir John ("Shan") Hackett (a paratrooper and survivor of the epic Arnhem battle) romantically described as "the British way of war." It was, he suggested, a style exemplified in the desert during the First World War by T. E. Lawrence ("Lawrence of Arabia"). As Hackett saw it, "The British way in war is not that of continental nations, whose natural tendency is generally towards massive frontal action. It lies more in looking for the open flank and then making use of it, often by distant action and deep penetration. The British method lies predominantly in the oblique approach. . . ." Hackett attributed this style to the fact that the British created an empire through command of the sea. "Wherever there was blue water, there was an open flank. . . ." In warfare, the desert, jebel, and jungle have much in common with the ocean.

America could lay claim to a similar inheritance. In the Revolutionary War against the British, Francis Marion ("the Swamp Fox") was one of many irregular warriors who harassed the Redcoats from the flanks. Sgt. Ezra Lee piloted the first submarine—*The American Turtle*—in an attack on the Royal Navy's HMS *Eagle* in New York harbor within weeks of the Declaration of Independence. Some of these lone rangers drew the short straw. In 1780, one of Washington's generals, Benedict Arnold V, deserted in a fit of pique to join the British, who made him a brigadier. John Champ, an Irish-born First Sergeant of Cavalry, was commissioned by General Washington to pretend to follow Arnold's example and switch sides. The real purpose of Champ's "defection" was to kidnap Arnold at gunpoint and bring him before American justice. Champ joined the British in New York, but his plan to snatch Arnold at gunpoint failed when Arnold changed his program, unexpectedly. Champ returned to his own lines, to be treated as if his desertion were genuine. The dirt clung to him for the rest of his life.

The groups that emerged from Churchill's initiative included the Special Operations Executive (commanded by Churchill to "set Europe ablaze"); the Long Range Desert Group, a deep reconnaissance team; the Special Air Service, a raiding regiment that became the godfather of America's Delta Force; the Special Boat Service; Lovat Scouts; Wingate's jungle commando, known as the Chindits, Laycock's Commandos in the Mediterranean, the Jewish-manned Special Interrogation Group (dressed in German uniforms), Popski's Private

Army, the Small Scale Raiding Force, Force 133, Force 136, Force 266, Rose Force, Ferret Force, Gideon Force and the Norwegian Independent Companies, among others.

Their progress was followed with interest from neutral America by Colonel (later Major General) Bill Donovan. In 1940 and 1941, Donovan made discreet trips to London, then under intensive aerial attack by the Luftwaffe, to assess British resilience. After meeting Churchill and the U.K.'s intelligence mandarins, he was persuaded that the U.S. needed a unified intelligence service similar to Britain's Secret Intelligence Service. He was also impressed by the old lion's adoption of unconventional warfare. In 1942, back in uniform as an army colonel, he created the Office of Strategic Services, modeled on the U.K.'s Special Operations Executive. Donovan's vision was even larger than Churchill's. He hoped to create "a new instrument of war" that combined psychological warfare, intelligence penetration, and propaganda—"the arrow of initial penetration"—with commando raids in support of conventional operations.[8] One of the most successful OSS teams was Detachment 101, operating in Burma with local Kachin warriors and initially led by British planters who knew the country. It was later described as "the only real military unit in the OSS."[9] Donovan had to ram support for the force through the opposition of conventional commanders. Other operational OSS groups were sent to the Pacific, Corsica, Italy, Greece, Yugoslavia, and France, usually in a reconnaissance role. The OSS also helped train Mao's Red Army and the Vietminh in French Indochina as allies against Japan. Like the training of mujahideen guerrillas in Afghanistan, it led to historical "blowback." By the time President Truman closed it down, OSS employed around 40,000 people (4,500 women), including desk analysts, psyops warriors, and spies, as well as guerrillas. Its functions and hundreds of its operators were inherited by the CIA. After the war, both CIA and postwar SIS inherited the OSS initiative

known as Gladio, a right-wing underground force operating in much
of western Europe.

There was another, less public, American inheritance from
Britain. In the spring of 1942, the U.K.'s Combined Operations
chief Lord Louis Mountbatten (assassinated by the IRA in 1979)
brought the attention of U.S. General George C. Marshall to an
Arctic warfare program that matured to include an American
tracked vehicle named the Weasel. "General Marshall concluded
that an elite force recruited in Canada and the United States would
be the best military organization for conducting raids and strikes;
he selected an American, Lieutenant Colonel Robert Tryon Fred-
erick, to assemble, organize, train and command the U.S.-Canadian
1st Special Service Force. Made up of three regiments of two battalions each, the unit became a separate branch of the service (as
did Special Operations Command much later) with the crossed
arrows of the Indian Scouts . . . as its insignia. The men were
trained in demolitions, rock-climbing, amphibious assaults and ski
techniques and were given basic airborne instruction. They fought
under Allied command with great bravery and considerable success
in the Aleutians, North Africa, Italy and Southern France. The 1st
Special Service Force got its nickname, 'the Devil's Brigade,' during
the Italian campaign from a passage in the captured diary of a dead
German officer who had written: 'The black devils are all around us
every time we come into line and we never hear them.'"

If the Second World War witnessed an unparalleled evolution of
irregular and special forces, the bonds formed during that conflict
were complicated by changing loyalties as Hitler's defeat came within
sight. On 5 June 1941, what British Communists perceived to be an
internecine blood feud between capitalist powers—a conflict of no
consequence to the British working class—was miraculously transformed into The Great Patriotic War as a result of Hitler's invasion of

Soviet Russia. British Communists, suddenly discovering a voice, called for "a Second Front, now!" to relieve Russia.

Until then, Britain had stood alone in defying Hitler. But now, with western Europe under the Nazi jackboot, Britain's only ally was Moscow. Churchill immediately promised Moscow "whatever help we can," though the U.K. was itself under U-boat siege and food in Britain was strictly rationed. Until then, Communist Russia had kept faith with the Nazis, with whom Stalin shared a non-aggression pact while the German blitzkrieg overran the West and the Red Army invaded Poland. The U.S., gripped by isolationism and anti-British sentiment personified by Joseph Kennedy (the most hostile U.S. ambassador ever dispatched to London), could not enter the fight, officially, until Japan's day of infamy and its destruction of America's Pacific Fleet at Pearl Harbor in December 1941.

In spite of the Bolshevik scare that permeated the U.K. Establishment for decades after the Bolshevik revolution of 1917, emerging British Special Forces (often regarded with fear and loathing by the Foreign Office and the Secret Intelligence Service) were prepared pragmatically to work with Communist partisans when that offered the best chance of victory over the Nazis. In the Malayan jungle, British officers such as Spencer Chapman found a valuable ally against the Japanese in the Communist guerrilla Chin Peng, who was awarded an Order of the British Empire (OBE) before he was hunted by the SAS in the postwar jungle as a terrorist. In French Indochina Lucien E. Conein, an American OSS officer, supported Ho Chi Minh. In Yugoslavia, Fitzroy Maclean, personally briefed by Churchill, was instructed to support the Communist Tito rather than a Yugoslav monarch. But, it was rumored, he was careful not to accept the first parachute his controllers offered him on his journey into Nazi-occupied Yugoslavia.

A sound Tory, Maclean had doubts about supporting the

Communist partisans in Yugoslavia, with obvious implications for what would happen in that country after the war. Churchill asked Maclean: "Do you intend to make Yugoslavia your home after the war?" Maclean said he did not. "Neither do I," snapped Churchill. "And that being so, the less you and I worry about the form of government they set up, the better. That is for them to decide. What interests us is, which of them is doing the most harm to the Germans."[10]

But in March 1946, when the war was won, Churchill—ever the pragmatist, so long as his side won—saw things differently, with a speech at Fulton, Missouri, recording the fact that a new Cold War had begun with the descent of an iron curtain across Europe from Stettin to Trieste. In truth he had been uneasy about his Soviet ally for some time. As the last shot was fired in 1945, he ordered General Montgomery "to be careful in collecting German arms, to stack them so that they could easily be issued again to the German soldiers whom we should have to work with if the Soviet advance [westward] continued." Others had the same idea. As Professor Richard Aldrich observed, "many components of Special Operations Executive marched out of the Second World War into the Cold War without breaking step." But if the old right wing of SOE had a postwar agenda, so did the West's wartime allies, including Mao Tse-Tung, Chin Peng OBE, and Zionists such as Chaim Herzog. They dreamed of independence and the day when the beaten men would come into their own.

Thanks to the evolution of Special Forces, the Second World War was one in which indigenous underground resistance movements also came of age. Their activities, like those of Commando raiding forces, started as little more than pinpricks which boosted morale, a drumbeat of hope, similar to the BBC's repeated Morse signal beating out dot-dot-dot-dash—the letter V, for Victory—on the radio. As time passed, and the chronic problem of resupplying guerrillas surrounded by highly efficient opponents was overcome, the Resistance took on a strategic importance, cutting enemy supplies before and after D-Day in France and undermining Japanese logistics in Burma and the Philippines.

There can be no doubt about the strategic impact of the SAS during the Western Desert War, or that of the American Detachment 101 in Burma. David Stirling, Paddy Mayne, and Jock Lewes, founding fathers of the SAS in 1942, led raids that destroyed around 300 to 400 German aircraft on the ground. By the end of the war in the Far East, Detachment 101 was a guerrilla army of 10,000 locals aided in the field by 120 Americans. It had killed or wounded around 15,000 Japanese, rescued 425 allied airmen, and wrought havoc on the coherence of the Japanese war machine in Burma.

In the Japanese-occupied Philippines, 1941–1944, Pentagon historians have concluded, "support to and in some cases leadership of irregular resistance to Japanese forces [by OSS] was an unqualified success. It stands as a premier example of what military planners today call operational preparation of the environment." An archipelago spread over 7,100 islands was impossible to control. Philippine resistance "collected and transmitted intelligence on adversary order of battle, conducted hit-and-run raids against Japanese forces and provided de facto government services in a number of villages." Like the British in Ireland prior to 1921, the Japanese resorted to "reprisals against villagers for attacks; imprisonment, torture or execution of suspected guerrillas, seizure of crops and livestock, turning the population against them."

Like Detachment 101, by 1944 the British General Wingate's Chindits were operating in divisional strength. In western Europe, German efforts to resupply defenses in Normandy were constantly sabotaged by the Maquis and SAS. The SAS historian Philip Warner reckoned that in France, Belgium, Holland, and Germany, 2,000 SAS soldiers killed or captured 7,733 enemy and captured 4,784, not including an entire division of 18,000 that surrendered to the SAS. Around 700 motor vehicles had been captured or destroyed, as were seven trains, 29 locomotives, and 89 individual trucks. Another 33 trains were derailed. Railway lines were cut 164 times.

In spite of these successes, Special Forces emerging from the Second World War were damned with faint praise, or none. When victory was won in Europe, a Foreign Office mandarin carped: "I know that the SOE have done good work in the past but I am confident that their time for useful work is over. Their contacts can only be dangerous." The ruler's fear of an untamed Praetorian Guard is a historical cliché. In 1831 the French packed the Foreign Legion off to North Africa "to remove from France those officers and soldiers, French or foreign, who were felt to be awkward, excitable or frankly dangerous to the new monarchy" of Louis-Philippe. Others among the top brass were ungenerous about the impact of Special Forces. Field Marshal Bill Slim, commanding the 14th Army in Burma, concluded in his memoir, *Defeat Into Victory*, "Such formations, trained, equipped and mentally adjusted for one kind of operation only, were wasteful. They did not give, militarily, a worthwhile return for the resources in men, material and time that they had absorbed." At the same time, Slim acknowledged that in future, there would be a place for small units behind enemy lines to kill or kidnap individuals and "inspire resistance movements." Inspiration requires only limited resources. Serious resupply by clandestine means requires commitment by high command, in the face of objections from more regular formations. Slim was not the only skeptic. The official British history of the war concluded that Orde Wingate's Chindits, operating far beyond the front line in Burma, had achieved nothing much more than proof that large numbers of men could be supplied by air.

Britain's Special Forces godfathers are still criticized by some historians. The writer Max Hastings comments: "These exotic elite groups ill served the wider interests of the British Army, chronically short of good infantrymen for the big battlefields. Thanks to Churchill, too many of Britain's bravest soldiers spent the war conducting irregular and self-indulgent activities of questionable strategic value."[11] As the war approached its bloody end, Special Forces received muted applause in messages sent indirectly to the men in the field, many still active behind the lines. Eisenhower described Donovan as "The Last Hero." In 1944, the future president also sent this message to an SAS brigadier: "I wish to send my congratulations to all ranks of the Special Air Service Brigade on the contribution which they have made to the success of the Allied Expeditionary Force. The ruthlessness with which the enemy have attacked Special Air Service troops has been an indication of the injury you were able to cause to the German armed forces both by your own efforts and by the information which you gave of German disposition and movements. Many Special Air Service troops are still behind enemy lines; others are being reformed for new tasks. To all of them I say, 'Well done and good luck!'"

Montgomery, in a radio message to troops behind the lines, shortly before the ill-fated Arnhem operation, relayed via Lieutenant General "Boy" Browning, said: "The operations you have carried out have had more effect in hastening the disintegration of the German 7th and 5th Armies than any other single effort in the army . . . which no other troops in the world could have done. . . . The strain has been great because operating as you do entails the most constant vigilance and cunning which no other troops are called upon to display. . . . To say you have done your job well is to put it mildly. . . ."[12]

The political compass, marking a decisive change of wartime loyalties, started to shift first in Italy in 1944 when Team X-2, an element of OSS led by the paranoid James Angleton, made common cause with Prince Valerio Borghese, whose men had "hanged [anti-Fascist] partisans from lampposts all over Italy" during the Mussolini years. Initially, Angleton's target was a German stay-behind unit in Rome, whose men were summarily rounded up and shot by their former Italian allies. Later, by devious means, the OSS became the CIA and former Fascists signed up to join the anti-Communist secret army known as Gladio funded by untraceable dollars siphoned from the Marshall Aid budget.

The political scenery changed rapidly elsewhere. Between 1946 and 1951 Britain smuggled 127 German scientists and engineers to Australia, including thirty-one Nazi Party members and six SS officers. These experts included the chief of the Messerschmitt aircraft team and a nuclear physicist working on Hitler's proposed atomic bomb.[13] Immediately after the Third Reich fell in 1945 the Gestapo war criminal Klaus Barbie—a torturer responsible for the deaths of 4,000 French patriots—worked for British and American intelligence services in Germany even as an SAS War Crimes Investigation Team known as "Secret Hunters" scoured Germany to track such people down. Secret Hunters, pursuing Germans who had butchered their wartime colleagues, made the "mistake," if mistake it was, of fighting yesterday's war against Hitler rather than today's new war against Stalin. They were appointed on 15 May 1945 by Lieutenant Colonel Brian Franks, whose soldiers of 2 SAS had been executed in Occupied France.

The Hunters stayed in business until January 1947, by which time the British Socialist government believed it had consigned the SAS brigade and Special Operations Executive, with its 2,000 agents, to history. Officially disbanded in 1946, SOE was able to transfer 280 of its operators to the Secret Intelligence Service (MI6) on 15 January that year. At first, they were part of a Special Operations Branch running agents and guerrillas into the Balkans and Russia. Many of them were betrayed by the British spymaster Kim Philby. Philby was also a KGB colonel, a senior SIS officer, and one of the Cambridge University spy ring. In a twist worthy of a le Carré novel, both Philby and one of the SIS agent-runners, Mark Arnold-Foster, a Royal Navy SF veteran, were doubling as journalists for the same London newspaper (the *Observer*) for some time, each still deeply entangled in the spying game. After Russia exploded its first nuclear weapon in 1949 and gradually deployed viable warheads, direct action, SOE-style, was regarded as too risky, though spying flourished.

In the United States, a similar process was happening. President Harry Truman, a Democrat, did not like the willful, freebooting style of the OSS leader Bill Donovan. The OSS was disbanded, only to re-emerge as a shiny, new Central Intelligence Agency employing many of the same people. Like the wartime SAS, it seems to have mutated in a series of steps. With its formal dissolution in October 1945 its identity was preserved by an entity known as the Strategic Services Unit until a year later, when the SSU became the Central Intelligence Group under Rear Admiral Sidney W. Souers and Admiral William Leahy. In 1948 the CIG was absorbed by the Central Intelligence Agency. The CIA's Special Operations Division then took on the mantle of the OSS, from early operations in Tibet in 1956 and Southeast Asia during the Vietnam War by way of Angola in the seventies, to the ongoing Afghanistan conflict.

In time, significant differences emerged between the fighting style of OSS and SOE on one hand, and the modern CIA on the other. Postwar Special Forces teams are usually just that: close-knit teams that sometimes act as the executive arm of the intelligence agencies. Frontline CIA and SIS personnel regularly function undercover as individuals in a hostile environment, a job requiring enormous emotional and intellectual stamina. As field officers they work at a distance from their controlling bureaucracies and sometimes, unsurprisingly, become alienated from it. One of these was John Stockwell, Angola case officer from 1974 to 2002, whose reflections on Agency incompetence at that time reflect pain (for Stockwell was an idealist who loved Africa) as well as anger. He is not alone in his emetic response to the moral ambiguities of *realpolitik*. But then, intelligence operations are often rough trade.

The survival of the British SAS, alone among wartime special forces teams, is a textbook example of political escape and evasion. Though the Socialist Attlee government had decreed that it must die, in the gloomy corridors of the War Office a cell was created in 1946 to consider the future of SF, if any. It concluded that in the next European war, there would be no static front lines. It acknowledged that small parties of stay-behind forces could punch above their weight, so long as they did not try to take over the functions of SIS or become a reborn SOE. In what was an obvious compromise between letting the government have its way over Special Forces and covering an unguarded military flank, the War Office gave its blessing, in principle, to the creation of a reserve, Territorial Army (National Guard) unit. This exercise was massaged by the ubiquitous Brian Franks, former boss of 2 SAS in Occupied France. Over later years, he would emerge as a key player in the continuance of special operations, not all of them not authorized by government. Between 1946 and 1947, Franks took two initiatives. First, he arranged for the Gladio network, promoted by the SIS chief, Sir Stewart Menzies, in various European capitals, to be serviced by British Liaison Officers who were former SAS and SOE operators.

He also arranged for a respected reserve regiment, the Artists Rifles, to be reborn as 21 SAS (Artists). Founded in 1859, the Artists accommodated such creative spirits as William Morris, Wilfred Owen, and Noel Coward and turned them into soldiers. It was disbanded in 1945 and reconstituted as an officer-training team two years later. By a process that is still not clear, Brian Franks arranged for the resurrected Artists to become 21 SAS (Artists) (Reserve). A humble national guard unit, 21 SAS was licensed to prepare for a stay-behind role in Germany, to wage guerrilla war against the Warsaw Pact invaders and identify targets for nuclear weapons. It was an awesome responsibility for weekend soldiers. The SAS reservists prepared by digging large holes in German soil for use as hides. In time, it found another role as a supplier of deniable soldiers for clandestine missions far from Europe and a recruitment agency for well-connected mercenaries.

On the other side of the world, in the Malayan jungle, a very different sort of conflict was about to have a decisive impact on the SAS phenomenon. In the spring of 1948, ethnic Chinese Malayans, armed with an arsenal of British and Japanese weapons, began an offensive to turn Malaya into a Communist state. The emergency had a shocking beginning. Small groups of armed Chinese entered rubber plantations, seized their Chinese foremen, and summoned villagers to witness the executions of these alleged enemies of the people. On 16 June, three young Chinese men cycled into Elphil Estate in Perak and shot dead a fifty-year-old British planter, Arthur Walker. A few miles away, Ian Christian and his manager, J. Alison, were bound to chairs and murdered in the same fashion.

One of the most charismatic leaders of the insurgency was Chin Peng, OBE. During the Japanese occupation, Chin Peng had worked with British agents from SOE's Force 136 and with Spencer Chapman, to whom he was "a true friend." It is believed that Chin took part in the London Victory Parade in 1945. But then he turned his guns on Britain. He became leader of the Communist guerrillas and took to the jungle. Chin Peng did not give up easily. His war against the British and Malayan governments continued until 1989. In 2008 he was living in exile in Thailand, hoping to return to Malaysia.

In 1950, to fight this latest jungle conflict, Brigadier "Mad Mike" Calvert, a wartime SAS commander and heavyweight boxing champion, was instructed to raise a force able to survive in the jungle for long periods, taking the battle to the Communists on their own ground. It was a novel idea at the time. Calvert was expected to create the new force almost overnight. He raised the Malayan Scouts, which he then renamed the Malayan Scouts (SAS). They were a very mixed bunch. There were some excellent veterans from SOE, SAS, Ferret Force, and Force 136. A squadron of 21 SAS reservists, on its way to the Korean War, was diverted to join the Scouts. Calvert also recruited 1,000 volunteers from Rhodesia (now Zimbabwe), a group that would re-emerge later as "C" Squadron, SAS. It still exists as a phantom squadron. Calvert also acquired some cowboys whose units were glad to be rid of them. A handful of National Service conscripts was added to the mix. At that time, the prolonged selection process for which the SAS would become a world leader did not exist. Calvert once told the author that the Scouts had similarities, in his mind, with the Black And Tans as an ad hoc formation that could be readily disbanded if it provoked a political row. No surprises there: most Special Forces units are ad hoc, temporary entities, dispersed when their work is done.

The Scouts were withdrawn in 1951 to be reorganized as 22 SAS Regiment under a new commander and retrained at the Jungle Warfare School, Kota Tingi, Malaya. This was an interesting establishment that subequently trained Australian SAS soldiers to fight in Vietnam. Run by a veteran jungle fighter named John Cross, it replicated some very evil jungle booby traps used by the Vietminh. Colonel Cross could imitate most of the bird calls to be heard in the jungle. During the Second World War, serving with the Gurkha Rifles, he heard a call that belonged to a nocturnal bird. It was mid-morning. He set up an ambush and waited for the Japanese patrol to walk into it. Did it work? "We killed every last one of them," he once told the author.

The reformed SAS returned to the jungle, fighting an often clandestine campaign until around 1960. Further changes from 1955 resulted from the appointment of Lieutenant Colonel George Lea, an Arnhem veteran, as commanding officer. Lea sacked the most ineffective officers and recruited some new talent including Lieutenant Peter de la Billiere. As a Lieutenant General, he led British forces in the first Gulf War in 1990–91. By 1956 five SAS squadrons totaling 560 men were operating in the Malayan jungle. But as yet, it was still an ad hoc force of the sort envisioned by Calvert.

There was always a darker side to the evolution of these forces. The same individuals who led by heroic example in the Second World War were thrust into counter-insurgency campaigns later perceived as "dirty wars" in which they matched evil with evil. Some of the Long Range Desert Group, having taken prisoners who were an embarrassment—since there was no provision for POWs in the Libyan desert—considered murdering their captives. They did not do so, releasing them to their fate in the wilderness instead. In the 1930s Wingate's Special Night Squads, hunting Arab saboteurs in Palestine, were disbanded because of the treatment of captives and because the SNS, like the Black And Tans in Ireland in the twenties, provoked rebellion rather than suppressing it. During the Vietnam War, the "Green Beret" affair arose from the unauthorized killing of a double agent in 1969.

The most dramatic moral breakdown, however, occurred not within the ranks of the SAS or SBS or their American counterparts in OSS, but within the U.S. Navy's equivalent, the Office of Naval Intelligence, which lubricated the Allied advance across Sicily in 1943 by cutting deals with the Sicilian Mafia, first in New York and later in Sicily itself. This morally ambiguous strategy was followed, as noted above, by OSS arrangements in Italy with Italian Fascists in the organization of shadowy anti-Soviet "stay-behind" units known loosely as "Gladio," The Sword. In Italy, Germany, and Belgium, assassins linked to Gladio teams took direct action against communists suspected of being part of a fifth column prepared to run Moscow-puppet governments should the Red Army overrun the country. The organic nature of the Gladio network after it was secretly adopted by NATO made it inevitable that some operators from these countries were trained in Britain and elsewhere by British and American Special Forces, just like the Afghan mujahideen in the 1980s.

For four decades after the Second World War, the British army had two commitments. The first, known as Priority One, was the defense of Western Europe from attack by the Red Army and its allies. These were edgy times. As Sir John Killick, British ambassador to NATO, told the author during those years: "We know their capabilities. We do not know their intentions." It does not seem to have struck Western governments that the Soviets, having lost 26 million dead following Germany's invasion, might have felt it needed buffer states in eastern Europe as an insurance against a repeat performance. Meanwhile, the scope for Special Forces activity in the frozen strategy of the Cold War in western Europe—a potential conflict between lumbering dinosaurs—was limited, but not impossible.

In Europe, throughout the forty-four years of the Cold War, a team unconnected with the wartime freemasonry founded by Gubbins and Stirling operated across the front line alongside the agent-running arm of SIS. It was known as Brixmis, or the British Commanders'-in-Chief Mission to the Soviet Forces in Germany. It answered to the intelligence secretariat of the Ministry of Defence and unlike the Foreign Office (vide Philby) or CIA (vide Aldrich Ames) it was never penetrated by the KGB. Its intelligence product was sent to Washington, sometimes before it reached London. From 1947 two similar, smaller missions worked alongside Brixmis. These were the U.S. Military Liaison Mission, which included Major Arthur Nicholson, and the French MLM.

Meanwhile in Northern Ireland, from 1969 onwards, following the explosion of resentment among the minority Catholic population in response to the government's failure to provide equal rights in voting, jobs, and housing, street politics boiled over to become an insurgency and full-blown campaign of terrorism. British intelligence was caught by surprise, asserting that the IRA was a long-dead, moribund force. After Gunner Robert Curtis, the first British casualty, was shot dead in Belfast in February 1971, elements of Britain's conventional "green army," configured for the European battlefield, adopted counter-insurgency methods including the use of civilian clothes, burglary of private homes to plant bugs, and assassination. For many soldiers it was a schizophrenic experience in which the Red Army's tank divisions were the threat during one operational tour, while at other times the Improvised Explosive Device teams of the IRA awaited them on the back streets of Belfast.

On the other side of the world, France and then the United States were fighting a war of attrition in Indochina. The French wanted to restore their pre-war colonial rule. The U.S. was persuaded by George Kennan and John Foster Dulles to adopt a policy of containment to rein in international communism. The locals wanted self-determination and were willing to take help from any quarter, as they had done during the Second World War. Step by reluctant step, the U.S. entered the Vietnam quagmire, unsupported, for once, by the U.K. Like Afghanistan today, it was a conflict fought against a guerrilla army, one in which the occupation of minds counted for more than the control of territory. It saw the emergence of strategic hamlets and free-fire zones (based on British experience in Malaya); civic action teams; recruitment of aboriginal tribes; and a steady buildup of Special Forces such as the Mobile Guerrilla Force and including, from 1962, the creation of Navy SEALs (described by their Vietcong adversary as "devils with green faces") on the orders of President Kennedy.

The same themes resonated in Afghanistan, but as Secretary of Defense Robert Gates pointed out: "Apart from Special Forces and a few dissident colonels there has been no strong, deeply rooted constituency inside the Pentagon or elsewhere for institutionalizing the capabilities necessary to wage asymmetric or irregular conflict."[14] By 1970, as U.S. planes began bombing the Ho Chi Minh trail and American combat troops invaded Cambodia, the British SAS focused on another Communist threat: the potential loss of Oman, gateway to the Gulf, as a result of the despotic, medieval regime of the Ruler, Sheik bin Taimur, a British client. A coup d'etat was engineered by SIS in which the Ruler was replaced by his son, Qaboos, then under house arrest. The first problem was to open a line of contact with Britain's chosen Ruler-in-waiting, Qaboos. His father grudgingly allowed him to receive cassette tapes of music. Qaboos, as a result of his service with the British army in Germany, liked Scottish marches, with bagpipe accompaniment. The tapes, purchased at Harrods store in London, were doctored so as to interrupt the music and relay voice messages from a friend who had shared his room at Sandhurst military college.

After a brief exchange of fire during which Bin Taimur shot himself through the foot, the deposed leader was spirited away by the Royal Air Force to live out his final years in London. The SAS then moved stealthily into Oman with a strategy that placed as much emphasis on winning hearts and minds as war-fighting. It included the extraordinary gamble of persuading the untamed hill tribes of Dhofar to change sides by arming them with the latest British rifles, and paying them. A similar strategy saved Western policy in Iraq in 2006 with the difference that in Oman, SAS officers and sergeants worked in isolation with these "turned" enemy, at great personal risk. The Oman Cocktail—a blend of bribes, development, and firepower—became a signature tactic of the SAS, out of sight of the

British public in a six-year war without limits that ended in 1976. This SAS victory had momentous implications. It ensured Allied control of the gateway to the Hormuz Strait, the Gulf, and its oilfields for decades.

The SAS phenomenon spread to postwar U.S. Special Forces thanks to Charlie Beckwith, a young American officer attached to 22 SAS from 1961 to 1963, during which time he took part in jungle operations in Malaya. The informal structure and idiosyncratic discipline of the SAS that paid little heed to rank, only quality, puzzled and fascinated him. He wrote later: "I couldn't make heads or tails of this situation. The officers were so professional, so well read, so articulate, so experienced. Why were they serving within this organization of non-regimental and apparently poorly disciplined troops? The troops resembled no military organization I had ever known. . . . Everything I'd been taught about soldiering, been trained to believe, was turned upside down."[15]

In 1977, having survived an apparently fatal gunshot wound in the abdomen in Vietnam, "Chargin' Charlie" set up an elite Special Forces known as Delta, carefully modeled on the SAS. Its first major test, Operation Eagle Claw—an attempt to rescue U.S. diplomat-hostages in Iran in 1980—was a fiasco caused by poor air support and a top-heavy command structure. Beckwith's ironic verdict, in a message to his British buddies, was: "You can't make chicken chow-mein out of chickenshit." Delta survived that disaster to become the cutting edge of U.S. unconventional warfare in Iraq from 2003 and Afghanistan after campaigns in Mogadishu, 1993, Central and South America. When the going got tough in Congress, ingenious spirits in Washington such as Marine Colonel Oliver North recruited plausibly deniable ex-SAS British mercenaries and others to operate in Nicaragua. They included Major David Walker, formerly of the SAS and later head of the enigmatic private military company KMS.

The creation of Delta Force was followed in 1979 during the Iran crisis by the Foreign Operating Group (later redesignated the Intelligence Support Activity, aka "The Activity"). In 1981 the ISA ran signals intelligence that led to the rescue of U.S. General James Lee Dozier, a prisoner of Italian Red Brigade terrorists for forty-two days, as well as the 1984 attempted liberation of Bill Buckley, the CIA station chief held captive, then murdered, in Beirut; and operations in Panama, Colombia, Somalia, Bosnia, Iraq, and Afghanistan. Like Britain's Special Reconnaissance Regiment, a unit with roots in the Irish conflict, the ISA also acts as the eyes and ears of an SF strike force such as Delta.

By the time the Soviet empire collapsed in 1989, Special Forces had emerged as the means to resolve political conflict without the penalties that would accompany the use of conventional armies. It was even, as M. R. D. Foot argued, a political safety-valve, a useful alternative to the mutually assured destruction of nuclear war. This history examines the validity of that novel proposition, and much else, including the extent to which the SF phenomenon licenses its operators, notably deniable warriors in the private sector, to enter a legal gray area where others dare not go, boldly or otherwise. In practice it uniquely inhabits an ambiguous zone between the politically acceptable and the officially deniable. Success comes at a cost, usually in civil liberties. Population control methods employed in the conflicts of Malaya, Vietnam, Kenya, Afghanistan, and Pakistan and internment without trial in Northern Ireland were all case studies in misapplied social engineering.

But in an age of asymmetric warfare, the techniques developed by Special Forces represent the future. The economic crash of 2008 forced the Obama regime to take a long, hard look at the Pentagon's spending. Hillary Clinton, Obama's Secretary of State, espoused instead Professor Joseph Nye's concept of "smart power," acknowledging that "most of the conflicts we are facing and will face rarely have a military solution." It was probably no coincidence that in the final months of the Bush presidency, after prolonged campaigns that ended in stalemate, at best, a blueprint for a new military strategy emerged from the Pentagon. Dated September 2008, the 280-page document is Field Manual 3-05.130, entitled *Army Special Operations Forces—Unconventional Warfare*. It defines the Bush administration's foreign policy aims as "furthering capitalism to foster economic growth . . . and promote the sale and mobility of U.S. products to international consumers" accompanied by such strategic tools as "global freedom of action" and "full spectrum dominance."

To create a new world order, after the American model, the authors concede, will be the work of generations. While orthodox military dominance, worldwide, is a given, the main thrust of policy is the use of Unconventional Warfare, "working by, with or through irregular surrogates in a clandestine and/or covert manner against opposing actors." It is also "a fundamentally indirect application of power that leverages human groups to act in concert with U.S. national objectives." That means training and supporting surrogates in "the full range of human motivation beyond narrowly defined actual or threatened physical coercion."

It is, essentially, war on the mind, manipulating public opinion. "The objective of Unconventional Warfare (UW) is always inherently political. . . . Some of the best weapons do not shoot." Furthermore, "A fundamental military objective in Unconventional Warfare (UW) is the deliberate involvement and leveraging of civilian interference in the unconventional warfare operational area. . . . Actors engaged in supporting elements in the Unconventional Warfare Operational Area may rely on criminal activities, such as smuggling, narcotics or human trafficking. . . . The methods and networks of real or perceived criminal entities can be useful as supporting elements of a U.S.-sponsored UW effort."

The foot soldiers in the new model army of irregulars will be "unconstrained by sovereign nation legalities and boundaries. These forces may include, but are not limited to, specific paramilitary forces, contractors, individuals, businesses . . . black marketers and other social or political 'undesirables'." The new doctrine also proposes a license to kill opponents pre-emptively, "against non-state actors operating within or behind the laws of nonbelligerent states with which the United States is not at war . . . or within a hostile state that harbors, either wittingly or unwittingly, these nonstate actors within its borders."

There is more of the same. The new doctrine also synthesizes the darker history of Special Forces: the ruthless use of surrogates including civilians, involvement in the international drug trade, compulsory relocation of civilian populations, the redirection of aid programs for political purposes, and the subversion of unfriendly governments lubricated by the dollar (as in Iran in 1951). It is a pragmatic handbook for illegal military activity to "ignite a new era of global economic growth through free markets and free trade." Its attraction to increasingly hard-up military planners facing an open-ended Global War On Terror, could be irresistible unless the Obama administration puts its foot on the ethical brake. Whatever the outcome, we cannot understand the complexities of modern, asymmetric warfare without an awareness of the sophisticated, multi-layered organism that we loosely describe as "Special Forces."

What began as Irish and American resistance to British rule, mutating into organized guerrilla warfare, terrorism, and propaganda-by-deed along the way, has now become a military discipline in its own right. It does not discard the old skills such as, for example, the British commando raid on the Bruneval radar station in 1942 to snatch enemy secrets. But it has matured into a matrix of intelligence-led military and non-military techniques requiring skills beyond the reach of the most talented conventional soldier including public relations, deception operations, undetectable burglary, and esoteric foreign languages—alongside, of course, high-altitude freefall parachuting, scuba diving, and a voluminous knowledge of exotic weapons. There is much more. SF medical specialists learn field surgery by practicing on anaesthetized, live animals freshly wounded by gunshot to ensure realistic blood pressure levels as the medics try to revive them.

The SF military agenda is now expected to include unconventional military operations as part of a conventional campaign (see Britain's amphibious South Atlantic War, 1982); counterinsurgency (Iraq, Afghanistan); combat rescue (Entebbe 1976); peacekeeping including weapons verification (Balkans); snatch operations to arrest wanted war criminals; rescuing allied pilots from enemy territory; and surrogate warfare using deniable paramilitaries. As an IRA joke about the SAS ran: "An SAS man is one who can speak half a dozen different languages while disguised as a bottle of Guinness."

Yet during the decades since 1945, Special Forces have won acceptance among governments at the pace of a funeral march and are sometimes—as in Yemen in the sixties—dependent on private funding. Official caution is understandable. Elements of the British Army in Northern Ireland during the Troubles, operating as armed men in civilian clothes, came chillingly close to resembling the death squads of South America. If democratic governments have a nightmare about their armed forces, it is that some adventurous spirits will act as a law unto themselves.

As we have seen, the SAS was officially reinvented with the inauguration of a reserve unit, 21 SAS (the Artists' Rifles) in 1947 and its merger with an ad hoc formation, the Malayan Scouts (SAS) in 1951. With the end of the Malayan Emergency, two of the regiment's four squadrons were axed. They were restored in the 1960s, following the regiment's successful cross-border secret war in Indonesia. Yet it was not until the regiment's unique skills were demonstrated during the Iranian Embassy siege in London in 1980—when what started as a terrorist "spectacular" became a British government "spectacular"—that it was accepted as a national institution. What little was published about the SAS until then, in postwar years, was almost universally hostile, the work of left-wing journalists.

American Special Forces, in spite of their many successes in defending a political lost cause in Vietnam, were also slow to win permanent status in America's order of battle. This time the leading opponents of Special Forces were the military top brass. "These [Special Forces] units," writes Colonel John T. Carney, one of their pioneers, "had been virtual pariahs within their own armed services . . . in the late 1970s" after Vietnam. "In the aftermath of post-Vietnam downsizing, funding for special operations forces had been cut by 95 per cent. Reaching a low point in 1975, special operations forces constituted only one-tenth of one per cent of the entire defense budget."[16] No official U.S. document even dared mention Special Operations Forces as such until 1981, when a Defense Guidance from the Pentagon directed all the armed services to develop an SOF capability.

Five years later, Senators Sam Nunn and William S. Cohen persuaded Congress to legislate for an independent U.S. Special Operations Command, to ensure that never again would "ad hoc rescue forces have to be cobbled together to meet the kind of time-urgent crisis that the Son Tay and Iranian rescue missions represented." Another year passed before Special Operations Command could begin work as the lead agency against terrorism, just in time for Afghanistan, America's first major Special Forces conflict since Vietnam. SF soldiers do not give up easily. As Colonel Bill Cowan USMC, one of the pioneers of the reborn Special Forces, told the author: "Following my retirement I went to serve as an aide on Capitol Hill. I got the last laugh with the bureaucracy. I was one of five key staffers who wrote the legislation which created the Special Operations Command in Tampa. The Pentagon and the White House fought the legislation tenaciously. But they lost and the command was formed, leading to Spec Ops being at the forefront as they are today."

The story of the CIA's paramilitary Special Operations Group followed a similar pattern. Following many misadventures involving coups and assassinations in the 1980s, the Agency retreated to intelligence analysis allied to satellite surveillance. The SOG "knuckle-draggers" were moribund. George Tenet, CIA Director, started the SOG renaissance in 1998. The process accelerated rapidly after 9/11. The budget grew by millions of dollars, equipment including jet aircraft, cargo planes reminiscent of Air America and Vietnam, speedboats, and Predator drones armed with Hellfire missiles.

Their remit, handed down by President George W. Bush, was to use "all necessary means" to track down and kill Osama bin Laden and his cohorts. Not everyone—notably Defense Secretary Rumsfeld—was happy about the duplication of effort that SOG—though tiny compared with SOCOM—represented. In 2005 he unveiled yet another weapon to be added to SOCOM's armory. The Marines had landed, in the form of 2,500 Leathernecks and sailors, to form an entity known as MarSOC (U.S. Marine Corps Forces Special Operations Command). The Corps was not happy, for it creamed off some of its best reconnaissance talent. It was also to lead to one of the most disputed firefights of the Afghanistan campaign, and an equally controversial court of inquiry that exonerated two officers.

The CIA, meanwhile, continued to recruit experienced Special Forces officers, training some of them for a year in spycraft, before sending them back to the Agency's preferred form of low-profile warfare, working through proxies. For a time after the invasion of Afghanistan in 2001, a symbiosis of CIA and SOCOM functioned well enough. But the two have continued to work in parallel, rather than together, with mixed results. Should President Barack Obama conclude some time in the future that U.S. strategy requires a change of emphasis, away from hearts-and-minds toward Howard Hart's nostrum ("Cut a deal with the Taliban") and Senator Biden's wish to concentrate America's fire on al Qaeda, it suggests a bigger role for the CIA's Special Operations Group. The McChrystal formula, publicly endorsed by the president at West Point on 2 December 2009 to safeguard civilians in the most populous areas of Afghanistan (and, by extension, Pakistan), will be a task that emphasizes the role of SOCOM, as well as the poor bloody infantry.

But we should note that Obama, a cautious cat, hedged his bets. He said: "The struggle against violent extremism will not be finished quickly and it extends well beyond Afghanistan and Pakistan. . . . Unlike the great power conflicts and clear lines of division that defined the 20th century, our effort will involve disorderly regions and diffuse enemies. So as a result . . . we will have to be nimble and precise in our use of military power. Where al Qaeda and its allies attempt to establish a foothold—whether in Somalia or Yemen or elsewhere—they must be confronted by growing pressure and strong partnerships." Note the language. For "nimble and precise," read "Special Operations Forces." At the military level, the symbiosis of CIA paramilitary and intelligence combined with Special Operations Forces was the future war-fighting model beyond the time-limited commitment to Karzai's Afghanistan.

CHAPTER 1

THE PRESIDENT'S DILEMMA

The president's dilemma was apparently insoluble. For nine years American Special Forces, working through corrupt surrogates in a faraway land unaccustomed to the ways of democracy, had fought a losing battle against well-organized insurgents prepared to lay down their lives. The ranks of the U.S. Army's own locally recruited irregulars were penetrated by spies. The local CIA headquarters had been blown up by a suicide car bomber. Washington's client head of state was a political liability, in office thanks to a fraudulent vote. There was also a healthy trade in illegal drugs, beyond everyone's control except, perhaps, the Mafia's. Yet for the White House to accept defeat and pull out would have catastrophic effects upon America's credibility and probably cause serious damage to the country's domestic security as enemies gathered strength from the belief that the U.S. giant was mortally wounded. The president's answer was to send thousands more GIs surging into a combat zone where it was often impossible to identify the enemy. Vietnam, 1963, was not a good place to be. Nor was Dallas. On 22 November that year, President Kennedy was assassinated there.

For years, it seemed, the Vietnam War was the Alpha and Omega of Special Operations Forces, years in which a renascence of SF tactics led to belief in the nostrum that small elite ground forces directing massive air power was a winning combination, until the strategy failed and Special Forces units were consigned to oblivion for almost two decades.

More than thirty years after Vietnam, while there were many apparent similarities with the West's involvement in Afghanistan— the commentator John Richardson, in *Esquire* magazine, was one of the first to identify "Six Signs That Afghanistan Could Be Another Vietnam"—there were significant differences. As President Obama noticed: "Each historical moment is different. You never step into the same river twice and so Afghanistan is not Vietnam . . . but the danger of not having clear goals and not having strong support from the American people, those are all issues that I think about all the time." In Vietnam, America's enemy was armed by both China and Soviet Russia. More than 320,000 Chinese soldiers served in North Vietnam, as did 3,000 Russians. Between 12 and 29 December 1972 Soviet-supplied missiles, possibly manned by Russian soldiers, shot down thirty-one U.S. B-52 strategic bombers over Hanoi. While the Taliban received covert backing from Pakistan's intelligence service from time to time, it could not match the external aid supplied to the Vietnamese communists. In any case, under U.S. pressure, covert Pakistani aid to the Taliban was a wasting asset.

According to Obama, to compare Afghanistan to Vietnam is a false reading of history. In his West Point address he said: "Unlike Vietnam, we are joined by a broad coalition of forty-three nations that recognizes the legitimacy of our action. Unlike Vietnam, we are not facing a broad-based popular insurgency. And most importantly, unlike Vietnam, the American people were viciously attacked from Afghanistan and remain a target for those same extremists who are plotting along its border."

Casualty statistics also have a tale to tell. During the Vietnam War, America sacrificed an average of 5,800 lives every year, for a decade or, to express the problem another way, 400 each week at the peak of attrition. During the first eight years of U.S. fighting in Afghanistan, the average was just over seventy. The nature of the enemy in the two campaigns also differed significantly. The Afghans were ferocious fighters conditioned to believe in suicide bombing. On home ground, in close-quarter battle, they were brave and clever tacticians. But even after thirty years of conflict, they remained unsophisticated warriors. The Vietnamese—contrary to the peasant image projected by some Western journalists—often proved themselves superior to the U.S. even on the arcane battleground of electronic warfare. "The Vietcong cryptographers learned their lessons well. While throwing an electronic fishing net into the ether, they regularly reeled it back in bulging with American communications, but they seldom used radios themselves. While they listened to broadcasts from Hanoi on inexpensive transistor radios, they sent messages back to their commands with couriers, except in dire emergencies. For local communications they often used radios with very low power, frustrating American eavesdroppers." They also cracked many American codes.[17]

The Vietnamese had been trained by, and had fought a successful war against, the French including the Foreign Legion. In those days, the Legion was buttressed by hardened German veterans who had fought the Soviets on the eastern front in the Second World War. When Vietnam was part of the French colony of Indochina, it was run during the Second World War by the

Japanese Army of occupation with the complicity of the Vichy French administration. As President Franklin D. Roosevelt said in 1944: "The case of Indochina is perfectly clear. France has milked it for one hundred years. The people of Indochina are entitled to something better than that."[18]

Resistance to Japanese wartime occupation in Vietnam was led by a founder member of the French Communist Party in Paris. His name was Nguyen Hai Quoc, which he later changed to "He Who Lights The Way" or, in Vietnamese, Ho Chi Minh. In that struggle, the Vietminh resistance movement received weapons, training, and moral support from America's Office of Strategic Services led locally by Colonel Lucien Conein, a Paris-born OSS warrior and former French soldier trained by the British. He was known, thanks to his sinister appearance, as "Black Luigi" among Corsican drug gangs in Saigon, who were his friends. Later, working for the CIA, he would play a significant role in the evolution of South Vietnam.

After a war of attrition lasting nine years from 1945 to 1954, the French were defeated by the Vietminh at Dien Bien Phu. French officers had resisted a recommendation from the U.S. Military Assistance Advisory Group in Indochina to train and arm a local army. In fact most American expert advice was rejected by French colonial officers who were still living, culturally, in the 1930s. Finally, during the last days of the epic fifty-five day siege of Dien Bien Phu, a French representative proposed to Douglas MacArthur II, a State Department official, a joint venture called Operation Vulture (Operation Vautur). This was "that the United States could commit its naval aircraft to the battle of Dien Bien Phu without risking American prestige or committing an act of belligerency by placing such aircraft, painted with French insignia and construed as part of the French Foreign Legion, under nominal French command for an isolated action consisting of air strikes lasting two or three days."[19] The

4

military options considered to bail out the French included the use of tactical nuclear bombs.

Congress argued that the British should be brought into the planning. Churchill vetoed the idea, reasoning that China might invoke a pact with Soviet Russia, provoking a reprisal nuclear attack on U.S. bases in England. The proposal ended there. Vietnam was then divided into two political entities at a Geneva peace conference. Though a dividing line was drawn on the 17th parallel, it meant little in practice for months, during which time thousands of refugees and agents of various sorts moved north or south and back again.

In this fluid situation, months of dynamic covert action followed. An American team under Lucien Conein, then a major, spirited out of North Vietnam fourteen paramilitary teams for training on allied soil. An American Special Forces officer known as Captain Arundel "engineered a black psywar strike in Hanoi: leaflets signed by the [Communist] Vietminh instructing Tonkinese how to behave for a Vietminh takeover in early October [1954] included items about property, money reform. . . ." This exercise terrified anyone with money in the bank. "The day following the distribution of these leaflets refugee registration [of people wishing to leave the country] tripled. Two days later Vietminh currency was worth half the value prior to the leaflets."[20]

In another psyops adventure, "the patriot we've named Trieu Dinh had been working on an almanac for popular sale, particularly in the northern cities and towns we could still reach. Noted Vietnamese astrologers were hired to write predictions about coming disasters to certain Vietminh leaders and . . . to predict unity in the south. The work was carried out under Lieutenant Phillips, based on our concept of the use of astrology for psywar in Southeast Asia. Copies of the almanac were shipped by air to Haiphong and then smuggled into Vietminh territory."[21] (In later years, the CIA would put the Koran to a similar purpose in Soviet-occupied Afghanistan and elsewhere.)

Back in Saigon, meanwhile, a team of Saigon Military Mission officers supported by CIA and Air Force personnel working like coolies, throughout the night, moved tons of cargo to build an anti-communist resistance movement in North Vietnam. "All officers pitched in to help as part of our 'blood, sweat and tears.'" By early 1955, the group had smuggled into North Vietnam 8.5 tons of materiel including fourteen agent radios, 300 carbines, 90,000 rounds of carbine ammunition, fifty pistols, 10,000 rounds of pistol ammunition, and 300 pounds of explosives. Around 2.5 tons were delivered to a separate team of agents in Tonkin, run by Major Fred Allen and Lieutenant Edward Williams, "our only experienced counter-espionage officer." The remaining materiel was cached along the Red River by Conein's Saigon Military Mission, helped by the Navy.

Conein's team in the north left with the last French troops on 9 October. It "had spent the last days in Hanoi in contaminating the oil supply of the bus company for a gradual wreckage of engines in the buses, in taking the first actions for delayed sabotage of the railroad (which required teamwork with a CIA special technical team in Japan who performed their part brilliantly), and in writing detailed notes of potential targets for future paramilitary operations. U.S. adherence to the Geneva Agreement prevented Conein's team from carrying out the active sabotage it desired to do against the power plant, water facilities, harbors and bridges. The team had a bad moment when contaminating the oil. They had to work quickly at night, in an enclosed storage room. Fumes from the contaminant came close to knocking them out. Dizzy and weak kneed, they masked their faces with handkerchiefs and completed the job."[22]

Fred Allen's group, meanwhile, "was able to mount a Vietnamese paramilitary effort in Tonkin from the south, barely beating the Vietminh shutdown in Haiphong as his teams went in, trained and equipped. . . ." A Navy team (Navy Lieutenant Edward Bain and Marine Captain Richard Smith) "became our official smugglers, as well as paymasters, housing officers, transportation officers, warehousemen, file clerks, and mess officers. . . .

"On 21 November, twenty-one selected Vietnamese agents and cooks of our Hao paramilitary group [run by Fred Allen] were put aboard a Navy ship in the Saigon River, in daylight. They appeared as coolies, joined the coolie and refugee throng moving on and off ship, and disappeared one by one. . . . The agents were picked up from unobtrusive assembly points. . . . The ship took the agents, in compartmentalized groups, to an overseas point, the first stage in a movement to a secret training area."[23]

The Vietminh, in their turn, were targeting the National Army of South Vietnam for subversion. "It was given top priority by the Vietminh Central Committee for operations against its enemy and about 100 superior cadres were retrained for the operations" months before the Geneva agreement was signed. "We didn't know it at the time, but this was the Saigon Military Mission's major opponent, in a secret struggle for the National Army. . . ."[24] Not only was much of South Vietnam's army penetrated by the communist woodworm. The civilian infrastructure was also subverted by thousands of communist sympathizers who were to be targeted, in due course, by a program of "neutralization." This, more often than not, meant the assassination of those holding public office in South Vietnam while wearing two hats, sometimes after a trial *in absentia* before a military tribunal, a process curiously similar to Israel's quasi-judicial process in dealing with terrorist suspects. The system, codenamed Phoenix, permitted interrogation, confession, and imprisonment where this was feasible. It was constructed by the CIA and run, in practice, by South Vietnamese entities in partnership with elements of U.S. Special Forces including the Studies & Observations Group (later the Special Operations Group).

The toxic effect of the North's subversion was to last throughout most of the armed conflict that was to follow. But the North's greatest ally in alienating a majority in the South was Ngo Dinh Diem, an American puppet, elected president in a rigged referendum. In Saigon, for example, Diem received 133 per cent of the vote. Diem had a talent for making unnecessary enemies, notably the Buddhists (the majority religious group) whom he persecuted and non-Vietnamese minority ethnic groups such as the Montagnards living in remote mountain areas, contemptuously dismissed by Saigon as savages unworthy of civil rights.

Communists including veterans of the Resistance against Japanese occupation were able to exploit the disaffection that resulted. A few years later, the British, saddled with a despotic local Ruler in Oman, faced a similar dilemma. In time, the CIA would orchestrate a coup against their client Diem followed by his assassination (possibly stage-managed by Lucien Conein). Both Oman and Vietnam became surrogate free fire zones as part of the Cold War. In 1954, the U.S. Military Assistance Advisory Group, Vietnam, still active after the French defeat, had a core strength of just 342 men. U.S. Special Forces based in Okinawa worked in Vietnam for the first time in 1957 to train fifty-eight Vietnamese commandos at Nha Trang. China and the Soviets had already offered help to the Vietminh in North Vietnam two years earlier. In South Vietnam, clashes between the Vietcong and Army of the Republic of South Vietnam (ARVN) rose gradually until 1960. From January 1960 to September that year, the number of "contacts" surged from 180 to 545. The heat was on.

As the stability of Vietnam cracked, then disintegrated over the next eighteen months, the role of U.S. Special Forces assumed increasing importance. Their number and variety flourished like exotic jungle plants. They included Green Berets of 5th Special Forces Group Vietnam (2,000 men training civilian irregulars in a multitude of camps, running offensive operations from 1961 to 1971)[25] and the Military Assistance Command, Vietnam—Studies and Observations Group (MACV-SOG), a mixed team, operating from 1964 to 1972. SOG was a rival of the Green Berets, with which it fought turf wars for resources. It was invented by the Joint Chiefs of Staff as an offensive cross-border raiding force and, some suspected, a Trojan Horse to take over many CIA functions. It included men from the CIA's Special Activities Division, which also had teams deployed elsewhere. There were also South Vietnamese Special Forces trained by the U.S.; the Army Security Agency, military arm of the signals intelligence National Security Agency; local mercenaries including ethnic Chinese tribesmen and Koreans; and Special Forces airmen and sailors including Navy SEALs.

This all-singing/all-dancing, bells-and-whistles lineup could be justified by the peculiar nature of the war, or rather the two wars being fought over the same soil. As Henry Kissinger glumly noted, after defeat in 1975, Vietnam "was both a revolutionary war fought at knife point during the night within the villages; it was also a main force war in which technology [including tanks, artillery and air power] could make a difference."[26] It was a war for territory which Vietnamese communists came to dominate on the ground in spite of America's air superiority. It was a civil war in the south and a guerrilla war everywhere else. It was a very complicated, confusing struggle meant to halt a "domino principle," through which, viewed from Washington, one anti-communist regime after another would fall to America's enemies if every one was not kept upright.

It was a conflict that required agile thinking as well as action. The Special Forces process was propelled enthusiastically forward by President Kennedy, who saw these unconventional warriors as the ideal tool for counterinsurgency. The U.S. Navy SEALs owed their foundation in 1962 to support from Kennedy, a wartime torpedo boat hero. In large areas of Vietnam such as the Mekong Delta, and elsewhere during the flood season, the SEALs became a riverine commando force. But in general, U.S. Special Forces were defined at that time by the job they were asked to do rather than by what they did best. The Green Berets learned quickly how to acquire, adapt, and exploit the uses of non-violent aid to the civilian community. Winning friends became an equal option alongside killing the enemy, though not by SOG. Theoretically, the Green Berets were in Vietnam as trainers and guests of the Diem government. Theoretically, South Vietnamese soldiers were in charge of operations. But when the shooting started, the South Vietnamese handed over command and control to their American Special Forces mentors, at the last moment. In Afghanistan, the local National Army sometimes behaved the same way.

In late 1961, the U.S. Mission in Saigon assigned Special Forces teams to train irregulars drawn from minority groups including the Montagnards to defend their own villages. It was a momentous decision that started very modestly in the strategic Central Highlands. In February 1962, after protracted negotiations with tribal leaders, the first team started work in the village of Buon Enao. Crucially, it included a Special Forces medical sergeant. Medicare, plus the right to carry and bear arms, were major inducements to persuade the aboriginals to cooperate. They had been disarmed by the Diem regime in Saigon in the late 1950s. Now their arms—crossbows and spears—were restored to them. Soon they were being trained to use the M15 Armalite rifle, approved because it was "compatible with the small stature, body configuration and light weight of the Vietnamese soldier."[27]

The villages were fortified and defended by civilian volunteers along lines developed by the British in Malaya. Weapons and pay were supplied outside the usual military accounting system, direct to Special Forces personnel and then filtered through local village headmen and tribal leaders. This unusual arrangement was described euphemistically by the Brits as "porter money," that is, funds originally used "to pay locals who were employed as porters to help carry the regiment's heavy equipment through the jungle."[28] (This revelation, if true, sheds a curious light on the legendary ability of the SAS to march through the jungle for many days without external support.) The system of unaccountable direct payment to friendly irregulars through Special Forces was open to fraud and, in the British case, was the subject of repeated internal enquiries. In Vietnam, formal accountability was replaced by "quick-reacting supply and procurement procedures."

In 1962, control of what was now known as the Civilian Irregular Defense Group (CIDG) program was transferred from the diplomats in Saigon—the U.S. Mission—to a new entity, U.S. Army Special Forces (Provisional) Vietnam. On the ground, training and—by default—leadership was the work of Army Green Beret teams. By December 1963, "Special Forces detachments, working through counterpart Vietnamese Special Forces units, had trained and armed 18,000 men as strike force troops and 43,376 as hamlet militia, the new name for village defenders."[29] The choice of "hamlet" was perhaps unfortunate, given the ambivalence of many village defenders about the Saigon government. As these statistics suggest, the village defense program had now mutated into an offensive entity, and another, the Trailwatchers, that was used as a tripwire to defend the northern border from incursions from Vietcong penetration.

"The Special Forces also helped train paramilitary forces in the 'fighting fathers' program, wherein resistance to insurgent activity centered on Catholic parish priests and a number of priests under the program made the arming and training of their parishioners possible

. . . By the end of 1964 the Montagnard program was no longer an area development project in the original sense of the term."[30] The concept of the militant priest would have been entirely acceptable to the Catholic laity, a minority in Buddhist-dominated Vietnam. Communism, a materialist creed, was anti-Christian. The U.S. president was a practicing Catholic and the Vietnamese president, Diem, was a militant Catholic who persecuted Buddhists. Irish Catholics would have understood. In their folklore, the legendary Father O'Flynn, in the tradition of muscular Christianity, lifted the lazy ones on with the stick.

The self-defense program had started as a successful Green Beret experiment at Buon Enao village in the Central Highlands. Once it was handed over to Vietnamese soldiers in 1963 it broke down, a pattern that was to be repeated. Defenders were sent away for "indoctrination," leaving settlements undefended, and pay agreements were not honored. The Vietnamese government attempted to reclaim weapons issued to the Montagnards. Ethnic Vietnamese Special Forces sometimes refused to take part in combat patrols with the "savages" because they had few trained leaders. At the same time, the Vietnamese "refused to allow leadership training in the camps."[31] Other reasons why transfers to Vietnamese control failed were summarized by the Green Berets as "mutual suspicion and hostility between the Rhade [tribesmen] and Vietnamese province and district officials; overly generous distribution by U.S. agencies of weapons and ammunition to tribesmen whose reaction to government-enforced repossession of some of the weapons was understandably hostile; apparent disregard on the part of the Vietnam government for the interests, desires, and sensitivities of the Montagnards; inadequate Vietnamese government administrative and logistical support; and, finally, failure of the U.S. authorities to anticipate these difficulties and avoid them."

In September 1964, Montagnard resentment exploded in an armed uprising. At five defended village camps, sixty-four CIDG militiamen disarmed and detained their U.S. Special Forces advisers and declared a rebellion against Saigon. At another center, irregulars belonging to a mobile strike force killed fifteen Vietnamese team leaders, then seventeen members of a "Popular Forces" group, militia absorbed into the regular South Vietnam army. In a third location, eleven Vietnamese SF soldiers were killed. Over the following year, American Special Forces brokered a better deal for the Montagnards, but the use of local surrogates to fight—a form of conflict-franchise— was always a delicate process that often left regular, conventional American forces to bear the brunt of the war.

The defended camps were themselves coming under increasingly heavy, concerted attack by Vietcong guerrillas and regular North Vietnam Army troops, assisted by militiamen who had switched allegiance, providing the attackers with precise plans of the camps. This left the American Special Forces advisers frighteningly exposed. Weaknesses exploited by the VC included the camps' isolation after nightfall. There was no reinforcement before daybreak. And as civilians in areas around the camps became intimidated by the VC, the enemy were able, with impunity, to preserve the element of surprise until large attacking forces were at the gates. The camps were now being overrun, though in some cases, such as Nam Dong, U.S. Special Forces and Nung tribesmen held their ground in spite of a heavy mortar barrage that destroyed key defensive positions including the camp radio post, followed by repeated ground assaults by hundreds of VC.

In July 1965 a team of four U.S. Special Forces Green Berets and a Vietnamese Regional Forces company holding Camp Bong Son was hit. The commander, Captain (later Major) Paris D. Davis, reported: "We had just finished a successful raid on a Viet Cong Regimental

Headquarters, killing upwards of one hundred of the enemy. The raid had started shortly after midnight. We had four Americans and the 883rd Vietnamese Regional Force Company participating in the raid. After the raid was completed, the first platoon of the 883rd company broke and started to run just about the same time I gave the signal to pull in the security guarding the river bank. I went after the lead platoon, MSG Billy Waugh was with the second platoon, SSG David Morgan was with the third platoon, and SP4 Brown was with the fourth platoon.

"It was just beginning to get light (dawn) when I caught up to the first platoon and got them organized, and we were hit by automatic machine gun fire. It was up front and the main body of the platoon was hit by the machine gun. I was hit in the hand by a fragment from a hand grenade. About the time I started moving the platoon back to the main body, I heard firing and saw a wounded friendly VN soldier running from the direction of the firing. He told me that the remainder of the 883rd company was under attack. I moved the platoon I had back towards the main body. When I reached the company, the enemy had it pinned down in an open field with automatic weapons and mortar fire.

"I immediately ordered the platoon I had to return the fire, but they did not. Only a few men fired. I started firing at the enemy, moving up and down the line, encouraging the 883rd company to return the fire. We started to receive fire from the right flank. I ran down to where the firing was and found five Viet Cong coming over the trench line. I killed all five, and then I heard firing from the left flank. I ran down there and saw about six Viet Cong moving toward our position. I threw a grenade and killed four of them. My M16 jammed, so I shot one with my pistol and hit the other with my M16 again and again until he was dead.

"MSG Waugh started to yell that he had been shot in the foot. I ran to the middle of the open field and tried to get MSG Waugh, but the Viet Cong automatic fire was too intense, and I had to move back to safety. By this time SSG Morgan, who was at the edge of the open field, came to. He had been knocked out by a VC mortar round. He told me that he was receiving sniper fire. I spotted the sniper, and shot him in his camouflaged man-hole. I crawled over and dropped a grenade in the hole killing two additional Viet Cong.

"I was able at this time to make contact with the FAC [forward air controller] CPT Bronson and SGT Ronald Dies. CPT Bronson diverted a flight of 105's and had them drop their bombs on the enemy's position. I ran out and pulled SSG Morgan to safety. He was slightly wounded, and I treated him for shock. The enemy again tried to overrun our position. I picked up a machine gun and started firing. I saw four or five of the enemy drop and the remaining ones break and run. I then set up the 60mm mortar, dropped about five or six mortars down the tube, and ran out and tried to get MSG Waugh. SSG Morgan was partially recovered and placing machine gun fire into the enemy position. I ran out and tried to pick up MSG Waugh, who had by now been wounded four times in his right foot. I tried to pick him up, but I was unable to do so. I was shot slightly in the back of my leg as I ran for cover.

"By this time CPT Bronson had gotten a flight of F4's. They started to drop bombs on the enemy. I ran out again, and this time was shot in the wrist but I was able to pick up MSG Waugh and carried him fireman style, in a hail of automatic weapon fire, to safety. I called for a MEDEVAC for MSG Waugh. When the MEDEVAC came, I carried MSG Waugh about 200 yards up over a hill. As I put MSG Waugh on the helicopter, SFC Reinburg got off the ship and ran down to where the 883rd company was located. He was shot through the chest almost immediately. I ran to where he was and gave him first aid. With SSG Morgan's help, I pulled him to safety.

"The enemy again tried to overrun our position. I picked up the nearest weapon and started to fire. I was also throwing grenades. I killed about six or seven. I was then ordered to take the troops I had and leave. I informed the colonel in the C&C ship that I had one wounded American and one American I didn't know the status of. I informed the colonel that I would not leave until I got all the Americans out. SFC Reinburg was MEDEVACed out. The fighting continued until mid-afternoon. We could not get the company we had to fight. The enemy tried to overrun our position two more times. We finally got reinforcements, and with them I was able to go out and get SP4 Brown who lay out in the middle of the field some fourteen hours from the start until the close of the battle."[32]

Colonel Kelly noted: "Major Davis received the Silver Star and the Purple Heart for his efforts in this action."

By now, the Green Berets of 5th Special Forces Group (Airborne), the cutting edge of the U.S. Military Assistance Advisory Group, Vietnam (MAAG) were being politically outflanked by the big battalions of the Marine Corps, the conventional Army, and changing geopolitics.

The murder of President Kennedy in November 1963 led to the inauguration of Lyndon Johnson, a credo of aerial bombing in North Vietnam and attrition on the ground in South Vietnam. MAAG was swallowed up in 1964 by a new entity, the "Military Assistance Command, Vietnam: Studies and Observations Group" or MACV-SOG. The bland title, with its academic nuances, masked a major switch of manpower and resources to the service of a new aggressive strategy that was ultimately to draw 500,000 conventional U.S. troops into the war. The Pentagon Papers revealed that three days after Kennedy's assassination on 22 November 1963, the Joint Chiefs of Staff proposed a twelve-month covert offensive in North Vietnam which would include harassment, diversion, political pressure, capture of prisoners, physical destruction, acquisition of intelligence, and diversion of Hanoi's resources. These hit-and-run operations would be non-attributable, "carried out with U.S. military materiel, training, and advisory assistance."

This would prove to be an understatement. The Pentagon Papers also record: "On 1 February 1964, the United States embarked on a new course of action in pursuance of its longstanding policy of attempting to bolster the security of Southeast Asia. On that date, under direction of the American military establishment, an elaborate program of covert military operations against the state of North Vietnam was set in motion. There were precedents: a variety of covert activities had been sponsored by the CIA since 1961. Intelligence agents, resupplied by air, had been despatched into North Vietnam, resistance and sabotage teams had been recruited inside the country; and propaganda leaflets had been dispensed from 'civilian mercenary' aircraft. But the program that began in February 1964 was different . . . because it was a *program* . . . placed under control of a U.S. military command."

This would prove to be more than mission creep. It represented a disastrous, open-ended commitment to a tottering regime in Saigon. Though the Green Beret mobile strike forces of the Special Forces Group (Airborne) soldiered on in the jungle, they were now in competition with the lavishly endowed MACV-SOG, which had its own aircraft and ships as well as ground forces including local mercenaries.

The impact of the new, covert policy was first felt in the Gulf of Tonkin on the night of 30/31 July 1964 when South Vietnamese commandos under SOG command attacked radar sites on two islands, Hon Mo and Hon Ngu, that belonged to North Vietnam. They were beaten off but then blasted away at the sites from their ships with machine-gun and cannon fire. What followed is still, in some respects, a riddle, a military whodunit. The Pentagon Papers suggest that "South Vietnam coastal patrol forces made a midnight attack, including an amphibious 'commando' raid'" on the islands. Cruising in the same area, the U.S. destroyer *Maddox* was trawling for signals and other electronic intelligence, her crew apparently unaware of the SOG raid. Intelligence intercepts were at the heart of the offensive. Cryptographers and linguists worked twelve-hour shifts inside a steel box bolted to the destroyer's deck.

From the outset, signals intelligence—SIGINT—had been part of a deadly game of hide-and-seek. The first American to be killed in this struggle, three years before, was a cryptologist named James T. Davis, from Tennessee, serving with 3rd Radio Research Unit. With a team of South Vietnam bodyguards, he was hunting Vietcong guerrillas in undergrowth near Saigon, using handheld direction-finding gear to identify the source of enemy signals. The enemy found him first. He died with his escort of nine soldiers.

At mid-afternoon on 2 August 1964, less than forty-eight hours after the strike on the islands, three North Vietnamese torpedo boats attacked the *Maddox*. "Two of the boats closed to within 5,000 yards, launching one torpedo each. . . . Maddox fired on the boats with her 5-inch batteries and altered course to avoid the torpedoes, which were observed passing the starboard side at a distance of 100 to 200 yards. . . . The third boat moved up abeam of the destroyer and took a direct 5-inch hit. . . . All three PT boats fired 50-caliber machine guns at *Maddox* . . . and a bullet fragment was recovered from the destroyer's superstructure."[33]

Fifteen minutes later, U.S. aircraft, responding to a call for help from the *Maddox*, swooped on the torpedo boats, immobilizing one and damaging the other two. All three craft limped back to port. The *Maddox* continued on her way. The following night, SOG unleashed another attack on a radar site at Vinh Son. This operation, like the first raid, was not co-ordinated with the *Maddox*'s SIGINT missions, which were run under separate U.S. Navy command.

Next day, 3 August, the *Maddox*—now accompanied by a second destroyer, the *Turner Joy*—sent a radio message claiming that it was being stalked in the darkness by sea and air. A mysterious "intelligence source" suggested that "North Vietnamese naval forces had been ordered to attack the patrol."[34] In the early hours of 4 August, colorful accounts of an onslaught by numerous enemy vessels were relayed back to the Pentagon. Later investigations, however, soon indicated that "there was no attack. But the original report of an attack was not a lie concocted to provide an excuse for escalation; it was a genuine mistake."[35] The mistakes started with inaccurate warnings from a Marine signals establishment in South Vietnam followed by misjudgments by radar and sonar analysts aboard the destroyers. Believing they were under attack, "the two destroyers gyrated wildly in the dark waters of the Gulf of Tonkin" firing at brief, suspect radar contacts as they did so.[36] The contact signals mysteriously disappeared almost as soon as they were spotted. Eventually, officers aboard the two vessels realized that their own maneuvers were the source of these apparitions. "The rudders of the two ships had caused the high-speed returns when they reflected the turbulence of the ships' own propellers." By now, however, the ships had sent word that they were under attack. This raw, uncorrected intelligence—always questionable in the fog of war—was put into the hands of Defense Secretary Robert MacNamara, who promptly called President Johnson. Three hours after the "attack" was over, the president had ordered a retaliatory air raid on North Vietnamese naval bases.

Early doubts were expressed within the National Security Agency, responsible for signals intelligence, but they were suppressed. What seemed to confirm the apparent reality of the attack was a later signal originating from North Vietnamese sources. This said that its forces had "shot down two planes in the battle area" and "we had sacrificed two ships and all the rest are ok." The signal in question, it transpired, related to the first, genuine attack of 2 August in response to the SOG raid on the islands, not the "attack" of 4 August, which never happened. It was also ambiguous. In better translation, the phrase "we had sacrificed two ships" probably meant "two comrades," which would be consistent with the casualties suffered by the communists on 2 August. The communist signal was itself inaccurate in claiming that two U.S. aircraft were shot down.

The mistake in translation had not gone unnoticed where it mattered. President Johnson later admitted: "The North Vietnamese skipper reported that his unit had 'sacrificed two comrades.' Our experts said that this meant either two enemy boats, or two men in the attack group." He went further with the acid comment: "Hell, those damn stupid sailors were just shooting at flying fish" or, according to another source, at whales. In an increasing atmosphere of war excitement, most of the raw SIGINT data was suppressed, some of it forever. As the NSA historian Robert J. Hanyok, having examined what was left of the record, concluded: "The extensive amount of SIGINT evidence that contradicted both the initial attack order and the notion that any North Vietnamese boats were involved in any 'military operations,' other than salvage of the two damaged torpedo boats, was either misrepresented or excluded from all NSA-produced post-incident summaries, reports, or chronologies. . . . What was issued in the Gulf of Tonkin summaries beginning late on 4 August was deliberately skewed to support the notion that there had been an attack. What was placed in the official chronology was even more selective. That the NSA personnel believed that the attack happened and rationalized the contradictory evidence away is probably all that is necessary to know in order to understand what was done. They walked alone in their counsels."[37] And, apparently, freely away from the war they had helped precipitate. The role of SOG in precipitating the extension of the war that resulted from its raids was concealed from Congress and the American public along with doubts about the reliability of signals intelligence and the very fact of the "attack" of 4 August. As black operations go, this was an unusually dark shade.

On 7 August, Congress passed the Tonkin Gulf Resolution, giving the president authority to take "all necessary measures" to prevent further aggression. He later asserted that thanks to the same resolution, he had legal authority to escalate the war in 1965, bringing America into direct conflict with North Vietnam. Until then, thanks to the use of Special Forces, U.S. involvement had been oblique and deniable. The political impact of this misadventure might bear comparison with the explosion that sank the U.S. battleship *Maine* in Havana harbor in 1898, triggering the Spanish-American War or the unfounded intelligence, stoked up by British sources, suggesting that Iraq possessed weapons of mass destruction in 2003.

From February 1965 a prolonged aerial bombardment of North Vietnam was launched to fulfill the threat by General Curtis LeMay, "We're gonna bomb them back into the Stone Age." To protect the bases from which the attacks were launched, the first 3,500 U.S. Marines were dispatched to Da Nang. By December the number increased to almost 200,000. The scene was now set for combat between regular U.S. and North Vietnamese ground forces. Initially, U.S. planners believed in the fiction that a ground war could be won by air power alone; or at least, that the North Vietnamese could be arm-twisted into an accommodation with the South. The nostrum of strategic air power was a venerable myth dating back to the British attempt to control Waziristan in the 1930s; the belief in Europe that "the bombers will always get through" after the attack on Guernica, discredited in spite of what Goebbels called "total war" against civilians in Europe during the Second World War.

Committing conventional ground forces ignored another lesson of history, including the recent French experience. This was that it is easier to put soldiers' boots on the ground in hostile territory and much more difficult to extract them.

In Vietnam, the U.S. faced the additional complication of the draft, the use of young conscripts who had not chosen to fight this war. To make matters worse, as General Alexander Haig remarked: "As a young officer in Korea, I was repelled by the policy of granting draft deferments . . . that primarily benefit the white middle class. In Vietnam, the system produced even greater abuses. A draft that was openly designed to favor the rich and the educated filled the ranks with soldiers who were neither."[38] Anti-war demonstrations at home, notably on the university campuses of Kent State and Jackson State universities in 1970, further complicated the politics of the conflict on the home front and military planning on the front line as war journalists, scenting a lost cause and political blood, were no longer on-message with the military.

Richard Nixon, elected in 1969, promised "peace with honor." His way out of the dilemma was "Vietnamization," a process of training the army of South Vietnam in sufficient numbers to enable an American withdrawal. In practice it was a politically plausible exit strategy. Whatever Special Forces might have attempted, however heroically, could no longer affect the outcome. In that sense, they could no longer have a strategic impact, or make a silk purse out of a pig's ear.

Nevertheless, they tried. After the Gulf of Tonkin incident, the Pentagon dispatched ever more conventional battalions to Vietnam. Optimism, like the odor of coffee and napalm in the morning, was in the air. In 1966, a high-level study concluded, "Within the bounds of reasonable assumptions . . . there appears to be no reason we cannot win if such is our will—and if that will is manifested in strategy and tactical operations."[39] Soon, the total

U.S. Army manpower committed to Vietnam was nudging toward 500,000. The Pentagon had plans to call up reservists.

In the fall of that year, U.S. Special Forces of 5th Special Forces Group (Airborne) were charged with setting up mobile guerrilla forces able to operate in enemy territory undetected for up to sixty days, supplied every five days or so by bomber aircraft dropping modified 500-pound napalm containers, using genuine air strikes as cover. It was a parallel operation to the SOG adventures.

The mobile strike forces were to run intelligence-gathering recce missions, raid enemy camps, mine roads, ambush convoys, direct air strikes, and even search (unsuccessfully, as it turned out) for American and allied soldiers held prisoner by the VC. "Once in the area of operations the unit became a true guerrilla force in every respect except that of living solely off the land. . . . Training was simplified to the utmost for the benefit of the largely illiterate ethnic and religious minority groups who comprised the forces," though many had already had experience with the CIDG cadres defending their villages. They started by qualifying for airborne operations, including, presumably, static-line parachuting. Six weeks of training that followed covered jungle warfare techniques including silent movement, tracking, navigation, use of "special" weapons, covert infiltration and exfiltration, and preparing helicopter landing zones.[40] Though unacknowledged, it is likely that the training also covered silent killing.

The mobile strike/reaction force ("Mikeforce") groups, salted with Green Berets, melded sometimes with Special Forces "project groups," known by ancient Greek codenames such as Project Omega and Project Sigma. Each had about 600 men from 5th Special Forces Group (Airborne), as well as an advisory command group, reconnaissance and quick reaction forces. Among their many successes, they rescued many U.S. airmen shot down over the demilitarized zone ostensibly separating North and South Vietnam. "BLACKJACK 33, a typical unconventional operation, was carried out between 27 April and 24 May 1967. . . . It was the first operation in which a mobile guerrilla force was employed in conjunction with the long-ranged reconnaissance capability of a project force, Project Sigma, Detachment B-56. The operation was highly effective; 320 of the enemy were killed."[41] Pentagon planners believed that the VC and their North Vietnamese ally would cave in under the pressure of a campaign of attrition. The enemy did not have the same mystical belief in the power of the body count. Around a million North Vietnamese, civil as well as military, died during the war.

The greatest tactical success among the Project teams was scored by Gamma, which did much in its brief two-year existence from 1968 to 1970. Operating from nine sites under the pretense of running civil aid projects, Gamma infiltrated agents, including friendly Vietnamese, into ostensibly neutral Cambodia in 1968 to identify Vietcong camps there. During the preceding two years, Prince Norodom Sihanouk, the country's ruler, hedging his bets in the event of a Communist victory, had allowed Vietnamese Communists to use areas of Cambodia near the border with Vietnam as resupply bases. The supplies, including weapons, were landed at the port of Sihanoukville, in spite of U.S. diplomatic protests. South Vietnamese and U.S. Special Forces began small raids across the border, prompting counter-protests from Cambodia.[42]

Project Gamma's men were not raiders. They were a force-multiplier for what was to follow, providing 65 per cent of the intelligence on North Vietnamese base camps in Cambodia, including the number of soldiers there. By early 1969, according to one historian, the Project "had developed into the finest and most productive intelligence-collection operation the United States had in Southeast Asia."[43] It seems almost certain that this intelligence was the basis for the B-52 bomber air onslaught on Cambodia that was to follow, though some sources link the information to a North Vietnamese defector, or even aerial photography that by some magic penetrated the jungle canopy. There was one other candidate. This was the SOG. There was intense competition between the SOG and the Green Beret/Vietnamese militia teams.

The U.S. Air Force had made limited raids on Cambodia for four years before the bombing offensive of 1969, during Johnson's presidency.[44] But the escalation in March 1969 was a step-change, a response to the North's shelling of Saigon in February. U.S. intelligence had long sought the enemy's secret jungle headquarters, known by the abbreviation COSVN (for Central Office for South Vietnam) HQ. The Army's best guess was that it was in Laos. But on 9 February 1969, soon after Nixon was inaugurated as president, General Creighton Abrams, C-in-C in South Vietnam, cabled the chairman of the Joint Chiefs of Staff, General Earle G. Wheeler, with the knowledge that COSVN-HQ was in fact in Base Area 353, inside the "Fish Hook" area of eastern Cambodia, so called because it was a salient that extended into South Vietnam, northwest of Saigon. It accommodated several enemy regiments and a field hospital.

Abrams wrote: "The area is covered by thick canopy jungle. Source reports there are no concrete structures in this area. Usually reliable sources report that COSVN and COSVN-associated elements consistently remain in the same general area across the border. All our information, generally confirmed by imagery interpretation, provides us with a firm basis for targeting COSVN HQs."[45] Abrams's opaque reference to "source reports" does not identify Project Gamma, probably to preserve the secrecy surrounding long-running Special Forces cross-border operations. His proposal was subject to a stratospheric discussion in Washington, to be finally approved by President Nixon after the enemy shelled Saigon. In the early hours of

19 March forty-eight B-52 bombers pulverized Base Area 353 with 2,400 tons of high explosive. The Hanoi authorities maintained an icy silence, in public. Over the following fourteen months, Abrams served up a list of another fifteen Base Areas for aerial assault. The first attack was codenamed Breakfast. The ensuing five operations were Lunch, Snack, Dinner, Supper, and Dessert, in which B-52s mounted 3,800 raids, dropping 108,823 tons of high explosive.

After any air raid, the planners need a Bomb Damage Assessment. Since this can best be made on the spot, on enemy or disputed territory it is a job for Special Forces. In this case, it was not the Green Beret-led mobile forces that did the job but their rival, the SOG, which provided 70 per cent of BDA intelligence after these attacks.[46]

The damage done to Cambodia was reassessed in 2000 when President Bill Clinton released classified BDA data previously concealed from public view by the Air Force. Between 4 October 1965 and 15 August 1973, a total of 2,756,941 tons of ordnance was dropped on 113,716 Cambodian sites. An expert Canadian analysis by Taylor Owen and Ben Kiernan concludes that more than 10 per cent of the targeting was indiscriminate. They suggest: "Civilian casualties in Cambodia drove an enraged populace into the arms of an insurgency that had enjoyed relatively little support until the bombing began, setting in motion the expansion of the Vietnam War deeper into Cambodia, a coup d'etat in 1970, the rapid rise of the Khmer Rouge and ultimately the Cambodian genocide." The data also demonstrated that "the way a country chooses to exit a conflict can have disastrous consequences."

The disastrous consequences in Cambodia included the failure of a succession of governments, culminating in the barbaric killing fields of Pol Pot. As General Haig revealed, in the 1980s President Reagan "continued to support the Khmer resistance movement as a means of opposing the Vietnamese military presence in Kampuchea [formerly Cambodia]. "It was with considerable anguish that we agreed to support, even for overriding political and strategic reasons, this charnel figure" [Pol Pot].[47]

In the short run, however, the attacks on Cambodian soil were effective. Vietcong attacks on the South, particularly the Special Forces/CIDG camps, dropped significantly. Raids on the ground by Mikeforce teams recovered huge quantities of enemy weapons and ordnance. On the waters of the Mekong Delta, using air boats—air-propelled inflatables—and sampans, another Mikeforce group kept enemy forces on the back foot.

For the Green Berets of 5th Special Forces Group (Airborne) the end game was reached with Vietnamization in 1970, when 14,534 tribal guerrillas of the Civilian Irregular Defense Group were absorbed into the regular Vietnamese Army as Ranger battalions. The SF goal had differed from that of the conventional battalions. "The goal of conventional forces was the conventional one of winning the war. For Special Forces, however, the goal was to help the South Vietnamese win what was really their war, and that goal was never forgotten."[48]

Civil action (assistance) programs were equally impressive. "A summary of the civil action missions of the 5th Special Forces Group in the period 1964–1970 shows that the group set up 49,902 economic aid projects, 34,468 welfare projects and 10,902 medical projects; furnished 14,934 transportation facilities; supported 479,568 refugees; dug 6,436 wells and repaired 2,949 kilometers of road; established 129 churches, 272 markets, 110 hospitals and 398 dispensaries and built 1,003 classrooms and 670 bridges."[49] By this time, the U.S. Marine Corps, not formally Special Forces, had also run a Civic Assistance Program during which they assisted thousands of sick or war-wounded civilians. Such figures might not make exciting reading for military buffs, but for almost half a million refugees and thousands of others, they were a welcome change from the carnage of war. It was time to go home, though not for everyone. "Generally, U.S. Special Forces men who had spent less than ten months in Vietnam—some 1,200 or sixty per cent of the group strength—were reassigned to other U.S. Army, Vietnam, units. The remainder returned to the continental United States."[50]

MACV-SOG, the parallel multi-force Special Forces group, remained in action in Vietnam until May 1972. The SOG was an extraordinary, heterogeneous task force energized by adventurous spirits from the CIA's Special Activities Division, SEALS, U.S. Air Force, Green Berets, Vietnamese Special Forces, local and foreign mercenaries and signals intelligence experts. Fathered by the Joint Chiefs, it also had much political clout. CIA chiefs feared that it represented a takeover. Lyman Kirkpatrick, the Agency's executive director, suspected "the fragmentation and destruction of the CIA, with the clandestine services being gobbled up by the Joint Chiefs of Staff."[51]

In spite of its political backing, SOG was either singularly unlucky or unwilling to learn from past mistakes, or both. The Gulf of Tonkin raid was not the only misadventure. Between 1959 and 1961, the CIA had parachuted 250 South Vietnamese agents into the North. Most were killed or turned by the enemy. For three years from 1965 SOG repeated the error. Once captured, the teams were turned by their captors. The intelligence they sent back was false. Information relayed in return, detailing the next parachute or helicopter insertion, including landing zones, was genuine. The outcome was predictable. Between 1960 and 1968 the CIA and MACV-SOG sent 456 South Vietnamese agents to their deaths or harsh imprisonment.[52] In 1965, SOG turned its guns on Laos, or rather, the Ho Chi Minh trail, a rabbit warren of tracks that lay beneath the jungle canopy and rode over rugged 8,000-foot mountains. SOG targeted and USAF bombed.

Within a few months, the number of air raids had increased from twenty to 1,000 a month. By now, the State Department and its ambassador in the Laotian capital—defending the country's notional neutrality—were in conflict with the Joint Chiefs, who claimed that the trail was part of "the extended battlefield."

In 1968, as the war dragged on and enemy supplies and manpower continued to flow in vast quantities from the North with 20,000 enemy troops infiltrating the South each month, SOG tried its luck again in North Vietnam, running intelligence agents in support of conventional forces. Unlucky as ever, SOG's new enterprise coincided with North Vietnam's Tet Offensive. A series of feints from the North in remote border areas succeeded in drawing the attention of the U.S. and South Vietnamese armies away from cities in South Vietnam. On 31 January 1968, at the start of the most important Vietnamese holiday, "the full scale offensive began with simultaneous attacks by the communists on five major cities, thirty-six provincial capitals, sixty-four district capitals and numerous villages. In Saigon, suicide squads attacked the Independence Palace (residence of the president), the radio station, the Vietnamese Army General Staff compound, Tan Son Nhut airfield and the U.S. embassy."[53] If the assault was meant to take and hold ground, it failed, at a cost: the lives of 32,000 communist soldiers were sacrificed. But like the hidden dimension of General Giap's siege at Dien Bien Phu—plus his unexpected use of anti-aircraft guns and howitzers—its true purpose was political and psychological. In that sense, the Tet offensive succeeded. "On March 31, 1968, President Johnson announced that he would not seek his party's nomination for another term of office, declared a halt to the bombing of North Vietnam (except for a narrow strip above the Demilitarized Zone) and urged Hanoi to agree to peace talks."[54] Johnson's credibility at home was mortally damaged and so was the public's belief in this war. "With U.S. troop strength at 525,000, a request by [General] Westmoreland for an additional 200,000 troops was refused by a presidential commission headed by the new U.S. secretary of defense, Clark Clifford."[55]

On 6 November, Richard Nixon, a Republican, won the presidential election with a promise of "peace with honor." This meant training the South Vietnamese armed forces up to a level where they could guarantee the security of their country. Meanwhile, the war was extended to Cambodia and Laos, assisted in both cases by regime change. Communist bases and the Ho Chi Minh trail were targeted by MACV using, among other tools, electronic sensors linked to computers in an attempt to automate intelligence collection. This endeavor, codenamed Operation Igloo White, has been described as "the keystone of the U.S. aerial interdiction effort of the Vietnam conflict." Enthusiasm for bombing Laos grew as a result to 433,000 tons in 1969. Devastating though that figure was, it was modest compared with what was happening in Cambodia. Within two years, MACV's clandestine operations in Cambodia and Laos were ended by Congress. MACV stayed in business by proxy, running local mercenaries known as Special Commando Units.

As U.S. Special Forces' involvement in ground operations in Vietnam neared its end, the Pentagon planned a spectacular that, had it succeeded, might have lifted morale back home. This was the airborne raid by fifty-six Green Berets and CIA paramilitaries on Son Tay, a sprawling military complex a mere twenty-three miles west of Hanoi, and identified as a prison holding seventy U.S. soldiers and airmen. The operation, though it cost only two minor casualties and one aircraft, was fatally flawed in two respects. First, intelligence on which the raid was planned was out of date. The prisoners had been moved to other locations when the rescuers arrived. Second, it took too long for the military bureaucracy to get its act together. SOG had suspected since 1968 that Son Tay held

POWs. In early May 1970, following an analysis of aerial recce photographs, planning began. The raid did not happen until 20 November 1970. The outcome provoked controversy for years afterwards. In March 1983, a Washington symposium brought together leading theorists and practitioners to discuss special operations in U.S. strategy.

Dr. Edward N. Luttwak, Senior Fellow at the Center for Strategic and International Studies, Georgetown University, suggested: "When a bureaucratized and engineering-oriented establishment attempts commando operations, it is always 'unlucky.' The action starts with the information that was received on May 9 1970: American POWs in Ap Loy and Son Tay. Had this information gone to a commando organization—consisting of, say, thirty or forty officers who have spent five or six years doing only commando work—their own self-contained planning group would have said, 'Right. This is where they are. What's the most prosaic vehicle that will get us there?' Then they would have gone in to take the POWs out.

"When a bureaucratized establishment receives the same information, it sets up a planning committee. When the planning committee advises how to . . . get the POWs out, the establishment sets up a feasibility planning group or an assessment group. This is followed by an evaluation group, and so on. Then, after six months or so" [and around seventy rehearsals] "all concerned are finally ready for the operation, which has been planned and prepared as a very small-scale D-Day. Then they go in, and they discover that the POWs are not there any more. Son Tay was a crushing failure of the planning system. The Israeli raid at Entebbe was planned and executed in five days."[56] Other participants saw Son Tay—"the first operation of its type ever undertaken by the United States, a long-range penetration by helicopter, deep into enemy territory . . ."—as "an outstanding success" from the tactical standpoint. Retired officers present at the symposium, some of whom were part of the Son Tay team, objected vigorously to Luttwak's thesis.

In January 1973, Nixon halted all U.S. combat operations in South Vietnam. Peace agreements with the various powers involved soon followed and MACV, along with its cutting edge, the Studies and Observation Group, was formally consigned to history, though the latter would be reborn, in time, as the CIA's Special Operations Group.

South Vietnam should have been safe. On paper it outgunned and outnumbered its northern adversary by two to one. Its air force had 1,400 aircraft. Its army had been fastidiously trained by U.S. Special Forces but—with a few honorable exceptions—it always showed a reluctance to fight. Its officers had a talent for retreat. So when the communists attacked with artillery and tanks in March 1975, it retreated. The retreat became a panic and panic engendered a rout to the sea. Under incessant shelling, civilians took their chance in trying to swim out to overloaded vessels as they weighed anchor. By the end of the month, 100,000 South Vietnamese soldiers joined the grateful dead at Da Nang and surrendered the city. There was courageous, if isolated, resistance by the Xuan Loc garrison some forty miles to the east of Saigon for two weeks in April. By the end of the month, the South Vietnam capital was surrounded by 100,000 enemy, who now enjoyed a three-to-one advantage.

Inside the city, martial law was declared, but it did nothing to dampen the panic as senior officials fought with dogsbodies to claim a place on evacuation helicopters. The testament to the failure of American policy in Vietnam was the image of the last helicopter to claw its way to survival from the roof of the U.S. embassy on 30 April, accompanied by surreal music—Bing Crosby singing "I'm Dreaming of a White Christmas"—that was the coded signal to leave. Henry Kissinger, an architect of the Cambodian bombing campaign, wrote the campaign's obituary in a secret memorandum to President Ford:

"In terms of military tactics, we cannot help draw the conclusion that our armed forces are not suited to this kind of war. Even the Special Forces who had been designed for it could not prevail."[57]

The war cost 60,000 U.S. dead or missing. Around three million Vietnamese also lost their lives. The conflict left America with a political hangover, expressed as "No More Vietnams!" or at best, "a very cautious approach that borders on a 'never again' approach."[58] That is, until 9/11 pierced the carapace of America's self-belief. The successes of U.S. Special Forces in Vietnam, like the better side of Julius Caesar, was oft interred with their bones. Green Beret veterans, given half a chance, will remind us: "At their peak, less than 2,300 U.S. Special Forces soldiers skilfully controlled and led about 69,000 indigenous fighters, denying their use to the enemy, and precluding what otherwise would have been classified as genocide if control had slipped to the other side. There would have been no other alternative but to wage an anti-logistical, primarily air campaign against them as these peoples supported the enemy. That in and of itself was a most successful special operation: control and denial of a remote population to the opposition."[59]

It is a bleak equation, yet one that matches M. R. D. Foot's argument that irregular warfare is the only sane way wars can be fought in a nuclear age or, for that matter, as an alternative to strategic air power to murder civilians. In spite of that, Vietnam impacted adversely on the evolution of U.S. Special Forces for decades afterward. Denigrated by conventional soldiers as "unprofessional" and by others as wild men, out of control and acting "unilaterally," U.S. Special Forces were all but eradicated during the 1970s.[60]

More than thirty years after U.S. Special Forces pulled out of Vietnam, that war continues to divide historians. Gordon Goldstein's *Lessons in Disaster* argued that President Johnson was "pressed by the military into escalating an unwinnable conflict," while Lewis Sorley's

A Better War proposed that "antiwar feelings and pressure from Congress forced Richard Nixon to reject a counter-insurgency strategy that could have succeeded."[61]

The asymmetric conflicts of Vietnam and Afghanistan were hardly understood by many professional, conventional soldiers whose careers had conditioned them for careful, orderly, and prolonged preparation for textbook warfare as in the Gulf, 1990, in which Operation Desert Shield was orchestrated as if the impending carnage were a Mahler symphony to be concluded triumphantly in the home key. Asymmetric warfare belongs on another planet. It is a conflict of ideas in which the battleground is anywhere and everywhere, with no firm criteria for victory or even, perhaps, a defined end to hostilities. It is a process that mutates according to its own rules, like a cancer. The only people who understand it are the lateral thinkers on the front line. They are not often to be found in the Pentagon or the Ministry of Defence.

In Vietnam, following a rigged election in 1967 that maintained a military junta in power, U.S. forces were perceived by most civilians as puppet-masters of an illegitimate, unwanted government. Political legitimacy was the missing ingredient to success in that campaign. The more military force was used to prop up the old, corrupt regime, the more credibility Hanoi enjoyed in characterizing America as an alien, neo-colonial power to which ordinary people owed no loyalty. Rufus Phillips, the dean among U.S. diplomats in Saigon (where he was the boss of Richard Holbrooke, Obama's special envoy to Afghanistan), notices similarities between then and now. Writing in advance of the return to office of Hamid Karzai, he endorsed the view that in Vietnam, the electoral fraud of 1967 proved to be "the most destructive and destabilizing factor of all." As they might have said in French-managed Indochina, plus ça change; plus c'est la même chose.

CHAPTER 2

DELTA, DESERT ONE, AND "THE ACTIVITY"

I n 1962 a burly Green Beret captain, Charlie A. Beckwith, formerly an all-state football player from Atlanta, was in the Malayan jungle feeling seriously unwell. He was no stranger to the hazards of jungle warfare. He had been an Airborne soldier for seven years and had two years' service with Special Forces in South Vietnam and Laos as a "military adviser." The local leeches, bloated on his blood, and only removable from the most intimate parts of his body with a burning cigarette applied by a buddy, were nothing special. He'd had dengue fever and a touch of malaria in Laos. But this sickness was unlike anything else he had known. To make matters worse, he was not even serving in his own army. With another Green Beret, a Sergeant Rozniak, Beckwith was on attachment to the British Special Air Service Regiment as part of an exchange program through which the Brits sent their brightest and best to Fort Bragg.

The connection had been made several years before by Colonel I. A. ("Boppy") Edwards of 7th Special Forces Group and a British legend named Colonel John Woodhouse. During the 1960s, the transatlantic exchange program involved three of the principal players subsequently caught up in the tragic failure of Desert One. As well as Beckwith, the SAS trained Dick Meadows, who operated in civilian clothes in Tehran on a DIA contract and Jerry King, Chief of Staff to the general commanding the doomed attempt to rescue fifty-three American diplomat-hostages. All that was over the horizon when Beckwith virtually collapsed in Malaya.

Special Forces are hard men. In Afghanistan in 2009, a medevac team from 55th Expeditionary Rescue Squadron USAF was astonished by the fortitude of a British SBS soldier who had been shot through the face. He declined an offer of morphine and, as one of the rescue team noted, "calmly picked pieces of bone and teeth from his own wound." In Malaya, the SAS commander John Woodhouse, dealing with one of his soldiers who had accidentally fired his weapon—in official language, an "accidental discharge"—gave the man a hand grenade to carry for the rest of the day. The firing pin had been extracted. To relax his grip for even a second would mean the victim's certain death. In Turkey in 2009, a similar experiment resulted in the death of a recruit. In such company, Beckwith felt impelled not to let America down. He staggered on. In fact, in their rough fashion, the twenty-odd men of Three Troop, A Squadron, 22 SAS, had taken to their American guest. His nickname, "Chargin' Charlie," meant something. As one of his troop once told the author: "He'd rather march through a tree than go round it." The SAS were teaching him stealth.

His team was now into its ninth day of living close to nature in a green twilight beneath a canopy of trees that excluded direct light, an apparently welcoming place that was full of hidden danger. In the jungle it is standard practice before lying under a tree to shake it, lest the tree fall and kill you as you sleep. Venomous snakes and a variety of hairy, poisonous six- and eight-legged creatures await the unwary. Some humans actually like it in there. Paddy B, an SAS veteran of the parallel campaigns in Borneo and the arid Radfan Mountains of Aden in the 1960s, when asked which environment he preferred, replied, in his Cork brogue: "Sure I'd say there, Mr. Geraghty, I like the jungle best. There's no shortage of water in the jungle and a man can get as much sleep as he needs. I'd call that a gracious living."

Before Beckwith fell sick, his patrol had already taken one casualty and had found it necessary to make a clearing with high explosive to enable a helicopter to take the injured man out. As a result, in a race against time, they had lost thirty-six hours and now had to chance compromise and exposure to CTs (Communist Terrorists) by snatching the only possible shortcut if they were to reach their rendezvous with another SAS patrol on schedule. The shortcut was the river. So they built rafts and traveled swiftly, without apparent trouble, to the RV.

It was at this point that Beckwith became ill. He did not know it yet, but he had contracted leptospirosis, also known as Weil's Disease, a deadly infection if an open wound, or sore, comes into contact with water carrying the urine of animals also suffering from the condition. (The author first learned about this hazard when he returned from a run through part of the Jungle Warfare School at Kota Tingi, in Johore Baru, barefoot). Chargin' Charlie, moving through dense rain forest, had picked up many minor cuts, then entered the river to launch the raft. It was his bad luck that his patch of water hosted leptospirosis.

He was hospitalized in the nick of time and after repeated doses of penicillin and thanks to his own will to live, he started to recover. After ten days, he could walk a few steps, unaided. The U.S. government sent a doctor from the Philippines to remove him to an American hospital. Beckwith told the man, in less than polite terms, to go to hell. His twelve-month attachment to the Brits had not yet run its course. Word got back to his SAS troop. They approved. He wrote later: "For once, I've done something right."[62] While he was recuperating, Beckwith had a bright idea. This was that the unorthodox methods of the SAS including deep penetration of contested territory by stealth, guerrilla warfare turned against guerrillas, was something America could usefully absorb into its own military doctrine. "The American Army not only needed a Special Forces capability, but an SAS one; not only a force of teachers [of native surrogates], but a force of doers."

His moment of enlightenment had an interesting precedent. In Cairo in 1941 the founder of the SAS, David Stirling, was hospitalized following a parachuting accident. For the time being, Stirling was paralyzed from the waist down. He passed the time scribbling a proposal for a tiny team to hit targets behind Rommel's lines in the Western Desert. It would replace a major commando outfit, now disbanded after a disastrous start, called Layforce. Stirling later explained: "The main thesis . . . was to plead that many objectives envisaged for Layforce . . . could be tackled by a unit less than one-twentieth the size of the 1,600-man establishment of Layforce. . . . The minuscule demand on the sources of the Middle East Command and the project's high potential reward decided the Commander-in-Chief to authorize me to go ahead. Thus was born the Special Air Service."

It would be fifteen years before a conservative U.S. military establishment understood Beckwith's message. This was that in spite of the separate skills and shared bravery of other Special Forces teams—Rangers, SEALs, Marines and autonomous Green Berets—there was a hole in America's military preparedness. That was the threat of international, global terrorism. Britain knew about it thanks to the support given to the IRA by the Libyan leader Colonel Gaddafi and the car bombs that shredded much of London as well as Belfast. Italy knew, thanks to the assassins of the Red Brigades. Germany and Israel had learned a bitter lesson through the Munich Massacre at the 1972 Olympics. In 1977, the Joint Chiefs of Staff were finally persuaded to endorse, in principle, the creation of a unit modeled on the British SAS, to prepare for a global war on terrorism. They were influenced by the latest terrorist outrage. A team of Palestinians, supported by German anarchists, had seized a Lufthansa airliner and taken it to Mogadishu. The siege there ended when a German anti-terrorist team, led by two SAS men, Major Alastair Morrison and Sergeant Barry Davies, blasted their way onto the aircraft and rescued the hostages.

During the years between Beckwith's first proposal, drafted on his hospital bed, and the JCS decision to endorse it, Beckwith had founded and led a special reconnaissance team in Vietnam which he called "Delta Project B-52." His formula combined deep jungle penetration by a tiny, elite force on SAS lines, with America's air power to take on the elusive warriors of the Vietcong and the regular North Vietnamese Army. In January 1966, a heavy caliber .50 bullet bored through Beckwith's body as he was about to land by helicopter in a jungle fortress besieged by hundreds of enemy. Defying a medical diagnosis of imminent death, he walked out of the hospital four months later to resume his career as a Special Forces adviser.

Following the JCS decision, Beckwith needed two years to bring his Delta Force up to SAS standards. He still had to overcome the mindset of existing U.S. Special Forces commanders, working by the book and wedded to the 260-page Field Manual 31-21, *Guerrilla Warfare and Special Forces Operations*. First published in 1961, FM 31-21 reflected the tactics of the Second World War. It defined Unconventional Warfare as "interrelated . . . guerrilla warfare, evasion and escape, and subversion against hostile states (resistance). . . . Operations conducted in enemy or enemy controlled territory by predominately [*sic*] indigenous personnel usually supported and directed in varying degrees by an external source."

The authors admit "the doctrine set forth in this manual is structured around a general war situation [in which] special forces organize guerrilla forces to support conventional military operations under the direction of a theater commander. . . ." The world had moved on by the 1970s, to one in which, to cite a 19th century Anarchist phrase, "propaganda by deed" was dramatically magnified by the evolution of worldwide television news. It was a world in which the hierarchy of big military formations could be outsmarted by nimble irregular cells. Beckwith, learning from the SAS, wanted to fight fire with fire. His new, superbly trained Delta force was not conceived as a large-scale raiding force. Events dictated otherwise.

On 4 November 1979, following the overthrow of the Shah of Iran, the return to Iran of Ayatollah Khomeini from exile in Paris, and the Shah's grant of sanctuary in America, a student demonstration directed against the U.S. embassy in Tehran got out of hand. The most venturesome demonstrators, armed with martial arts nunchaku sticks, a croquet mallet, and a broken wooden board, climbed the embassy gate and, to their surprise, encountered little opposition from within other than a token volley of riot gas cartridges fired by Marine guards wearing shiny dress shoes.

The Marines' Rules of Engagement did not permit shooting into a crowd of civilian demonstrators led by women who claimed they intended nothing more serious than a sit-in. Initially, the Iranian government promised to do what it could do to arrange a peaceful outcome. The deception was complete as the embassy was surrendered without a shot. It was a misplaced, naïvely Quaker defense. While they had the chance, the embassy's CIA team of four burned classified documents. The siege became a circus of political humiliation that lasted 444 days and fatally undermined the Carter presidency.

America boiled with anger during the siege and expected a military response as well as the safe return of fifty-three embassy staff held hostage. These were barely compatible objectives. In total secrecy, a rescue task force was built around Delta and an ad hoc collection of Air Force and Marine pilots, plus a sprinkling of CIA and Pentagon secret agents at large in Iran. Responsibility was divided between Delta, which would run the ground rescue and evacuation, and the air element, handling movements in, around, and out of Iran. By the time the team was assembled under the codename "Operation Eagle Claw" in April 1980, it had grown to 120 men. It was also, according to some observers, saddled with a top-heavy bureaucracy including four separate commanders on the ground. The rescue scenario was complex. It proposed inserting the Delta rescue team on an apparently isolated hard runway codenamed Desert One by three C-130 aircraft 200 miles from the target; a laying-up position fifty miles from Tehran, to which 118 members of Delta plus six drivers and six translators would move in darkness by eight Navy Sea Stallion helicopters, normally used for minesweeping, flown from the carrier *Nimitz* and piloted by Marine Chinook pilots who had little experience of night flying under radar and little chance to adapt to the machines they were to fly.

Another trio of C-130s would act as fuel tankers for the helicopters at Desert One. A two-man Pentagon team, covertly inserted ahead of the main mission, would provide trucks for road movement on the second night into Tehran. The Delta assault team would make a *coup de main* strike on the embassy compound as a Ranger company held the perimeter. The hostages would be carried to a stadium where they would be picked up by helicopter and flown to another airfield seized by Rangers. There, Starlifter transports would be waiting to fly the hostages to safety.

The mission was in trouble from the start. In bleak, terse language the Holloway Report tells us how it started to go wrong: "On the evening of 24 April, after 5½ months of planning and training under very tight OPSEC [operational security], eight RH-53 helicopters took off from the aircraft carrier *Nimitz* and began a journey of nearly 600 nautical miles at night and low altitude to a preselected refueling site, Desert One, in the desert. The C-130 element with the ground rescue forces was also in the execution phase on a different track and time schedule to Desert One. Approximately two hours after takeoff, the crew of Helicopter No. 6 received cockpit indications of an impending rotor blade failure; landed; verified the malfunction (an automatic abort situation); and abandoned their aircraft. The crew was picked [up] by another helicopter, which then continued the mission individually.

"Approximately one hour thereafter, the helicopter formation unexpectedly encountered a dust cloud of unknown size and density. The helicopters broke out of the first area of suspended dust but, within an hour, entered a second, larger and denser area. While attempting to navigate through this second area with severely degraded visibility, a second helicopter (No. 5) experienced a failure of several critical navigation and flight instruments. Due to progressively deteriorating flight conditions that made safe flight extremely questionable, the helicopter pilot determined that it would be unwise to continue. He aborted the mission, reversed course, and recovered on *Nimitz*. Eventually six of the original eight helicopters arrived at the refueling site in intervals between approximately 50 minutes and 85 minutes later than planned.

"While en route, a third helicopter (No. 2) experienced a partial hydraulic failure, but the crew elected to continue to the refueling site believing repairs could be accomplished there. Upon landing, however, the crew and the helicopter unit commander determined that the helicopter could not be repaired. A hydraulic pump had failed due to a fluid leak, and no replacement pump was available. Even if a pump had been immediately available, there was insufficient time to change it, repair the cause of the leak, service the system, and complete the next leg prior to daylight. The helicopter was unsafe to continue the mission unrepaired.

"Earlier, it had been determined that a minimum of six operational helicopters would be required at the refueling site to continue the mission. Since at this point there were only five operational, the on-scene commander advised COMJTF [Commander, Joint Task Force] by radio of the situation, and he in turn communicated to Washington the status of the force and his intention to abort the operation and return to launch base. The President concurred in the decision that the mission could not continue, and preparations began for withdrawal of the five operational helicopters, the C-130s, and the rescue force."[63]

The first helicopters to arrive would have had no trouble in spotting Desert One. This was not because a CIA-contract pilot, at great risk, had landed there in a Twin Otter aircraft a month before to plant infrared landing lights to be activated as the task force approached. By the time the helos arrived, the scene was illuminated by a blazing road tanker, a sign that on the ground as well as in the air, the operation was already compromised. The element of chance—bad luck—struck almost as soon as Delta landed. Beckwith spotted a Mercedes bus approaching the landing zone, ordered his men to halt it and, leading by example, fired at its tyres. Some 45 passengers, most of them women and children, clambered out, bewildered. One who spoke English asked the black Ranger guarding her where the armed men came from. "We're African commandos," he joked.

The next civilian vehicle to blunder into what was, by now, a war zone was the fuel tanker. One of Beckwith's team fired an anti-tank missile at it. The tanker exploded and burned for hours, illuminating the runway, the waiting aircraft, and the herded bus passengers. The tanker was accompanied by a smaller vehicle which paused long enough for the tanker driver to escape into the darkness on foot. Eagle Claw had now been compromised on the ground three ways within, perhaps, 30 minutes.

Speculation continues, thirty years later, that sand filters to protect the helicopter engines had been removed to reduce weight and increase range. The hazard of dust in the desert is no novelty. If this was a factor in the calamity that followed, Beckwith did not address it in his account. Nor did the unclassified version of the Holloway report. But Colonel John T. Carney, Jr., an Air Force Special Operations officer who took part in Eagle Claw, suggests that MC-130 Combat Talon pathfinder aircraft should have led the helicopters safely to the target, as they did in the Son Tay raid. They were on the scene and might even have passed within sight of the ill-fated Sea Stallions.

There was another problem. Navigation equipment that would have helped blind-flying was removed to reduce weight. "Thus," writes Carney, "they were literally flying blind and could not advise one another of the actual weather conditions, which were much more benign than the pilots believed. . . . The [Marine] pilots should have broken radio silence for a second or two to query the Combat Talons, regain their bearings, and find better weather." According to Beckwith, high command suggested following these technical failures that he should proceed with five helicopters. The sinister implication of that was that Delta would be obliged to dump as many as twenty of its own at Desert One. As Beckwith put it: "In a tight mission, no one is expendable *before you begin!* [his emphasis]. Which twenty would I leave?"[64]

Other factors were at work to undermine the mission. Feuding between the CIA, then headed by Admiral Stansfield Turner, and the

National Security Agency prompted fears among the Joint Chiefs of Staff about a loss of security. NSA was headed by a Vice Admiral, Bobby Ray Inman, and had been excluded from the prolonged planning for Desert One. In spite of that, NSA got wind of what was going on as a result of insecure communications by some of the planners. Inman, in charge of NSA, later suggested that Air Force General David C. Jones, JCS chairman, "was so stunned by the potential of blowing the security at the beginning that he imposed awesome communications security constraints and it probably directly impacted on the readiness of the forces. The fact that the helicopters were put on carriers, sent for five weeks, never flown until they left the carrier, all of this out of concern that they would be detected in the process . . ." along with total radio silence, lack of pre-mission helicopter training, and the choppers' condition after they sat unused on the carrier deck for so long all contributed to the disaster.[65]

To abort the operation rather than write off twenty men was a bitter decision for Beckwith, but it was, at least, one that did not reinforce a calamity in the making, a calamity that might have resulted in the deaths of many of the hostages as well as their would-be rescuers. Beckwith's choice required moral courage as well as military cool. Yet fate had one last evil card to play. As Admiral James Holloway put it, in laconic, deadpan language: "While repositioning one helicopter to permit another to top off his fuel tanks for the return flight, the first helicopter collided with one of the refueling C-130s. Both aircraft were immediately engulfed in flames in which eight crew members died and five other members of the team were injured. Since the C-130 was loaded with members of the rescue force awaiting extraction, even greater injury and loss of life were avoided only by swift and disciplined evacuation of the burning aircraft. Shortly afterwards, ammunition aboard both aircraft began to explode. Several helicopters were struck by shrapnel from the explosion and/or the burning ammunition, and at least one and possibly more were rendered non-flyable. At this point, with time and fuel running out for the C-130s, the decision was made to transfer all helicopter crews to the remaining C-130s and to depart the area."

The Iranians, remarkably, were able to recover several of the grounded Navy helicopters intact. Holloway reported:

"*Destruct devices on mission rescue helicopters:* Helicopter No. 6 developed mechanical problems en route to Desert One and landed in the desert short of destination. Ground personnel tasked with responsibility for helicopter destruction were not available. An unforeseen accident and ensuing conflagration at Desert One prevented the on-scene commander from implementing the helicopter destruction plan because he perceived it to be too risky. As a result, five RH-53Ds [Sea Stallion helicopters] were abandoned intact.

"As planning proceeded, an option to destroy the helicopters in Iran, should a contingency situation warrant, was considered. This contingency called for individuals to place thermite grenades in the helicopters if their destruction was called for and then to detonate them. This option was never implemented at Desert One because of the perceived danger of exploding helicopters and ammunition to personnel and aircraft evacuating the site and to Iranians aboard a nearby bus."

This was not the only choice, Holloway suggests. There is good reason to believe explosives, when properly installed, are no more dangerous to crew and passengers than the onboard fuel supply. Moreover, explosives for use in destroying the helicopters and breaching the Embassy walls had to be carried aboard several, if not all, helicopters. Therefore, it is a moot point as to what explosives were carried onboard and where they were placed. On the Son Tay mission, explosives for helicopter self-destruction were placed onboard at the outset. The helicopter to be abandoned was fitted with explosives and detonators. Electrical initiators were placed apart from the explosives, and the electrical leads left disconnected. Aircrew members destroyed the helicopter, when necessary, by simply connecting the initiator to the explosives and activating a built-in timing device. With regard to aircrew reluctance to have similar devices to the ones used in the Son Tay raid aboard their helicopters, Iranian-mission aircrews interviewed stated that this procedure was acceptable to them. Moreover, they admitted that most explosives were less of a danger than other hazardous material carried on-board mission helicopters—e.g., fuel.

"Equipping rescue mission helicopters with easily removable, separated, and disconnected explosive devices and initiators should not have jeopardized safety and would have enhanced the ability to destroy helicopters at any point in the mission. . . ."

As the C-130s, rumbled away south from Desert One, a dawn sun caught their wings as if to remind the survivors of the fires they had left burning. By the time they touched down at the sanctuary of Masirah Island, part of friendly Oman, an Iranian army team was searching the site. It found eight American and one civilian Iranian dead. Much worse, it discovered documents that compromised an American agent on the ground in advance of Eagle Claw. This was retired Major Richard Meadows, one of the first Americans to serve with the SAS in 1960 and son-in-law of an SAS warrant officer. Born in 1931, Meadows enlisted at the age of sixteen and emerged from the Korean War three years later as the Army's youngest master sergeant. He joined Special Forces in 1953 and in 1970 led the Son Tay rescue attempt. He extracted his team safely. The need for better intelligence in the future, and quicker reaction to what intelligence there was, was not lost on Meadows. By the time the U.S. Embassy in Tehran was occupied in 1979, Meadows had been in retirement for two years. The Pentagon invited him to act as the forward eyes and ears of Beckwith's mission on the ground in Tehran, and he accepted.[66] After the mission was aborted, using an Irish passport in the name of Richard H. Keith supplied by the CIA, he kept his cool, checked in at Tehran airport, and flew out on a civil airliner, undetected.

A final indignity awaited Beckwith back in the Pentagon's press briefing room. He was to address a press conference. What gutted him was not the prospect of talking to journalists. He'd done that in Vietnam from time to time. But "what kicked the wind out of me was losing my cover and having to answer questions about sensitive classified matters."[67]

The failure at Desert One prompted a major re-examination of the role of Special Forces in the U.S. A fundamental flaw was the ad hoc nature of its order of battle. It was a cherry-picking, mix-and-match process, conditioned by the availability of air and intelligence assets. It was not organic. Following the Holloway inquiry, another level of bureaucracy was added: a counterterrorist joint task force and an advisory panel. On the sidelines, battalions of experts offered their sometimes-conflicting advice.

In March 1983, the National Strategy Information Center, the National Security Studies Program at Georgetown University, and the National Defense University sponsored a two-day symposium on the role of Special Operations in U.S. strategy for the 1980s. Dr. Edward N. Luttwak, for example, suggested that the Eagle Claw rescue plan was "clearly designed by people without a clue as to the realities of war." It is worth noting that in his own book, first published in 1983, Beckwith blamed "political considerations" in Washington for delaying the mission from mid-January, when Delta was ready, when "the weather favored us," until April, the season of sandstorms and dust. "National resolve is weakened by many forces," he wrote. "The longer the crisis is allowed to run, the more such forces come into play. The longer a government waits to respond to a terrorist incident, the harder is the rescue by military means." His solution, a counsel of perfection, was "predictive intelligence," with contingency plans to cover a crisis before it happened.

The structural changes in U.S. preparedness were still being worked through when President Barack Obama took office in 2009, but in the shorter term, useful reforms were introduced. In 1982, the Army consolidated its Special Operations Forces (known as ARSOF) in a Special Operations Command. On 1 January 1984, following the Hizbollah bombing of a Marine barracks in Beirut with the loss of 237 men, the Pentagon created a Joint Special Operations Agency without any command authority over any SF element [see Special Operations Command.com online]. After years of debate in Congress, President Ronald Reagan signed off the establishment of U.S. Special Operations Command (USSOCOM) on 13 April 1987, almost exactly seven years after Delta set off for Desert One. The CIA's Special Activities Division (known as SAD) continued, meanwhile, to run its own high-risk, plausibly deniable operations involving subversion and unconventional warfare using surrogates. The sub-group concerned was inherited from the MAC/SOG era in Vietnam and was now known as the Special Operations Group.

Beckwith had been ordered not to trust the State Department because it could not keep secrets. Who could? As the Holloway Commission Report made plain: "intelligence drove the operation from the outset," but "certain elements of the Intelligence Community seemed slow in harnessing themselves initially for the tasks at hand." Could it be that this criticism was aimed at the Central Intelligence Agency, whose role is never mentioned in the unclassified version of Holloway? Since the Agency provided Meadows with his bogus Irish passport, it clearly gave some support to Eagle Claw. A month before the mission was launched, "a CIA Twin Otter had flown into . . . Desert One. A USAF Combat Controller had rode [sic] around the landing area on a light dirt bike and planted landing lights to help guide the force in. That insertion went well. . . ."[68]

Yet the suspicion that the CIA had somehow let down the Pentagon's rescue team festered for more than twenty years. The pain was finally revealed in 2003 by Carney himself. He asserted: "Eighteen years after the rescue attempt some of us learned that the CIA had received a covert communication that detailed some of the most important information we needed: the exact location of three hostages [in addition to those held at the embassy compound] being held in the Iranian Ministry of Foreign Affairs. The CIA claimed that it had stumbled only by providence on detailed information on almost all the other hostages who were being held in the American embassy compound when a Pakistani cook who had been working in the embassy happened to be on the last leg of a flight from Tehran to Frankfurt and found himself seated next to a CIA officer. The CIA apparently fabricated the Pakistani cook story in order to protect its own sources inside the embassy and gave up its information only after it was absolutely certain that the rescue mission could be launched."[69]

The British author Michael Smith suggests: "The Agency had someone in Tehran all along, a very good source supplying his bosses at CIA headquarters in Langley with top-grade intelligence. But it held back the wealth of intelligence he was providing until the very last minute because it feared that the existence of their agent and his sub-agents would leak out, putting its only source of information at risk."[70]

One CIA expert working the streets of Tehran when the Shah fell was the veteran Howard Hart, whose unfashionable warnings to Langley of what was to come were put under the blotter. Hart, it is claimed, advised the Desert One team, whose effort, according to Anthony Quainton, Washington's chief counter-terrorism co-ordinator from

1978 to 1981, "relied heavily on the CIA." Unnoticed by the Agency's critics was the CIA's separate success in conjuring six Americans out of the Canadian embassy in Tehran, where they had taken refuge during the siege. Tony Mendez, a CIA technical operations officer expert in providing disguises, invented a film crew called Studio Six.

Collateral cover for its existence went deep. The CIA opened a Los Angeles Office for the fictitious company. It advertised its upcoming sci-fi movie *Argo* in the theatrical media and sent its Canadian film crew to Iran, with the blessings of the revolutionary government, to do location shots. Led by a genuine CBC cameraman, Dennis Packer, and equipped with Canadian passports, the six American hostages, freshly disguised and absorbed by the "film crew," left Iran unscathed. The Agency, employing elaborate deception, achieved what Special Forces, with all their expertise and firepower, could not. That said, it was easier to smuggle six men out of Iran than fifty-three. Mendez received the CIA's Intelligence Star from President Carter soon after the operation.

After the failure of Desert One, the Iranians dispersed their hostages to a variety of locations, rendering a follow-up operation impossible. William J. Daugherty, a Marine veteran on his first CIA tour, was compromised by documents uncovered in a search of the embassy. He was in solitary confinement for nine months, with barely enough room to move, a skeletal figure when the Iranian government released him with the other fifty-two hostages the day after Carter ceased to be president.

For Eagle Claw to have had a chance of success, the bravery of a few individuals on the ground in advance of the operation led by the retired Major Richard Meadows was clearly insufficient. The gap was to be filled in the future by a dedicated, expert team of Special Forces people capable of providing real-time intelligence in a variety of scenarios including hostage rescue. It was to be filled in January 1981 by the Pentagon's creation of an ultra-secret surveillance organization known as the Intelligence Support Activity or, more simply, "The Activity."

"Our Own CIA, But Like Topsy"

Eight months after Desert One, in December 1980, Lieutenant General Philip Gast, USAF, Director for Operations for the Joint Chiefs, sent a top-secret memorandum to the Director of the Pentagon's Defense Intelligence Agency. Subject: Intelligence Capability. A redacted version of the document asserts: "A review of the intelligence collected during the past year to support Iranian contingency planning revealed a serious and persistent information deficiency. This revolves around the need of military planners to have accurate and timely situation-oriented and environmental data such as . . . [words redacted]."[71]

The "intelligence collected during the past year" reflected plans for a proposed second attempt to save some of the Tehran hostages, codenamed Honey Badger. The ingredient missing from intelligence identified by General Gast was the sort of ground truth that only human agents, inside enemy walls, could provide. Under President Carter and Stansfield Turner, pursuing the Holy Grail of an ethical foreign policy, the CIA had favored electronic systems over the sometimes uncontrolled violence exercised by deniable agents in Central America. They took the view that he who dines with the Devil must have a very long, technological spoon. So as many as 2,800 intelligence officers, mostly paramilitary specialists, were ditched by the CIA in 1977, in a purge known as "the Halloween Massacre." As a secret DOD history of ISA, drafted in 1983, observed, "the ill-fated attempt in April, 1980 to secure by military force the release of . . . Americans held hostage in Tehran revealed institutional shortfalls in U.S. national intelligence and special operations capabilities. At the time of the initial rescue attempt, there existed nowhere in the national capability an organization to provide this vital support."[72] And as General Gast's memorandum drily noted: "Although technical systems can and did provide some of the information needed, the nature of the required data puts the burden of collection on reliable human observers. . . . The current Department of Defense/Service HUMINT structure is not organized to satisfy these requirements. . . ."

The short history quoted above takes the story on. "As the second [rescue] effort matured, a formal force to conduct this intelligence operation, *a combination of intelligence collection and operational support to a striking force* [author's italics], emerged in the form of the Field Operations Group (FOG). FOG was prepared and in place to support a second rescue attempt when the hostages were released." How many hostages might have been sprung, in view of the fact that the Iranians had now spread their captives over many locations, is not addressed. The document continues: "FOG did not, however, disappear with the disbandment of the Iranian rescue force. Bridging a crucial gap in national capabilities to execute nationally directed missions, FOG's capability was institutionalized in a DoD special unit to establish a worldwide, immediately responsive capability similar to that developed over a one year period in the Tehran crisis. FOG was redesignated as the Intelligence Support Activity (ISA) in March 1981."

What emerged was an instrument of tactical intelligence, the view, let us say, from somewhere close to the action, from under the bed, rather than strategically, from the street outside. The Pentagon's solution—inserting its own eyes, ears, and wallets beyond the front line—required "selected personnel who were trained to fill critical intelligence and operational units." Unlike FOG, which was yet another ad hoc collection of Special Forces veterans, the new, permanent entity was to run both human agents and—ironically, in view of Stansfield Turner's early conversion to electronics so as to keep the administration's hands clean—SIGINT (signals intelligence), but obtained from low, slow-flying aircraft.

Both FOG and its successor, the ISA, were commanded during the formative years by Colonel Jerry King. King was rigorous in his choice of volunteers. As an official "brief history" recognized, "training of operative personnel is among the most intensive in the Army and includes Assessment & Selection: a rigorous program to place the candidate in a sufficient number of different physically and mentally stressful situations to . . . form the basis for a selection decision by the Commander."[73] After Selection, a core training course, believed to involve CIA facilities, taught the successful volunteers the arts of professional espionage.

ISA's role was to support America's elite of elites among Special Forces as they confronted a new style of warfare, global counter-terrorism. After earlier irregular warfare scandals accompanied by the abuse of human rights, the last thing the Pentagon needed was yet another feral SF unit operating without accountability to higher authority. To reduce the risk, it was made answerable to the Assistant Chief of Staff for Intelligence, Lieutenant General William E. Odom. Odom was an austere Russian expert who had penetrated much of Soviet Russia undetected during the Cold War. As Zbigniew Brzezinski's military adviser—a hawk's hawk—Odom was known as "Zbig's Super-Hawk," later taking control of the electronic eavesdropping service, the National Security Agency.

The ISA's first commander, Jerry King, was a hardened Special Forces veteran who had led cross-border forays from South Vietnam into North Vietnam, Laos, and Cambodia. King was an abrasive action man who did not suffer fools, or nervous military bureaucrats, lightly. He and Odom clashed regularly about his methods. King selected individuals on the basis of their resilience, endurance, specialist knowledge, and ability to act on their own initiative. His physical selection tests, like those of the SAS and Delta, pushed volunteers beyond their apparent limits. They were also expected to learn the infiltration skills of all Special Forces soldiers including high-altitude parachuting and underwater diving. Yet their forte was not combat but concealment and electronic intelligence-gathering, often by tapping telephones or scanning the radio wavebands of a potential enemy at close quarters, detecting low-level, localized signals that even the National Security Agency or its British cousin GCHQ could not reach.

It was this sort of magic that enabled them to identify the Italian "people's prison" near Padua in which General James Lee Dozier, America's senior man at NATO's southern command, had been held captive by members of the Italian Red Brigades for forty-two days. An Italian anti-terrorist squad raided the apartment on 28 January 1982, rescued the general, and arrested Dozier's captors without firing a shot. The role of ISA in Dozier's salvation was concealed for years afterward. Diplomacy required that this be seen as an exclusively domestic, Italian triumph. The ISI went on to run similarly successful operations in El Salvador, penetrating, from the air, the operational security of left-wing guerrillas and right-wing death squads. This campaign ran successfully for three years.

But the sweet smell of success was overlaid by a less palatable odor in Washington as a result of the ISA's involvement in a freelance operation proposed by James "Bo" Gritz, a retired Special Forces lieutenant colonel with an obsession about rescuing American prisoners of war, if any there were, still captive in Vietnam in 1981, six years after the war ended. Gritz and others campaigning on the MIA ("Missing In Action") issue stirred a profound sentiment in yellow-ribbon mid-America. Gritz claimed that he was asked to stand down his proposed operation so as to give a clear run to ISA, to achieve the same object. A former ISA officer quoted by the author Michael Smith "said the discussions were all designed by the Activity to find out where Gritz's agents were and whether they might produce valid and useful intelligence on the POWs issue. . . . He [Gritz] was provided with one camera . . . and a broken polygraph machine" rather than the $40,000 Gritz claimed to have received. The reason for supplying a polygraph machine that did not work is not explained.

The Activity's double bluff did not impress General Odom, the senior staff officer to whom Jerry King was answerable. King wanted to continue to play Gritz along so as to identify and take over Gritz's intelligence sources. Odom overruled him and stopped the game. The outcome was an inquiry by the Pentagon's Inspector General, which landed on the desk of Frank C. Carlucci, Deputy Secretary of Defense. As a result, on 26 May 1982 Carlucci sent a memorandum to Richard Stilwell, Deputy Under-Secretary for Policy. More in sorrow than in anger, Carlucci found the report on ISA "disturbing in the extreme." He continued:

"We seem to have created our own CIA, but like Topsy, uncoordinated and uncontrolled. Unquestionably ISA contains much talent and probably even more dedication. There may also be a need, but that is less clear. But we should have learned the lesson of the 70's on control over . . . [words redacted]. Accountability is the essence and we have created an organization that is unaccountable.

"Action will be taken to terminate all ISA operations within 30 days; or effect transfer thereof to other competent organizations. If it is desired to continue ISA in some form, the following will be submitted for my approval not later than 15 June:

1. A concept plan.
2. A list of requirements.
3. A command structure, indicating to whom it is accountable and how.

4. A list of controls to be established, particularly over . . .
   [words redacted]
5. A fiscal management and accountability plan.
6. A program for working with appropriate committees of
   Congress.
7. A funding plan, fully coordinated with the Comptroller.
8. The concurrence of the DCI [Director Central Intelli-
   gence] and the General Counsel for all of the above."

Carlucci's concern about financial control probably reflected references in the IG's report to "ill-advised" acquisitions, including a hot-
air balloon and a Rolls Royce limousine. The ISA did not assist its
own case by claiming that the hot-air balloon, no longer wanted by
another part of the army, would be of use in basic parachute training
along the lines of the British system of teaching jump novices. The
British have always used sealed helium-gas ("barrage") balloons,
tethered to the ground by a cable and winched to a jump height of
800 feet. On the order "800 feet, four to jump!" the trainees and
their instructor have a chillingly silent ascent followed by an adrena-
line-filled drop on the end of a static line during which, in the
absence of an aircraft slipstream, the student is surprised to see his
boots rise slowly in front of his nose, before sinking back to where
they belong. It is a safe, well-tried system that had been in use for
decades when the ISA discovered, naïvely, that a hot-air balloon
"didn't work out, too unstable and difficult to maintain a predeter-
mined altitude." What about the Rolls? The Drug Enforcement
Agency had seized it from smugglers. The ISA thought "it might be
useful in the event of a counter-terrorist operation in an unfriendly
country . . . disguised as the car of a prominent politician . . . to transport Delta troops surreptitiously to the scene of the anti-terrorist

operation." The opinion of Delta, a unit dedicated to the low-profile approach, is not recorded but it is clear that aside from 5th Avenue, Knightsbridge, or the Champs d'Elysee, there are few places in the world where an advance by Rolls Royce limousine would qualify as covert. Israeli Special Forces tried the limousine trick at Entebbe. It did not go undetected for long.

Following the Gritz affair, the future of ISA hung by a thread. The few friends it had in the Pentagon played for time and promised reforms. The team was hung out to dry while the reforms, promulgated in July 1983, were codified in a dense thirteen-page Charter of U.S. Army Intelligence Support Activity. The ISA was brought firmly under the control of the Pentagon and, obliquely, the DIA, CIA, and NSC. The text identified the Activity as "a Field Operating Agency of Headquarters, Department of the Army, under the operational control of the ACSI" (Assistant Chief of Staff, Intelligence, General Odom, the only person who could authorize, in the future, ISA expenditure exceeding a modest $10,000).

Furthermore, ISA activities, "especially those involving U.S. persons, will be pursued in a responsible manner that is consistent with the Constitution and respectful of the principles upon which the United States was founded." This was more than rhetoric. It reflected the view of President Carter and CIA director Stansfield Turner to "conduct intelligence operations within Constitutional limits." Potentially, the most crippling clause in the charter insisted that the ISA would undertake activities "only when other intelligence or operational support elements and resources are unavailable or inappropriate to accomplish the tasking."

In spite of all, the Activity lived to fight another day, under another president, though, in spite of hawkish pronouncements from President Reagan and his Secretary of State, George P. Shultz, little changed. The early eighties were not good for America, or

President Reagan's reputation as a hawk. In April 1983, Hizbullah terrorists bombed the U.S. embassy in Beirut, wiping out an eight-man CIA team there along with fifty-five others. The following October, a U.S. Marine barracks near Beirut airport was attacked by a suicide bomber driving a massive truck bomb. The bomb flattened the three-story reinforced concrete building, killing another 241 Americans, most of them Marines. The survivors of a U.S. peace-keeping force were withdrawn.

Might these attacks have been anticipated? Bill Cowan, a retired Marine and Special Forces lieutenant colonel, was a member of a small ISA team trawling the back streets of Beirut for intelligence after the embassy attack.[74] From the outset, Cowan detected a lack of commitment for action in Washington. "It took five weeks for the co-ordination process and the Pentagon to finally allow us to get on airplanes and go. . . . So, we sent a small team into Beirut whose primary purpose was to ascertain the intelligence situation. Was there sufficient intelligence being acquired? How was it being acquired? Was it moving around? Were the right people seeing it?"[75]

With the CIA's team wiped out, the ISA proposed a more focused intelligence-gathering operation that would protect the U.S. peace-keepers in Beirut. Here is Cowan again: "We sent back a report to the Secretary of Defense . . . that if there were not something done to improve the intelligence-gathering, sharing of information in Beirut, that in fact, a military presence was at risk. Well, nothing was done. . . . We ran into bureaucratic stonewalling about making any changes. No changes whatsoever from our recommendations were implemented until after the bombing of the Marine compound. At that point, every recommendation was implemented, but it cost 241 servicemen to get there."[76]

The ISA team returned to Beirut a second time after the Marine deaths "because the President had said we were going to retaliate and the Secretary of Defense wanted us to go over and see about retali-ating." Though the CIA team in Beirut had been eliminated, Washington was still receiving information—probably courtesy of Mossad—to identify the ringleaders and their locations. "We took that information, got on the ground and tried to verify what we could. . . . We had a number of targets that we had no problem identifying," said Cowan. "We had a list of people provided by the CIA and that's because the CIA had good information on people that were involved in the bombing. We were not looking specifically for those people inasmuch as we were looking for where they were located. What houses were they living in? What buildings were they frequenting? . . . The CIA really had a handle on the folks. We were looking to have a handle on the locations." The surveillance targets also included two Syrian anti-aircraft positions (probably in the Bekaa Valley, from which Hizbollah operated) "nowhere close to any place where somebody who was not party to the military action could not have been hit. . . . They were in Lebanese territory. . . . In terms of the rest of the terrorists, the people we were after, the buildings they ran it out of, were clearly identifiable. A precision bombing in any one of those would have created some collateral damage."[77] Cowan skirted around the possibility that a policy of retaliation combined with close-in targeting of a terrorist's base might amount to assassination. He reminded his interviewer, "We had an executive order [from several presidents] at that point banning assassination. . . . Assassination is where you specifically target that one person, and you focus on taking him, and only him, out. And that was never where we were looking." With his soldier's eye, he was identifying an enemy position, confirming intelligence supplied from elsewhere.

Cowan and others returned to the Pentagon with "a rather substantial report." It must be assumed that others on the ISA team remained on station, to be certain that the terrorist targets were at home if and when a bomb struck them. Yet when Cowan arrived with a report that described "the options we could do—not just in terms of striking back, but other rather good intelligence operations that we could have activated, we were met with anger. We were not welcomed. We had people who absolutely berated us for even suggesting that we retaliate. We were surprised, to say the least." The report "was put away in a back drawer very, very quickly. There was absolutely no follow-up to anything we recommended."

From this, Cowan learned a hard lesson about the reality of realpolitik. "Every time somebody has struck at us, we've threatened, we've stood up, we've pounded our chest, we've blown out fire out of our mouths, smoke out of our ears, and then within a couple of weeks we've sat back down and gone back to business as usual. So we've sent a message over the years that we weren't quite serious. . . ." Cowan was speaking from the heart, eighteen years after the deaths of his fellow Marines in Beirut. Believing the lesson of that disaster had still not been taken on board, he finally unburdened himself, courtesy of public service broadcasting, soon after 9/11/01.

The years following the 1983 Charter were a time of dogged effort by the Activity, taking operations that went to the wire only to be halted at the last moment. The unit focused on two war zones: Central America (El Salvador and Nicaragua) and Lebanon. There was success in El Salvador in 1985 where four members of ISA's signals intelligence (SIGINT), flying from Honduras, intercepted hostile—and unencrypted—militia messages. The Activity's efforts to assist the rescue of the latest crop of American hostages, held this time by Hizbollah in Lebanon and constantly moved from one location to another, presented an intelligence-gathering challenge which the team met with the help of the right-wing Christian Phalange movement and, one may surmise, its Israeli ally.

During the Reagan years, a total of fourteen American hostages were snatched in Beirut alone. In March 1984 they included Bill Buckley, the ageing CIA veteran sent to rebuild the intelligence network wiped out by the bomb that destroyed the U.S. embassy. The loss of Buckley was a personal blow to CIA Director William Casey and President Reagan. Casey had persuaded Buckley, a known Agency spy, to enter the dragon's lair. Casey later received a tape recording—played to Reagan—containing the piercing screams of Buckley, under torture before he died, probably of heart failure. Buckley also left a long "confession," inevitably compromising his network. Seven other hostages remained alive. The CIA set up a Hostage Location Task Force which seems to have monitored the labyrinth of Lebanese politics, but little else.

Yet in spite of the Activity's success in identifying the location of most of the hostages, somewhere within the Washington machine the brakes were regularly put on a Special Forces rescue. This might have had something to do with the fact that the Reagan administration had a cunning plan of its own. This was to do a deal with Hizbollah's Iranian backers, then at war with Iraq, by selling the Iranians 504 TOW wire-guided anti-tank missiles (and later, several thousand Hawk anti-aircraft missiles) in exchange for hostages. The point man in this operation, serving the National Security Council, was a charismatic Marine colonel called Oliver North. North's embroidery on the scheme was to divert funds generated by the Iranian deal to fund a covert, surrogate war waged against the Nicaraguan government by right-wing Contra guerrillas. Funds for this clandestine war had been denied in Congress by the Boland Amendment. In spite of that, supported by plausibly deniable assets including a retired SAS major and ageing ex-CIA veterans, the Contras' unsuccessful Nicaraguan campaign continued.

North luminously described Casey's scheme, cooked up with a shyster Iranian middleman and riding on Israeli logistics, outside the

U.S. Constitution and its chain of command, as "a neat idea." President Reagan shared his enthusiasm. As a congressional inquiry concluded, in spite of Boland "the President felt strongly about the contras, and he ordered his staff, in the words of his national security adviser, to find a way to keep the contras 'body and soul together.' Thus began the story of how the staff of a White House advisory body, the N.S.C. [National Security Council], became an operational entity that secretly ran the contra assistance effort, and later the Iran initiative. The action officer placed in charge of both operations was Lieutenant Colonel Oliver L. North."[78]

Some hostages were released. By July 1986 the number in captivity was just four. There was a problem. It was that the Casey/North formula had generated a hostage-takers' market. Colonel Cowan, in his radio interview, ironically explained: "That policy was a great deal for the Iranians: 'We'll give you two hostages and we'll go pick up two more.' It's an endless source of money. I'd be happy to run an operation like that. You keep paying me for something, I'll make sure I've got plenty of it." The arms-for-hostages scam was "Unbelievable. I think people in the State Department, clearly people at the CIA, certainly people at the Department of Defense who understand terrorism and counterterrorist operations were aghast at the whole thing. It was . . . absolutely amateurish."

North's Contra campaign in Nicaragua unraveled spectacularly on 5 October 1986 when a cargo plane was shot down by a conscript soldier who got lucky with his shoulder-fired missile. The aircraft was carrying arms to the rebels. The only survivor, who parachuted to safety, revealed the involvement of an American military adviser in El Salvador. His trial generated useful propaganda for the Nicaraguan government. Less than a month later, the Lebanese newspaper *Al-Shiraa* revealed the arms-for-hostages trade, still continuing. By then, Iran had acquired 1,500 missiles. Three hostages had been released and three new ones snatched by Hizbollah in what Secretary of State George Shultz described as "a hostage bazaar."

The ISA finally abandoned its reconnaissance/planning mission to rescue the Beirut hostages, codenamed Project ROUND BOTTLE, almost a year later in October 1987. The unit's report for that year bleakly noted: "Project ROUND BOTTLE was terminated without evaluation of information . . . even though the DCINST [Deputy Chief of Staff, Intelligence] personally requested same."[79] Meanwhile the ISA was obliged to prove itself yet again in a series of exercises. In 1986, simulating a hostage rescue operation, it provided HUMINT and SIGINT intelligence and acted as pathfinder for the counter-terrorist strike team, probably from Delta. According to the Activity's 1986 Historical Report, the job involved "locating, surveying, reporting and operating landing zones [for helicopters] and drop zones [for parachutists]." "ISA executed their mission primarily through tradecraft means," that is, in civilian dress and maximum deception. "ISA's success was very impressive and well received."[80]

ISA soldiers also conducted twenty-nine airborne operations in FY 86. Airborne operations consisted of static-line [low-level parachute drops] and HALO [high altitude freefall drops, using oxygen from above 12,500 feet down to low opening at around 3,000 feet]. These were night jumps, with a full load of combat equipment, carried in rucksacks mounted below the parachute pack, a highly dangerous process even if, as is likely, these jumps were not live operations but exercises. It is normal SF practice to go into freefall at night from high altitude. If the parachutist loses grip of his stable, face-to-earth posture at terminal velocity, as his canopy opens, the result can be fatal as the canopy snags on his boots (a "horseshoe" malfunction), collapsing the canopy instead of allowing it to rise cleanly from the backpack to "breathe." The presence of a 100-pound rucksack, if it shifts, can make it very hard to maintain stability in freefall.

There were other difficulties at ground level. "A major problem occurred in that eight personnel were surveilled and later apprehended by State Bureau of Investigations (SBI) personnel, who thought they were involved in drug smuggling-type operations." The matter was resolved when two senior officers "were dispatched from headquarters to the exercise area." The forces of law and order were usually more obliging. "In January and February 1986, two . . . personnel were dispatched to Miami to talk to U.S. Customs Services and the Drug Enforcement Administration about concealment devices and techniques currently being used [by smugglers] and to obtain their views on how to do it better. These trips came to the personal attention of the Secretary of the Army who was advised of the results, which were primarily, we would have to do each on a case by case basis, depending on what, where and when it was needed."[81]

It was an elegant coincidence, perhaps, that the Activity should take lessons from the DEA in the methods used by drug smugglers. In 1986, President Ronald Reagan revived the Nixonian concept of a war on drugs, but this time, it was more than a metaphor. As the Cold War ended, it gave the armed services of the U.K. and U.S. an identifiable conflict zone and a new raison d'etre. In September that year the Pentagon announced that it would "lead the attack on the supply of illegal drugs from abroad."[82]

Like other White House declarations of war on drugs, before and after, it was doomed to fail but it provided the British SAS and American Special Forces including the Activity with an opportunity to test themselves in live operations against a real enemy. Such adventures are sometimes known as "operational exercises." The principal battleground was Colombia.

Over the next three years, using airborne intercepts siphoned electronically out of the Colombian jungle, the ISA tracked two cocaine barons controlling the apparently omnipotent Medellin Cartel: Jose

Rodriguez Gacha and Pablo Gavria Escobar, men whose business turnover was greater than the gross domestic product of some countries, men who commanded private armies equipped with missiles and heavy machine guns, and a ruthlessness matched only by the Mafia. Gacha was the first to die. Thanks to the ISA's intercepts, a local paramilitary team hit his hideaway, a farmhouse on the border with Panama, with helicopter gunships. Gacha tried to escape into the jungle with his son and five bodyguards. On the ground, a captain in the Anti-Narcotics Police used his SAS training to identify Gacha's likely escape route. He set up an ambush and waited. Gacha and his party walked onto the guns. There were no survivors. In 1993, it was Escobar's turn. Again, ISA identified the target's location and called in a hit team of Colombian police. Some sources suggest that the coup de grâce was delivered by a member of Delta.

The victory over the Medellin cartel triggered the law of unintended consequences. Alfred W. McCoy points out: "After the Medellin cartel's terror ended with Pablo Escobar's death in December 1993, the rival Cali cartel's quiet infiltration of the state culminated in its secret contributions to the 1994 campaign that helped elect President Ernesto Samper and half the Colombian Congress. Within two years, however, Cali's leaders too were jailed and the traffic fragmented among dozens of smaller syndicates. In this vacuum, the leftist FARC guerrillas and their blood rivals, the rightist paramilitaries, soon captured the drug trade, using rising coco profits to buy arms for civil war. . . . As FARC's influence grew, the military countered by backing the violent paramilitaries, particularly the United Self-Defense Forces commanded by Carlos Castano, a former lieutenant to drug lord Pablo Escobar."[83] Not for the first or last time would a finely honed Special Forces team achieve a brilliant tactical success in furtherance of a failed strategy thanks to a political wishlist that was none of its making. The Activity's pursuit of enemy big fish failed repeatedly in Somalia, Bosnia, and the pursuit of bin Laden as the targets learned to avoid using vulnerable cell phones, relying on human couriers instead. In Somalia in October 1993, the target was Mohammed Farah Aideed, a warlord and clan chieftain disinclined to go along with a Western-imposed plan for nation-building in his country. Allegedly, Italian military sources in Somalia tipped off the wanted man, who eluded capture. The attempt to snatch two of his lieutenants in Mogadishu as an alternative to Aideed resulted in the trauma of Black Hawk Down: the loss of first one helicopter, then another, and eighteen GIs as more assets were thrown into a battle which also took the lives of around 500 Somalis. In Bosnia, from 1996, the big fish that got away was Radovan Karadic, the Serb leader who allegedly presided over the massacre of 8,000 people at Srebrenica, as their UN protectors stood idly by. The British SIS had a plan to assassinate him, never put into effect. Karadic, bearded and disguised as a practitioner of alternative medi cine, was finally arrested by Serbian paramilitary police in 2008 after thirteen years on the run and put on trial a year later at The Hague. His chief executioner, Ratko Mladic, was still at large, protected by the Serbian army brotherhood. Bin Laden was repeatedly sighted and targeted by a number of intelligence agencies, notably the CIA, whose historian and critic Tim Weiner quotes an Agency veteran, John MacGaffin: "The CIA knew bin Laden's location almost every day, sometimes within fifty feet." But, Weiner records, while at least fifteen American special forces soldiers were killed or injured in training missions for an anticipated assault on bin Laden, "commanders in the Pentagon and civilian leaders in the White House continually backed down from the political gamble of a military mission against bin Laden."[84]

The U.S. National Commission's report on 9/11 confirmed that it was the ghost of Desert One that inhibited conventional military commanders. "General William Boykin, the current deputy under-secretary of defense for intelligence and a founding member of Delta Force, told us that 'opportunities were missed because of an unwillingness to take risks and a lack of vision and understanding.' . . . One Special Operations commander [Boykin] said his view of 'actionable intelligence' was that 'if you give me the action, I will give you the intelligence.'"[85]

CHAPTER 3

BLOOD, OIL, AND DOLLARS

America's affair with Iraq took a serious turn when Saddam Hussein confronted April Glaspie, the U.S ambassador to Baghdad, on 25 July 1990. It was the start of a confrontation with an Arab powderkeg that was to continue to drain Washington's military resources twenty years later. Saddam had not forgotten Irangate and the aid supplied to his Iranian enemy as part of Oliver North's arms-for-hostages deal four years earlier. Now he complained that Kuwait, with American complicity, was stealing Iraqi territory and oil. Alongside expressions of respect, he added menace: "I do not belittle you but . . . yours is a society which cannot accept 10,000 dead in one battle." Eight days later, Iraq invaded Kuwait.

This war, like the one that followed in 2003, was essentially about oil. In 1990, U.S. experts noted that Iraq controlled more than 10 per cent of the world's accessible oil reserves. Invading Kuwait added another 9.6 per cent to Saddam's resources. If he were to follow this through and invade Saudi Arabia, it would give him almost 26 per cent more. The arithmetic was very bad news for Western economies. Oil was still the issue in 2003. Four years after the second Gulf War, Alan Greenspan, chairman of the Federal Reserve and an icon of capitalism, wrote: "I am saddened that it is politically inconvenient to acknowledge what everyone knows: the Iraq war is largely about oil."[86]

For the allied build-up that followed Saddam's seizure of Kuwait in August 1990, five months were needed to create an expeditionary force of almost a million men and women, poised to strike in January 1991 from bases in Saudi Arabia. The process was perceived by bin Laden's fundamentalists as defilement of sacred land, made worse by the presence of healthy American females, armed, booted, in uniform and driving trucks on the streets of Riyadh. The local morality police were not pleased. One was unwise enough to challenge an American Amazon who happened to be a karate black belt. He lost and discovered horizontality. Virtually no place in this massive invasion force, the biggest since Vietnam, was allocated to allied Special Forces. The U.S. C-in-C, General Norman ("The Bear") Schwarzkopf, made no secret of his reservations about SF operations, which he saw as pinprick initiatives, marginal to the main action.

He told journalists during the buildup: "The Vietnam experience left a lot of scars. I was on the Cambodian border at a time when the rules were that the enemy could attack across the border and beat up on you and do anything he wanted. But when you started to get the upper hand you weren't allowed to chase him. That's not my favorite way to fight a war. When you go to war, you're going to war all the way." General Colin Powell, chairman of the Joint Chiefs, shared Schwarzkopf's opinion: "Light and lethal is good but you also need heavy and lethal." Powell's belief in overwhelming force gave his name to the Powell Doctrine. But it was a decision by the JCS, faced with the first Scud attacks on Israel, that finally tipped the balance in favor of giving Special Forces a limited role in this conflict.

By a piquant coincidence, the general commanding British forces in the Gulf was Sir Peter de la Billiere, a lifelong SAS soldier, who labored to persuade his American partner to accept a role for Special Forces. The SAS were not given their chance until almost a week after the shattering allied air offensive began on 17 January 1991. In general, in spite of total dedication and courage by British SAS non-commissioned officers, their regiment did not have a good war in Iraq (see chapter 7). Both U.S. and U.K. Special Forces put much effort, and took huge risks, to find the Scuds. In one case, a tanker carrying hundreds of gallons of fuel was misidentified, in darkness, for a mobile Scud launcher and destroyed. The presence of Western commandos deep inside Iraq, before the main ground offensive, prompted a change of tactics by the Iraqis. They withdrew their missiles further north, putting Israel out of Scud range. An NCO from the U.S. Air Force 24th Special Tactics Squadron was greeted by Defense Secretary Dick Cheney. "So you're one of the men who kept Israel out of the war."[87]

The opening salvoes of the Gulf War were fired by soldiers of 101st Airborne air assault division, flying heavily armed Apache helicopters. Eight of them, guided by two U.S. Air Force MH-53 helicopters capable of blind-flying, wiped out Iraqi radar sites, blinding the country's air defense system. One of the first SF operations on 25 January (D+8) was a largely British Special Boat Service (U.K. SEALs) attack on Iraqi ground communications less than twenty miles from Baghdad. Deep-buried cables had to be dug up and then destroyed. The SBS team of twenty was augmented by three Green Berets and a USAF combat controller, Master Sergeant Steve Jones, to handle close air support. They cut out a length of the cable for expert analysis, then detonated 400 pounds of high explosive. "In 90 minutes the SBS had

crippled the Iraqi communications grid with no casualties. The lieutenant leading the team grabbed one of the markers for the cable
route and presented it to General Schwarzkopf on their return."[88]
This was a remarkably short ground war—just 100 hours—and
inevitably left Special Forces, given their late start, on the sidelines.
Observers noted that although Iraqi militia units (the fedayeen)
sometimes fought bravely, even fanatically, the regular army—aside
from local actions at Nasaryiah and elsewhere—imploded. After
Saddam's reference to 10,000 dead in one battle and the Iraqi Army's
sacrifices in the war with Iran, it was an enigma. Was the Iraqi Army's
apparent change of personality due to the most remarkable Special
Forces/CIA operation of all, and the most uncelebrated? In May
2003, General Tommy Franks, Assistant Division Commander
(Maneuver) with the 1st Cavalry Division during Desert Storm, was
interviewed by *Defense News* editor Vago Muradian. A reliable summary of that interview suggests that before the first Gulf War began,
"U.S. Special Forces had gone in [to Iraq] and bribed Iraqi generals
not to fight." Franks was quoted: "I had letters from Iraqi generals
saying, 'I now work for you.'"[89] The article quoted an anonymous
"senior official" (possibly American) saying: "What is the effect you
want? How much does a cruise missile cost? Between $1m and
$2.5m. Well, a bribe is a precision-guided missile. It achieves its aim.
But it's bloodless and there's zero collateral damage." Another told
the journal: "We knew how many of these Iraqi generals were going
to call in sick." General Franks's own memoir *American Soldier* makes
no reference to this episode

There was also the anomalous political end to this war, leaving
Iraq's regime, including enough military force intact and fit to fight
an internal war against dissident Marsh Arabs in the South and Kurds
in the North. A theory circulated at that time suggested that once
Kuwait's sovereignty was restored, Saddam's Iraq was still needed as

a counterweight to likely Iranian domination of the Gulf region. However, if bribery was the secret weapon of Desert Storm, it might provide an alternative theory to explain Saddam's survival for another twelve years.

By the time America and Britain resumed their onslaught on Iraq, the world had changed. The gulf between the two wars was more than chronological. The post-9/11 world was a different place in which the clash of cultures, led from the West by a president who believed in a crusade, was worldwide and open-ended, and tailor-made for irregular military forces. A war had been fought success-fully in Afghanistan against the Taliban, apparently confirming that. Yet in 2003, dismantling Saddam Hussein's regime along with his alleged weapons of mass destruction was a misplaced experiment in "invasion lite,"[90] turning upside down the post-Vietnam policy known as the Powell doctrine. This, as the Senate Foreign Affairs Committee report on the Tora Bora battle points out, advocated "overwhelming and disproportionate military force to achieve con-crete political gains."

Anyone who took part in operation Desert Shield will recall that the counter-attack on Iraq following Saddam's occupation of Kuwait in 1990 required an American expeditionary force of 500,000 to occupy only a small part of Iraq. The first men in during the days immediately after the invasion—a tripwire force of the 82nd Airborne—shared a mordant joke about the "General Custer battle plan." Some fatalistic Saudi males were said to believe in the "Insh'Allah"—"If God Wills"—battle plan. By contrast, the invasion of 2003 was an act of faith, or worse, one that depended on the belief that 248,000 soldiers could seize and hold down five times as much territory as Desert Storm by audacity, speed, and deception.

Pentagon planners led by Defense Secretary Donald Rumsfeld gambled on the hope that Iraqis would greet Westerners as liberators and that within three years, only 5,000 U.S. soldiers would be needed in the country.[91] Other unstable elements in the invasion gamble included the decision of Paul Bremer, head of the Coalition Provisional Authority, to disband the regular Iraqi Army, losing control of its armories and to purge the Baathist apparatus that ran the country's civil, secular government. Priority was given to safeguarding oil assets. As Sir David Manning, Tony Blair's foreign policy adviser, told a U.K. inquiry: "It took us completely by surprise and judging from my conversations with Dr. Condoleezza Rice, it took her by surprise too. It was a mistake. The assumption that the Americans would have a coherent plan after the war was obviously proved to be unfounded."

Planning for the war of 2003 began soon after a tiny band of Special Forces operators, combined with an even smaller advance party from the CIA's Special Operations Group, achieved a lightning victory over the Taliban in Afghanistan, using local surrogate militia and air power as force multipliers. It was an attractive formula: not many U.S. lives at risk and maximum benefit to be derived from America's superior (and vastly expensive) technology, a process best described as Invasion Lite/Capitalism Heavy. When America and its allies, led by the U.K., invaded Iraq in 2003 the same formula was employed, though on a larger scale. Ahead of the main invasion, a Special Operations Group team helped construct a Kurdish guerrilla army. SOG also identified potential targets for U.S. air power and built the sinews of escape routes for airmen shot down over enemy territory. The Special Operations Command component, meanwhile, was increased from 350 Green Berets to 10,000, welded onto the big, regular battalions in Iraq.

Special Operations commanders wanted to prove that their small units (typically, a twelve-man Operational Detachment Alpha, or ODA) could play a significant role in a large-scale conventional

campaign. For them the war was an experiment that largely succeeded in establishing their style of soldiering as the way to the
future, the major growth industry of the American military and a
larger slice of the Pentagon budget. The reverse happened. As the war
developed, the regular army often operated in support of Special
Forces, rewriting the norms of the game. As an official history points
out: "Integrating these formations raised the kinds of issues expected
when units do not habitually train together. SOF and conventional
infantry approach the battlefield from two fundamentally different
perspectives. Moreover, the Army's doctrine on how to integrate SOF
and conventional units is not mature enough to provide adequate
guidance. Additionally, since they had not trained with each other to
any degree, they had not developed the trust and procedures so critical to working through the unknown issues. Finally, the command
and control relationship created potential for disagreement since
conventional forces are traditionally the supported force and not the
other way around. . . . But the troops worked through these friction
points."[92]

Before the invasion, key roles identified for Special Forces were to
protect Iraq's oil facilities by preventing the environmentally disastrous sabotage inflicted on Kuwait by Saddam's troops in 1991; to
provide forward reconnaissance for conventional ground forces; and
to stalk the most-wanted leaders, starting with Saddam and his two
sons. U.S. and allied SF accomplished all those things. But a more
crucial strategic victory was achieved out of sight, against the odds
and in a situation not anticipated by planners. The plan had been
that an attack by British and American forces from the north, across
Turkey into the Kurdish region of Iraq, would pin down thirteen
Iraqi divisions otherwise available to resist the advance on Baghdad
from the south.

This scheme was blocked at the last moment by Turkey's refusal to permit its territory to be used in this war. Ankara probably calculated that if—as happened—the Americans armed Turkey's Kurdish enemy in northern Iraq, then the strategy would leave the Turks with a legacy of trouble. America responded to this crisis by calling on 5,200 SF soldiers, including a British Special Boat Service team, to lead 70,000 Kurdish guerrillas against thirteen Iraqi divisions. A division is around 10,000–12,000 men. In the most critical battles, an average of two SF soldiers was allocated to 360 guerrillas.[93] In northern Iraq, as in Afghanistan and Orwell's *Animal Farm*, some animals were more equal than others. The apparent inequality in manpower was smoothed over by the West's ability to call down fire from heaven, without a politically embarrassing allied body count.

America enjoyed some street cred among the Kurds. After Saddam Hussein's defeat in the Gulf in 1991, his forces punished the Kurds for their support of the Coalition's offensive, Operation Desert Storm. It was not the first time the Kurds were hammered. In 1988, Saddam had used poison gas in an indiscriminate attack on Halabja. In April 1991, three battalions of the 10th U.S. Special Forces Group had been sent on a UN humanitarian mission to provide shivering refugees with food and shelter. General John R. Galvin asserted: "The Group saved a half million Kurds from extinction."[94] A number of officers and NCOs from the 10th were still serving when their advance guard sneaked into northern Iraq ahead of the main invasion in 2003. The Kurds greeted them as trusted friends. As in Afghanistan, the Green Berets were met and supported by officers from the CIA's paramilitary team, the Special Activities Division (SOG). The Kurdish welcome was probably tempered by the CIA's doomed attempt, in 1995, to stir up a Kurdish rebellion against Saddam that ended in disaster. Hundreds of Kurdish agents were executed.

Planning the 2003 invasion ran into an acute, last-minute complication when two fighting divisions—the U.S. 4th Infantry and British

1st Armoured—were blocked out of Kurdish northern Iraq by Turkey's veto. At short notice a substitute force had to be found to enter and hold enemy territory without crossing Turkey. No less than thirteen Iraqi divisions held their positions in the north, convinced by an elaborate American deception plan that this was the region which the U.S. Army would strike first and hardest. The key player in this spoof was a U.S. officer known as April Fool who, for almost two months ahead of the event, had been selling the Iraqis genuine but outdated invasion plans, crown jewels that were really mere paste. The spoof was given its final cutting edge by a decision to commit the 173rd Airborne Brigade, which should have been attached to the 4th Infantry Division, to a classic coup de main parachute drop onto a strategically valuable airfield at Bashur in the far north of Iraq, near the Iranian border.

The 173rd was now officially under Combined Forces Special Operations and part of the northern command titled Task Force Viking. As an official U.S. Army history concedes: "Without the 4th Infantry Division, Special Operations Forces troops would be wholly responsible for northern Iraq until the conventional forces could fight their way north from Kuwait."[95] It is unlikely that the parachute soldiers knew of April Fool, whose success focused Iraqi eyes on the area into which they jumped. The main invasion was mounted from Kuwait, to the southeast. For anyone within the magic circle that did know of this deception, and with a memory of doomed enterprises, a parachute operation in Northern Iraq in these circumstances must have been haunted by specters of Arnhem, 1944 (where clear intelligence that a Panzer division lurked near the drop zone was ignored) or Dien Bien Phu, 1954 (where French and Foreign Legion men jumped, some without parachute training, into an area already surrounded by a superior enemy force).

As it turned out, this latest operation—Operation Northern Delay, the 44th combat jump in U.S. history—got lucky. A mixed team of Special Forces, CIA Special Operations Group agents, Kurdish Peshmerga guerrillas, and drop zone pathfinders was in place at the undefended airfield on the evening of 26 March, three days after the main ground offensive began in the south, when a fleet of five C-17 Globemasters approached Iraqi air space at 30,000 feet, then dived to 600 feet so fast, to elude enemy ground fire, that the paratroopers experienced negative gravity. The Globemaster is a big bird with a wingspan of 170 feet, not designed for dive bombing or dogfights. Nevertheless, in one pass, the C-17s dropped ten heavy drop platforms of vehicles and equipment. The first man to jump after this was 173rd's commander, Colonel William Mayville. During the next 57 seconds, another 962 paras followed him. It was probably a record. The total might have been close to 1,000, had not thirty-two men been prevented from jumping as the Globemasters "powered up to make their violent escape back up to altitude." The DZ was now 10,000 feet long.[96]

This journey to war had been no picnic: a five-hour flight from Aviano, Italy to a drop zone that was glutinous mud, in total darkness on a moonless night. Thirty minutes from the drop zone, internal lights in the aircraft were switched off to be replaced by red lights over the doors, a signal that the time to jump was not far off. Tension inside the aircraft rose further as Air Force jumpmasters took the men the men through the exit drills. One of the paras recalled: "By the time we stood up to wait for the green [jump] light, my stomach was doing somersaults. I thought for a second I might throw up and had to put my head on the parachute of the guy in front of me to get my bearings. We stood up and our rucksacks [carried in front of the body for the jump] were as heavy as hell, so we were leaning on everything and trying not to stand up straight because it was horrendous."[97]

Bodies crushed together, the paras hooked up their static lines to a wire cable above them and checked the parachute container of the man in front. Then the jumpmasters opened the doors on each side of the fuselage. A cold blast of air hit them and so did swirling desert dust. One of the soldiers recalled: "We were already standing and hooked up when they went into this crazy dive. When they started to pull out of it I couldn't stand up with all the weight I had on. All I wanted to do was to get out of the bird." As the aircraft leveled off, the sensation was as if an elevator had descended at speed from a sky-scraper to hit the basement without pausing. At the same moment, the green light came on and voices shouted "Go! Go! Go!" Adrena-line time. "That's when all the fear left me and I just wanted to get out of the plane. Everybody is screaming to get out of the door because nobody wants to be left behind."

At such low level, with so many men under canopy in the same place at the same time, there was a risk of mid-air entanglement, though that does not seem to have happened. Instead, on the ground, there was mud that swallowed up some men to their waists. Some were extracted at the price of losing a boot, with the prospect of a long march ahead. It was dark, dead silent, and cold. One man recalled, "My weapon was a big chunk of mud. The barrel was clogged and I couldn't get to the trigger. It was all over my uniform, my skin and my hair. I spent the rest of the night pulling people out of it. It was crazy."

As the official U.S. Army history notes, the sun rose on "'LGOPPs—little groups of pissed off paratroopers'"—linking up with anyone they could find to form ad hoc fighting teams.[98] But fif-teen hours after the jump, 173rd was once again a coherent brigade, preparing the runway for an airborne bridge that brought in twelve Globemasters each day. The U.S. Air Force delivered 2,160 soldiers and 381 pieces of heavy equipment including tanks and artillery in ninety-six hours. With the airhead secured, the 173rd moved forward to link up with a Special Operations task force and their Kurdish allies to confront the Iraqis near Kirkuk and its vulnerable oilfields.

On 5 April, a forward reconnaissance team—twenty-six Green Berets, three Air Force controllers, and two intelligence officers driving southeast from the territory now held by their Kurdish allies—approached an enemy-held crossroads on the main road linking Kirkuk and Mosul. The approach was blocked by minefields and Debecka Ridge, a feature that defined the Green Line separating the semi-autonomous Kurdish region from the Iraqi Arab heartland to the south. Iraqi soldiers stood on bunkers on the ridge, apparently unconcerned by the appearance of such a tiny enemy force in thin-skinned Humvee's and Range Rovers. The Iraqis had confidence in the knowledge that their armory included Russian T-55 main battle tanks, equipped with 100mm guns. That night, the Americans called down B-52 strikes on the ridge. It shattered the morale of many of the Iraqi defenders, who deserted.

The recce team was now joined by only eighty Kurdish Peshmerga fighters rather than the 200 they expected. Faced with a defensive earthen berm and a minefield, the Kurds drove a Jeep armed with a recoilless rifle, clearing mines as they went, to the top of the ridge. Led by some of the team on foot, the Green Berets, with their heavier vehicles, followed through to a secondary ridge that they called, with good reason, the Alamo. Iraqi infantry opened fire on them. Under heavy enemy fire, Staff Sgt Jason D. Brown lowered his profile by squatting down, a Javelin anti-tank missile on his shoulder. He had fired only one practice round before this moment. Hoping that the missile's fire-and-forget infrared guidance system would do what the Army promised, he lined up an enemy truck full of troops at a range of 3,000 meters. The vehicle exploded in a fireball. In the battle that was to follow, the Javelin was "worth its weight in gold" according to Sergeant 1st Class Frank Antenori.[99]

The team now drove forward at 70 mph to occupy the crossroads. Then, out of the morning haze, three Iraqi utility vehicles—SUVs—came toward them, headlights flashing. For a moment it seemed that they wished to surrender, but then they released smoke grenades to cover the rest of the convoy: three armored personnel carriers on each side of the SUVs. They were followed by a column of tanks. As Staff Sergeant Bobby Farmer said: "I couldn't believe what I was seeing."[100] As bullets and shells exploded around them, it was time to retreat to the nominal sanctuary of the Alamo ridgeline. Once there, Brown jumped from his Humvee, carrying a loaded Javelin, sat down, and sighted the weapon on the leading armored personnel carrier. For a brief, heart-stopping moment the missile appeared to hesitate as it left the tube, moving a safe distance from the firing point before its main motor fired up and hurtled like an avenging angel toward the target. When flame and smoke cleared, little remained of the vehicle but a charred chassis.

Brown was joined by two of his comrades who also carried Javelins. They were Staff Sergeant Jeffrey M. Adamec and Master Sergeant Kenneth Thompson. By the end of a five-hour battle, the team had unleashed nineteen missiles. According to Sergeant Antenori, "sixteen hit enemy vehicles; two hit other structures (mud hut, monument) as a result of gunner error (accidentally locking on the wrong target), and one missile actually missed." Discovering their vulnerability, Iraqi infantry left the cover of their APCs only to be cut down by the Green Berets' machine guns.

Undeterred, in tactics reminiscent of their sacrificial war with Iran, the Iraqis "just kept coming and coming" according to the team leader, Captain Eric Wright. A later estimate by Antenori is that the allied team was indeed outnumbered. As well as five tanks, the Iraqi force totaled up to 200 men. The tanks, concealed behind a berm, were out of the reach of the Javelins, but their 100mm guns were able to maintain a dangerous barrage on the Green Berets' exposed Alamo position. The SF team summoned an air strike. The result was disastrous. A Navy F-14 bombed the wrong position, killing sixteen Peshmerga and wounding at least forty. Two Green Berets were also wounded, as was the BBC war correspondent John Simpson, who was traveling with the Kurds. Simpson's translator, Kamaran Abdurazaq Muhammed, lost both legs and bled to death. Simpson said he witnessed a scene from hell as bodies littered the dusty road amid burning wrecks. "I saw the bomb coming out of one of the planes and then, extraordinarily, I saw it as it came down beside me. . . . I saw people burning to death in front of me."[101] Had Simpson not worn his flak jacket, which was riddled with shrapnel, he also would have died.

Led by Captain Wright, six of the recce force including the team medic raced to the scene. Their first, macabre job was to sort the dead and dying from potential survivors, whose wounds they treated. On the ridge, the battle continued. An Iraqi tank moved from cover toward the handful of Special Forces soldiers facing them across the Kirkuk road. Staff Sergeant Eric Strigotte hit it from a range of 3,700 meters, substantially more than the Javelin's theoretical effective range of 2,500 meters. More air attacks, on target this time, broke the Iraqi advance. They fled on foot, leaving eight tanks and sixteen APCs behind them.

Next day, recalled Antenori, "we were counterattacked by a larger force of six T-55 and sixteen armored personnel carriers. We took out the lead tank with a Javelin and dropped some bombs on the rest. The counterattack stalled when the enemy turned around . . . later abandoning their vehicles about three kilometers away."

The road to Kirkuk was now open. The city was taken in a virtual walkover by the Kurdish Peshmerga and their Green Beret friends, supported by U.S. air power, followed up by the Paras of the 173rd. No one was spoiling for a fight at Kirkuk, a city with a large and long-established Kurdish population, living alongside Arabs, Turkmen, Assyrians, Christians, and Muslims. An Iraqi army officer, Amir Sahib Aziz, who had sworn to die to defend the city, admitted: "The Peshmerga came and they called out to us and said, 'We are your brothers and your countrymen. If you give up, we will not hurt you.'"[102]

The next strategic target, Mosul, was another matter. This city of two million people included thousands who were fiercely loyal to Saddam. In due time, Saddam's two sons would seek sanctuary in Mosul and die there under the guns of American Special Forces. In April 2003 the senior U.S. officer in the region, Lieutenant Colonel Robert Waltemeyer, had only 380 Green Berets from 2nd Battalion, 10th Special Forces Group, to take over the city. Suddenly, his Kurdish allies were a political embarrassment. Had they led the occupation, Turkey might have fulfilled its threat to invade northern Iraq. Invasion Lite was unraveling. The 2,000 men of the 173rd Airborne were now committed to one of Washington's top priorities, seizure and protection of oil refineries at Kirkuk. The result was general mayhem in Mosul and within a year, much of Iraq descended into a chaotic, unstructured conflict that mocked President Bush's boast "Mission accomplished!"

The campaign in northern Iraq in March and April 2003 bears closer scrutiny by believers in the refashioned doctrine of Unconventional Warfare. UW is defined in that document as "a broad spectrum of military and paramilitary operations, predominantly conducted through, with, or by indigenous or surrogate forces organized, trained, equipped, supported and directed in varying degrees by an external source."[103] If Special Forces and ethnic surrogates are used as a means of reducing the number of regular American or Allied soldiers, then there are manifold risks in employing the surrogates as an army of occupation rather than a useful extra tool on the battlefield.

There is another sort of surrogate, used to the same effect but not discussed in FM 3-05.20. This is the private military contractor, whose employment in Iraq provoked controversy. On 31 March 2004, the Blackwater company sent two two-man teams (including former SEALs) into Fallujah as guards for a catering company. They were ambushed at a position later renamed Blackwater Bridge, dragged from their vehicles, lynched in scenes reminiscent of Mogadishu, murdered, their bodies mutilated and set on fire. The incident detonated a bloody siege lasting a month during which twenty-seven U.S. soldiers and an unknown number of civilians and insurgents were killed. The verdict on Special Operations Forces in northern Iraq in 2003, nevertheless, must be that yet again a tiny, elite force—thanks to its versatility and intelligence as well as courage—had a strategic impact on the course of events. If, at times, too much was expected of Task Force Viking, that was no novelty either.

So far as the American government was concerned, there were two objectives of greater priority at the other end of the country. These were strategic "decapitation"—the assassination of Iraq's leadership, starting with Saddam—and the preservation of Iraq's oilfields. For President Bush, removing Saddam seems to have been a personal issue, linked to his determination to nail any perceived ally of al Qaeda after 9/11. For neocons the war was about oil.

In the event, removing key leaders, a policy of decapitation, won out, if narrowly. It missed its targets but had the unexpected result of triggering a premature ground invasion ahead of the "shock and awe" attack from the air. On 19 March, the U.S. high command received "highly perishable intelligence reporting that Saddam Hussein and several key subordinates were gathered together in a known location. . . . Unsure if such an opportunity would present itself again," President Bush authorized a strike by Nighthawk Stealth bombers and Tomahawk cruise missiles."[104] The target was a farm complex known as Dora, identified by the CIA. The only casualty was the CIA's own spy.[105]

Within hours, this preemptive attack seems to have triggered an Iraqi plan to sabotage oilfields in the south of the country and offshore in the Gulf, an event that in turn prompted ground force commanders to launch their operation ahead of the agreed deadline and in advance of the air onslaught in yet another gamble. The invasion timetable was brought forward twenty-four hours when Army intelligence analysts, studying images provided by a Predator drone, detected the beginning of sabotage in Iraq's southern oilfields. As the U.S. Army's history of the campaign makes clear: "Early on the morning of 19 March, a small group of intelligence analysts located at Camp DOHA, Kuwait, made the key intelligence call that launched the ground war on the 21st. Protecting . . . the Iraqi oil wells was so important that detecting indications of sabotage was a 'priority intelligence requirement.' . . . Determining if the oil wells were in danger of destruction—before they were destroyed—was a vital question and difficult to answer. The decision on when to start the ground war rested on that answer."[106]

The oil issue had a further impact on U.S. strategy. The Air Force could not meet the accelerated timetable as it put the final touches to its fine-tuned "shock and awe" assault on Iraq. Turning this problem to its advantage, General Tommy Franks, now chief of CENTCOM, decided that the Iraqis would expect a massive air assault before the main ground attack went in. Reversing the order—ground first, air second—would surprise the enemy. Or so it was hoped. Once more, Special Forces were invoked to save the situation, just as they had been during the Scud attacks in the First Gulf War. It was preceded by an episode that should be worth its place in any history of military intelligence.

The man who alerted the high command to the start of the sabotage was Major David Carstens, an intelligence officer with fifteen years of experience in Haiti, the Balkans, and Afghanistan. Responsible for an elite team of forty analysts, Carstens had learned to distinguish between false reports that the oil wells were on fire (when the flames were normal, precautionary burn-offs) and the real thing. He taught himself by studying video images of Saddam's destruction of Kuwait's facilities in 1991. When he received images relayed from a Predator drone of "oil well fires with pressure-backed flames reaching 60–310 feet into the air" on the morning of 19 March 2003, he called senior officers and obtained confirmation for his diagnosis from a civilian oil expert. At 0830 hours he was summoned into the presence of Colonel Steven Rotkoff, his superior.

"Dave, what do you think this is?" asked the colonel. "Do you think it is the beginning of the sabotage we talked about?"

"Yes, sir."

"Dave, I just want to be sure because we are getting ready to launch 60,000 Marines across the border."

"Yes. I'm sure."

Shortly thereafter, the authors of *On Point* observe, General Franks gave the ground forces the order to go "and 1 Marine Expeditionary Force attacked to seize the oilfields on the night of the 20th." They "achieved tactical surprise and quickly secured the oilfields, preventing the Iraqis from igniting more than a few small fires." Though successful—only nine out of 1,000 oilfields were torched—the operation to save the oil was not straightforward. It required an airborne/amphibious task force comprising U.S. SEALs, Marines, fast Navy craft, helicopters, U.K. Special Boat Service, Royal Marines of 3 Commando Brigade, and Polish Grom commandos trained by the SAS. With 250 men committed, it was the SEALs' biggest operation since Vietnam.

Oil protection in southern Iraq was a two-pronged affair. Swooping in by helicopter, a *Sunday Times* team reported, "British and U.S. forces dropped behind enemy lines north of Basra and struck south. . . . Other forces moved on Umm Qasr, a port just over the border from Kuwait whose deep-water docks were seen as vital for bringing in humanitarian aid. . . . In the al-Faw peninsula to the east, helicopters were skimming low through the night, ferrying U.S. and British commandos over the border. . . . AC130 gunships circled giving fearsome covering fire as the commandos established beachheads. . . ."[107]

The most daring attacks were on two vulnerable oil platforms offshore, fifty miles apart. One was taken by an elite SEAL team known by the acronym DEVGRU (for the enigmatically named "Development Group"). The second rig was targeted by a Polish commando known as "Grom" ("Thunderbolt"). Twenty men moved by fast open craft fitted with machine guns until they were within a mile of the target. They then switched to a pair of dinghies propelled by silenced engines and, finally, paddles. As they nosed against the steel supports of the rig, a diving team slid under the water to check for demolition charges. This time, the intelligence was correct. The explosives were found, carefully unpicked and made safe. The rest of the team, observing no signs of life on the rig, began the long climb up the structure using, according to one source, magnets as a climbing aid on the smooth superstructure.

Exactly on time, a U.S. Black Hawk helicopter flying just above sea level swept up and hovered as the SEAL snipers on board it lined up their night sights on the rig. Guards appeared, possibly alerted by a telephone that rang in their watchroom. The snipers picked them off as if this was a duck shoot. Three minutes later, the operation was over, the rig secured.[108]

The SEALs' extraordinary marksmanship was demonstrated to the world on 12 April 2009 when Captain Richard Phillips, captain of a

U.S. container ship, was held hostage by Somali pirates. Beaten off the vessel, three of the pirates escaped in one of the ship's lifeboats, taking Phillips with them. As ransom negotiations began, the hijacked lifeboat was held in tow by a U.S. warship. In the darkness, the SEALs parachuted into the sea and were picked up. Subsequently, when it seemed that Phillips—held with an AK-47 to his head—was about to be executed, three SEAL snipers, perched on superstructure above the tail of the towing vessel, fired simultaneously, killing three pirates. The fourth surrendered. Synchronised sniping to eliminate multiple targets is a finely honed art. If it works, it ensures that no enemy survives to kill a hostage. But in this case it was complicated by the movement of both ships involved, separated by thirty meters, and reliance on night sights.[109]

It was not only the route through the maritime minefields of the Shatt al Arab that made the ground invasion of Iraq on 21 March 2003 a high-risk option. Only one major ground formation—3rd Infantry Division—was ready to move at H-hour on G (for ground force operations) Day. As the official history confirms, when the 3rd ID advanced to cross the berm originally erected to stave off a second Iraqi invasion of Kuwait, "it was the only Army division ready to fight out of the four that the original plan required. The remaining units were still moving into the theater, linking up with their equipment, or moving forward to attack positions." In spite of that, "the ground war actually started two days before formal air operations began . . . General [Tommy] Franks made the deliberate decision to start the ground fight before some of the designated forces were available and ready for combat. He balanced the strategic, operational, and tactical benefits of a rapid, early advance against the risk inherent in not having sufficient combat power to achieve the campaign's objective at the start of operations. The tensions within this balance affected the campaign's execution and are a defining characteristic of the entire operation." In retrospect, the importance of Special Forces operations in the north of the country, pinning down thirteen Iraqi divisions (approximately 130,000 men), was even greater than most commentators appreciated at the time.

Initial SF maneuvers involving Delta Force, Australian and British SAS soldiers, U.K. SBS, and American Green Beret Alpha teams had started around forty-eight hours or more before. The initial heliborne assaults were on Iraqi command posts and vital communications. As in the first Gulf War in 1991, the teams identified and dug up fiber optic cables on which the enemy depended for secure communications.

Special Forces patrols emerged like desert ghosts to meet the incoming invaders. On 22 March, the second day of the ground invasion, an American cavalry team approaching the city of As Samawah encountered a group of small pickup trucks mounted with heavy machine guns, flying large American flags. "They were an SOF team conducting linkup. The team had been in the town for several days conducting reconnaissance and surveillance. . . . The SOF troopers effected the linkup in accordance with an established recognition signal worked out with the special forces liaison element. The SOF team confirmed that the bridges were intact and not wired for demolition. The SOF troops had developed a contact in town who reported on the infiltration of Republican Guard troops in town and the presence of paramilitary forces as well."[110]

The risk of fratricide, given the ambiguous appearance of Special Forces mingling on the battlefield with friendly forces, never goes away in this kind of warfare. American SF tried to minimize it by carrying tracking devices that enabled a joint command to avoid confliction. Sometimes it required heroic intervention on the ground. Special Forces soldiers often took the risk of becoming targets from their fellow Americans when they intervened in stand-offs between one U.S. force and another.

This super-cool approach was sometimes misapplied. One infantry team faced with an obstacle was joined by SF soldiers who proposed, before the firefight began, talking to tribal chiefs, "the men with beards" to settle the affair peacefully. It was a Woody Allen moment. Earlier arrivals on the scene had come under heavy fire and could not believe what the SF proposed. When the Special Forces men also encountered a withering barrage, they dressed in full battle kit and went to work to do the business the hard way.

Some SF operations became media spectaculars, good for morale back home. These included the removal from an Iraqi hospital of Private 1st Class Jessica Lynch by Special Forces supported by Marines and the subsequent recovery of other lost personnel including two valuable Apache pilots. Lynch and some of her comrades, part of a supply convoy, came under fire near An Nasiriyah on 23 March. A multiple road crash resulted, fatally injuring two men. Another two died after capture in unknown circumstances. Lynch, seriously injured, was alive but unconscious. Her captors took her to a hospital in the city, where she received medical care. The official history records: "On the evening of 1 April 2003, SOF, supported by marines, assaulted the hospital in which Private Jessica Lynch was being treated. Although there have been news stories subsequently suggesting that the assault was unnecessary since Iraqi troops had left the day before, one fact is clear: the SOF brought Lynch out."

Alongside the northern campaign and oil protection, allied Special Forces mounted a major operation in the west of the country to reduce the threat that Iraqi Scud missiles might be unleashed yet again, indiscriminately against Kuwait or Israel. This vast area, thousands of square miles of desert, became the exclusive preserve of a family of Special Forces units from the U.S., Britain, and Australia known as Task Force Dagger, under the command of General "Shooter" Harrell. In their search, they were disappointed. There is no publicly available evidence that any Scuds were fired during this war, though seventeen smaller weapons—the Ababil-100, with a range of 90 miles and a payload of 300 kg—were aimed from the Basra area at coalition assembly points in Kuwait. They missed their targets or were intercepted by defensive Patriot missiles. But as in the first Gulf War, 1991, it was the fear of what-might-happen that made the Scuds a potent psychological weapon.

The campaign in the west opened on the night of 20 March with sorties against border positions by Little Bird helicopters, which shot up their targets and returned unscathed. Iraqi soldiers got the message and began evacuating airfields that the allies needed as forward operational bases. Fired up and ready for battle, British and Australian SAS soldiers, arriving from Jordan by Chinook or desert vehicles to occupy the bases (known as H2 and H3), met little or no resistance. They probably experienced a sense of anticlimax. Certainly that was how an American close air support expert, Technical Sergeant Ed Shulman, felt about target H3. He said: "We had a team in place watching H3 as the rest of us were converging on the airfield. They watched a thirty-vehicle convoy leaving H3 and they couldn't get permission to hit it. The FOB [forward operational base] was saying, 'Don't fire until you are fired upon. Don't initiate contact.'"[111] As time passed and no Scuds were found, though around 100 possible launch sites were inspected, more aggressive tactics were permitted. Meanwhile, the abandoned airfields were crowded with Allied C-130 transports and Chinook helicopters. The once-mighty Iraqi Air Force was nowhere to be seen. The auguries were good for the U.S. 75th Airborne Rangers to parachute into yet another desert air base, H1, an operation that went smoothly enough on 25 March.

But all was not quiet on the western front, all the time. Unconfirmed reports suggest a fierce battle near Qaim, close to the Syrian border, in which SAS soldiers and Green Berets fought Republican

Guards for control of a chemical fertilizer plant once suspected of being a nuclear facility.[112] There is no public collateral to support a claim that on 22 March, in the same area, an Australian patrol of six SAS men took on an Iraqi force of between thirty and fifty, killing twelve, forcing the rest to surrender without any losses.

Meanwhile, the main coalition forces thrust from the south, up the Euphrates and main supply routes toward Baghdad, encountered their heaviest resistance, less from the regular Iraqi army than the paramilitary fedayeen, fundamentalists who would later continue the fight as guerrillas after the regulars accepted defeat. Repeatedly, at such places as Nasiriyah and Najaf, fanatical paramilitaries deserted their natural battlegrounds—urban areas—to expose themselves to American firepower during frontal attacks on allied supply lines. But in spite of such determined resistance, the advance paused only briefly as Coalition air power, night vision, and electronic surveillance made this an unequal contest. Baghdad fell on 9 April. Hostilities against the Baathist regime officially ended on 30 April. On 1 May, on board the carrier *Abraham Lincoln*, President Bush announced victory. Behind him, a banner proclaimed: "Mission accomplished!" In one important sense, that was correct. Regime change had happened and Paul Bremer was about to take over as Bush's proconsul in Baghdad. The fighting was not over by a long way, but the nature of the conflict had changed, decisively. From mid-April, this was no longer a war between nation-states but an insurrection led by several factions against the new order, one in which Special Forces would turn their strategy around 180 degrees, from acting as a destabilizing force to one that picked off opponents of government and defended the status quo.

The opposition included an army without leadership, pensions, promotion or future, and access to many tons of armaments. From having the initiative and a fine-grained plan of attack, U.S. forces were now plunged into a conflict with no front line and no fixed military doctrine. Instead, it involved a chaotic war of modern cowboys, a free-play contest in which the man, or woman, who was quickest on the draw was the one who lived to fight another day. It was Northern Ireland all over again, complete with car bombs, but on a grander scale and the added horror of suicide bombers. The first phase of the war had lasted twenty-one days and cost America 109 soldiers killed in action, with 116 wounded and unfit for further service. Phase II, the counter-insurgency war, from 1 May 2003 until 31 August 2010, when America's combat mission would end, would see around 4,000 body bags returning home. (The author's estimated figure is conservative and could well be greater. It was unlikely to be less.)

The top priority of the counterinsurgency ("coin") campaign was the former enemy's leadership, starting with Saddam Hussein and his sons, Uday and Qusay. The difference now was that leaders of the regime were no longer targets for death in battle, unless they chose that road to glory, but were fugitives from victor's justice. Having eluded Tomahawk missiles and smart bombs dropped on his palace and a remote farm during the official war, Saddam would be tried by an Iraqi court and clumsily hanged for crimes against humanity on 30 December 2006. Uday and Qusay would opt for the glory road on 22 July 2003.

The hunt for all "high-value targets" was spearheaded by a dedicated team of various SF skills, from close-in surveillance to silent killing, known as Task Force 20, later redesignated Task Force 121 and then Task Force 145. Delta's C Squadron made a point of picking up anyone closely connected to the Hussein clan in Tikrit, a town full of the dictator's kin. They got lucky when one of these revealed Saddam's hideout. By 6 P.M., under cover of darkness, the Army had a 600-man cordon around the area. The sharp end of this operation was run not by Special Forces but by Colonel James B. Hickey, son of

Irish immigrants, a scholar-soldier and boss of a conventional unit, 1st Brigade, 4th Infantry Division. At 8:30 P.M., 150 meters from Hickey's command post, some of his men searched a run-down adobe hut that contained a camp bed. It might have been a tramp's shelter but for the $75,000 in a box beneath the bed.

Nearby, one of the hunters noticed an abnormality in ground levels. Closer examination revealed a polystyrene trap door covered by a kitchen mat. Ready for a firefight, one of the soldiers pried the lid open, ready to hurl a grenade into the void. Then two supplicatory hands appeared. Saddam responded to the soldiers' challenge not with gunfire but an announcement that deserves its place in the history of bathos: "My name is Saddam Hussein," he said in English. "I am the President of Iraq and I want to negotiate."

Hickey, embarrassed by media acclaim back home in America, dismissed the coup in a television interview. "It pretty much went off as we had planned and we got the guy we were looking for," he said. The soldier who discovered Saddam's hole has never been identified. There were no citations or medals for this man. It was a minor anomaly, perhaps, but the sort of thing that gave rise later to a seemingly plausible conspiracy theory, that the real heroes of the hunt for Saddam were not Americans but Kurdish Peshmerga. There was another loose end. Senior officers advised CNN that "it is unclear whether anyone will receive the $25 million bounty on Saddam because the information leading to his capture came under duress and from more than one person." Major General Ray Odierno, commander of the 4th Infantry Division, told the network: "Over the last ten days we brought in about five to ten members of these [Tikriti] families, who were then able to give us even more information and finally we got the ultimate information from one of these individuals."[113]

Five months before Saddam surrendered so ignominiously, his sons had died in a hail of gunfire. From mid-July, the Hussein brothers had been hiding in a fortified compound in Mosul, a city that had resisted American occupation. British SAS soldiers, well practiced in the arts of concealment and deception, dressed as locals and speaking excellent Arabic, as well as electronic surveillance, had confirmed the presence of the two wanted men. The original tip had come from an inside source for whom a bounty of $15 milllion for each of Saddam's sons had proved greater than his loyalty to a defeated leader.

The use of bounty in this way originated in a U.S. Supreme Court judgment of 1873, legalizing the role of bounty hunters. In 2007 a British barrister representing the U.S. government in a case heard in London confirmed that it was acceptable under American law to kidnap people if they were wanted for offenses in America. "The U.S. does have a view about procuring people to its own shores which is not shared," he said.[114] In November 2009, an Italian court sentenced twenty-three former CIA agents up to eight years in prison for their part in abducting a terrorist suspect, Abu Omar (aka Osama Mustafa Hassan Nasr), an Egyptian on a Milan street, in February 2003.[115] The practice of paying bounty was widely used in Pakistan during the War on Terror, resulting in some suspects becoming "rendered" for interrogation elsewhere.

In the case of the Hussein brothers, no local legal framework existed. No U.S. warrant seems to have been issued for their arrest. They were about to be taken into custody, therefore, as enemy combatants. It was not a very subtle process. Rather than follow the SAS style of stealth, silence, darkness, distraction, and sudden, shocking force, the Delta Force team, backed up by a cordon from 101st Airborne Division, positioned an Iraqi interpreter in the street, equipped with a bullhorn, ordering the brothers to come out with their hands up.[116] It might have been a remake of a 1935 black-and-white movie about the G-men, starring James Cagney. The Hussein brothers, faithful to their role in the drama, responded with a burst of ill-directed automatic fire that wounded a civilian spectator. Delta failed to take the fugitives alive. This was not surprising since "in the end," after a four-hour gunfight, "it took almost all the firepower the Army could muster—TOW (wire-guided anti tank missiles), Kiowa helicopter rockets and Mk. 19 grenade launchers—to punch through the fortress-like inner walls of the villa and kill Uday Hussein and his brother, Qusay."[117]

With the end of conventional warfare, the counterinsurgency pattern that emerged followed a pattern: huge bribes available to defectors and informers, occasional arrests, and, less frequently, the use of timely information to kill a particularly dangerous opponent by Special Forces combined with air power. Seven fugitives, former Baathist leaders, got the message and gave themselves up. By 2005 only eight of the fifty-five people on "Iraq's Most Wanted" list, identified with the help of playing cards at the beginning of the campaign, were still at large. The majority, thirty-five, were pursued and captured. The fate of three was unknown though one, Saddam's right-hand man, Izzat Ibrahim al-Douri, was rumored to have died in an air raid. The two Hussein brothers were the only ones on the original list to have been killed by Coalition forces.

With the *ancien regime* accounted for, the insurgency came under different brand names. Embittered former Army officers and Baath Party officials constituted only one of these. Much more dangerous were the emerging sectarian forces of the former Sunni ruling class, notoriously led by a Jordanian psychopath whose nom de guerre was Abu Musab al Zarqawi, and the Shi'ite Mahdi Army loyal to the charismatic preacher Moqtada al-Sadr. Al-Sadr's family traditionally opposed the Saddam regime. The two private armies represented ancient fault lines in a country invented by the U.S., Britain, and France after the First World War following the collapse of the

Ottoman empire. Their potential for trouble, post-Saddam, went unnoticed during the planning of Operation Iraqi Freedom. With the conventional war officially over, the job of containing the activities of Sunni and Shi'ite terrorism—a mirror image, to some, of the IRA/Loyalist war—would keep U.S. and U.K. Special Forces busy for years, until final Western withdrawal.

The most bloodthirsty guerrilla leader, Zarqawi was an acolyte of Osama bin Laden who wanted to outdo his better-educated mentor in the politics of horror. Zarqawi's triumphs included his beheading, personally, of a 62-year-old British civil engineer, Kenneth Bigley, and Nicholas Berg, a jobless 26-year-old American from West Chester, Pennsylvania. Zarqawi deliberately engineered suicide bomb attacks on civilian Shia areas, including shrines and mosques, in order to provoke a religious war between the communities. The atrocity that finally marked the beginning of the end of his career, and his life, shocked the Arab world, including, it was rumored, bin Laden. On the evening of 9 November 2005 three suicide bomb attacks on separate hotels in Amman, capital of Jordan, killed around seventy people including guests at a wedding party. Most of the dead were Sunni, the people Zarqawi claimed to lead in Iraq. One American was killed. A former British SAS commander, a veteran of the French Foreign Legion on his way to Iraq, survived because he was shielded from the blast by a concrete pillar in the room where the wedding banquet bomb exploded.

From this point on, Jordan's intelligence service joined a hunt already controlled by Task Force 145, a group that loosely covered four autonomous Special Forces teams, one of which, Task Force Black, was built around a British SAS squadron and support forces from the U.K.'s Parachute Regiment. Task Force West had as its core the SEAL unit known as DEV-GRU. Task Force Central was a Delta squadron with Rangers as backup, and Task Force North was a Ranger battalion attached to a Delta cadre. The driving force behind this small empire was the boss of Joint Special Operations Command, Lieutenant General Stan McChrystal, later put in command of a new U.S. strategy in Afghanistan.

Prior to the Amman bombs, Task Force 145 had come close to capturing Zarqawi several times. By August 2005, the team had captured or killed 200 of his most loyal fighters. The man himself proved almost as elusive as bin Laden. He escaped one ambush by driving at speed through a checkpoint manned by Rangers before they could react. At other times he melted away dressed as a woman or a policeman. In April 2006, Zarqawi released a video that presented him as a figure as charismatic as bin Laden, delivered with all the flowery rhetoric—"Where are the lions of Anbar? Where are the lions of Salah ud-Deen?" (or Saladin)—that comes with the Arabic language.

Task Force 145 was closing in on his circle. The same day that the video was released, a Special Forces team attacked a house in Yusufiyah, twenty miles from Baghdad, killing twelve of Zarqawi's men. Zarqawi himself was now worth $25 million to a lucky bounty hunter. Helped by a prisoner picked up on the border with Jordan in May, satellite intercepts probably provided by the NSA, and a Predator drone, the hunters identified the chink in Zarqawi's armour. This was his spiritual adviser, Abdul-Rahman. Thanks to the Jordanians, the team had collateral for the movements of people close to their quarry. One was a courier known as Mr. X. When both Rahman and X turned up in a hamlet thirty miles north of Baghdad, Delta force moved in for the kill. On the evening of 7 June, from the cover of date and palm trees, they watched as Zarqawi's people came and went from the farmhouse, where their target was about to share dinner with his inner circle, including Rahman and X.

Using the license given them by McChrystal, the team did not seek clearance from higher authority for their decision to kill Zarqawi and anyone close to him. They summoned a passing Air Force F-16 to bomb the house. This it did with cool precision, with two 500-pound bombs from 20,000 feet. According to one eyewitness, Ali Abbas, a local laborer: "We saw the bodies of two women that had been fleeing away from the blast. . . . Another body was totally destroyed and in pieces. Then we heard a moan coming from another part of the house. We found the body of a big man, middle-aged. There was life in him still. It took seven of us to move him out. . . . He just moaned over and over again. He had an injury to the back of his head."[118] First Iraqi security forces, then seven U.S. helicopters descended on the scene. It seemed as if Zarqawi, on a stretcher, would still refuse to die. He became briefly conscious and recognized the uniforms looming over him. He tried to roll off the stretcher as if to make a final escape. When he did so, it was into the next world. Next day, a newly elected Iraqi Prime Minister, Nouri al-Maliki, said the $25 million dollar reward would be honored. "We will meet our promise," he said enigmatically. While Special Forces pursued the strategy of decapitation, Iraq descended steadily into growing chaos between 2004 and 2007. Abu Khalaf, Zarqawi's successor as leader of the Sunni terrorist movement (calling itself "al-Qaeda in Iraq"), commanded an army of 12,000. Khalaf was killed by SF Task Force 88, including British SAS, in Mosul on 24 June 2008.

General David Petraeus, installed as military supremo in Iraq during the last year of the Bush presidency, adopted a classic Special Forces technique, refined by the British during their war in Oman, 1970–1976, to turn the tide. He bought out the Sunni opposition. He did so by inventing local groups of "concerned local citizens," paying them and giving them authority to protect their neighborhoods. It is likely that much of the strategy was inspired by Petraeus's SAS deputy, the Scottish General Graeme Lamb. (As Colonel Kurt Pinkerton, commanding 2/5 Cavalry Regiment, said of his experience in

Baghdad: "When I first got here, a sheikh told me that anyone wearing my uniform deserves to be shot. Then after General Lamb approached community leaders who said they were prepared to do something, this same guy is thanking me for my persistence.")

Two other factors were vital if this hearts-and-minds strategy was to work. First, there was the brutality of the self-styled local al Qaeda against their hosts, alienating local people. Equally important was a surge in military force, agreed to by President Bush on 10 January 2007, of up to 30,000 more troops. Terrorist car bombs, averaging forty-two a month in Baghdad in the summer of 2006, dropped to twenty-three by September 2007. In Oman, the British had armed their recent enemy with the latest self-loading rifle. In Iraq, no weapons were handed out, but the men signing up to join the new militias, sometimes called "Awakening Councils," had plenty of those. In the disordered economy of Iraq, they needed dollars. At first, the U.S. taxpayer provided each man with $130 to $300 per month. Later, when the Iraq government took over, the pay evaporated, leaving the door open to a return by the dissidents.

Nevertheless, by the summer of 2009, the situation in much of Iraq had stabilized sufficiently for the U.S. Army to withdraw street patrols and for President Obama to propose an entire withdrawal from the country by December 2011. While the Iraq government presented this as a victory over America, many local people feared that once the foreign soldiers disappeared, the nightmare of a *de facto* civil war, accompanied by ethnic cleansing, would return. It would be surprising, however, if agents from the CIA's Special Activities Division and the U.K.'s MI6 did not maintain their street knowledge by one means or another. The U.S.-Iraqi agreement permitted the Pentagon to continue unspecified military operations, if necessary.

In 2007, well before the end of operations in Iraq, General Barry McCaffrey, an adjunct professor at West Point, reported that the SF elite there was "simply magic. . . . Deadly in getting their target—with normally zero collateral damage—and with minimal friendly losses or injuries. Some of these assault elements have done 200 to 300 'takedown' operations at platoon level. The comprehensive intelligence system is phenomenal. We need to rethink how we view these forces. They are a national strategic system akin to a B1 [Stealth] bomber."

This was not the whole picture. The Special Forces culture also included an American (and possibly even Israeli) trained Iraqi Counterterrorism Bureau, a stand-alone entity distinct from Baghdad's armed forces and the police. By April 2008 the Iraq Special Operations Force, ISOF, had 3,709 trained warriors. According to Shane Bauer, an Arabic-speaking freelance journalist based in the Middle East, an eight-man team from ISOF raided a house in Sadr City, Baghdad's rundown Shiite district, during a drive against the Mahdi Army. They smashed their way into the home of Hassan Mahsan, a police officer, accusing him of terrorist links.

"The men didn't move like any Iraqi forces he'd ever seen. They looked and spoke like his fellow countrymen but they were wearing American-style uniforms and carrying American weapons with night-vision scopes. They accused him of being a commander in the local militia, the Mahdi Army, before they dragged him off, telling his wife he was 'finished.' But before they left, they identified themselves. 'We are the Special Forces. The dirty brigade,' Hassan recalls them saying."[119]

There was one other deeply clandestine Special Forces priority during the allied occupation of Iraq. This was the movement of enemy guerrillas and terrorists across Iraq's borders with Iran and Syria. By their very nature, such operations are, or should be, invisible. But the motivation and political architecture were present to make such cross-border operations at least credible. For a start, many of the Improvised Explosive Devices used to kill and maim American and British soldiers on Iraqi roads were anything but improvised. They were factory-made anti-tank missiles, probably in Iran, and supplied to their co-religionists in the Mahdi Army. Interdicting those supplies would be a natural function of Special Forces assisted by the CIA's Special Activities Division.

U.S. and U.K. Special Forces could rely on knowledgeable allies in the Kurdish north of Iraq, to cross back and forth across Iran's exposed border in that area. On their own account, Kurdish guerrillas belonging to the PJAK (Party of Free Life in Pakistan) clashed repeatedly with Iranian security forces from 2004 onward. Links with U.S. or U.K. Special Forces, however, would need to be more than usually "black." The Obama administration declared the group a terrorist organization in 2009, forbidding contact between PJAK and U.S. citizens. This was in line with Obama's "extended hand" policy toward Iran at the time.

When 132,000 U.S. soldiers were withdrawn from the crowded, jostling streets of the country's urban areas on 30 June 2009, the Baghdad government declared a national holiday to celebrate a great victory, but feelings about the transfer of security were mixed on both sides. A total of 4,321 American soldiers, 179 Brits, and many thousands of Iraqis were dead. The fault lines of Iraq's disordered social architecture splintered into four separate, polarized entities subdivided into clan loyalties and criminal fraternities, all driven by anger and fear. More blood flowed. During the last ten days of Coalition presence on the streets, more than 250 people, most of them civilians, were murdered by terrorists. By October 2009, the insurgency was still killing 300 people each month, a reduction of 90 per cent on the previous year. But on the countdown to Iraq's election in 2010, the bombers were back. A truck and a car carrying bombs were driven undetected through a series of checkpoints manned by Iraqi security forces to kill 155 people, injure another 500, and destroy three government buildings in the capital.

The U.S. withdrawal from the streets of Iraq was far from being as ignominious as the last helicopter out of Saigon, or the British surrender to the militias at Basra, or the British retreat from Palestine. Indeed, after the double bomb attack in Baghdad on 25 October, the question in many Iraqi minds was whether it was a good idea to say farewell to American protection. A majority of Iraqis were more than satisfied with Pax Americana. They now wanted it to work. As one close observer in Baghdad noted, the more violent Iraq became, the harder it would be to justify a full U.S. withdrawal in 2011.

If regular, conventional U.S. soldiers were not to return to restore order and hold the line for an indefinite period, then the obvious Special Operations remedy would be Iraq's own, U.S.-trained Special Forces supported by American intelligence to arrange—who knows?—a return to the Phoenix Program? After extraordinary rendition, Abu Ghraib, and Guantanamo, it would probably be a step too far for most Americans, and their friends, to accept. It would assuredly need to be more scientific, more accurate, and more plausibly deniable than America's earlier assassination agendas. The name of Fidel Castro comes to mind. History looms like Nemesis over such notions. During the Algerian War of the 1950s, the French Foreign Legion achieved a military victory over terrorism in Algiers by torturing terrorists. The French Army lost their war politically and morally, back home in Paris, when the news got out, as it usually does.

CHAPTER 4

CLOAK-AND-DAGGER DONS THE GREEN BERET

T he story of America's thirty-year military campaign in
Afghanistan, led by Special Forces and the CIA, has been one of
expediency camouflaged as strategy, from the destabilization of
a Soviet client ruler and arming mujahideen guerrillas in the 1970s so
as to draw the Russians into "their own Vietnam" (Zbigniew
Brzezinksi) to the mutating strategies—none convincing as yet—
addressing the Islamist threat; from the moral certainties of Charlie
Wilson's war against the Soviets to the carefully limited commitment
of President Obama; from eight wasted years of military inconsis-
tency after 2001, to the search for political legitimacy in Kabul thereafter; from the canonization of Hamid Karzai ("a future national
leader who could unite the disparate ethnic factions," according to
General Tommy Franks) to Karzai's diminished status as just another
mediocre politician; from the spread of drug dependency as a

weapon against Russian soldiers to the demonization of poppy barons now placed on a U.S. death list . . . the meandering policies continued as American casualties mounted.

By 2014, according to one expert analysis by Deloitte, the figure could reach 5,400 including 927 killed, but not including 300,000 military victims of post-traumatic stress disorder among veterans of this conflict if—and it was a big if—American boots were still on Afghan soil by 2014. By way of comparison, the Red Army during its nine-year occupation lost 14,427 men killed augmented by 576 KGB dead. The financial cost of the war to the U.S., by the fall of 2009, was running at $3.6 billion per month.

It did not have to be like this. In 2001, following the 9/11 assault on America, an initiative led by a handful of Green Beret Special Forces and CIA operators gave the West effective control of Afghanistan. But then, in an exercise of monumental hubris immortalized by the phrase "Mission Accomplished!" America and Britain turned their attention away from nation-building in Afghanistan and their guns on Iraq. When Obama took office in January 2009, as he points out, "We had just over 32,000 Americans serving in Afghanistan, compared to 160,000 in Iraq at the peak of the war." Along the way, much of Pakistan was also radicalized in the madrassas of Quetta. Benazir Bhutto was assassinated and her country plunged into its own dark night of the soul. Secret contingency plans were made in the Pentagon to deal with Pakistan's nuclear arsenal, should that be compromised.

In "Af-Pak," a shorthand name for this now-complex geopolitical problem, the war could not be won by military means alone. Nor could it be won without military muscle. Militarily, Obama switched budget priorities and military command toward Special Forces. Politically, he banged together two heads of state: Afghanistan's fleet-footed, sinuous Hamid Karzai and Pakistan's money-grubbing Asif

Ali ("Mr Ten Per Cent") Zardari, in an effort to plug the gap through which Taliban and al Qaeda warriors were able to attack Western forces and then back off, with impunity, to fight another day. A medallion of generals on both sides of the Atlantic lined up to declare that the war was not being won and, possibly, might never be. It could be that the West might have to think the unthinkable and settle for what a British minister (Reginald Maudling) proposed during the thirty-year Irish insurgency: "A tolerable level of violence." In that case, it might succeed in keeping Islamist terror on the back foot until, like the Provisional IRA, this enemy also tired of an unwinnable war of attrition and settled for the best deal it could get.

The new strategy, placing imaginative, lateral thinking at the heart of military policy, was most dramatically expressed with the removal from office of America's military commander in Afghanistan, General David McKiernan, in May 2009. McKiernan, a distinguished soldier with a background in conventional warfare, was replaced by Lieutenant General Stanley McChrystal, a Special Forces veteran with a proven track record in Iraq. The new administration introduced a political rottweiler into the diplomatic arena in the form of Richard Holbrooke. During the Balkan wars in 1995, Holbrooke revealed how the Serb army was defeated by the Croats, with American help. He said: "We hired these guys [the Croats] to be our junkyard dogs because we were desperate. We need to 'control' them. But this is no time to get squeamish. . . . That is essential for us to get stability, so we can get out."[120]

The reconstruction of all U.S. Special Forces including those controlled by the Pentagon following 9/11 rolled through the defense budget before and after Obama's inauguration. As Obama pointed out in his West Point speech of 2 December 2009: "By the time I took office the cost of the wars in Iraq and Afghanistan approached a trillion dollars. Our new approach in Afghanistan is likely to cost us roughly $30 billion for the military this year." Special Operations Forces, once the little brother of U.S. defense, had already emerged as the main actor in a new, asymmetric style of conflict demanding a realignment of planning priorities and budgets. In November 2007, Michael G. Vickers, a former Green Beret NCO and CIA paramilitary officer who rose to become Special Forces supremo under President Bush, revealed that funds allocated to Special Operations Command had doubled to $6 billion for 2008, while its strength was to increase from 54,000 to 67,000 by 2011.[121] Todd Harrison, an expert on military budgets, confirmed in May 2009 that the winners in President Obama's $534 billion core defense budget for FY 2010 "are Special Forces and programs that are designed to help fight irregular wars." Marching in step, the U.K.'s Defence Minister announced that "the next decade must see a major rebalancing of our armed forces toward Special Forces in response to the new threats." Britain and America, he said, were conducting an urgent joint analysis to identify how their armed forces could best work together.[122]

Even before Obama took office, in spite of anxieties about constitutional niceties, the clear separation of duties, roles, and powers between the CIA's front line Special Activities Division and the Special Forces of the U.S. Navy, Marines, Army, and Air Force was largely eradicated by the brutal realities of GWOT, the Global War On Terror. Which element within the USA—CIA or military Special Operations Command (SOCOM), an entity independent of other services— would ultimately dominate the irregular warfare empire was unclear. The rivalry continues. In 2004, the main arm of the Army's Special Force team, the Green Berets, claimed that it could do better than the CIA in running agents in contested areas. At Fort Lewis, near Tacoma, it opened an advanced intelligence course resembling the CIA's Camp Peary ("The Farm") near Williamsburg, VA. The thinking blades of the Agency, an organization which recruits, almost exclusively, university graduates, were also looking at the options when, in 2005, following the intelligence failures preceding the Iraq War, a shiny new organism emerged to coordinate clandestine activities and, in effect, swallow up the Agency's entire Directorate of Operations. This included the agent-running and covert warfare Special Activities Division and its sub-unit, the paramilitary Special Operations Group, a child of the Vietnam conflict. The new organism was called the National Clandestine Service.

In a press release, Intelligence supremo John D. Negroponte and the CIA Director, Porter J. Goss, said that the takeover "reflects the thinking of some the most seasoned veterans in human intelligence collection, men and women with decades of experience in the field." It also "represents a grant of trust and an expression of confidence in CIA from the President, the Director of National Intelligence (Negroponte) and our partners throughout government."[123] The statement made much of coordinated Humint operations. It said nothing about the covert war-fighting activities of the Agency's Special Activities Division.

The de facto coalition of Army/Agency guerrillas had not gone unnoticed elsewhere. In 2002 a U.S. Army lawyer, Colonel Kathryn Stone, was working on an analysis of the implications of "employing CIA operatives in a warfighting role alongside Special Operations Forces."[124] Taking 9/11/2001 as her starting point, she noted that President Bush, backed by Congress, ordered the CIA to "use all necessary means" to destroy Osama bin Laden and al Qaeda. The focus of U.S. paramilitary operations at this time was Afghanistan, identified as al Qaeda's training ground. The distraction of Iraq did not occur until two years later.

Stone correctly asserts that a small number of CIA operators had been on the ground in Afghanistan since September 1999, supporting anti-Taliban warlords in the Northern Alliance such as the

Afghan-Uzbek Abdul Rashid Dostum, in a non-combat role. The pioneers included a former Marine captain and CIA operator named Johnny (Mike) Spann. A handsome, boyish all-American hero, he was destined to be the first American to die after the U.S. intervention in Afghanistan in 2001. Before 9/11, the assistance Spann and his colleague Dave Tyson could offer to their local allies usually amounted to intelligence derived from America's satellite and electronic spy systems, tactical advice, better communications, and money.

In practice, the Agency had been covertly fishing in the troubled waters of the region for much longer, certainly for months before the Soviet invasion of Afghanistan in December 1979. The CIA's most experienced field operator in Afghanistan, Gary C. Schroen, had been involved in that country's affairs since 1978.[125] By 30 March 1979 Under Secretary of Defense Walter Slocombe, thinking aloud at a meeting of the National Security Council, wondered whether "there is value in keeping the Afghan insurgency going, 'sucking the Soviets into a Vietnamese quagmire.'"[126] On 3 July that year, President Jimmy Carter ordered the CIA to start secret operations to undermine Russia's puppet regime in Kabul. Zbigniew Brzezinksi, Carter's National Security Adviser, in an interview with a French journal, later revealed that Carter's strategic objective was "to draw the Soviets into the Afghan trap. . . . Their own Vietnam War."[127] The chief strategist for this indirect war on Russia was probably Michael G. Vickers.

On behalf of America, British SF teams, including members of the Special Boat Squadron (Royal Marine Commandos, the U.K.'s SEALs) and deniable ex-SAS men working for a military company known as KMS were covertly training friendly mujahideen from 1979. In 1982, twenty potential leaders among these guerrillas, members of Ahmed Shah Masood's Northern Alliance, were trained by the SAS at privately owned estates in Britain and Oman. One of the most successful British operators in this deniable campaign was Richard Adamson, an

SBS instructor at the U.K.'s Commando Training Centre, posted to Iran in the early 1970s to set up a commando school for the Shah's government. For this assignment he learned Farsi, then Pashto. When the Shah was overthrown 1979, Adamson escaped from Iran and was chosen by Prime Minister Thatcher to join an undercover team in Afghanistan training mujahideen to fire U.S. Stinger missiles. Working subsequently for a private military company, he was a hostage in Somalia, survived that, and returned to Kabul after the overthrow of the Taliban in 2001. He was murdered by gangsters in Kabul in 2007.

Limited by the doctrine of plausible deniability in the early eighties, the CIA increasingly turned to British Special Forces veterans. In London in 1982, two SAS veterans were invited to meet a team from the Agency, which wanted unattributable advice: a battle plan for an attack on a Soviet air base in Afghanistan. The Brits, one of whom was a long-serving sergeant-major named Ken Connor, studied reconnaissance photographs of 24 MiG-21 aircraft, parked in a line. They wrote a detailed plan of action itemizing untraceable plastic explosive, weight to carry, time to target, entry and exit methods, and force requirements. A month later, the CIA team contacted Connor again and showed him photographs of the same air strip. The MiGs were still there, but their backs had been broken as if a scimitar had sliced through them.[128]

In July 1983, working on behalf of the Defense Intelligence Agency, a five-man British team infiltrated Afghanistan from Peshawar. Their controller was the British Secret Intelligence Service head of station on the Pakistan border. Unwisely, they carried electronic eavesdropping equipment supplied by the U.S. National Security Agency, NSA. They had been operating for three months when they were detected and hunted down. Radio Kabul identified them by their *noms-de-guerre* as Stuart Bodman, who was shot dead during the pursuit, Roderick Macginnis, Stephen Elwick, and three others known only as "Tim," "Chris," and "Phil." Their fate remains unknown. The U.K. government denied all knowledge of the team, who carried false passports.

From the mid-eighties, U.S. Green Beret soldiers were cleared to enter Afghanistan. They spent seven months there on a CIA-led mission. Following 9/11 and Bush's declaration to use all necessary means, CIA paramilitary operators entered Afghanistan on 26 September 2001 ahead of the Army's Special Operations Forces teams. They included Gary C. Schroen, the CIA's most experienced Afghanistan hand. During the anti-Soviet campaign, he had gone alone into the country, carrying bags full of dollars to encourage resistance leaders and warlords to participate in the West's version of jihad. They included Ahmed Shah Masood. Two days before 9/11, Masood was assassinated by agents of Osama bin Laden. Schroen had known Masood well. The CIA veteran was now expected to establish working relations, neglected after the Soviet withdrawal in February 1989, with Masood's successors.

Aged 59, deferring his retirement, Schroen was accompanied by seven other CIA veterans including, according to some sources, the redoubtable Billy Waugh, a soldier from 1948 until 1972 and member of the Agency's Special Activities Division from 1962. In September 2001, Waugh was aged 71 and still battle-fit. The team's orders included the instruction: "Your job is to capture bin Laden, kill him and bring his head back in a box full of dry ice."[129] For some of them, it was their most dangerous assignment. They updated their wills before they set off.

Schroen flew into Afghanistan in a Russian-made helicopter, carrying a war chest of $3 million to encourage leaders of the Northern Alliance to join the hunt for bin Laden. It required energetic diplomacy. Three weeks later, the first joint CIA/SF operations in

Afghanistan got off to a mixed start. In the early hours of 20 October 2001, a Special Forces Operational Detachment Alpha Team—code-named 555 and therefore nicknamed "Triple Nickel," led by Chief Warrant Officer David Diaz—landed somewhere in the Panshir Valley. Two helicopters carried the eleven-man group and a heavy load of equipment including laser designators to direct missiles onto targets. Each designator weighed around 90 pounds. Though Schroen's people had carefully marked the landing zone with lights that should have been identifiable even without the aid of night-vision goggles, placed at coordinates known to the pilots, both helicopters landed in the wrong place. The Alpha team, burdened with up to 300 pounds of equipment per man, exited the choppers and went to ground.

Diaz, spotting flashlights moving toward their impromptu landing zone, moved forward alone, machine gun ready. As the *Washington Post*'s Dana Priest later recounted,[130] Diaz told his men: "I'm going to try to talk to these guys. If I hit the ground I expect you guys to start shooting." The leader of the group coming toward them was "a monster of a man." He stretched out a welcoming hand to Diaz and his unquestionably American voice boomed: "Hi! I'm Hal. Damn glad to meet you!" Hal was also known as Murray. A former SEAL, he was now a freelance working on contract for the CIA, having resigned from it earlier in his career. In another context, Diaz might have joked, "Dr. Livingstone, I presume?" The encounter in Afghanistan marked the symbiosis of CIA and Special Forces as a new warfighting organism that nevertheless shared some common features with the MAC/SOG (Military Assistance Command Special Operations Group) of Vietnam days.

After a slow start due to political maneuvers in Washington and Islamabad to hobble the anti-Taliban Northern Alliance, the first twelve of a Green Beret "Alpha" team, having landed by helicopter, had to ride on horseback for eight hours to link up with General

Abdul Rashid Dostum. With them went two operators from the U.S. Air Force's own commandos, the Special Tactics team. Only two of the party had ridden a horse prior to their introduction to Afghanistan. The combined CIA/SF teams called in U.S. airstrikes against closely packed formations of Taliban tanks and artillery. They also secured helicopter landing grounds for Green Beret Special Forces and acted as guides to the newcomers, "who arrived with their arsenal of laser target designators to enable U.S. aircraft to strike [more accurately] Taliban positions."[131] During the following forty-nine days, a mere 316 SF soldiers with three CIA teams, and a handful of Air Force air controllers with godlike powers to call down fires from heaven, turned the tide in Afghanistan. Taliban forces retreated from their last redoubt, the southern city of Kandahar, before the Northern Alliance on 6 December.

Behind this dramatic victory, a massive logistical exercise had taken place controlled by General Tommy Franks at U.S. Central Command and closely monitored by Defense Secretary Donald Rumsfeld. It involved 40,000 men and women, 393 aircraft, and thirty-two ships co-ordinated with the help of thirty-one nations. Alongside attacks on suspected al Qaeda bases with Tomahawk cruise missiles, 200 men from 75th Ranger Regiment parachuted onto a high-altitude drop zone to secure it for a force of incoming Marines.

But as U.S. policy became obsessed by Iraq—by its mirage of weapons of mass destruction, the refined cruelty of Saddam Hussein's regime, and the lure of cheap oil—the early victory in Afghanistan was foregone. America's mistake in walking away from the Afghanistan power vacuum after the Soviet withdrawal in 1991 was repeated in 2003. Little by little, like the ragged-trousered army of the Vietcong, the Taliban returned. It also mutated from a vulnerable force equipped with tanks and artillery into a world-class guerrilla army.

The initial U.S. operations, successful as they were militarily, converted CIA paramilitaries into de facto fighting soldiers, at times embedded with regular army formations in the Global War on Terror. Colonel Kathryn Stone concluded: "The full spectrum dominance bought with this CIA-SOF integration of warfighting capabilities has produced a new, successful battlefield synergy. Improving the *ways* of warfighting by integrating all *means* has not only succeeded, but that has transformed the traditional view on the prosecution of armed conflict."[132]

But, as a judge advocate who believes that the rule of law and defense of America are synonymous, she offered a warning that the synergy of plausibly-deniable CIA methods and more lawfully accountable Army strategies could go badly wrong if the process were not handled carefully. She had a point. CIA operators, if taken prisoner, are deniable by their government and pay the price. Special Forces soldiers enjoy at least the fig-leaf of the Geneva Conventions. The problem with this impeccable logic, however, is that special operations, usually beyond the front line, are often unstable and not easily resolved by reference to the classic risk-versus-gain equation of intelligence-gathering theory. Luck, for which there is no legal remedy or reward, often plays a major part in the outcome. The death of the CIA field officer Mike Spann on 25 November 2001, less than a month after the first U.S. fighting unit went into action, illustrates the point.

Dostum had corralled hundreds of Taliban prisoners in the courtyard of a 19th century fort north of Mazar-I-Sharif. The prisoners had not been searched and Dostum's men in control of the fort were apparently unaware that the cellars, accessible to the prisoners, concealed an armory of thousands of automatic rifles. Spann and Tyson had heard that the prisoners included an exotic individual who spoke excellent English. Armed with Kalashnikov rifles and pistols, they went into the courtyard to find the foreigner. The man was a bearded Caucasian with black shoulder-length hair. He resembled the mass murderer Charles Manson. His local name, a nom de guerre, was Abdul Hamid. Spann noted that the suspect was wearing a British army sweater. In this part of the world, the garment might just have been worn, at some time, by a British Special Forces operator. In the fort that day, it was a sinister souvenir.

Spann repeatedly asked the man: "Where are you from? Who brought you here?" "Hamid" blanked him. Spann snapped his fingers in front of the prisoner's face. "Hey! Wake up!" Still the man said nothing. The CIA men conferred, then explained their deal to the prisoner, who was subsequently identified as a twenty-year-old Californian. Ironically, having espoused a faith that rejects alcohol, the prisoner shared his original, American name with that of a well known brand of Scotch whisky. Once upon a time, "Hamid" had been "Johnny Walker." His second surname was Lindh.

"I explained to the guy we just want to talk to him, find out what his story is," Spann told his comrade Tyson in a stage whisper directed at the prisoner's ears. "He's got to decide if he wants to live or die and die here. . . . He's going to fucking sit in prison the rest of his fucking short life. It's his decision, man."[133] Still Hamid/Walker Lindh said nothing. A necessarily short, tactical interrogation ended there. Walker rejoined the other prisoners. A very short time after that, a burst of automatic fire inside the compound triggered a gun battle that was to last three days. One of the first to die was Spann.

Tyson shot his way out of the compound and summoned reinforcements. Soon, the courtyard became an abattoir as a C-130 gunship arrived and rained down lead. On the ground, reinforcements included a team of six British Special Boat Service commandos. They joined other guards on the high wall surrounding the courtyard and blazed away with machine guns. Someone called for close air support.

A guided bomb exploded on the position from which the call was made, killing several of Dostum's men. It was not the first, or last, own-goal of this sort in Afghanistan. As the battle drew to its end, a handful of Taliban fighters retreated to the cellars. Dostum flooded the place to flush them out. Around eighty recaptured prisoners included John Walker Lindh. Later, he entered a plea bargain in the U.S. and received a twenty-year prison sentence.

The victory lost through neglect was not foreseen when the new, combined CIA/Green Beret units—initially seventy-eight men operating from Bagram airfield—repeatedly directed deadly air strikes on Taliban positions. Victory-into-defeat might have been anticipated had successive U.S. administrations identified the source of its troubles as a philosophy—Islamist fundamentalism—rather than its messenger, Osama bin Laden. Yet the CIA had itself used the idea of Islam (or a version of it) as a psychological weapon. In the mid-1980s the Agency, in alliance with Pakistan's Inter-Service Intelligence Directorate (ISI), had stoked the theocratic fires in Afghanistan and neighboring Soviet republics such as Uzbekistan. The CIA translated the Koran into local languages and printed thousands of copies that were smuggled into the region as part of the ongoing Cold War.[134] British Prime Minister Margaret Thatcher, on a high-profile visit to the border between Pakistan and Afghanistan, was also on-message. She reminded Afghan refugees: "You left your country because you refused to live under a godless Communist system which is trying to destroy your religion and your independence."

Soon after the prisoners' revolt in the fort compound at Mazar-I-Sharif, there was a second catastrophe involving a guided bomb known as JDAM (for "Joint Direct Attack Munition"). The victims were a 14-strong Green Beret team escorting the prime minister, Hamid Karzai, on his advance into Kandahar as the Taliban retreated. They identified a cave complex in which Taliban guerrillas were thought to be hiding. They called down an air strike. Flying high over-head, a B-52 crewman pressed the button to release the 2,000-pound bomb onto its target. There was a problem. This was that the target identified by the guidance system was the position occupied by the Green Berets calling the strike. Two of them were killed outright. Others lost limbs or suffered multiple injuries. Karzai was knocked unconscious and suffered a number of cuts. Three of his fighters, sit-ting on a wall a few yards away, were vaporized. How could this have happened? The most plausible theory is that at some point, a battery in the GPS receiver, from which target coordinates were sent, was replaced. The system would then go into default mode to display the only coordinates it recognized: its own. If this went uncorrected, then the team inadvertently targeted itself.

The first U.S. soldier to be killed by enemy fire was Nathan Ross Chapman, aged 31, of Georgetown, Texas. A Green Beret communi-cations expert, he was working alongside a CIA agent on a high-risk contact assignment with tribal leaders near Khost, on the border with Pakistan. Making contacts and gathering intelligence are central to the role of Special Forces in a guerrilla war. The British have lost a number of their most talented people on just such assignments, among them Sarah Bryant, aged 26, a Pashtu-speaking corporal in the Intelligence Corps. On 4 January 2002, as Nathan Chapman and his CIA companion left their meeting, they were ambushed. The Agency's man, though wounded, survived.

In 2002, after the Taliban were temporarily expelled from most of Afghanistan, the new CIA/SF synthesis did not always produce the right result. There were growing pains and mutual recriminations. The heat was on Osama bin Laden. It had been since at least 1996 when a team within the Agency's Counterterrorist Center, code-named Alec Station, had dedicated itself obsessively to the sole objec-tive of nailing him. As a result of the 1998 bomb attacks on two U.S.

embassies in Africa, President Clinton wanted bin Laden, alive or dead. After 9/11, that sentiment was shared by Clinton's successor, George W. Bush. Repeated efforts were made to assassinate fundamentalist Islam's prophet of doom. But like those earlier targets Castro and Gaddafi, he was not around when the moment came to strike. He had the same sense of impending danger as T. S. Eliot's mystery cat Macavity ("He's called the hidden paw. . . ." Whenever retribution was imminent, "Macavity's not there.") The U.S. Navy, relying on CIA intelligence, struck bin Laden's main training camp in Afghanistan with 75 Tomahawk cruise missiles. Bin Laden, tipped off—perhaps by allies in Pakistan—was not present.

Arguments continue about the failure of the world's most sophisticated intelligence and military machine to assassinate bin Laden. He had been in their sights many times. At the top of the military pyramid, clearance to proceed was never given until 9/11 happened. Some commentators believe that the bruising experience of Somalia and the spectacle of American bodies being desecrated there in 1993 had infected the Joint Chiefs of Staff with a risk-averse culture during the Clinton years. Special Forces, with their gung-ho testosterone energy were perceived as "'cowboys' whose operations would only get senior officers into trouble and damage their careers."[135]

Risk avoidance was not part of President George W. Bush's agenda after 9/11. His finding directed the CIA to use all necessary means to destroy Osama bin Laden and al Qaeda. Yet, as the Senate Foreign Relations Committee would conclude in November 2009, serious efforts to nail bin Laden before he escaped from entrapment in the rabbit warren of Tora Bora, near the Pakistan frontier, mean putting American lives on the line. The committee's report, *Tora Bora Revisted. . .* , notes: "The injection of more U.S. troops and the resulting casualties would have contradicted the risk-averse 'light-footprint' model formulated by Rumsfeld and Franks. But commanders on the scene and elsewhere in Afghanistan argued that the risks were worth the reward."

Tora Bora is "a fortress like section of the White Mountains that stretches about six miles long and six miles wide across a collection of narrow valleys, snow-covered ridgelines and jagged peaks reaching 14,000 ft." Bin Laden, scion of a prominent engineering enterprise in Saudi Arabia, built a road into the area, excavated new tunnels, and reinforced existing ones to create a military honeycomb. Around 30 November, he retreated to this redoubt with 1,000 or so Spartan warriors prepared to die in his defense, in their own, last-stand Thermopylae.

In the valley, a handful of CIA had established a base in a schoolhouse, from which they dispensed gold coins to two local tribal leaders and their militias. In early December, ninety Delta Force commandos joined this team, dressed as Afghans. Major "Dalton Fury," commanding them, told the Senate inquiry that bin Laden's communications were constantly monitored, partly thanks to an al Qaeda radio retrieved from the body of one of bin Laden's jihadists. A CIA specialist confirmed that one of the voices was that of bin Laden. It was just one gem in a jewel box of intelligence confirming that the Americans had the world's leading terrorist within their grasp.

The Tora Bora assault began with an intensive aerial bombing offensive in which Special Forces, moving in pairs, played a key role, creeping close enough to the enemy positions to be able to target them precisely with global positioning devices and laser designators. The hired Afghan warriors "insisted on retreating to their base at the bottom of the mountains each night, leaving the Americans alone inside al Qaeda territory." Nevertheless, two Delta Force soldiers got close enough to al Qaeda positions to call down air strikes for seventeen continuous hours, forcing the enemy to retreat. One attack used a 15,000-pound Daisy Cutter bomb—capable of sucking oxygen from the air around the massive explosion over a wide area—rolled from the tailgate of a C-130, in a return to the tactics of the Vietnam War. The bomb "shook the mountain for miles around."

By 14 December, bin Laden was writing his will, a remarkable document later recovered by the CIA: "Allah bears witness that the love of jihad and death in the cause of Allah has dominated my life and the verses of the sword permeated every cell in my heart, 'and fight the pagans all together as they fight you altogether.' How many times did I wake up to find myself reciting this holy verse!" In his own reinterpretation of the Koran, he left orders that his wives should not remarry. He apologized to his children—whom he had treated harshly—for devoting himself to jihad. And then he escaped into Pakistan.

The reason, as the Senate committee explains with a wealth of supporting evidence, was that repeated requests from the CIA and Delta for more American boots on the ground, to ensure that the back door into Pakistan was firmly blocked, were rejected in Washington. It asserts: "The decision not to deploy American forces to go after bin Laden or block his escape was made by Secretary of Defense Donald Rumsfeld and his troop commander, General Tommy Franks, the architect of the Afghan battle plan known as Operation Enduring Freedom. Rumsfeld said at the time that he was concerned that too many U.S. troops in Afghanistan would create an anti-American backlash and fuel widespread insurgency. . . . The Afghan [military] model emphasized minimizing the U.S. presence by relying on small, highly mobile teams of special operations troops and CIA paramilitary operatives working with the Afghan opposition. Even when his own commanders and senior intelligence officials in Afghanistan and Washington argued for dispatching more U.S. troops, Franks refused to deviate from the plan."

General Tommy Franks, leader of U.S. Central Command at the

time, has always contended that there was no hard intelligence about bin Laden's whereabouts at the time and, further, that it was best to leave the fighting to Afghans because they knew the Tora Bora terrain best. That view is not shared by the British SAS soldiers who fought alongside their Delta Force blood-brothers at Tora Bora.

Bruce Anderson, an influential British journalist, describes a visit by former Secretary of State Henry Kissinger to the SAS base near Hereford in January 2002, soon after bin Laden's latest feline disappearance. "Kissinger rapidly realised that he would have to defend his country. He was talking to men with a grievance, who believed that American generals had let bin Laden escape. Some of Dr Kissinger's audience had just come back from Afghanistan. They had taken part in the attack on the cave complex at Tora Bora, where two squadrons of the SAS [around 120 men] went into action: a significant proportion of its total strength. . . . The SAS was fighting alongside Delta Force . . . the SAS was happy enough with Delta Force. It was the American high command which let their own men down, and everyone else. The SAS and Delta Force won a victory for the West. The American generals then ensured that the full fruits of victory could not be harvested.

"By the end of the battle, the SAS was certain that it knew where bin Laden was: in a mountain valley, where he could have been trapped. The men of the SAS would have been happy to move in for the kill, dividing themselves into beaters and guns. Going round the side, the guns would have positioned themselves at the head of the valley to cut off bin Laden's retreat. The beaters would then have swept up the glen. If such a drive had taken place, the SAS is convinced that bin Laden would not have escaped. It would have been happy to fight alongside Delta Force and would have been glad of the assistance of American ground-attack aircraft. But it would also have been confident that it could finish the job on its own.

"It did not get the chance. The SAS was under overall U.S. command, and the American generals faltered. Understandably enough, they wanted Delta Force to be in at the death. They would have preferred it if bin Laden had fallen to an American bullet. So would Delta Force; every bit as much as the SAS, its men were raring to go. It was their commanders who held them back.

"Being in at such a death involves the risk of death. It seems unlikely that bin Laden could have been bagged without casualties. The men on the ground did not quail at that prospect; the generals on the radio did. They wanted Delta Force to kill bin Laden; they were not prepared to allow their men to be killed in the process. They would not even allow USAF ground-attack aircraft to operate below 12,000 feet. As far as the SAS could tell, their hope was that the ragged-trousered militants of the Northern Alliance would do most of the dangerous stuff—and take most of the casualties—while Delta Force came in for the coup de grace. Nor were the American generals willing to allow the SAS to win the glory which they were denying to American troops.

"So strategy was sabotaged by schizoid irresolution. There followed hours of fiffing and faffing, while gold coins were helicoptered in, to encourage the Northern Alliance. The USA is the greatest military power in the history of the planet, spending well over $300 billion a year on defence, yet everything was paralysed because it would not allow its fighting men to fight. While the generals agonised about bodybags, bin Laden was escaping. Henry Kissinger tried to put all this in context. He told the SAS that in his first five weeks as National Security Adviser, the U.S. lost at least 400 lives every week in Vietnam, and that was only a small percentage of the total casualties. The scars of those losses in a lost war take a long time to heal."[136]

If Tora Bora was mishandled, then the battle known as Operation Anaconda that followed a few months later was worse. Like Tora

Bora, it depended heavily on local militia known as the Afghan Military Forces, assisted by Special Forces and backed up by air power. It was to prove a deeply flawed order of battle. Many of the Afghan militia were not up to the job and air power was critically restricted by bad visibility, poor coordination with ground forces, and refueling problems. The attacking forces, yet again, had no artillery other than mortars. To win a mountain battle, fighting uphill, would depend on good luck, the element of surprise, coordination, and overwhelming firepower. In the event, most of these ingredients were not available in the right order, or time.

Following bin Laden's escape, the remnants of his army held out in the Shahi-Kot Valley, a killing zone on the Pakistan border surrounded by 10,000-foot mountains. It was familiar terrain to mujahideen who had twice whipped Soviet soldiers there. Bin Laden's veterans stayed there through a freezing Afghan winter, stoically awaiting the next Allied assault and their tickets to paradise. In February 2002, they were joined by al Qaeda volunteers from Uzbekistan and Chechnya as well as the Middle East and further afield. Britain's signals intelligence center, GCHQ, detected a flurry of cell phone traffic centered on the river running through the valley. A Special Forces recce on 10 February detected an enemy presence. There was also human intelligence that was hard to evaluate. An initial estimate of 1,000 enemy fighters was reduced to 200.[137] That was a mistake. The original figure was nearer the mark. To an optimist, the revised intelligence seemed a gift that offered the chance to crush the last of the Taliban in open battle. As ever, the coalition believed that thanks to technology, it could count on an unequal fight in favor of the coalition, adding a new luster to the phrase "asymmetric warfare." As an old SAS joke went, "I don't believe in dying for my country. I believe in allowing the other guy to die for his."

But in practice, Taliban intelligence about coalition forces was as accurate, if not more so, than that of the allies. Well in advance of the operation, the Taliban evacuated women and children from local mountain villages.[138] They prepared a defense in depth, with machine guns, mortars, and rocket launchers on the heights, and fall-back sanctuaries in caves. What Western forces expected—a three-day action with few casualties—became a 17-day pitched battle notable in American history as the highest-altitude battle its soldiers ever faced. The engagement involved 1,700 U.S. conventional soldiers, Army Special Forces, Navy SEALs, and the CIA's Special Activities Division. It also drew in hundreds of allied forces: men from the Australian and New Zealand SAS Regiments, British Royal Marines, Canadian snipers, and Special Forces contingents from Norway, Denmark, and—in spite of political inhibitions—Germany. Afghan friendly forces totaled 1,000. The air assets included French Mirage aircraft. The number of Taliban fighters is guesswork, something between 150 (the initial estimate) and 1,000 or more. A thousand was a healthy number to fight a well-prepared defense.

Operation Anaconda was probably compromised from the start. A five-man Delta Force reconnaissance team, codename Juliet, was inserted by helicopter as a preliminary move. Its lightweight, all-terrain vehicle imprinted tracks in the snow like Man Friday's footprint that were spotted by local guerrillas. The element of surprise was now lost. The five-man Delta team, perched on a high point with a lordly view over the hostile villages, lost sight of the opposition that stalked them as a snowstorm began. A day or so later, as an official report put it with masterly understatement: "Increased enemy activity in the valley seemed to indicate that the enemy forces were aware that something was afoot."[139]

As it dawned on the top brass that Anaconda required a major operation, a grand and complex plan of attack was composed. Basically, one force of Afghan militia, with Special Forces liaison teams able to summon air strikes would be Task Force Hammer, attacking enemy positions. A second would be Task Force Anvil, a stop-party to intercept Taliban fugitives. Western forces would provide circles of containment: the anaconda that would devour its prey. Objectives to be seized by heli-borne commandos were painstakingly identified. In the event, Hammer came to grief before it made contact with the enemy. "As the trucks moved off the main road [in darkness] and onto the muddy track that was the main approach route to the valley, things began to go wrong. One of the large 'jinga' trucks tipped over, halting the convoy. After cross-loading the troops and equipment, the convoy began to move out again, only to have other vehicles become stuck, break down, or tip over. Hours were consumed extricating the vehicles. . . ."[140] The militiamen, in desperation, threw hundreds of combat rations under the wheels of vehicles to provide a stable platform for wheels that spun in snow and ice. Many of the Afghan friendlies gave up this struggle and marched toward the official battle start line.[141]

Thanks to the use of headlights, as well as shouted voices, the element of surprise was now lost on this part of the battlefield. The convoy came under heavy fire. A mortar bomb scored a direct hit on the leading Special Forces vehicle. Worse, a C-130 USAF Spectre gunship lurking above the Hammer team mistook the convoy for enemy and shot it up, killing Chief Warrant Officer Stanley Harriman, aged 34, belonging to the Third Special Forces Group. Two Afghan militiamen were also killed and up to fifteen wounded. Evacuating them delayed the advance by another hour. Promised air support produced only a handful of bombs on the heights surrounding the convoy, from which Taliban fire, including artillery, rained down. The lack of support "demoralized the Afghans and frustrated the Special Forces."[142]

Unaware of this shambles, elements of the U.S. 10th Mountain and 101st Airborne divisions were delivered by helicopter to a flat, exposed area near the targeted villages that was, in truth, a killing zone. Two Australian SAS soldiers were attached to this group. Martin Wallace, a signaler, knew he was in trouble the moment his boots touched the ground. The smoke trail of a rocket-propelled grenade fired from 300 meters fizzed toward him, missing him by inches. He said later: "The RPG round hit the ground and slid through the mud, chasing us up the hill as we ran from it. It just lay there steaming in the ground as we scrambled for cover." In a later interview he recalled: "We hadn't moved 100 meters from the choppers when we started taking heavy fire from machine guns and RPGs. It was relentless. There was no cover and 82 people were looking for some." He watched, horrified, as a mortar round struck a group of Americans. "I was just lying there, watching them out of the corner of my eye and about five or six of them [U.S. soldiers] disappeared in a puff of gray smoke. It was basically a direct hit on the American mortar from the al Qaeda mortar." Under fire, Wallace ran forward and dragged those who were wounded but alive into a ditch where he had found shelter.

Wallace had one weapon that saved the day. In the confusion that followed their landing, most of the American soldiers, following normal procedure in such a tight corner, dropped their backpacks so as to be more mobile. Wallace had not discarded his pack because "we didn't have as far to go for cover." It contained his radio. He was able to call for air support. He told his headquarters: "We are in a bit of a shit-fight. We need help." Tactical air-hq obliged and sent a B-52. "I was lying on my back, watching the B-52 come overhead and you could see the bomb bay doors open and the bombs as they started to fall. You're just hoping that they're going to be on target."

The ground shook, but the bombs silenced enemy fire for only 15 minutes. The combined airborne force, codenamed Rakassan, was pinned down for more than 18 hours before Wallace was able to bring in a Spectre gunship. This gave the team covering fire as helicopters rescued the assault team, with its wounded. Having heard the story, General Frank Hagenack, overall commander of Anaconda, acknowledged: "I would not have wanted to do that operation without the Australian SAS folks on that ridge side. I mean they made it happen that day."[143]

During the following 24 hours, 3–4 March 2002, the action shifted to an 11,000-foot peak named Takur Ghar overlooking the entire Shahikot Valley. At 3 A.M. on 3 March, two Chinook helicopters tried to land near the summit to deliver two SEAL teams on a recce mission. They were advised that the place was undefended. As the first machine touched down, it was shredded by small arms fire. The Taliban were dug in and waiting for this moment. Three RPGs hit the Chinook. Petty Officer 1st Class Neil C. Roberts, on the tailgate, was hurled out of the aircraft under the impact, taken prisoner, and later shot dead. The crippled Chinook crash-landed in the valley four miles away. A second Chinook dropped another SEAL patrol on the same mountaintop to search for the missing petty officer. For the Taliban it was a turkey shoot. They killed Technical Sergeant John A. Chapman, a USAF Special Forces combat controller, and wounded two of the newly arrived SEALs. This patrol, codenamed Mako 30, retreated down the mountain. Shortly before dawn, yet another rescue team—25 Rangers on two helicopters—made another attempt. The first to land was disabled by heavy fire. Three Rangers and a member of the helicopter crew died immediately.

The second heliborne Ranger team was put on the ground "several hundred meters away." But "these Rangers were forced to move slowly up the steep slopes of Takur Ghar as their comrades were engaged in sharp fighting at the top."[144] The two parties linked up but came under attack from enemy reinforcements that had contrived to climb to the summit unnoticed. By now, al Qaeda had declared jihad and every able-bodied man in the region was expected to join the fight as a religious duty. The renewed battle continued all day. The Rangers had found the body of the missing SEAL. The bitter cold wore down one of the wounded, an Air Force medic. He became the seventh and last American to die on Operation Anaconda. The Rangers dug in and held on until they were extracted as darkness fell on 4 March. The U.S. Army's history of the battle records that the rescue was at a final cost for the U.S. of seven dead: two Army, two Air Force, and one Navy (as well as the first fatal casualty, CWO Harriman victim of friendly fire). "The fight on Takur Ghar was the most deadly firefight during Operation Anaconda."

Opinions differed about the true nature of this battle. General Tommy Franks, commander of Central Command, saw it as "an unqualified and complete success." His aides believed that 800 enemy had been killed, though there was no body count to substantiate that. The journalist, author, and pathologist of military mishaps Seymour Hersh dismissed it as "a debacle, plagued by squabbling between the services, bad military planning and avoidable deaths of American soldiers, as well as the escape of key al Qaeda leaders, likely including Osama bin Laden."[145]

Did it have to happen this way? That this became an unexpected battle of attrition was due to an intelligence failure of some sort. Why was the first estimate of enemy strength—1,000 fighters—massaged down to a more optimistic 200? The Pentagon does not say. An exhaustive review of the battle, completed in September 2003, was passed from one DOD office to another and underwent "an extensive security review" before being cleared for publication in February 2009. The review did note: "Anaconda shows the liabilities of relying on questionable human intelligence and of trying to use communications intelligence (COMINT) when the enemy has good communications security. The best solution is often better 'boots on the ground,' reconnaissance by Special Operations Forces and Army units, *which was not heavily pursued at Anaconda owing to the desire to surprise the enemy*"[146] [author's emphasis]. The Anaconda battle was a success for American forces and their allies in that an unknown number of enemy were killed and a terrorist base area was eliminated. But the affair increased the credibility of the Taliban and al Qaeda as a well-organized fighting force capable of taking on the best from the West. It was, arguably, a pyrrhic victory in spite of the heroism of the men sent to win it.

Soon after Anaconda, in the spring of 2002, there were renewed tensions about the quality of intelligence when the CIA came up with a possible location for bin Laden's latest hideout in Pakistan. Another target in the same area was his deputy, Ayman al-Zawahiri, an Egyptian doctor. Military top brass questioned the accuracy of the CIA's intelligence and, given the political risks inherent in a clandestine cross-border operation, were reluctant to sanction a reconnaissance. Unfortunately, shared intelligence with Pakistan was also fraught with the risk that what the CIA shared with Islamabad's intelligence service might be promptly shared by some within the ISI with bin Laden. Nevertheless, a Green Beret reconnaissance team tiptoed across the border with Afghanistan. Bin Laden was not at home. The hit team tiptoed out again. An anonymous Pentagon spokesman seemed to regard the latest failure as some sort of vindication of the Army after Tora Bora and Anaconda. He or she told the journal *USA Today*: "We like to underpromise and overdeliver. That other agency likes to overpromise."[147]

Alongside Anaconda, sniping between the Pentagon and the CIA's futuristic portals at Langley had continued as usual. In February 2002 an Agency-controlled Raptor loosed a missile at a white-clad figure in eastern Afghanistan, apparently on the basis that he was tall and so was Osama. Defense Secretary Donald Rumsfeld allegedly commented:

"God help anyone over five-foot-four in that country." In some of his later public statements he was more generous about the Agency. But when the bruises of Tora Bora were still fresh, the Pentagon went on the record with a litany of complaints about its CIA comrade-in-arms. These were that the Army was held responsible for air strikes and ground attacks based on faulty intelligence, leading to civilian deaths; the Agency had wanted to arm warlords who then used the weapons in local feuds or worse, perhaps, against U.S. forces; optimistic CIA leaks about the hunt for bin Laden undermined confidence in operations when the hunt produced another false lead.

The complaints reflected, at best, naïvety about the nature of this irregular conflict, with its constantly shifting loyalties, loyalties shaped by two often-incompatible factors. These were tribal dedication to some longstanding local blood feud versus the lure of the dollar as Uncle Sam's inducement to stay onside. Differing interpretations of the Koran and its additional doctrinal work, the Hadith, complicated matters further. Then there was the burgeoning heroin trade. And endemic corruption at every official level. The CIA was familiar with all this and had learned to live with it. During the campaign to defeat the Soviets, one of its surrogates was Gulbudding Hekmatyar, a warlord who received hundreds of millions of CIA dollars by way of the Pakistan intelligence agency ISI. Langley might have detected a hint of things to come when Hekmatyar, having taken the money, refused to travel to New York to shake hands with Ronald Reagan. Instead, he espoused Islamist fundamentalism and became an enemy of the West and ally of bin Laden during the civil war that followed Soviet withdrawal. Identified by the U.S. as "a global terrorist," Hekmatyar was the target of an agency-launched missile attack on his convoy in Kunar province on 6 May 2002. The missile missed its intended target but killed ten civilians.[148]

There was also the Stinger saga. During the anti-Soviet war of

1979–89, the Agency's Afghan Task Force had supplied around 2,000 of these anti-aircraft, shoulder-fired missiles to the resistance movement. When that war was over and the risk to U.S. military and civilian aircraft became apparent, case officers were dispatched in secret to buy back any missiles still in circulation. The going rate ranged from $80,000 to $150,000. This was not a CIA misjudgment. The Agency had initially opposed the introduction of such a deadly, Western weapon into a Cold War conflict but was overruled by the administration. The initial outcome was a military success. As the French analyst Olivier Roy concluded: "A staff of around 100 CIA officers; no American citizens killed or imprisoned; no retaliation against U.S. interests and the nominal expense of $2 billion over ten years: these were relatively low costs for one of the most important post-World War II conflicts."[149] The anti-Western jihad that followed the Soviet defeat was regretted at Langley, no doubt. But the CIA knew from long experience that you have to lose some to win some.

In the hunt for bin Laden, it lost two valuable paramilitaries, ostensibly working as civilian contractors, on 25 October 2003. They were Glenn Mueller, aged 32, of San Diego (a former SEAL) and William ("Chief") Carlson, aged 43, of Southern Pines, North Carolina. Soon after joining the CIA, Mueller spent a year living like a vagrant, "rocking 'n' rolling," as he told a friend, in Western Iraq. Shortly before he died, he telephoned home and told a lifelong friend: "We're looking for the golden ring," meaning bin Laden's inner circle. The day he died, he and Carlson were in the badlands adjoining the Pakistan border when they were trapped in a Taliban ambush. An Afghan commander with whom Mueller had established mutual trust was hit and went down. Mueller broke cover, entered the killing ground, and dragged his buddy to safety. In doing so, he stopped a bullet in the chest. Carlson died with them. Known as "Chief" in recognition of his heritage as a member of the Blackfoot

Nation of Montana, Carlson was a former Delta Force soldier who had retired after twenty years in the Army and still thirsted for action when he signed the Agency contract.

At the CIA headquarters, just inside the imposing entrance, on the north side, they have a Wall of Honor, decorated with stars. Each represents a life sacrificed in the line of duty. Some, such as the one commemorating William Buckley, the Agency's station chief tortured to death in 1985, are clearly identified. Many others remain anonymous, even in death. For their names to be revealed, posthumously, could compromise ongoing operations. In February 1991 there were sixty-nine stars, dating from 1950. By the time Carlson and Mueller were commemorated at Langley in 2004, the number had increased to eighty-three. They included three stars that were added following the Carlson ambush. But *three* stars? The extra one was a tribute to a man whose name was still withheld. At the commemoration, Director of Intelligence George J. Tenet said: "Chris and Chief put the lives of others ahead of their own. That is heroism defined." These deaths underscored the risk of Special Operations of all kinds. One expert assessment is that although SF men comprise only two per cent of U.S. armed forces, they record thirty-one per cent of combat casualties.[150]

The hunt for bin Laden was downgraded in 2005, when Alec Station was formally disbanded. Its analysts were reassigned to other duties within the Counterterrorist Center—though, subsequently, retired CIA veterans were brought back into service to sit in caves in the badlands of the Pakistan border with Afghanistan. The CIA briefed journalists to suggest that al Qaeda was no longer as hierarchical as it once was. Nevertheless, it was also a move away from a longstanding American fondness for personalizing complex political issues, as if the troubles of the world were a manichean cowboy movie inhabited by good guys in white hats (with or without the cattle) and the bad guys in black ones. The Tom Mix/John Wayne approach and its concomitant demonization of bin Laden probably contributed more to his legend than did his deeds.

During the first few years of the war in a region to be renamed by Obama's team as "Af-Pak," the symbiosis of Green Beret and Agency Special Activities operators was contradicted by increasing rivalry between the Pentagon and Langley. As Rumsfeld's people at the Defense Department saw things, if the CIA could exercise a military role, then DoD could run an intelligence business. It deployed clandestine teams from the Defense Intelligence Agency "to deliver intelligence that's finer-grained than what the CIA provides, for example, architectural details of a building that commandos must storm."[151] In 2005, the defense analyst William Arkin identified more than a hundred secret units, intelligence initiatives and linked operations invented by the Pentagon as part of the Gobal War on Terror. They included, for example, Joint Task Force Aztec Silence, set up in December 2003 to counter international terrorism in North Africa.

In Tampa, Florida, the Army's Special Operations Command, SOCOM, had 50,000 commandos, most of them Green Berets for strike operations. It also controlled an ultra-secret intelligence team that regularly changes its name, chameleon-like, every two years, to confuse everyone. Variously known as the Intelligence Support Activity, "The Activity," "Gray Fox," and "Capacity Gear," it was based at Fort Belvoir outside Washington and, for that reason, acquired yet another, informal name, "The Army of North Virginia." The ISA's primary role, what it does best, is covert surveillance of terrorists, which enables other security forces to strike hard and true, to kill terrorists and, sometimes, rescue hostages.

The ISA also uses lethal force on its own account, when necessary, but as observers including Douglas Waller have pointed out, "the Defense Department has had a checkered history with cloak-and-dagger work. The Pentagon set up intelligence units in the early

1980s that were kept secret from Congress. They became rogue out-fits, using tax dollars for questionable operations, to pay for expensive hotel rooms, first-class airline tickets and, in one instance, a hot-air balloon and a Rolls-Royce. . . ." For Rumsfeld and his successors, the test would be whether the soldier spies "can do better than the CIA overseas and keep out of trouble at home."

As hundreds of Special Forces operators, Agency Special Activities artists and freelance guns hired from the private sector penetrated the undefined battlefields of Af-Pak, the sort of fine-tuning expected by Congress was usually overtaken by events, many of them lethal. The first strategic error was to switch Special Operations resources from Afghanistan to Iraq. As Gary Schroen has pointed out: "In early 2002, in the immediate aftermath of the battle at Tora Bora . . . CIA and specially trained U.S. military Special Operations units began to organize teams in the provincial areas east and southeast of Kabul along Afghanistan's border with Pakistan. These teams, relatively small and mobile, operated out of temporary compounds protected by local commanders, who provided manpower, intelligence and firepower as the teams tracked down terrorist elements. . . . Initial results were promising.

"However, as early as March 2002, the U.S. military began to withdraw many of the key units involved in this effort, in order to allow them to regroup and train in preparation for the coming war with Iraq. These special units were replaced, for the most part, with members of conventional U.S. military forces, such as the 10th Mountain Division. While staffed with excellent, brave soldiers, these forces lacked the training and the agility in guerrilla warfare of the Special Operations units."[152]

Later, though the CIA's increasing use of Hellfire anti-tank missiles fired from Predator drones caused dismay to Islamist foes, critics claimed this strategy also brought about so many innocent civilian deaths that its employment, like strategic B-52 bombing in Cambodia and elsewhere, became politically counterproductive. Irregular warfare, after all, is about winning hearts and minds rather than occupation of territory or, as in Vietnam, computing success by reference to the body count. As the CIA prepared to increase Predator strikes on "high value human targets," officials claimed that in eighty such attacks between the summer of 2008 and mid-December 2009, more than 400 militants had been killed, as well as twenty civilians. Human rights groups believed the civilian death toll was 260.

Targeted assassination from the air, combined with ritualized regret about "collateral damage," was perfected by Israel. But then, Israel seeks not to persuade its enemies but—witness Operation Wrath of God, the international manhunt for the Munich Massacre terrorists—to suppress them.

Within a Pentagon think tank called the Defense Science Board, the philosophy was taken a stage further in 2002 with a proposal for a Proactive Pre-emptive Operations Group (P2OG) to "proactively, pre-emptively evoke responses from adversary/terrorist groups."[153] This could be interpreted to mean that a clandestine unit, similar to the pseudo-gangs employed by the British in Kenya in the 1950s, would launch false-flag operations aimed at stimulating reactions among terrorists. The defense analyst David Isenberg believed it would "prod terrorist cells into action, thus exposing them to 'quick response' attacks by U.S. forces. The means by which it would do this is the far greater use of special forces."

Such blue-sky thinking probably appealed to the Bush administration, contributing to the creation of the National Clandestine Service in 2005. But in this conflict, the underlying assumption—that by flushing out the enemy so as to kill him in large numbers, a political victory could be achieved—failed to recognize the potency of the cult of death and martyrdom that underpins Islamist terror. The immediate impact was to make the Pentagon, not the CIA, the lead agency in operations that could be characterized as "black." The new doctrine evolved into a belief in decapitation. This did not mean the physical removal of victim heads (though the British did chop them in Malaya, to identify dead terrorists more easily than removing an entire body from the jungle by helicopter). In Iraq and Afghanistan, "decapitation" was used figuratively and politically to describe a policy of removing key players on the opposition team. The Pentagon's decision to issue packs of playing cards to soldiers in Iraq, bearing portraits of the most-wanted fugitives, gave physical expression to the process. The jury must still be out on the result of this strategy in the Af-Pak War. The strategy worked for Michael Collins in Ireland back in 1919/20, but then he led an indigenous resistance guerrilla army, not an alien counterinsurgency force.

In terms of attrition, decapitation seemed to have something going for it by 2007. In that year, according to a source within the rebel movement, the insurgency lost half its deputy commanders. U.S. field commanders claimed to have killed or captured 100 middle ranking enemy and a number of top people in addition. This was achieved by a variety of means developed by the Israelis as well as British and American signals intelligence specialists at the National Security Agency and its English counterpart, GCHQ. Cell phones and satellite phones were like a tin can tied to a dog's tail, and more easily pursued. British Special Forces in the wilderness of Afghanistan received real-time guidance about the locations of their adversaries from a base in England. In the field, infantry units were able to employ their own Unmanned Aerial Vehicles such as Hermes to watch the enemy prepare hides for roadside mines known in the jargon as IEDs (for Improvised Explosive Devices). The British problem was that they were under-resourced. There were more IEDs than UAVs.

The Taliban response to Anaconda was to cut the number of sacrificial frontal assaults. It also ordered commanders to use couriers in preference to cell phones and to limit the number of men in most operations to between five and eight. a policy that worked for the IRA in Northern Ireland between 1970 and 1998. After 2002, the indirect warfare strategy represented by IEDs, perfected by Islamists in Iraq and reliant on technical know-how from Iran and Pakistan, was one of the most effective weapons employed by the Taliban in this second phase of the Afghanistan war. Out of 21 Green Berets killed in action between 2001 and 2009, twelve fell victims to roadside bombs. In 2009, at least 175 American and allied troops were killed this way, double the number the year before. In Iraq and Afghanistan, many British Special Forces were killed by roadside bombs, largely due to their country's failure to invest in hardened vehicles and helicopters. There were also numerous coalition victims among conventional military units not engaged in the higher-risk operations that SF teams accepted as part of the job.

The price of stalemate in Afghanistan as the Bush era came to an end was being paid in civilian lives as well as those of combatants on both sides. Most civilian casualties, as Human Rights Watch acknowledges, were caused by Taliban fighters including suicide bombers. This conclusion was confirmed by a UN report that found that militants were responsible for 55 per cent of the deaths. The greater political damage was suffered by U.S. and NATO forces as wedding parties in obscure villages came under deadly aerial bombing.

The New York-based advocacy group Human Rights Watch (HRW) concluded after dogged research: "The combination of light ground forces and overwhelming air power has become the dominant doctrine of war for the U.S. in Afghanistan."[154] The same analysis distinguished between pre-planned strikes on suspected Taliban hideouts ("Interdiction" in soldier-speak) and the forces' response to unexpected contacts with the enemy ("Close Air Support") whether by accident or as a result of ambush. In cases that HRW categorized as "unplanned" air strikes, U.S. Special Forces were prominent, if only because they often acted as the forward reconnaissance team for a sweep by regular soldiers. Sometimes outnumbered and surrounded, their only recourse was to call on air power, a legitimate reaction in a free-fire zone but inappropriate in densely populated civilian areas. In another scenario, as HRW noted, Taliban fighters occupied villages so as to use them as bases for attacks on U.S. forces, effectively using local people as human shields.

The concern increased after a suicide bomb attack on a U.S. Marine Corps Special Operations team near Jalalabad on 4 March 2007. Human rights groups alleged that the Marines' response was to kill nineteen unarmed civilians and to wound another fifty as the convoy drove away from the scene, shooting at everything that moved over a six-mile route. The unit was ordered out of Afghanistan by Army General Frank Kearney, commander of Special Operations in the region. A court of inquiry followed in the U.S. The Marine Lieutenant-General commanding U.S. Marine Forces at Central Command ruled that the convoy "acted appropriately and in accordance with the rules of engagement and tactics, techniques and procedures in place at the time in response to a complex attack."

Germany's response to a similar nightmare was less robust. In September 2009, two petrol tankers were hijacked by the Taliban and taken to the banks of the Kunduz River, where they were bogged down. A German officer in charge of the area called an air strike by two USAF F-15s, whose bombs wiped out the tankers and killed around 142 people, including a number of civilians. Was it a legitimate call? Some civilians were looting the petrol, either for their own benefit or on instructions from the Taliban. Was it clear enough that to hit the target would cause unacceptable civilian casualties, contravening

McChrystal's new policy of avoiding such incidents? A leaked report on the affair back in Germany coincided with America's appeal to allies to send more soldiers into this war. A political rumpus provoked the resignation of Germany's Defense Minister, Franz Josef Jung.

The ramifications of the affair did not end there. Though the German Army was slow to follow up the air attack on the ground, to confirm the facts and head off a Taliban propaganda coup, an Anglo-Irish journalist named Stephen Farrell, working for *The New York Times,* and his interpreter, Sultan Munadi, did reach the scene the following day. They were promptly taken hostage by the Taliban. An urgent, joint Anglo-American Special Forces rescue operation was mounted. Aided by radio and telephone intercepts provided—almost certainly—by The Activity, British SAS soldiers launched an attack on the compound where Farrell and Munadi were held. An intense gun battle followed. Farrell dived into a ditch and shouted to his rescuers he was a British hostage. Munadi was killed, as was an SAS soldier. The incident revived a debate among British Special Forces about the role of reporters, and whose responsibility it was if, on high-risk assignments of their choosing, they became prisoners.

In 2008, the UN concluded, a total of 2,118 civilians had been killed in Afghanistan, the worst year since the 2001 invasion. While insurgents were responsible for the majority of these, 828 of the casualties were caused by pro-government forces. Two thirds of that group died as a result of air strikes. The impact of these deaths sent ripples of indignation through the coalition. In an unsourced statement, HRW claimed: "Beyond violations of international humanitarian law, the political cost of each bombing that goes awry is high. In one district, a senior British commander asked U.S. Special Operations Forces to leave his district due to the mounting civilian casualties caused when the U.S. repeatedly called in airstrikes to rescue small numbers of special forces during firefights with insurgent forces. Each civilian death for which U.S. or NATO forces are perceived to be responsible increases hostility to the U.S. and NATO forces and may increase support for anti-government forces." In December 2008, Kai Eide, the UN's special representative in Kabul, suggested that harsh criticism of allied strategy by Hamid Karzai (by then into his first tour as the country's president) was "authentic."

For a time, the bombing and attacks on civilian houses continued after President Obama's inauguration. U.S.-led air strikes in Farah province early in May 2009 destroyed houses "packed with terrified civilians," killing more than a hundred people. Yet with the Obama factor came the first signs of a dramatic change of strategy. Covert Special Forces operations, including nocturnal raids on the homes of Taliban suspects, were halted on the orders of Special Operations Command. The only exceptions permitted were "the highest ranking leaders of the Taliban and Al Qaida."

Soon after this decision, the senior American soldier in Afghanistan, General David D. McKiernan, was forced to resign to clear the way for a new approach to the conduct of the war. He had been in command for only eleven months. He was replaced by Lieutenant General Stanley A. McChrystal, commander of the Joint Special Operations Command, a Green Beret soldier and qualified Ranger who liked to lead from the front. In Iraq, Delta Force, under his command, was credited with capturing Saddam Hussein and with the hunt that ended with the death of Abu Musab al-Zarqawi, an al Qaeda chieftain. Both operations were remarkable for their precision.

It would be some time before the new strategy could be expected to achieve a military victory while retrieving the catastrophic loss of popular support for the anti-Taliban campaign that had occurred in both Afghanistan and Pakistan over the preceding eight years. Some commentators believed that McChrystal represented "a more aggressive and innovative" approach, though what the Afghanistan strategy needed, after decades of conflict, was a rapier rather than a cosh. This implied even greater reliance on Special Forces of every sort, but limiting their use of air power as a form of instant and often self-defeating artillery.

The Maudling formula, "a tolerable level of violence," if that was to be a component of future of U.S. strategy, would require a stoic, if not resigned, acceptance of the normality of body bags returning from Af-Pak's poppy-laden killing fields. Certainly, at that time, the nation's military planners expected the Global War on Terror to be a very prolonged business indeed, stretching over a generation or more. General McChrystal was the first to recognize, publicly, another consequence of the new strategy, combining Special Forces finesse to reduce civilian casualties while killing foreign enemy fighters. As allied casualties resulting from the surge in Afghanistan rose sharply in the summer of 2009, McChrystal "ordered his forces to reduce aerial bombing because of the risk to civilians." One outcome was that "the additional risks to soldiers were a price worth paying. If the Afghan people swung behind the Taliban this would make the war unwinnable," he said. "In the long run it is more economical in terms of loss of life to operate this way because we can gain the support of the population."[155]

Meanwhile, the cost in U.S. lives was rising. On 26 October 2009 a Chinook helicopter attempted to rescue a Special Forces team that had made a nocturnal raid on a drug smuggler's compound in Badghis Province, western Afghanistan. The operation was supported by Afghan commandos and civilians from the Drug Enforcement Agency. The helicopter crashed on takeoff, landing in a local bazaar. Taliban sources claimed they had shot it down. A U.S. military spokesman revealed: "Seven U.S. service members and three U.S. civilians were killed." At least eleven American soldiers were wounded, as were fourteen Afghan soldiers and one American civilian. "More than a dozen enemy fighters were killed in the ensuing firefight."[156] The "ensuing firefight" was a hectic affair in which the Islamists pressed home their attack. It was not clear how the survivors were finally extracted.

There was less doubt about the reasons why the attack was launched. In a radical tactical shift away from poppy eradication toward interdicting the drug supply train and in collaboration with Britain and Australia, the Pentagon had recently placed fifty of the most powerful drug barons on a "kill or capture" agenda, officially described as "the joint integrated prioritized target list." The list included another 317 individuals. The reason the drug barons now rated equally with leading terrorists as legitimate military targets was that the Taliban depended increasingly for funds on the narcotics industry. The narcos, for their part, could not function without Taliban protection and logistics. To qualify for inclusion in the list, the suspect must have "proven links to the insurgency" confirmed by two "verifiable human sources." They could not be killed off the battle-field, but "battlefield," in this context, was not defined. Because of these caveats, in Pentagon eyes, the agenda could not be described as an assassination plan. As Rear Admiral Gregory Smith, senior U.S. military spokesman in Afghanistan, confirmed: "The list of targets are those that are contributing to the insurgency—the key leadership— and part of that obviously is the link between the narco-industry and the militants."[157] In the Pentagon's eyes, the targets were not assassinated, since their deaths occurred on the battlefield.

America's allies in this strategy were Britain and Australia. It was unclear whether all the British participants knew what they were getting into. Little or no public discussion took place in the U.K. An investigator representing the country's Serious Organized Crime Agency suggested: "In the past, the military would have hit and evidence would not have been collected. Now, with law enforcement present, we are seizing the ledgers and other information to develop an intelligence profile of the networks and the drug kingpins," to which an American military officer dryly replied: "Our long-term approach is to identify the regional drug figures and corrupt government officials and persuade them to choose legitimacy or remove them from the battlefield."[158] They might be lucky to have a choice. In 2002, a senior Pentagon legal official suggested to the Crimes of War Project: "When we have a lawful military target that the commander determines needs to be taken out, there is by no means a requirement under the law of armed conflict that we must send a warning to those people and say, you may surrender rather than be targeted," though U.S. policy "did not try to kill people who could be detained."[159]

Whatever the legalities, the new strategy had some early success. An official report discloses: "The village of Marjah in southern Afghanistan has long been an insurgent stronghold and bustling hub of drug smuggling about fifteen miles southwest of Lashgar Gah, the capital of poppy-rich Helmand Province. The Taliban felt safe gathering and training there, and they often stored weapons and explosives in the village bazaars.

"In late April 2009, U.S. military intelligence picked up information that a spectacular attack on Lashgar Gah had been ordered by the Taliban's leadership in exile, safely ensconced across the border in Quetta, Pakistan. The target appeared to be Gulab Mangal, the new governor who was having some success persuading farmers to turn away from poppy to other crops. Marjah was designated by the Taliban leadership as the staging ground for the attack, and fighters from across Afghanistan and as far away as Waziristan in Pakistan began filtering into the village. Along with the usual arsenal of AK-47s, grenade launchers, and explosives, they towed in four Soviet-era anti-aircraft guns, a sign the operation was going to be big.

"As the contingent grew, the Taliban bosses in Quetta pressed to launch the attack. But the local commanders insisted on delaying because many of their fighters were working in the fields, harvesting the last of the poppy crop. 'We still have poppies in the field,' one commander said in a conversation picked up by military intelligence. 'We do it when we come out.'

"As Afghan and U.S. troops prepared for their surprise assault on Lashgar Gah, an opportune distraction occurred. British forces killed a local tribal leader in an unrelated skirmish, causing the Taliban to postpone the attack for three days of funeral services for the leader, who had ties to the insurgency. The Taliban fighters were in the midst of the second night of mourning on May 19 when they heard the prodigious thumping of a fleet of military helicopters approaching. Within minutes, the night sky was ablaze with the first shots in what would become a fierce three-day firefight on a deadly piece of ground not far from the border with Pakistan.

"The composition of the coalition force that attacked Marjah says a lot about how far we have come in Afghanistan. Eighty percent of the 216 troops were American-trained commandos from the Afghan National Army. They were augmented by U.S. Special Forces and NATO soldiers. The presence of a twelve-man DEA paramilitary team also reflected a new level of cooperation between the military and law enforcement; the DEA was there to identify the drugs and processing chemicals that intelligence had said were hidden in the local bazaars.

"After three days of intense fighting, about sixty militants lay dead and coalition forces had seized roughly 100 tons of heroin, hashish, opium paste, poppy seeds and precursor chemicals used to turn opium into heroin. The troops also uncovered a cache of weapons, suicide belts and explosives as well as sophisticated communications equipment inside the opium bazaar, indicating that the Taliban had used it as a command center. The haul was dragged into a huge pile on the outskirts of the town and plans were made to have a jet fly over and bomb the material. But a senior U.S. military officer said that . . . the resulting explosion would be the equivalent of an 80,000-pound bomb, which would have wiped out everything in a wide swath. So the cache was divided into smaller piles and blown up from the ground." An equally large store of drugs was spirited away before the attackers could get to it. Who owned the drugs? "There is strong evidence the drugs belonged to a former police chief now living in Kabul."[160]

By the time the Marjah operation happened, a police colonel identified only as Commander S. was in custody in Kabul awaiting trial on drug charges. His property was raided in November 2008 by Special Forces soldiers who discovered forty tons of cannabis plants. His lawyer said the plants were being kept "for use as winter fuel." He was not arrested until eight months later, when CIA and British SIS agents enticed him into a meeting at Kandahar airport, where he was separated from his bodyguard by local Special Forces, the 333 Commando Brigade, mentored by the British SBS. British officials alleged that 80 kilograms of opium was found in the commander's home and that instead of congratulations, there were "howls of protest" from President Karzai's palace. The commander's defense lawyer pleaded guilty on his behalf to assisting smugglers but denied he ran a network in Arghestan, near the Pakistan border.

The emphasis on a strategy of decapitation was sometimes counterproductive. During the summer of 2009 the son and wife of Abdul Wahid Baghrani, described as "the most senior former Taliban commander in Helmand to have been reconciled" to collaboration with the West, were killed in a "mistargeted ambush by Special Forces operating in the British zone." The killings caused outrage among Helmand's tribes. Baghrani was no longer reconciled. Such episodes also left unresolved the depressing possibility that the presence of foreign troops on Afghan soil might become the problem, not the solution.

President Obama spent months weighing the implications of a report from General McChrystal, proposing a new surge of 40,000 men to drive the insurgency out of population centers to protect civilians. An alternative strategy envisaged a minimal presence on the ground accompanied by maximum hunt-and-kill missions targeted on al Qaeda leaders using Special Forces. Obama's planning was also bogged down by Afghanistan's stolen election and the confirmation of Hamid Karzai's re-election as his country's president.

As he pondered, like Rodin's Thinker, a parallel strategy of striking local deals with the enemy was lapping around the back of the White House. An incoming tide of new facts was embracing Cnut's throne; and a throne, as Cnut might have said, is not a beachhead. There were rumors that the Italian contingent had bought peace in its area of responsibility (Sarobi, forty miles east of Kabul), leaving its French successors to walk unwittingly into a hail of bullets when the bribes ceased. Ten French soldiers were killed and twenty wounded in one ambush. A local warlord allegedly on the Italian payroll, Ghulam Yahya Akbari, did not live long enough to spend the money before he, too, was killed by U.S. Special Forces.[161] Even the British produced a new doctrine proposing: "The best weapons to counter insurgents don't shoot. In other words, use bags of gold in the short term to change the security dynamics. But you don't just chuck gold at them. This has to be done wisely."[162] This, like many other confusions, was not the result of the fog of war. It reflected an uncoordinated military command. As the British experience of Malaya had demonstrated fifty years earlier, an overarching, unified civil/military command structure was vital if this sort of war was not to be lost to the guerrillas.

Meanwhile the CIA had apparently reverted to its old habits, running its war in its own way in Afghanistan, lubricating warlords with dollars. In October 2009, *The New York Times* claimed that a tribal leader was being paid by the Agency to arrange contacts with the Taliban to permit U.S. Special Forces and local paramilitaries known as the Kandahar Strike Force to use a large compound near that city. The compound was a former home of the Taliban founder, Mullah Omar. The tribal leader on the payroll, it was alleged, was none other than the Afghan president's controversial brother, Ahmed Wali Karzai. As a Senate committee report put it: "Stories about him are legendary—how Afghan police and military commanders who seize drugs in southern Afghanistan are told by Ahmed Wali to return them to the traffickers, how he arranged the imprisonment of a DEA informant who had tipped the Americans to a drug-laden truck near Kabul, how his accusers have often turned up dead. No proof has surfaced, and he and President Karzai have denied the accusations."[163]

In targeting the drug industry's big players—or at least those believed to be in bed with the Taliban—Obama's strategy seemed to be moving toward a revival of the Phoenix strategy of selective assassination in Vietnam. It raised complex legal issues about human rights and rules of engagement. No doubt Obama, a skilled, experienced lawyer, had thought of that. But talking to the enemy, while still killing his grunts, is a classic stratagem in any counter-insurgency, as the British demonstrated in Northern Ireland. It has been tried once and might have succeeded but for the Kabul government. In 2007 Michael Semple, an Irish diplomat working as a UN political officer, established a discreet dialogue with a Taliban former general. Their shared objective was practical reconciliation through rehabilitation camps for former enemies. The Afghans involved were arrested on Karzai's orders. During the Christmas break a few weeks later, Semple and a colleague from Northern Ireland were expelled for "actions prejudicial to the security of Afghanistan." It was another missed chance of peace.[164]

In 2010, President Obama tried again, dispatching another 30,000 soldiers on a limited mission, to regain the military and political initiative from the Taliban in eighteen months. But he also predicted a longer, continuing global struggle beyond that deadline in which Special Operations Forces would be the cutting edge yet again.

CHAPTER 5

PLAUSIBLY DENIABLE (AND OTHER WAYS INTO TROUBLE)

T he darkest, most sensitive Special Forces operations are linked to official, or quasi-official, intelligence agencies while remaining plausibly deniable. The relationship between free-lance soldier and government is akin to that of the ventriloquist and his dummy. It is also sometimes competitive, sometimes symbiotic. While the CIA has its own direct action team, the Special Activities Division/Special Operations Group, it also depends for many of its operations on the multi-service Special Operations Command. Neither of those sources might be armed with sufficient deniability to make them plausible comrades in arms on black operations. In any case, critics of the CIA such as the espionage historian David Wise argue: "The CIA would be much better serviced by getting out of the paramilitary business altogether and strengthening its clandestine intelligence gathering. It was, after all, created to avoid another Pearl

Harbor. It should concern itself now with preventing another 9/11."[165] Even some former insiders argue that the Agency should stick to its main job of running agents and collecting intelligence, leaving it to SOCOM to carry out the derring-do.

The CIA's problem, of course, is that SOCOM is under Pentagon control. So for the most controversial black operations, such as armed coups and assassinations, the Agency still has a tendency to sub-contract to the paramilitary private sector. In June 2009, Leon Panetta, newly appointed to run the CIA, exposed to Congress a program through which the controversial security company Blackwater—now rebranded as "Xe Services"—would help train CIA assassins to kill al Qaeda leaders. Though the secret program ran for seven years, it seems to have produced a zero body count. Blackwater would have "helped the Agency with planning, training and surveillance."[166] The millionaire boss of Blackwater, Erik Prince, felt betrayed. He told *Vanity Fair*: "When it became politically expedient . . . someone threw me under the bus." It became apparent that Prince, a right-wing patriot, offered more than advice to the Agency. He claimed to have been a vetted CIA asset for five years, developing at his own expense covert means of penetrating hard-target countries and stalking potential targets, including al Qaeda operatives, for assassination. A source close to Prince disclosed: "This program died because of a lack of political will." And, it might be added, fear of legal trouble in spite of President George W. Bush's license to the CIA to use "all necessary means" against Islamist terrorists

News of this arrangement was broken by the *New York Times* almost two months after Panetta informed Congress. The paper conceded that it was unclear whether the CIA had planned to use the contractors to capture or kill al Qaeda operatives in practice or just to help with training and surveillance. Questions about accountability also hung in the air. Robert Baer, a veteran CIA case officer, mid-East expert, and skeptic of misplaced direct action, surmised: "I suspect that if the agreements are ever really looked into—rather than a formal contract, the CIA reportedly brokered individual deals with top company brass—we will find out that Blackwater's assassination work was more about bilking the U.S. taxpayer than it was killing Osama bin Laden or other al Qaeda leaders. More than a few senior CIA officers retired from the CIA and went to work at Blackwater. . . . But Blackwater stood no better chance of placing operatives in Pakistan's tribal areas, where the al Qaeda leadership was hiding in 2004, than the CIA or the U.S. military did."[167]

This is not entirely accurate. The CIA-driven drone offensive in Pakistan fired more than fifty missiles at Islamist targets in the tribal belt of Pakistan during the year preceding Panetta's disclosure, killing numerous enemy including the Taliban commander in Pakistan, Baitullah Mehsud. Part of the price of that strategy was the innocent blood of an unknown number of civilians caught in the crossfire of this war. At the same time, up to 100 CIA and Special Forces operators spent months staring at computer screens inside the caves of Waziristan, scanning hours of video footage of suspect houses, vehicles, and faces in the ongoing hunt for bin Laden and his associates. CIA veterans brought out of retirement, back to the front line, are known as "The Cadre." Their freedom to roam was limited by their "hosts," Pakistan's own intelligence agency the ISI, elements of which have been been accused of secretly supporting the Taliban. Instead, The Cadre did their best using human surrogates, who were regularly assassinated. One agent on this beat was Art Keller, who told a British correspondent: "These old hands, despite their age, are willing to spend many months in conditions most people would say is akin to prison. The divorce rate is through the roof. Yet it's part of the allure that keeps driving them back. A lot of the time you are just sitting reading stuff but you are also in the right area. It's the big show. You are at retirement age, but are you really going to sign up for the bowling league?"[168]

If things go wrong for agents manning such outposts, the covert extraction plan is invoked. It is usually risky. Its political origins are hard to conceal combining, as it does, the joint efforts of an intelligence agency, Special Forces and, occasionally, freelances drawn from the private sector. Britain, for example, relies upon "The Increment," an elite drawn from the SAS and SBS, to provide tactical support for the Secret Intelligence Service (MI6) as well as the Royal Air Force Special Duties Flight. Using specially equipped Puma helicopters, C-130 Hercules transports, and a variety of civilian aircraft, Increment groups can usually smuggle agents into alien territory at night and in all weathers and retrieve them from remote airstrips identified in advance. Nearby, there is a prearranged emergency rendezvous. A plastic beer keg, buried underground, contains emergency survival rations and other items enabling the compromised spy to hide out for several days until the rescue team arrives. The agents in their turn are trained to use standard NATO flashlights fitted with infrared filters. Arranged in a T, these help the Special Duty pilots to identify the covert airstrip. Members of the maritime SBS, as well as running miniature submarines, take civilian qualifications enabling them to command a variety of non-military craft including trawlers as part of the same organization.

A former SIS officer, Richard Tomlinson, described how, during a training exercise in darkness and heavy rain, "the Hercules screamed into view. . . . With its props on full reverse thrust and its tires screeching in protest, it halted in an astonishingly short space. The rear ramp dropped and a Range Rover burst out and tore off down the runway toward the control tower. As briefed . . . we ran to the aircraft and clambered into the spacious hold. The aircraft executed a sharp U-turn and accelerated back down the runway as we clung to the webbing seats inside, took off, flew a tight circuit, and landed again. The rear ramp was already half-open as the plane touched down, giving a view of the Range Rover hurtling down the runway after us. With the aircraft still rolling, the Range Rover hurtled up the ramp at alarming speed. The [Increment] crew strapped it down and only seconds after touching down we were airborne again. 'That was an example of how we do hot exfiltrations,' Barry [one of the Increment] shouted over the roaring engines."[169]

The greater the risk of compromise, the greater is the need for plausible deniability. It is also the area where freelance soldiers, many of them ex-Special Forces veterans, continue their military lifestyle beyond the limits of accountability. Sometimes they are formally released from regular military service for the duration of a black operation through an informal re-identification process known as "sheep dipping." Intelligence agencies will employ freelances only when there is no alternative. Blocks on the use of regular Special Forces may be legal and financial, as in the case of Nicaragua, when Congress turned off funding for the Contras. They may be geopolitical, in cases where the fingerprints of Washington, London, Paris, or Tel Aviv must not be traced to a black operation. The attempt to blow up Sheikh Fadlallah, the spiritual leader of Hezbollah, on 8 March 1985 in Beirut was manipulated through various cutouts including, possibly, a British planner and Lebanese foot soldiers.

There are also, in the subtle world of intelligence warfare, degrees of deniability. A spy using diplomatic cover as, say, his embassy's commercial secretary, is likely, when caught, to suffer nothing worse than a declaration that he is *persona non grata* and sent home, though the loss of face and diplomatic cover can be substantial. In 2005 four British SIS men were filmed at different times in a Moscow park while retrieving data from an electronic device concealed inside a dummy rock. This was described by the Russian counter-espionage service, the Federal Security Service, as "the 21st century version of the dead-letter drop." Using a palmtop high-speed transmitter carried by a Russian intelligence "asset," the secrets were downloaded to the rock as the agent strolled past. The device, 30 centimeters wide, hollowed out to accommodate a waterproof box containing the electronics to fit inside the "rock," had a range of twenty meters.

The data was retrieved electronically by one of the agent's British controllers. The British agents were filmed in action and the rock itself opened and displayed on Russian television. Nikolai Zakharov, a spokesman for Russia's FSB intelligence, said that the U.K.'s Secret Intelligence Service had promised in 1994 that it would stop spying on Russia, "but still as a rule they send their most talented men." Surprisingly, no formal complaint was made by Russia. For diplomatic reasons, the Russians concluded that television exposure and the arrest of the British "asset," along with international ridicule, sufficed.

For other spies, using a natural cover as a doctor, journalist or businessman—cases where the cover is fact—the risk is the greater since diplomatic immunity from trial and punishment is not an option. British intelligence uses a tiny band of patriots known as "UKN." These people have a variety of skills as civil pilots, sailors, veterinary surgeons, and medical specialists. When SIS blows the bugle, they volunteer to work at short notice in hostile situations. If they are caught, the British government denies all knowledge of them. Extracting them might be delegated to the private sector, to a company such as Control Risks. Following Iraq's invasion of Kuwait in 1990, a number of British citizens working in Iraq became hostages. Some were alerted by secret radio messages to arrive at a prearranged rendezvous at a given time. They were then smuggled out by way of Kurdish northern Iraq, into Iran and flown from Tehran back to Britain. Deals of that sort usually form part of the K&R—Kidnap and Ransom—industry.

At the extreme end of deniability is the use of assassination. As a political instrument, it is usually of little value except in those cases where the target commands unusually centralized political power. The killing of the Taliban chieftain Baitullah Mehsud was such a case. After his death, a power struggle began within the Pakistani Taliban, setting off a series of terrorist attacks in Pakistan by factions claiming leadership. If power is diffused, democratically, then it makes little sense to pick off one or two individuals. The IRA's near-success in wiping out Prime Minister Thatcher and a number of her ministers with a bomb at their Brighton hotel in 1984 came close to achieving a decisive political success. The terrorists succeeded, obliquely, in 1990, by assassinating Thatcher's former aide, Ian Gow, a Member of Parliament. His death led to a by-election in a safe Conservative constituency. The Conservatives lost. It was a shock result that finally provoked Thatcher's own supporters to turn against her. She was forced to resign in 1990 during Operation Desert Shield, when Britain was on the brink of war.

In spite of the unwisdom of assassination as a tool of political change, it happens. "In unguarded moments" Major Andre Dennison, a former SAS officer, serving the white supremacist regime in Rhodesia, "hinted of dark deeds, like the elusive IRA leader holed up in his Londonderry 'safe house,' where the frustrated SAS could not 'legally' reach him for months on end. Then the mysterious, never-explained shotgun blast in the dark of night, snuffing out the IRA man on his own doorstep when he answered the coded knock known only to his mistress."[170]

The former British spy Tomlinson, claimed he was shown three plans to assassinate the Serbian President Slobodan Milosevic. These did not bear fruit but the third plan interested conspiracy theorists who studied the death of Princess Diana in a car accident in the Alma Tunnel, Paris in 1997. Milosevic Plan 3 envisaged an arranged car crash, in a tunnel, triggered by use of a flashing strobe gun wielded by a member of UKN, disguised as a papparazo, to blind the chauffeur. While some people were disposed to believe the theory that Diana was assassinated by agents working for SIS, the long, official inquiry into her death dismissed it.

American doctrine on political assassination has wobbled over the years. For some time, heads of state were held to be untouchable, though the notorious plots against Fidel Castro (at least eight, constructed by the CIA) suggest otherwise. The U.S. aerial bombing of Gaddafi's Libyan tent in 1986 was carried out because Gaddafi qualified, in Washington's eyes, as a certified terrorist. In the world of plausible deniability and cut-outs, there is no doctrine except pragmatism. It might be no more than the by-product of an agenda aimed at political change (and pursuit of profit) by ex-CIA and Special Forces mercenaries doubling as patriots. The anti-Castro movement, enthusiastically supported by Cuban exiles in Florida, became an integral part of the disastrous invasion attempt on Cuba known as the Bay of Pigs fiasco.

This operation was a triumph of optimism and disorganization over experience. It rested on two fallacies: first, that in 1961, around 30,000 dissidents would take up arms against Castro if they were encouraged by a token occupation of part of the Cuban coast by a small invasion force based in the USA; second, that 1,500 paramilitaries, after an amphibious landing without close air support, could take on Cuba's Revolutionary Army of 30,000, backed by 200,000 militia newly furnished with 40,000 tons of Warsaw Pact weapons. The CIA wrongly assumed that any civilian opponent of Castro was an insurgent. Substitute "Saddam Hussein" for "Castro" and it was a miscalculation repeated in Iraq in 2003. In Cuba there was no meaningful Resistance of the sort that Eisenhower—who first approved the operation—applauded in Occupied Europe during the Second World War.

By the time the invasion plan was transferred to the incoming President Kennedy in January 1961 it was already mired in administrative chaos, its political front composed of exiles torn by internal feuds, its secrecy blown in the press. As an official report noted: "'Plausible denial' was a pathetic illusion."[171] Radio Moscow announced the impending invasion four days before it happened. All that was required to ensure failure was a decision by Kennedy, after the invasion fleet had set sail from Nicaragua, to deny the force proper air cover. An official report, classified top secret for many years, reveals: "Late on 16 April, the eve of D-Day [in Cuba], the air strikes designed to knock out the rest of Castro's air force on the following morning were called off. The message reached the field too late to halt the landing operation, as the decision to cancel the air strike was made after the landing force had been committed." The outcome was predictable. As the invasion fleet approached Cuba, Castro's B-26 light bombers, Sea Fury and T-33 fighters sank a supply ship, caused a transport to beach uncontrollably and damaged an infantry landing craft. A projected beach landing was abandoned, its assets transferred to another beach. Cuban air attacks went on throughout D-Day. At a third beachhead, Blue Beach, "enemy ground attacks, supported by aircraft, began from three directions on the afternoon of 18 April [D+1]." Six of the invaders' B-26, two flown by American freelances, "inflicted heavy damage on the Castro column . . . using napalm, bombs, rockets and machine gun fire to destroy several tanks and about twenty troop-laden trucks. Air support to the Blue Beach troops was continued on the morning of 19 April, when three friendly [anti-Castro] B-26s including two piloted by Americans were shot down by Castro T-33s. . . ."

"In spite of a reported 1,800 casualties suffered by the Castro forces, the [exile] brigade's ability to resist depended in the last resort on resupply of ammunition which had now become impossible. . . ."

In the last hours of resistance the brigade commander sent a series of terse and desperate messages to the task force command ship pleading for help:

"'We are out of ammo and fighting on the beach. Please send help. We cannot hold.'

"'In water. Out of ammo. Enemy closing in. Help must arrive in next hour.'

"'When your help will be here and with what?'

"'Why your help has not come?'

"'Am destroying all equipment and communications. Tanks are in sight. I have nothing to fight with. Am taking to woods. I cannot repeat cannot wait for you.'"[172]

During the following days, two freelance Americans and some Cuban frogmen rescued twenty-six survivors from the beach and nearby islands. The invaders lost 118 killed and 1,202 captured. Cuba lost 176 dead.

The Bay of Pigs left the memory of a nightmare that still haunts America. This is the well-grounded but unproven suspicion that Kennedy's belated decision to withhold air support from the Cuban Exile Brigade, to ensure Washington's plausible deniability, lay at the root of the president's assassination in Dallas on 22 November 1963. At least 100,000 Cuban exiles flooded into the U.S. during Castro's first year of power in 1960. They included small but extremely violent mafias such as Alpha 66 that continued raids on Cuba after the Bay of Pigs fiasco. When Kennedy ordered those to stop, the exiles—some linked to the CIA as well as organized crime—saw this as a further betrayal. As one investigator reminds us: "By 1963, an intense bitterness pervaded the community of anti-Castro Cubans toward the man they believed betrayed them, John F. Kennedy. That hatred was, at the least, as great as their hatred of Fidel Castro."[173]

In 1979, after a three-year investigation, the House Select

Committee on Assassinations reported that there probably was a conspiracy to kill Kennedy and that the exiles "had the motive, based on what they considered President Kennedy's betrayal of their cause, the liberation of Cuba from the Castro regime; the means, since they were trained and practiced in violent acts, the result of the guerrilla war they were waging against Castro and the opportunity, whenever the President appeared at public gatherings, as in Dallas on 22 November 1963."[174] However, the committee stopped short of identifying any Cuban group as such as being a formal part of the conspiracy. It concluded: "The committee believes, on the basis of the evidence available to it, that anti-Castro groups, as groups, were not involved in the assassination . . . but that on the available evidence does not preclude the possibility that individual members may have been involved."[175] If, indeed, Cuban-exile bitterness was what fueled the Kennedy assassination then it was one of history's more lurid examples of the law of unintended consequences, known in military circles as "blowback," that can result from ill-advised and clandestine paramilitary operations.

Assassinations can even happen in Washington—perhaps a mere fourteen blocks away from the White House—as well as in Dallas when an intelligence agency, or a conspiracy of intelligence agencies, puts their minds to it. Between 1973 and 1977 an international, anti-Marxist crusade shared by numerous South American governments embarked on Operation Condor, to hunt down perceived enemies around the world. Leading the pack was President Augusto Pinochet of Chile and his secret police chief, Manuel Contreras, who received a payment from the CIA officially explained away by "miscommunications in timing."

On 21 September 1976, Orlando Letelier, his country's former ambassador to the U.S., and Ronni Karpen Moffitt, his American colleague in the Institute for Policy Studies, were assassinated by a car bomb at Sheridan Circle, Washington, D.C. Hundreds of other opponents of Pinochet were dying suddenly, violently, at the time. After the Pinochet regime fell, Contreras was convicted of Letelier's murder. He claimed he was acting under orders from Pinochet, with CIA complicity. In fact, he was brought to trial for this crime in Chile in 1995 as a result of U.S. pressure. He served seven years for this crime and in June 2008 was further convicted of the assassination of Carlos Prats, former Chilean Army chief, and his wife in Buenos Aires in 1974, also by car bomb, and given two life terms.

When Letelier and Moffitt were murdered, the CIA was being prodded by the Nixon administration into promoting anti-Communist coups in Central and South America, with a beatitude of dollars to promote the right sort of publicity and influence. The Agency was also encouraged to stop short, just, of actual assassination, leaving it to surrogates to do the dirty work. The dilemma Operation Condor presented to the CIA was made plain in an Agency report dated 18 September 2000. It conceded: "In addition to information concerning external threats, CIA sought from Contreras information regarding evidence that emerged in 1975 of a formal Southern Cone cooperative intelligence effort—'Operation Condor'—building on informal cooperation in tracking and, in at least a few cases, killing political opponents. By October 1976 there was sufficient information that the CIA decided to approach Contreras on the matter. Contreras confirmed Condor's existence as an intelligence-sharing network but denied that it had a role in extra-judicial killings. . . . As a result of lessons learned in Chile, Central America and elsewhere, the CIA now carefully reviews all contacts for potential involvement in human rights abuse against the potential intelligence value of continuing the relationship. These standards, established in the mid-1990s, would likely have altered the amount of contact we had with perpetrators of human rights violators in Chile had they been in effect at that time."[176]

But that sentiment, of course, predated 9/11 and the sea change that overtook many liberal Western regimes afterward.

Sometimes, in an untidy world, who dares wins. Shortly before Kennedy was assassinated—some veterans suggest the day before—Kennedy told the British prime minister, the 14th Earl of Home (pronounced "Hume")—that he was concerned about rumors concerning a force of Anglo-French mercenaries running a private war in Yemen. That this operation shared some of the characteristics of the Bay of Pigs concept did not strike Kennedy as anomalous. He had his Frontiersman's dream of a world in which decaying European empires would be replaced by newly independent, democratic states that had to be brought on-side before Soviet Russia impregnated them with Communism. In Yemen, a medieval monarchy had been overtaken by a Marxist republican revolution supported by an Egyptian expeditionary force. The republicans controlled the country's few urban areas including the capital, Sana'a. The royalists, headed by Imam Mohammed al-Badr, were fighting a rearguard guerrilla war in the mountains.

British SAS and French Foreign Legion veterans, with the complicity of both their governments, were training and leading the royalist resistance. Britain and France did not trust the word of the Egyptian leader Colonel Gamal Abdel Nasser, whose country they had invaded in 1956. Nor did they sign up to Kennedy's vision. The Brits, with effective control of Aden and its hinterland, feared the domino effect of Yemen on access to Gulf oil. Saudi Arabia feared Egyptian expansionism by way of Yemen. But Kennedy recognized the new regime in Sana'a. The British held off. For the Western alliance, it was a can of worms. Kennedy's events diary for the time reveals how heavily Yemen weighed on his mind, even alongside Vietnam, following the downfall and murder of President Diem.

"October 4, 1963, 10.30-11.25: Meeting with British Foreign

Minister, the Earl of Home [later prime minister] and Ambassador David Ormsby-Gore, the White House." In that conversation, Home gave his personal word to Kennedy that "Britain has given no aid to the Imam" and was not, therefore, running a secret war in Yemen.[177]

"October 10, 1963: President Kennedy directs the Secretaries of State and Defense to keep pressing Saudi Arabia and the United Arab Republic to disengage from the civil war in Yemen."

"October 28, 1963: 5:25–6:00 P.M.: Meeting with advisers to discuss Yemen, Morocco and Algeria."

Twenty-four days later, Kennedy was dead, replaced as president by Lyndon Johnson, whose sympathies lay more with Israel than emerging Arab republics. Macmillan had been replaced as British Prime Minister by Lord Home. It is now apparent that when Lord Home told Kennedy that Britain had not assisted the Imam in Yemen, he was—to use a phrase later conjured in London—being economical with the truth. For many months, a cabal of right-wing politicians, including government ministers and serving and former SAS soldiers, had been running a war of attrition in Yemen in a campaign that Nasser would describe as "my Vietnam." It was a war that sapped Egypt's fighting strength on the countdown to the 1967 war with Israel.

The London circle was known as the Aden Group. Before that, it had been the Suez Group, political cheerleaders for the Anglo-French invasion of the Suez Canal Zone, with Israeli complicity, in 1956. One of the group was Neil ("Billy") McLean, a British Member of Parliament, wartime veteran of SOE in Albania and the Far East, and SIS "asset." Another was Air Minister Julian Amery, son-in-law of the then Prime Minister, Harold Macmillan. Amery would later double, secretly, as "Minister For Yemen." In September 1962, King Hussein of Jordan visited London, met Amery, and appealed for non-recognition of the Yemen Arab Republic (YAR). Amery asked McLean to visit the country to obtain ground truth about the war. Could the royalists hold out? Was the Egyptian Air Force using chemical weapons against civilians? Using journalistic cover, McLean took to the hills of Yemen with enthusiasm. In December, he returned to advise Macmillan that the Egyptians could be defeated. In January 1963, the British cabinet received an unsourced intelligence assessment, based on McLean's report, suggesting that to recognize the YAR would be to surrender control over the Gulf to America. Diplomatic recognition of the Sana'a regime withheld, the movement toward a deniable military intervention began.

The operation had a slow start, possibly because McLean and others depended on the Secret Intelligence Service to handle recruitment, while the Saudis acted as banker for this enterprise. In mid-April, at White's, a gentleman's gambling club in London, Amery and Home (then Foreign Secretary) met SAS founder Colonel David Stirling, Brian Franks, by now Colonel-Commandant of the SAS, and McLean. By this time, McLean had visited Yemen again. British positions in the Aden Federation were coming under guerrilla assault from Yemen, confirming the worst fears of the U.K. government about recognizing the YAR. A delegation from the Yemeni royalists had visited Israel, which was now delivering arms into areas under royalist control.

One of those involved in the later operation recounts what happened. "McLean told the gathering, 'Whatever the Egyptians are telling Washington, the coup in Yemen is not a success. Resistance continues. We have to get some sort of operation going.' Home reported that SIS was having difficulties. Alec [Home] said, 'I will talk to SIS but they say they have no agents in Yemen and it will take six months to set something up.'"

Stirling snorted: "Rubbish. I can produce a guy in London who has just given up command of 21 SAS [the reserve regiment ostensibly dedicated to stay-behind actions should the Warsaw Pact invade western Europe]. He could put something together." The man Stirling had in mind was Jim Johnson, former Guards officer and a broker at the insurance market, Lloyds. Franks telephoned Johnson immediately and invited him to have a drink at the club. As they exchanged regimental small talk, Franks asked Johnson: "Do you fancy going into Yemen and burning the MiGs which are upsetting the tribes and bombing them? The tribes have no defense against them." Johnson thought this was a good idea. At a later meeting in London, Johnson and McLean met the Imam's foreign minister, Ahmed al-Shami. Johnson asked what funds were available. Al-Shami laid his checkbook in front of them and wrote a check for around $10,000. The money trail, which ultimately led back to Saudi Arabia, had to be concealed. Franks picked up the check and funneled it through the Hyde Park Hotel account, a process made easier by his role as chairman of the hotel board.

Johnson took leave of absence from Lloyds and opened a secret headquarters near the headquarters of 21 SAS. The commander of the regular, full-time 22 SAS Regiment obligingly provided unattributable weapons including Swedish submachine guns, which were stored in Johnson's fashionable London home on Sloane Avenue. Stirling drummed up his wartime comrade and one-time driver, Major John Cooper, now working as a contract officer for the Sultan's Armed Forces in Oman.

On 6 June, the anniversary of D-Day, Johnson, Stirling, and Cooper were at a mansion in Paris to meet two mercenaries nominated by the French Secret Service. These were Colonel Roger Faulques, a scarred veteran of a Vietnam prison camp and the Algerian war, and Robert Denard, a hulking freelance soldier from the French Atlantic coast. The gathering also included senior government officials from London and Paris. If Kennedy was mentioned, it was in less than reverent tones. The SIS also probably came in for its share of criticism. Much wine was drunk. Johnson later told the author: "We were entertained royally. The French side said they had a lot of ex-Foreign Legion Paras who had served in Algeria and spoke Arabic. But it was the wrong Arabic, Maghrib Arabic. They were unintelligible to everyone but themselves."

What emerged from this gathering was a decision to send an advance party of four French and four British freelances on a reconnaissance mission to Yemen, led by Cooper, whose experience with the French Resistance during the Second World War would be useful in calling in Israeli supply drops. Back in London, the word was sent to Morse signals specialists serving with 21 SAS. On arrival, they were "invited" to join Johnson's secret army. Three regular soldiers serving with 22 SAS—Geordie Dorman, a mortar expert; Corporal Chigley, a medical orderly; and Trooper Richardson, all-round firearms expert—were given leave of absence, or sheep-dipped (nominally discharged from the Army), to join the team.

The French volunteers drove from Paris in an official staff car, with a uniformed military driver and concealed weapons. One of them was Tony de Saint-Paul, alias Roger de Saint Prieux, a tall, sinister figure with deep-set eyes who went into battle dressed as an Arab, a curved dagger at his waist. He was to meet a painful death in Yemen soon afterward.

Shortly before they were to leave, Johnson received word that the U.K. government had taken fright. Scandals in high places, including the forced resignation of War Minister John Profumo, meant that there could be no other source of political embarrassment for the time being. Risky military adventures were not wanted. Nevertheless, Johnson hastily booked the team in ones and twos onto any flight available out of Britain, in the direction of Aden, before the British government could intervene. In a duplicitous farewell that night, Lord Home dined with Johnson and the team.

Cooper flew first to Tripoli, in Libya. He later recalled: "We had just collected our baggage from our various incoming flights when one of the cases broke open, spilling out rolls and rolls of plastic explosive." Some of the Libyan security guards, he added, "actually helped us repack the stuff. I told them that stuff was marzipan, because of the smell, for various Arab heads of state."

In Aden, the mercenaries and their dangerous cargo were able to bypass the usual formalities with the help of a young officer serving with British forces there: Captain (later Lieutenant-General) Peter de la Billiere. DLB, as he is known in SAS circles, arranged for the team to move by a Dakota of Aden Air to a border area controlled by an ally among local rulers, the Sharif of Beihan. Then the party of six, dressed as Arabs, with two guides, loaded their camels and joined a train of 150 camels carrying supplies to the royalists to cross the border. It was a hazardous journey, moving by night to avoid Egyptian aircraft, in single file through minefields.

From a mountain village called Gara, headquarters of Prince Abdullah bin Hassan, Taylor sent out reconnaissance patrols stiffened by his mercenaries in spite of continuous air raids in which attacks with iron bombs were followed with low strafing runs by Yak fighters using machine guns. Next, he set up an ambush for Egyptian infantry and tanks obliged to climb a gully to reach Hassan's redoubt. Each gun position was camouflaged and sheltered by rocks, with additional shelter nearby in case of air attack. Cairns were built as markers, or orientation points for the defenders. Cooper wrote later: "As the enemy reached our markers, our men opened up with devastating effect, knocking down the closely packed infantry like ninepins. Panic broke out in the ranks behind and then the tanks started firing, not into our positions but among their own men. Then the light artillery opened up, causing further carnage."[178]

The mercenaries' campaign ran for the next three years, during which the Egyptians were increasingly confined to paved roads. They hit back with air power and poison gas. For example, on 4 July 1963, McLean, back in Yemen, reported to the U.K. ambassador to Saudi Arabia on his visit to a village called Kowma. "I went to the exact spot where two bombs had landed. . . . Even after an interval of about . . . five weeks during which heavy rains fell . . . I was immediately aware of, from between twenty and thirty yards away, an unusual, unpleasant and pungent smell . . . rather like a sweet sour musty chloroform mixed with a strong odour of geranium plant . . . I was told that all of the 120 people in the village still have severe coughs, irritation of the skin and of the twenty-two people injured, many still vomit black blood after severe coughing."[179]

A gradual stalemate developed. The Egyptians placed a bounty on the heads of the mercenaries. Just before he was blown up by an enemy shell, the Frenchman Tony de Saint-Paul wrote: "The Egyptians' price on my head has now grown from $500 to $10,000. I hope they increase it even more." His companion, known only as "Peter," blinded by poison gas, survived a two-week journey by camel to Aden, before being flown home to France. Though outgunned, the royalists enjoyed two powerful advantages thanks to the mercenary force. First was the use of tactical communications, which gave the Imam's men flexibility the Egyptians usually lacked. Second, the supplies parachuted by Israel into drop zones controlled by Cooper gave the royalists an increasingly sophisticated edge. Jim Johnson, the political commander of the mercenary force, flew on some of these missions, using a new identity supplied by Israel with a Canadian passport and an escape kit including gold sovereigns. Serial numbers on the weapons Israel supplied had been filed off. Wood shavings in the containers were imported from Cyprus and the parachutes from Italy. A total of 50,000 British rifles was also dropped by civilian aircraft piloted by former Royal Air Force pilots, one of whom was now on Johnson's team.

In 1965, 300 camels were used in the buildup for a royalist ambush on a road linking Sana'a and the Saudi border at a defile known as Wadi Humaidat. The ambush would need 81-mm mortars to destroy an Egyptian convoy and cut the road. The historian Clive Jones writes: "In what was perhaps the most efficient battle fought by the Royalists, 362 soldiers of the First Army, backed by 1,290 tribesmen . . . directed by two British and three French mercenaries cut this main supply route and, despite several days of determined Egyptian counter-attacks, held on to their positions."[180]

In 1966, the French mercenaries launched a barrage of covering fire to assist a royalist advance on Sana'a, but the Imam's men did not move. The royalists' lack of resolve went beyond the front line. Johnson, after conferring with the Saudis who bankrolled the operation, concluded that a stalemate that pinned down 70,000 Egyptian soldiers in a war of attrition suited the Saudis nicely. With a new, Socialist government in London, SIS was also lukewarm about the right-wingers' Yemen adventure. So in October 1966, Johnson wrote a memorandum describing "the apparent lack of interest by HMG [Her Majesty's Government] and the stated indifference to our activities by MI6 [SIS] coupled with the absolute disinterest . . . of HRH [Saudi Prince] Sultan we appear to have three courses open to us. . . ." He nominated the first of these, "to withdraw as soon as possible from the Yemen before disaster overtakes us," for "there is no indication that HMG wants us to continue now."

On 6 October he confronted the Saudis and asked: "Do you want us to win this war or not? The British have announced the date to leave Aden. If I go before they leave, it will be a shambles."

The stalemate became a political fact in 1970, recognized by Egypt and Saudi Arabia, backed with a $300 million bribe from Kuwait and Saudi Arabia to compensate Egypt for lands lost to Israel during the 1967 war, the outcome of which was affected by the absence from that battlefield of Nasser's lost army in Yemen. The timing of this event oozed with dramatic irony. It was the year in which Communist guerrillas, based in the Peoples' Democratic Republic of Yemen (formerly the British-controlled Aden Federation), launched an offensive on Oman, coming close to bringing that kingdom into Moscow's orbit. The SAS were to spend the next six years defending this gateway to the Gulf. No one now sought to defend Kennedy's idealistic, unquestioning support of newly independent former colonies with a taste for republican government. Such countries were now part of a global battlefield over which the Cold War was being fought for real.

In 1975 the CIA spotted an opportunity to give the Soviets a bloody nose in Africa, specifically in Angola, using plausibly deniable British assets. By this time, according to the Church Committee, the Agency had run 900 major interventions and 3,000 minor ones around the world during the preceding fourteen years. With the withdrawal of Portuguese colonists, Angola was the latest ripe African fruit toward which both superpowers were reaching. Kissinger, witnessing Cuban intervention, warned the NSC and the Agency that unless something were done, "the whole international system could be destabilized." In any case, in the wake of the Vietnam fiasco, it would be good for morale to score in Africa. Bill Colby, director of the CIA, gave the message to the National Security Council from the shoulder: "Gentlemen, this is a map of Africa and here is Angola. Now in Angola we have three factions. There's the MPLA [Popular Movement For the Liberation of Angola, including the Communist Party]. They're the bad guys. The FNLA [National Liberation Front, Angola], they're the good guys, and there's Jonas Savimbi [leading Unita], we don't know too well."[181] As a geopolitical model it had the merit of simplicity.

John Stockwell, a lifelong Africa hand and chief of the CIA Angola task force, believed that in backing FNLA leader Holden Roberto, the most violent of the warlords, the Agency ensured that "the fate of Angola was cast, written in blood."[182] The operation was also fatally flawed. A war chest of $31.7 million was conjured from contingency funds, out of sight to Congress. In this respect, the phantom budget anticipated Oliver North's plan to recycle funds from the Iran arms-for-hostages deal to fund the war in Nicaragua after Congress blocked funding for that campaign. The problem with the Angola deal was that the Russians took up the challenge, played poker and—uninhibited by democratic issues—raised the stakes to $400 million. The CIA ran out of money and blinked first.

The strategy was also designed for losers. A memorandum prepared for the CIA Director, George Bush, Sr. in the Agency's Africa Division stated, in the second paragraph, that large supplies of arms to Roberto in northern Angola and Savimbi in the south "would not guarantee they could establish control of all Angola, but that assistance would permit them to achieve a military balance that would avoid a cheap Neto victory" (Agostinho Neto was president of the MPLA).[183] Stockwell, reading the proposal, noted: "This memo did indeed state a no-win policy . . . I wondered what 'cheap' meant. Would it be measured in dollars or in African lives?"

The Angola program was then coordinated by Frank G. Wisner, Jr., whose father had been chief of the OSA and CIA covert operations a generation earlier. Wisner Jr. was now working for Kissinger in the State Department. He reasoned: "We had been forced out of Vietnam. There was a real concern on the part of the [Ford] Administration that the U.S. would now be tested" by the forces of Communism worldwide.[184]

The CIA recruited, at extravagant cost, some French mercenaries through the quality-control mechanism of Robert Denard. It was all profit for Denard, but there is no evidence that it benefited the operation known at Langley as IAFEATURE. Meanwhile Roberto, by some occult means, was advised to make contact with British mercenaries. The gang he recruited was led by Red Beret psychos who had served together in Northern Ireland and had been dishonorably discharged from the army. One was convicted for selling army weapons to Loyalist Ultras and was deemed mentally unstable. Another had robbed a post office using army weapons and an easily identified army vehicle. These two rounded up a ragbag collection of Walter Mitties and dreamers including two former road sweepers as well as a tiny kernel of professionals. The latter included one SAS expert, an SIS man, and a former submariner. News of their recruitment became public knowledge. Though many of them had no passports, the British and Belgian authorities waved them through open doors on their way to Angola via Zaire. Later, they were joined by a handful of naïve American crusaders against Communism.

Once established in Angola, the British contingent set about massacring civilians for sport, or to test their weapons on human targets, before turning on one another. (One of their intended victims was the author, the subject of an assassination contract.) Even by the standards of mercenaries in Africa, it was a macabre story which ended with a show trial in Luanda, a firing squad for captured leaders, and prolonged imprisonment for the surviving grunts.

A few had tried to fight their well-armed, professional Cuban enemy who, after the Bay of Pigs, were giving the West another bloody nose. One mercenary recalled: "Men literally threw themselves at tanks though we had no real equipment to knock them out. The only way was to get on the turret, open the hatch, and drop a grenade inside. Unfortunately, the T54 hatch locks from the inside." The same man tried to incinerate the tank crews, "but we did not have enough petrol."

And yet, at the start of the campaign, the view from Washington was that everything was going just fine. On 11 November 1975, as the

FNLA advanced on the capital Luanda, a celebration was under way at the CIA's Langley headquarters. The Angola task force office was decorated with crepe paper, as if for Christmas, the wine and cheese delicately laid out. Stockwell reported: "People came from all over the building, from the Portuguese Task Force, the French Desk and the Special Operations Group to drink to the program's continued success. Then the Cubans' 122-mm rockets began to land in the Quifangondo valley, not like single claps of thunder but in salvoes, twenty at a time." The devastation was witnessed by CIA case officers from a nearby ridge as the FNLA men "fled in panic, abandoning weapons, vehicles and wounded comrades."[185] The Angolan civil war outlasted the Cold War by a decade. The government that was still standing in Luanda was the MPLA, characterized by Colby as the bad guys. Having survived, the MPLA hired a team of South African mercenaries to secure the country's oil assets. It was symptomatic of a movement by governments toward the private market for black operations and intelligence-gathering.

The use of the British firm KMS in Nicaragua (where a devastating bomb attack on an army barracks in the capital Managua was attributed by Colonel Oliver North to a former SAS major, David Walker, a link he denies) and in Afghanistan, where KMS operators trained the mujahideen, was merely the tip of a covert warfare iceberg. It did not, of course, do much for open government or the American tradition. The majority report from a Congressional Committee Investigating the Iran Contra plot, issued on 18 November 1987, quoted a long-dead Supreme Court judge, Louis Brandeis: "Our Government is the potent, the omnipresent teacher. For good or ill, it teaches the whole people by its example. Crime is contagious. If the Government becomes the lawbreaker, it breeds contempt for law, it invites every man to become a law unto himself, it invites anarchy." The committee added: "The Iran-Contra affair resulted from a failure to heed this message."

During the presidency of George W. Bush, the market in officially licensed privatized warfare, far from diminishing, grew at the expense of the very agencies that were charged with covert operations as special forces soldiers quit to join the private sector. The failure of the CIA and British SIS to establish the facts about Saddam Hussein's non-functioning weapons of mass destruction, or to anticipate the threat of Islamist terrorism on the streets of New York and London, were symptoms of their weakness. Intelligence (and the covert operations that often flowed from it) was "just another form of politics." It was also to become a marketable commodity.

A purge of CIA veterans that began with the appointment of Porter Goss produced a crisis through which, by 2005, half the CIA's workforce—operators and analysts alike—had five years' experience or less. Their experience had now moved to private corporations that the Agency was obliged to hire. As the writer Tim Weiner points out: "Corporate clones of the CIA started sprouting all over the suburbs of Washington and beyond. Patriotism for profit became a $50-billion-a-year business by some estimates—a sum about the size of the American intelligence budget itself."

As the West became bogged down in the ill-comprehended global war against Islamist terrorism, the CIA and Special Forces were obliged by force of circumstance to share their expertise and personnel. But in that process, diplomatically as well as militarily, it was the culture of Special Forces, personified by General Stanley McChrystal in Afghanistan, that dominated the agenda. In the increasingly shared culture of private and public covert warfare, the first victim was public accountability. This was good for clandestine operations but, given the history of plausible deniability, inevitably treated with suspicion by a skeptical public.

CHAPTER 6

JOSEPH'S COAT OF MANY DISRUPTIVE PATTERNS

America, Ireland, and Israel share a secret. This that in every case, their successful resistance to British rule depended, initially, on irregular military forces. Revolutionary America had its Minutemen and less accomplished state militias. Ireland had Sinn Fein and the IRA. Zionists working to undermine the British Mandate in Palestine had Haganah. The military traditions that followed independence were strongly influenced by the idea that special forces operations, as they later became known, were the military norm, the template for defense. By contrast, most European models, following the Peace of Westphalia in 1648, invested the state with a monopoly of lethal force, a deal requiring regular, standing armies. Conventional warriors regarded Special Forces with suspicion. So did their political masters. In Ireland and America, many former guerrillas moved smoothly enough into the conventional fold, adopted formal dress, and took the salute at public events, but the sons of Zion never quite gave up the champagne taste of clandestine warfare. Like Don John of Austria, they were never quite legit, except in Israel. In Israel, military SF and intelligence units proliferate. At the latest count, there were around thirty of them.

Alongside the remarkable but real evolution of Israel's Special Forces—the external intelligence service Mossad, its military cousin Aman, and domestic espionage service the Israeli Security Agency (Shin Bet)—pervasive myths were cultivated and administered like a magic potion to successive generations of Israelis. In 2009, *Time* magazine interviewed Jewish settlers on the Palestinian West Bank, where Zionist migration had increased from 138,000 in 1995 to nearly 300,000 within fourteen years. One typical family, from Woodmere, New York, "believe Arabs arrived in the area only in the 1970s."[186] Other great minds made the same mistake. Even as Colonel T. E. Lawrence ("Lawrence of Arabia") was leading his Arab Revolt against the Turks, Arthur Balfour, the British prime minister who committed his country to support for a Jewish homeland in 1917, professed he "did not know there were Arabs in that country" [Palestine].[187] In those days, Jewish resistance to Turkish rule in Palestine led to the formation of *Netzah Yisrael Lo Yeshaker* (or NILI), an espionage team that made common cause with Britain until one of NILI's carrier pigeons was intercepted, with disastrous results for its human controllers as well as the pigeon.

The true story of Mossad and Israel's special military agencies, though often embellished by enthusiastic myth-makers (and what is a myth other than a poetic extrapolation of truth?), does not need— to quote Churchill—a bodyguard of lies. In Israel as in Ireland, a sense of destiny backed by attachment to the sanctified earth (personified by fundamentalist Irish republicans as "Cathleen ni Houlihan") helps to mold martyrs. So does the brutal reality of diaspora. The extraordinary story of Bricha—the secret escape line for survivors of the Holocaust after 1945, from Eastern Europe into the American sector of Occupied Germany, with U.S. complicity—contains all these elements and more. In a new Exodus, Bricha engineered the migration of 250,000 European Jews to Palestine, 170,000 of them Poles.[188]

America was rewarded for its support with an invaluable intelligence by-product: ground truth about conditions behind the Iron Curtain that could only come from those who had experienced it. As Black and Morris noted, "Military installations, factories and railways behind the Iron Curtain were of no interest to Israel. For the CIA the product was priceless."[189] It included Soviet identity cards, handed over to the CIA for use in secret operations inside Russia. In May 1951, with a little help from James Jesus Angleton, this harvest led to a formal U.S./Israel agreement on Intelligence co-operation.

There are other elements that shape a unique Israeli culture and its defense forces. Unlike most developed countries, Israel retains the draft, compulsory military service for virtually all citizens of fighting age, something that binds the nation organically to its army. Then there is The Book, religious doctrine perceived as divine revelation. In Israel's case, divinely inspired holy text is a potent element to unite a diaspora of the disinherited, spread across centuries and continents, though—even after more than 2,000 years—it can still generate confusion about what territory actually constitutes Israel. Among Zionists, God's guidance about this matter is to be found in Genesis 15:18: ". . . the Lord made a covenant with Abram, saying, 'Unto thy seed I have given this land, from the river of Egypt [the Nile] unto the greater river, the river Euphrates'" [in modern Iraq.] There is also the book of Numbers, one of the five works that form the Torah. "The Lord spoke to Moses, saying: 'Send men that they may spy out the land of Canaan, which I give to the children of

Israel; of every tribe of their fathers shall you send a man, every one a prince among them.'" (The resonant phrase *Every Spy a Prince* was adopted by an American journalist and an Israeli scholar as the title of a "warts-and-all" history of Israeli intelligence operations in 1991.)

The notion that, in the right circumstances, every man is a prince-in-waiting matches perfectly the Special Forces philosophy of SAS founder David Stirling: "We believe, as did the ancient Greeks who originated the word 'aristocracy,' that every man with the right attitude and talents, regardless of birth and riches, has a capacity in his own lifetime of reaching that status in its true sense. . . . All ranks in the SAS are of 'one company,' in which a sense of class is both alien and ludicrous."

Canaan encompasses contemporary Israel, much of Lebanon, Gaza, and the Palestinian territories. This is not the so-called Greater Israel comprising the State of Israel and the Palestine of Mandate times. Nor is it the UN's nostrum for partition in 1947; nor the Israel enlarged by the 1967 Six Day War, doubling Israeli-controlled territory to incorporate the Golan Heights, Sinai and the Gaza strip, Jerusalem, and the West Bank. As a result of that feat of arms, materially helped by freelance British and French mercenaries in the Yemen civil war, the UN sought "withdrawal of Israeli armed forces from territories occupied in the recent conflict" in exchange for Arab recognition of Israel's right to exist.

If there are biblical ambiguities about Israel's geography, there are bigger questions about the authenticity of a universal Jewish identity, raised significantly by Shlomo Sand, a teacher of contemporary history at Tel Aviv University, who challenges the veracity of one of his country's creation myths, that there was a golden age before the Romans evicted Jews from their country after the fall of the temple in the year 70 C.E. He does not believe that the Jews occupied the land of Canaan in the era of David and Solomon; or even that there was a diaspora. He argues that there was, instead, a diffusion of Judaic culture by merchants and missionaries far beyond Jerusalem, long before the fall of the temple.[190] As the English historian Max Hastings commented, reviewing Sand's work: "The legend of the ancient exile and modern return stands at the heart of Israel's self belief."[191] For the foreseeable future this will have no impact on the special fervor of Israel's armed forces, particularly its most dedicated warriors, the Special Forces. As the Irish know, what matters is not the fact behind the ancient legend, but its current vitality, refreshed by new suffering.

There is one other characteristic of Israel's Special Forces that makes them unique. This is a religious mission to save and protect Jews wherever they are endangered, whether by military intervention beyond Israel, such as at Entebbe, Uganda, in 1976, or in the 1985 exodus of Falashas from Sudan, or by changing the demography of Palestine through the Jewish right of return. Predating the Holocaust, from the 1930s onward, tens of thousands of Jews were imported, often in defiance of local, British-administered laws and later, to take over land previously occupied by Arabs. The process continued into the 21st century. From the resulting backlash, three forms of resistance emerged. There was first the secular, political Palestinian response personified by Yassir Arafat's Fatah organization after the 1967 defeat; the international terrorism of warlords such as Abu Nidal and Imad Mughniya; and finally Islamist fundamentalism, often perverting Muslim doctrine, embodied by Osama bin Laden. Had the Arab states adjoining Palestine in 1947 accepted the UN-brokered deal—to partition the country into separate Jewish and Arab entities joined in an economic union—the outcome might have been different, though the guerrilla wars on both sides created a less than optimistic climate. (The British Field Marshal Montgomery did not expect the new state of Israel to survive more than three weeks.) Twenty-four hours after Israel came into existence, the armies of

Egypt, Syria, Jordan, Iraq, and Lebanon attacked from three points of the compass. Against all the odds, Israel survived to fight another day, and another. If this seemed like a miracle to some, it was perceived as a sign of god by dedicated Zionists.

The pact between Israel and the diaspora was not a one-way deal. According to one former case officer (a *katsa*) and later critic of Mossad, loyal Jews, wherever they are to be found, in whatever job or profession, are part of the *sayanim*, a secret international army offering safe houses, arms, intelligence, and whatever else is required by Mossad and its agents.[192] This might be an exaggeration. If it is not, it calls into question the reliability of many Jews in the eyes of their host governments, making them objects of suspicion as were Roman Catholics in post-Reformation England. The case of Jonathan Pollard, an American Jew employed by U.S. Navy intelligence, sentenced to life imprisonment in 1987 for passing secrets to Mossad, makes the *sayanim* issue a legitimate topic for public discussion, but that should come with the caveat that generations of anti-semites have fed on a "world Jewish conspiracy." That said, it is historical fact that hundreds of Jews who served with the British army in the war against Hitler used their knowledge and contacts within British forces to betray their former comrades-in-arms when Hitler was defeated.

Dedicated Zionists would not perceive this as betrayal, but as a regrettable necessity resulting from their religious duty to the greater priority of patriotism. As Pollard's first wife, Anne, memorably put it: "We did what we were expected to do, and what our moral obligation was as Jews, what our moral obligation was as human beings, and I have no regrets about that."[193] Most warfare, particularly within the world of intelligence and special operations, is morally dubious. As Isser Be'eri, the first head of Haganah's intelligence service, told his court martial: "The moment an intelligence service begins to act according to law, it will cease to be an intelligence service."[194]

The use by Western intelligence of former Nazis (Gehlen et al.) in postwar Europe and beyond could also be seen as a betrayal of the ideals that underpinned the Second World War. The ambiguities of the postwar world of intelligence and Special Forces were to be found in the friendships of people such as James Jesus Angleton, the OSS/CIA officer, with former Italian Fascists as well as with David Ben-Gurion; or between Maurice Oldfield of MI5 (the U.K.'s internal security service) and Teddy Kollek, a Mossad liaison officer; or Otto Skorzeny, the Nazi commando who liberated Mussolini, and Mossad agents running a "false flag" operation. In spite of that, the clandestine campaign of Haganah in pre-independence Palestine is seen by some romantics as a golden age of Jewish resistance, aided by worthy *goyim* in a process that retrieved Jewish dignity from the ashes of the Holocaust.

The British Mandate was a poisoned chalice handed down by the League of Nations, timed to expire after twenty-five years, on 24 May 1948. For years before the deadline, Jewish underground forces led by Haganah and its intelligence bureau anticipated a war for survival. By 1947, Zionist intelligence was running sixty British and Jewish agents (many of them working for U.K. agencies) and eighty Arabs. A British army captain gave Haganah a list of 5,000 of its members who were to be arrested, in exchange for a love nest where he could be with his Jewish mistress.

The moral authority of the Jewish resistance movement was not enhanced by the activities of two splinter groups, the Irgun Svai Leumi and the Lehi, known to the British as The Stern Gang, after its leader Avraham Stern, who did not "disqualify terrorism as a means of combat."[195] With the British withdrawal, Israel's declaration of statehood, and the Arab armies' attacks in 1948, Haganah became the basis of the emerging Israel Defense Force while its intelligence agency was reorganized as the Army's intelligence arm, Aman. In a further reorganization Mossad was formed in 1951 to coordinate the competing teams of internal security (Shin Bet), the military intelligence wing Aman, and the Political Department of Israel's Foreign Office as part of the Prime Minister's office. The reform was bitterly opposed by the existing intelligence freemasonry, many of whom resigned en masse in a "spies revolt" similar to the British officers' Curragh Mutiny in 1914.

From a few dozen case officers, Mossad grew to 1,200 by the early 1990s, augmented, according to Ostrovsky, by many thousands of Jewish-Zionist *syanim* sleepers outside Israel. The astonishing scale and scope of Mossad operations around the world—particularly "direct action" missions by Mossad's Metsada combatants and its sub-unit Kidon (Bayonet) team, responsible for assassination and kidnap—suggests a much higher force level even when allowance is made for augmentation of Kidon hit teams by the Special Forces.

The most important and daring among the military Special Forces is the "Sayeret Matkal," an army reconnaissance and commando unit modeled on the British SAS even to the extent of adopting the SAS motto, "Who Dares Wins." In practice many, perhaps a majority, of the spectacular Israeli raids, rescue operations, and coups de main attributed to Mossad were the work of the Sayeret Matkal (also known as General Reconnaissance Unit 269). The Israeli prime minister, Benjamin Netanyahu, served with it, as did his two brothers. Another veteran of Sayeret Matkal was Ehud Barak, Israel's tenth prime minister. Sayeret units are now routinely built into Israel's other military arms, including the infantry. For example, Sayeret Yahalom "is a special elite combat unit of the Engineering Corps. It specializes in accurate demolitions and planting pinpoint explosives along with other high-scale engineering operations in and outside the Israeli borders." Over the years many other Special Forces teams have been created in response to Israel's wars of survival. According to Israeli military sources, they include the following:

Mistaravin: Pseudo-Arabs trained in counter-terrorism, used for "surprise, hit-and-run missions" within the Occupied Territories. Israeli military sources assert that the Mistaravin use force economically and precisely, containing the threat of greater violence. "Undercover riot control is a good example. . . . A couple of undercover operators, who infiltrate the riot, can quickly take out the riot's leaders, preventing the need to use riot control techniques on the participants using large uniformed forces. . . . During the first Intifada (1987–1994) and the second Intifada (2000–2005) the units conducted thousands of missions, killing or capturing hundreds of terrorists. . . . Today . . . there is a distinct preference to capture the terrorists alive when possible so they can be used as intelligence sources."

Sayeret Egoz: "Originally a counter-guerrilla force set up in the 1960s for retaliatory cross-border missions, principally in Lebanon."

YATA (Urban Tactical Units) created in 2004 "to fight surgically and effectively against insurgents in urban areas."

LOTAR (Counter-Terror) Eilat: Based in Israel's most southern city, it is "the only Israeli Defense Force unit which specializes in hostage rescue. . . . Especially renowned for its snipers."

Sayeret Shaldag (Special Air Ground Designating Team): An SF unit within the Israeli Air Force set up after the Yom Kippur War in 1973—in which the IAF lost 100 aircraft—as a reserve to Sayeret Matkal to direct air strikes using laser designators. It is described as "the IDF primary airborne assault force," modeled on the British SAS. In 1982, in operations in Lebanon, Shaldag destroyed missile sites and anti-aircraft batteries, ensuring Israeli air superiority. In 1986–87, the first years of the Intifada, "Shaldag was among the very first units to conduct undercover missions wearing typical Arab clothing." In September 2007, the unit was thought to be involved in an attack by F-15 Israeli Air Force strike aircraft on a cache of nuclear materials supplied by North Korea to Syria.

Shayetet 13: Naval commando unit formed in 1949. During its early decades, until the 1980s, the unit suffered from insufficient training and specialization; but then, in Lebanon, it had "an excellent track record of dozens of successful operations each year, without casualties" including "interdiction of terrorists' vessels, blowing up enemy headquarters and key facilities, conducting ambushes and planting explosives in terrorists' routes." Against that record, "it lost twelve of its operators in a botched raid in Lebanon in 1997." In November 2009, a flotilla of Shayetet 13's speed boats intercepted the Antiguan-flagged freighter *Francop* off the coast of Cyprus. It carried a large consignment of missiles, rockets, shells, grenades, and assault rifles hidden in containers in the hull "bound for Hizbollah from Iran," said Israel's Deputy Foreign Minister Danny Ayalon. The haul was the biggest of its kind for seven years. In the Red Sea in 2002 Shayetet had intercepted the *Karine A*, also carrying arms from Iran to its Hamas ally in the Gaza Strip.

This list is far from exhaustive. Other teams include Army Unit 8200 (signals intelligence); Unit 504 running agents in occupied territories; even faceless establishments such as Facility 1391, known as "Israel's Guantanamo." There, according to the newspaper Ha'aretz, "detainees are blindfolded and kept in blackened cells, never told where they are, brutally interrogated and allowed no visitors of any kind. . . . No wonder Facility 1391 officially does not exist."[196] Brassey's most recent International Intelligence Yearbook (2003 edition) adds to this list the Nativ, or Liaison Bureau, still assisting Jews to leave Russia while acquiring that useful by-product, intelligence; deep reconnaissance units 5707 and 669; and Malmad, operating from the Defense Ministry and allegedly responsible for computer espionage. Its predecessor, Lekem (or Lakam), was disbanded as a result of Pollard's betrayal of the U.S. Navy.

Mossad, the Israeli state's intelligence service, comprises ten

separate departments. It is still primarily an intelligence agency similar to the CIA and the British Secret Intelligence Service (MI6), on
which it was originally modeled. Its covert strike force, Kidon, is part
of a "Mossad-Within-Mossad" operational branch known as Metsada.

This is probably not a complete, up-to-date list; but it is possible, by
identifying the operations in which these agencies have taken part, to
replicate Israel's Special Forces agenda. This would include (on
Mossad's part) *Strategic Intelligence* (such as disclosure of Khrushchev's
secret denunciation of Stalin in 1956); *Direct Action* including assassination (in conjunction with Army Special Forces); *Kidnap* (with agencies such as Shin Bet); *Rescue Operations* (largely military SF);
Acquisition of Military Hardware (including Operation Noah's Ark, the
mysterious escape from Cherbourg on Christmas Day, 1969 of Israel's
impounded gunboats; and acquisition of a MiG-23, after its Syrian
pilot was turned, 12 October 1989); *Interdiction Operations* (such as
Operation Sphinx, the air attack on Iraq's nuclear facility, 1981; or
Operation Plumbat, the theft at sea of an entire cargo of 200 tons of
uranium oxide); *Invisible Military Exports*, including arms deals and
training teams for the Kurdish Peshmerga; Chilean special forces;
Colombian guerrillas and simultaneously—Tamils and Sinhalese,
then at war with one another. There were some spectacular failures
along the way but, by and large, more gains than losses.

What follows is a far from complete account. It is indicative, however, of the nature of the operations run by Mossad and its allies,
combining courage, ingenuity, and—thanks to the belief that the ultimate Commander-in-Chief is God himself—sublime indifference to
the niceties of international law or international opinion. Two operations dominate the history of Israel's special operations, operations
linked by daring and public exposure. One was an exercise in Jewish
vengeance; the other, the preservation of precious Jewish blood.

For two decades from the 1960s onward, Western institutions were plagued by violent, "chic" revolution whose icon was Che Guevara, a movement that swept university campuses from Berlin via France, the Netherlands, and Northern Ireland to Ohio. Some protests had their origin in extreme left-wing politics. Others opposed military conscription for war service in Vietnam. In Ulster and elsewhere, there was a legitimate issue of civil rights. Some of these events, particularly in Ireland, began with the politics of provocation and spilled over into lethal civil war. Extremists of every kind made common cause to overturn the established order. They were often from wealthy backgrounds, part of a generation that had not been chastened by the Second World War. Libya's leader, Colonel Gaddafi, supplied the IRA with assault rifles and explosives. Palestinian extremists merged with West German Marxist terrorists. Starting with the hijack of four airliners bound for New York but blown up on Dawson's Field, Jordan in September 1970, air travel was perceived as a very bad idea. A Terrorist International had come into being.

In Germany, the imprisoned leaders of the Baader-Meinhof group (the Red Army Faction) called on the Palestinian terrorist group Black September for help. The Palestinians spotted their chance during the countdown to the 1972 Olympic Games in Munich. Hostage-taking and prisoner exchange were part of the landscape of terror practiced on all sides. Black September (named after the defeat of Syrian-backed Palestinians attempting to subvert Jordan two years earlier) sent a team of eight into the Olympic village in the early hours of 5 September where many of the Israeli team were quartered. Having taken eleven hostages, the terrorists issued their demand: release and transfer to Egypt 234 Palestinians and others held in Israel, as well as Andreas Baader and Ulrike Meinhof, in prison in Germany. The Israeli prisoners, weight-lifters and wrestlers, did not go quietly. In some of the fights that followed, two of them were shot dead.

Hours of negotiation followed. The German authorities persuaded the terrorists to travel with their hostages by helicopter to Fürsten-feldbruck NATO air base, ostensibly to be flown by a Lufthansa civil airliner to Egypt. In the febrile atmosphere at the airport, the terror-ists smelled a rat. After inspecting the Lufthansa jet, two of them started running back to the helicopter. It was now dark. An unquali-fied police sniper opened fire. In the chaos that followed, the remaining hostages were murdered and five of the terrorists shot dead, the last one after a manhunt that continued into the early hours. Three terrorists survived, only to be handed over by the West German government to Libya, following the hijack of another Lufthansa airliner.

The West Germans' loss of control at Fürstenfeldbruck, where only five untrained, badly deployed police snipers were initially outnum-bered by their enemy, was observed from the control tower with cold anger by Mossad's director, Zvi Zamir, and Victor Cohen, Shin Bet's senior interrogator. They were allotted a grandstand seat on condi-tion they remained passive observers of their countrymen's murders. The surviving terrorists and their dead comrades were received by most of the Arab world, aside from Jordan, as heroes.

The stage was now set for the next part of this bloody drama. In spite of the fact that one of Mossad's operations to hunt down and kill the Munich terrorists and their key planners was codenamed "Wrath of God," General Zamir denied that vengeance had any place in Israel's thinking. In an interview more than thirty years later, he said: "We are accused of having been guided by a desire for vengeance. That is non-sense. We acted against those who thought that they would continue to perpetrate acts of terror. I am not saying that those who were involved in Munich were not marked for death. They definitely deserved to die. But we were not dealing with the past; we concen-trated on the future." Elsewhere, he used the phrase "prevention of future threats" to describe the campaign of selective assassination outside Israel as a result of West Europe's failure to halt a succession of airline hostage-taking operations by Arab terrorists.[197]

Around twelve suspects were assassinated during a campaign that lasted several years. Preparation for the first strike against those held responsible for Munich took little more than five weeks. Captured Palestine Liberation Organization prisoners were persuaded, by bribes, blackmail, or other means, to identify some of the suspects. Others were already known to Mossad as "the usual suspects." Accurate identification depended heavily on the belief that Black September, originally backed by the Syrian movement known as al-Saiqa, was an arm of Arafat's PLO. To reduce the possibility of error, each assassination was preceded by a quasi-legal tribunal in Israel colloquially known as "Committee X." Over a fifteen-month period, at least eight Arab terrorists were slain. The first man to go, on 16 October 1972, was Abdel Wa'il Zu'itar, the Palestine Liberation Organization's man in Rome. As he waited for the elevator in his apartment building, he was shot twelve times at point-blank range, probably by a two-man team from Mossad's Kidon hit team. On 8 December, Mahmoud Hamchari, the PLO's man in France, answered the telephone in Paris: "Oui?"

"Est-que c'est Monsieur 'Amchari qui parle?" the caller asked.

"Oui. C'est lui," Hamchari replied.

At that moment, a bomb, concealed inside a bedside table on which the telephone rested, exploded. Hamchari died a month later. Six weeks passed, and in January 1973 Hussein Al Bashir, a senior member of the PLO's guerrilla arm, Al Fatah, was preparing for bed at a perhaps aptly named Olympic Hotel in the Cypriot capital, Nicosia. His assassins watched and waited for his bedroom light to be turned off. They then detonated the bomb planted under the bed.

On 9 April, a joint operation involving Mossad and the Army's

Special Forces commando Sayeret Matkal assassinated three more top PLO men in their Beirut homes. A week ahead of the attack, six Mossad agents (three using British passports) arrived on civilian flights from different capitals, to prepare the way with hired cars, safe houses, and target reconnaissance. The commandos came in by sea, the last mile by small inflatables, guided by a flashlight code from the agents onshore. Their surprise attack on the enemy apartments in downtown Beirut was total. Almost simultaneously, Muhammed Najjar, Kamal Adwan—allegedly senior Black September leaders— and Kamal Nasser, the PLO's spin doctor, were gunned down by their masked attackers as other Sayeret commandos struck at alternative Palestinian centers in the city in diversionary operations. Before the smoke had cleared, Israel's Special Forces had vanished like phantoms, collecting new clothes and passports before they passed "Go" on their indirect way home by civil flights. Others linked to the Munich massacre, taken out during the wave of Mossad assassinations, included Ziad Muchessi (Athens, 12 April 1973) and Mohammed Boudia, an Algerian terrorist organizer with links to many disparate groups (Paris, 28 June 1973).

It was not for these exploits that operations Wrath of God and Springtime of Youth would be remembered in most histories of the Arab-Israeli conflict. Mossad's apologists including Zvi Zamir assert that prior to Munich, "there was no need for illegal Israeli activitiy in Europe."[198] Munich traumatized Israel as 9/11 traumatized America and internationalized the conflict. In Israeli eyes, such actions were henceforth illegal but unavoidable. Much international opinion was prepared, tacitly, to tolerate this position so long as Israeli reprisals generated no innocent victims. As an English wit, Mrs. Patrick Campbell, once said: "I don't mind what people do so long as they don't do it in the street and frighten the horses." At Lillehammer, Norway, on 21 July 1973, the horses and much else were scandalized when a

Moroccan waiter named Ahmed Bouchiki was misidentified by a Mossad informant as Ali Hussein Salameh, the rich, flamboyant operations chief for Black September, known as the Red Prince.

Lillehammer is a crisp, neat, and very provincial resort favored by cross-country skiers. During the Cold War, British SAS men, training for Arctic warfare, were posted there dressed as civilians to learn from Norwegians, whose idea of a Sunday morning family outing was a brisk twenty-five-mile journey over rolling countryside while towing the youngest in a plastic ski buggy. It is a place where strangers are noticed and where, in the seventies, the presence of foreigners—to say nothing of a hidden arsenal of unguarded weapons for local stay-behind forces in the event of a Soviet invasion—lent the place a certain edge.

Bouchiki was gunned down by two members of the assassination team as he returned home from the cinema with his pregnant wife. Though some members of the Mossad squad escaped, six, including two women, were arrested. Five were convicted of murder. Huge damage was caused to Mossad's legend as the long, invincible arm of Israeli justice. The real target, the Red Prince, was not the sort of personality to hide himself away in obscure Lillehammer. He was blown up in a car bomb in Beirut, with eight other people, almost six years after Bouchiki's assassination on 22 January 1979.

Between 1976 and 1988, the Army's Sayeret Matkal Commando did much to restore the reputation of Israel's Special Forces, in a series of daring rescues and high-risk retributive operations far from home. On 22 June 1976, an Air France airliner took off from Tel Aviv bound for Paris, pausing at Athens, where it was seized by two members of the Baader-Meinhof group (whose leaders were still in prison in Germany) and two terrorists belonging to Popular Front for the Liberation of Palestine, which shared Baader-Meinhof's belief in Marxism. The crew of twelve and 246 passengers were now hostages.

A friendly welcome awaited the terrorists at Entebbe airfield, Uganda, whose ruler, Idi Amin, a convert to Islam, was reputed to store the heads of former political opponents in his refrigerator. The hijacked aircraft was met at Entebbe by another seven terrorists. Non-Jewish passengers were promptly released, providing Israeli intelligence with useful information about the architecture of the airfield and the chances of rescue. The 108 hostages who remained were Jews.

If any rescue was to have a chance of success, 3,000 miles from Israel with no red-carpet access to the target, deception was the key. The man who devised the deception plan, and much else, was Major-General Dan Shomron. His bleak assessment, he later explained, was: "You had more than 100 people sitting in a small room, surrounded by terrorists with their fingers on the trigger. They could fire in a fraction of a second. We had to fly seven hours, land safely, drive to the terminal area where the hostages were being held, get inside, and eliminate all the terrorists before any of them could fire."[199] When he revealed his plan to the Chiefs of Staff, "all those around me weren't enthusiastic. They said that the program was brilliant but the risk was too great. James Bond, they said." When he briefed the team who would do the business, he said: "We're going out 4,000 kilometers. We're alone, but we're the strongest force in the field. If anyone is afraid, he may leave." No one moved.

The deception—the Trojan Horse for Operation Thunderbolt—was a black, shiny Mercedes limousine, Idi Amin's preferred form of transport, flying a Ugandan flag but still carrying Israeli number plates. If the pseudo-VIP convoy, Mercedes and outriders, led the assault, it might, with luck, bluff its way through the outer cordon of Ugandan guards without firing a shot. The convoy was led by Sayeret Matkal's commanding officer, Lieutenant-Colonel Jonathan ("Yoni") Netanyahu, elder brother of the man who would become their country's prime minister in 1996 and later. The planners were blessed with good intelligence. Intricate details of the now-derelict old terminal where the hostages were held were supplied by the Israeli company that had constructed the building, enabling a crude mock-up to be built in Israel on which the commandos could practice. Meanwhile, a Mossad pilot made a simulated forced landing on the airfield in a light aircraft before the operation began, and, by unspecified means, contrived to relay photographs of the target to Shomron.

Six aircraft—two Boeing 707s and four lumbering Hercules transports—made up the force. One of the Boeings circled above Entebbe, providing secure communications to Tel Aviv and for the men on the ground. The second, converted into a field hospital, was parked at neutral Nairobi. The fourth Hercules was empty, allocated to the hostages if any could be brought out. Other space was meticulously provided for casualties, dead or alive. A team of pathfinders was the first to land, planting beacons to mark the runway in the event that when the action started, the main runway lights would be extinguished. That happened.

Then, as the Hercules fleet approached Entebbe, the leading aircraft slotted in behind a scheduled British cargo flight, as planned, and touched down in its wake. The other three flew in a holding pattern as the lead Hercules dropped its ramp on final approach. The Mercedes and its escorts—two Land Rovers—rolled onto the tarmac before the aircraft halted in front of the terminal where the hostages were held.

Two Ugandan sentries challenged the convoy and were immediately picked off by the Sayeret with silenced pistols. Around forty meters from the building, Netanyahu's deputy, known as "Muki," jumped from the Mercedes with his team and in quick succession killed a Ugandan guard and two of the terrorists, now on their feet and firing at the intruders. Outside the building, Netanyahu was hit in the back by a sniper bullet fired from a disused control tower and fatally wounded. In other contacts, six terrorists—two armed with grenades—and two more Ugandan guards were killed. As the team broke into the terminal, one of the guards fired a burst of automatic fire. He was unused to the weapon's tendency to aim high unless it was gripped firmly. His bullets shattered glass windows above the hostages before he, too, was cut down by the attackers.

As one of the rescuers, using a loud-hailer, ordered the terrified hostages to keep their heads down, the other three Hercules landed. The rescue had taken just three minutes. Early the following morning, "the lead Hercules flew low over Eilat at the southern tip of Israel. The tired airmen in the cockpit were astonished to see people in the streets below waving and clapping."[200] If terrorists had hoped to achieve a propaganda-by-deed, a "spectacular," this latest exercise in hostage-taking was an own-goal. "Entebbe," for years afterward, was no longer a place in Africa but a fanfare that celebrated the professionalism of Israel's Special Forces worldwide.

Over the next two years, Sayeret Matkal pulled off at least three other rescues, one known as the bus hostage rescue, before going onto the offensive with an assassination operation in conjunction with Mossad and its military arm, Metsada. The target was Khalil al-Wazir (nom de guerre, Abu Jihad), Arafat's deputy in the PLO. He had settled in Sidi Bou Said, a placid suburb of Tunis, when, on 16 April 1988, Israeli commandos—replicating the Beirut attack on Black September leaders in Operation Spring of Youth thirteen years before—smashed their way into his home and gunned him down in the presence of his family. Yet again, Mossad agents speaking fluent Arabic prepared the ground. The assassination team again came ashore in dinghies. A Boeing 707 circled overhead as a communications center and command post.

Equally dramatic were Israel's snatch operations, exercises in hostage-taking or the unlawful arrest of individuals outside Israeli jurisdiction. The abduction of the Holocaust bureaucrat Adolf Eichmann by Shin Bet operatives in May 1960 led to his trial and execution in Israel and an international outcry about Argentina's territorial integrity. Eichmann's trial generated a memorable phrase to describe his dutiful, no-questions-asked attention to detail in compiling his balance sheet of death: "The banality of evil." It also left a bad taste in the mouths of some Israelis, thanks to claims made by the legendary Nazi-hunter Simon Wiesenthal that he had traced Eichmann to Argentina before anyone else. Isser Harel, a Mossad founding father controlling the search, challenged Wiesenthal's claim. In 2009, the writer Guy Walters went further. Wiesenthal's reputation, he wrote, "was built on sand. He was a liar—and a bad one at that. From the end of the Second World War to the end of his life in 2005, he would lie repeatedly about his supposed hunt for Eichmann. . . ."[201] The history was further darkened by the suspicion that the CIA did not try too hard, if at all, to pursue Eichmann at a time when hundreds of unreformed Nazi war criminals were working for the agency against Communism in Europe.[202] In spite of some failures along the way, Mossad/Special Forces abductions continued. In Operation Crate 3, carried out by the Sayeret Matkal on 21 June, 1972, five Syrian intelligence officers with Palestinian resistance men, on a guided tour near the Israeli border, were seized as hostages. They then became bargaining chips to secure the release of three Israeli airmen held captive in Syria. The world's media paid little attention to this one, perhaps because it was a "domestic" affair within the opaque Middle East, where even participants did not always comprehend what was happening. The kidnap of Mordecai Vanunu in Rome in September 1986 made bigger waves. Vanunu, according to taste, is either a traitor to Israel, having betrayed its most cherished military secret, or an heroic whistleblower meriting a Nobel Peace Prize.

Vanunu, a rabbi's son, worked from 1976 until 1985 as a technician at his country's top-secret nuclear plant in the Negev desert at Dimona. During those years, disenchanted with Israel's manufacture of plutonium sufficient for up to 200 nuclear weapons, he made his way around the underground plant, taking photographs and making notes, apparently unnoticed by security staff. Soon after being laid off with 180 others in 1985, he was in Australia, undergoing a process of conversion to Christianity. He encountered a British journalist and after prolonged debriefing by the *Sunday Times* Insight team in London, he provided the newspaper with a densely detailed description of the Dimona plant.

Mossad learned of this disaster before the *Sunday Times* published *The Secrets of Israel's Nuclear Arsenal* on 5 October 1986, though just how that happened is unclear. It might have something to do with the fact that much of the British media is under constant surveillance by security agencies including MI5, the D-Notice Committee, and the Ministry of Defence. In addition, in a gossipy profession, a minority of journalists collaborate with the intelligence services. Leaks happen regularly, sometimes as "spoiler" stories that appear ahead of scheduled publication as a means of limiting damage to an intelligence agency, or as an abuse of legal process to stifle dissent. (The author has extensive experience of the phenomenon.)

The *Sunday Times* reprinted Vanunu's disclosures on 21 September 2008 with the additional note: "Before publication Vanunu, now 63, was lured into flying to Italy by a Mossad agent named Cheryl Bentov. He was captured by Israeli agents, smuggled to Israel and put on trial on charges of treason and espionage. He was released in 2004. . . ."[203] While some humanitarian organizations regarded the eighteen-year sentence imposed by a closed tribunal on Vanunu, ten of those years in solitary, as harsh, Mossad believed he had gotten off lightly. The director of Mossad at the time of Vanunu's abduction,

Shabtai Shavit, told an Australian broadcaster that assassination was an option that he had considered. "I would be lying if I said that thought didn't pass through our heads," said Shavit. It did not happen "because Jews don't do that to other Jews."[204] Shavit would also have been aware of the ground rules for a Mossad assassination. At any one time, according to the former Mossad case officer Ostrovsky, there might be 100 names on an execution list. Some cases are more urgent than others. An operational emergency might require shortcuts in obtaining clearance for the execution. Otherwise, permission is sought by Mossad's director from the prime minister, who would send it to a secret judicial committee. This sits as a military court. The accused, unaware of the hearing, is represented by counsel, as is the state. A guilty verdict means that the accused might be brought to Israel for trial (as were Eichmann and Vanunu) "or if that is too dangerous or simply impossible, execute him at the first possible opportunity," but only after the prime minister has signed the execution order. "One of the first duties of any new Israeli prime minister is to read the execution list and decide whether or not to initial each name on it."[205]

For Israel, the abduction/assassination option had a respectable history, if only because elements of the British 8th Army's Jewish Brigade made common cause with a handful of Holocaust survivors in hunting down Nazis in postwar Europe. These retributive squads, known as Nokmin, or Avengers, summarily executed many hundreds of former Gestapo and SS officers in Italy, Austria, and Germany, probably assisted by former colleagues of the targeted men. The British SAS had its own, unofficial War Crimes Investigation Team known as the Secret Hunters, operating in France and Germany immediately after the war. It claimed to steer clear of extra-judicial killings, preferring to hand over Nazi fugitives, particularly those involved in the murder of SAS prisoners-of-war in France, to due judicial process. The complete truth of that might never be known. Meanwhile, as we have noted, former Nazis recruited by the Gladio organization and other shadowy outfits enjoyed Allied protection in their joint prosecution of the emerging war on Communism.

Within the U.S., the idea of abduction in a just cause was taken up by Washington in the 1980s as a response to Arab terrorism. Two new laws sponsored by President Reagan in 1984 and 1986 and a secret legal opinion gave the FBI "extraterritorial jurisdiction over terrorists acting against U.S. nationals and property outside the United States."[206] These laws, and an executive order, became known as "the Presidential Snatch Option." Debate focused on two kidnaps. In September 1987, a team involving staff from the Pentagon, CIA, Drug Enforcement Agency, and State Department lured Fawaz Younis, a Lebanese, onto a luxury yacht in the Mediterranean. The bait was an illegal drug deal. Younis's crime was his part in hijacking a Royal Jordanian airliner, carrying, among others, American passengers. Though he was small fry and no casualties were caused, Younis was convicted on three counts and sentenced to thirty years. A federal appeals court found that his arrest met necessary standards of international law.

Following the Mossad's example, the road to extraordinary rendition in the War on Terror now lay open to thousands of cases similar to Younis's. One of these was the kidnap of Osama Mustafa Hassan Nasr ("Abu Omar"), a Muslim Imam, snatched on a street in Milan on 17 February 2003 in an operation coordinated by the CIA and Italian military intelligence. Omar was held for four years in an Egyptian prison where, he alleges, he was tortured. After his release in February 2007, he settled in Italy. A trial of those allegedly involved in Omar's kidnap opened in Rome in 2009. A total of twenty-six American defendants—twenty-five CIA agents and a U.S. Air Force colonel—were tried *in absentia*. In court were seven Italians including the former head of Italian military intelligence, Nicolo Pollari.[207] The issues of jurisdiction and state legitimacy were now emerging as the horns of a dilemma that was to trouble international lawyers for decades. Though President George W. Bush expressed a popular sentiment when he said, "I don't care what the international lawyers say,"[208] the rule of law remained at the center of the battle for international opinion and for hearts and minds among the uncommitted majority.

But not in Israel, hermetically sealed from such considerations along with Facility 1391, "Israel's Guantanamo." As Dan Yakir, legal adviser to the Association of Civil Rights in Israel (ACRI), put it: "The existence of a lockup like this gives rise to a double concern: first, of secret arrests and 'disappearances' of people; and second, an abuse of power, unfair treatment, violence, and torture."[209] In theory, Israeli law—specifically the Israeli Security Agency (Shin Bet) Law, adopted by the Knesset in 2002—"restricts the use of force against terrorists during their interrogation." One of the Special Forces units responsible for interrogation, as well as running agents outside Israel, is the Army's Intelligence Corps Unit 504, whose cadre of *katamim*, "officers for special tasks," includes some who undergo additional training to become *hakshabim*, or interrogators.

Following the occupation of Iraq in 2003, there were reports that the U.S. used Israeli interrogators to break top-level Iraqi prisoners, including former intelligence chiefs, using "a variety of techniques that did not cause physical damage."[210] Notionally, such techniques could include the use of drugs, hypnotism, deception, and blackmail, pioneered by British Intelligence in Cairo during the Second World War. In December 2003 Julian Borger, *The Guardian's* diplomatic editor, reporting from Washington, alleged that Israeli urban warfare specialists were helping to train U.S. Special Forces in counter-insurgency techniques, including assassination of guerrilla leaders. None of Borger's sources was identified.[211] Clear proof of Israel's direct involvement in the Iraq adventure is lacking, but it might be in the interests of both Israel and the U.S. to work together on specific, short-term, acute problems. If so, Special Forces would be the obvious candidates for such deniable operations. By the turn of the century, before 9/11, international opinion was turning against Israel's assassination policy—as if the world was its legitimate hunting ground—but even then, the Israeli intelligence historian Benny Morris told the *Sunday Telegraph*, an Israeli parliament would never take the Mossad to task for carrying out assassinations. "Israel has no limitations in that respect," he said. "Even in the 21st century it would be possible for a prime minister to say, like Golda Meir, just go and kill them."

Much of the history of Special Forces—anyone's Special Forces—is a story of dirty, morally reprehensible—if effective—work. In terms of presentation, rescue operations, whether by the SAS at the besieged Iranian embassy in London in 1980, or the rescue of several hundred Falasha Jews from Ethiopia four years later, play very much better. For the professional Special Forces soldier, it all comes down to the same thing: a job to be done. The Falashas are a mysterious people, possibly the remnants of the lost Israel tribe of Dan, finally acknowledged as Jews by Israel in 1972. In the 1980s, thousands of them sought sanctuary from local wars in Sudan. As an exit strategy for these people, Mossad, disguised as a Belgian holiday company, constructed a successful Red Sea diving resort on the coast of Sudan. Unnoticed by European holiday makers, over a six-week period, almost 8,000 Falashas were smuggled by Hercules from an airfield near the resort and flown to Israel. A news leak blew Mossad's cover and Operation Moses, as it was codenamed, was hastily wound up. In a follow-up operation (Joshua) run by the CIA, another 800 were extracted. After a political stalemate lasting six years, Israel overcame a tight political deadline in Operation Solomon to airlift around

5,000 more Falashas from Sudan in thirty-six hours. Absorbing 36,000 agrarian Ethiopian Jews who practiced animal sacrifice and spoke no Hebrew into a densely urban culture presented a double challenge for Israel: one part, practical, the other, the issue of identity, of what it means to be an Israeli and to what century Zion belongs. The Falashas left the Jewish homeland around the 2nd century B.C.E. In Operations Moses and Solomon, Mossad—uniquely among intelligence agencies—had demonstrated that it could even transcend the time barrier. Using various ingenious devices, Mossad's colleagues in Special Forces demonstrated that they could also, virtually, walk on water. The list of successes is greater than this chapter records. In addition to Entebbe, there were hostage rescues in 1972 (Operation Isotope); 1974 (school children saved at Ma'alot); 1975 (Operation Savoy: hotel guests extracted from captivity); 1978 (bus rescue); 1980 (Misgav Am kibbutz rescue). Kidnaps, in addition to Vanunu and Operation Crate 3, included the abductions of Sheikh Abdul-Karim Obeid (Lebanon, 1989) and Mustafa Dirani (1994) as well as Adolph Eichmann in 1960. These unorthodox military/intelligence exploits represent a style of warfare which the U.S. and Britain only started to rediscover after their interventions in Afghanistan and Iraq, and then with more legal caveats and moral inhibitions. Even some loyal Israelis had misgivings. On 21 December 2003, thirteen reservists serving with Sayeret Matkal placed before Prime Minister Ariel Sharon a formal protest about military suppression in the Occupied Territories. It said: "We have come to tell you, Mr. Prime Minister, that we will no longer be accomplices to the reign of oppression in the Territories and the denial of the most elementary human rights of millions of Palestinians, nor shall we be the shield of settlements erected on confiscated land."

The protesters, the most senior of whom was a major, were expelled from Sayeret Matkal. Such episodes are not unique among

Special Forces operators, whether they are asked (as were members of B Squadron, 22 SAS, to embark on a clearly doomed mission during the South Atlantic War) or stand by without protest as at least one SAS observer was asked to do (fruitlessly) during the massacre of Muslim men by Serbs at Srebrenica. The Sayeret Matkal dissidents— three officers and ten soldiers—suffered no further sanction than expulsion. They represented a degree of legitimate moral unease among some sections of Israeli society elsewhere in the military community. Nearly 600 members of the Israeli Defense Forces signed statements refusing to serve in the Occupied Territories. They included a decorated Air Force general who was also an air ace and twenty-six other serving or former pilots. As one expert in military studies put it: "It's a difficult type of war. It's harder to uphold ethics. There are no books on moral regulations for fighting terror." Just so. When the chips are down, Israel's Special Forces will point out that for sixty years, their country's enemies have sworn to destroy the country. Israel, with varying help from a few friends, was still standing at the end of the first decade of the 21st century. Whether it might have survived without black operations involving civilian casualties is another question. In a global war on terror, it is one which increasingly challenges liberal Western governments far from Jerusalem. Israel represents in an acute form a very contemporary dilemma.

CHAPTER 7

BIG BOYS' GAMES,
BIG BOYS' RULES

On 30 April 1980, just six days after the disastrous failure of Operation Eagle Claw to rescue U.S. diplomats in Iran, a new siege began. This time the victims were seventeen Iranian diplomats working at their country's imposing London embassy across the road from Hyde Park, plus eight visitors and an unassuming London policeman, a "Bobby," armed with a revolver. Their captors were six Iranian Arabs, armed with submachine guns and hand grenades and sent by the Iraqi dictator Saddam Hussein. The terrorists had arrived in London on 30 March, time enough to do some energetic shopping in the belief that their mission would be successfully completed within twenty-four hours. On British television, they watched reports of Delta's doomed operation at Desert One. The stage was now set for yet another hostage spectacular in London, in which Western security forces, constrained by tight rules of engagement (no indiscriminate shooting, etc.) would be perceived as odds-on losers.

The British had handled two sieges in the recent past, one in London, the other in Belfast, both linked to the Irish War. They had ended with the surrender of IRA terrorists to the SAS, which had been training in close-quarter battle for just such an operation for years beforehand. They developed special snap-shooting techniques on the move, in a crowded environment, that no Wild West shooter could match, except in the movies. Some of the soldiers admitted, privately, to a sense of anti-climax when there was no gunplay. Their practice runs, in a concrete building known as The Killing House, used real VIPs as hostages who were bound and held as "prisoners" during an assault in which hundreds of rounds of live ammunition were fired. This high-risk training had taken the life of at least one instructor.

Saddam's purpose in seizing the Iranian embassy was to enforce his claim to the Iranian province of Khuzestan—which the Arab minority described as "Arabistan"—and the release of Arabs imprisoned in Iran. Khuzestan was oil-rich. Ten years before Iraq's invasion of Kuwait, Saddam's claim to Khuzestan was another megalomaniac gesture by the Iraqi dictator. It was mid-morning when the terrorists rang the bell on the outer door of the London embassy, then wrestled Police Constable Trevor Lock to the ground. One of the intruders started the operation clumsily, firing a bullet through the glass of the inner door. Lock, bleeding from a face wound, managed to send an emergency signal on his personal radio before he was overcome. The SAS, at their Hereford base 150 miles to the west of London, were alerted unofficially by one of their own veterans now serving with the police. Within thirty minutes, before the public was aware of the drama building inside the embassy, a troop of twenty-four men led by a captain from the regiment's Counter Revolutionary Warfare Wing, at a peak of training for just such an emergency, was on its way

Men of 1st U.S. Ranger Battalion tackle the challenge of a punishing assault course at the British Combined Operations commando training center in Scotland, February 1943, where the originals of the SAS and many other emerging Special Forces teams were selected. Live ammunition was used in training. The Rangers were among the first to storm ashore at Omaha Beach, Normandy on D-Day, 6 June 1944. *The Times 21 April 2009*

Men of the Australian SAS Regiment, camouflaged for jungle operations in Vietnam, armed with a variety of weapons including 7.62-mm Self-Loading Rifles and grenade launchers. Other weapons in use in the confines of jungle warfare included machine-gun shotguns. *Private collection: Anon*

SAS soldier in HALO (high-altitude, low-opening) freefall at 120 mph from 30,000 feet, carrying a 100 lb rucksack beneath his parachute container. His rifle is on the left-hand side of his body. Parachute is deployed by an automatic opening device with manual override if there is a system failure. Oxygen mask and bottle containing six minutes' supply needed from this altitude. Risk of instability in freefall with this weight of gear is high. *Private collection*

Lieutenant-Colonel Jim Johnson, SAS soldier and mercenary organizer in Yemen, c. 1966, during deniable U.K./French government operation with covert Israeli support to contain Egyptian and Soviet expansion. U.K. government lied to President Kennedy about the operation shortly before his assassination. *Private collection*

Tony de Saint-Paul, French mercenary killed by Egyptian shell during Johnson's Yemen operation. With a $5,000 price on his head, he hoped the Egyptians would double it. *Private collection*

In the freezing conditions of a South Atlantic autumn, an SAS soldier prepares to bring down an Argentine aircraft with a U.S.-supplied Stinger missile during the Falklands War, 1982. The Stinger, supplied by the CIA to the Afghanistan mujahideen resistance, was a key weapon in defeating the Soviet Army in 1988. *Private collection*

SAS soldier in Arab dress (right) in the Dhofar Mountains, Oman, c. 1972 with former enemy turned ally to serve in a "firqa" militia, left. Winning over former foes was practiced by the SAS in the Falklands and Iraq and is part of the McChrystal strategy in Afghanistan. *Private collection*

Inside the SAS Killing House, where simulated hostages are rescued by soldiers firing live ammunition at very close quarters. The masks accompany the use of CS riot gas. The SAS rescue of Iranian diplomat-hostages in London in 1980 was a turning point in counter-terrorism but also stripped the SAS of its long-protected secrecy. The Iranian government's thank-you was a demand for compensation for damage done to the embassy building in saving its diplomats. *Private collection*

SAS soldiers Scud-hunting in Iraq, 1991. Note the unarmored desert Land Rover, dependent for its survival on mobility and luck. The men's faces are obscured, as usual, for security purposes. *Private collection*

Cold War East Germany, 22 March 1984: French army Regimental Sergeant Major Mariotti lies dead alongside his tour car after being deliberately rammed by a heavy Ural-375 East German Army truck which crossed the central reservation as another army vehicle boxed in Mariotti from the other side. The victim was serving with his country's military spy mission, working alongside the U.S. Military Mission and the U.K. Brixmis team. Such incidents were commonplace. *Private collection*

Parachute drop by 170 men of 173rd Airborne in an operational exercise onto Kru-
sevo Airfield, Kosovo, 2002. These are low-level (800-foot or less) static line jumps
involving a high risk of collisions among the parachutists. The heavy gear each man
carries is dropped on a nylon rope attached to the soldier's harness and released
200 feet above ground with the aid of a quick-release device and luck. Landing with
the load still closely attached is a certain way to serious injury. *KFO*

to London. By early evening, it had moved covertly into a building adjoining the embassy. At a location nearby, a hastily constructed mock-up of the building was being assembled. The soldiers called it Operation Pagoda.

Storming the embassy was close to mission-impossible. As one of the planners told the author: "Basically, we were facing a fortress situation here. You have to bear in mind this was a big, mid-terrace building on six floors (four above ground) with fifty rooms, easily defended at the front and back because of the open spaces on either side of it; twenty hostages and six terrorists who got increasingly jumpy as time went by, moving the hostages from one room to another."

The drama followed two paths that converged, after five tense days, in an explosion of violence. At first, the London police, faithful to a scenario practiced many times, called in a hostage-negotiator to seek a peaceful end to the confrontation. He was also buying time for the SAS to get prepared, should the worst happen. The "worst" would be clear evidence that the terrorists had started to murder hostages. Efforts to monitor what was going on in the embassy included hand-drilling through walls, to implant listening devices. Tell-tale sounds of that process were overcome by arranging for civil airliners to divert their flight paths over the building, creating as much noise as possible. It was a trick the SAS had used at a terrorist siege in Holland three years earlier. The SAS had another useful asset: the blueprint for security devised by the regiment for the embassy during the years of the Shah's government in Tehran. Explosive charges estimated to blow in the heavy metal window frames on much of the building were calculated, and—in case of unexpected problems—doubled. This was to generate unwelcome complications when the moment came to strike.

The SAS rapidly increased its strength around the building,

including an expert sniper team in Hyde Park. Two groups—Red and Blue—prepared for the assault. Red Team, following an Immediate Action Plan, was to storm the embassy at ten minutes' notice if the killing started. Red had already made its first reconnaissance of the embassy roof and was preparing abseil ropes and harnesses so as to make an assault from above. Blue Team would strike with more sophistication if the initiative lay with the rescuers, once the location of the hostages was identified. The negotiations dragged on as the terrorist leader, Salim, became increasingly jittery, goaded by one of his captives, the embassy press officer Abbas Lavasani, who challenged Salim to kill him. The terrorists demanded, and got, one concession: a propaganda broadcast by the BBC Overseas Service, stating their cause.

At 6:30 P.M. on Sunday 4 May, the fifth day of the siege, the front door of the embassy was flung open and a dead body rolled out onto the steps as television cameras focused on the horror of that moment. Salim had threatened to kill hostages earlier that day. The man he shot, claiming martyrdom, was Lavasani. Salim had fired other shots at random, to give the impression of more deaths. As a bluff, it failed dismally. The police immediately handed over control to the SAS, while maintaining the pretense of negotiations, by telephone, with Salim. By now, deserted by his Iraqi controllers, Salim's demands had shrunk to a guarantee of safe conduct out of the country.

"Salim," said the police negotiator. "Listen carefully, please. We want to talk about the bus."

Distracted by the squeaking sound of a drill in the wall alongside him, Salim said: "What bus?"

"The bus that will take you to London Airport."

On the roof, the Red Team were poised in black masks and overalls, abseil harnesses fitted to the ropes down which they would swoop like hungry carrion. At ground level, Blue team were ready with ladders and explosive charges to blow out windows. Across the road, in the park, the snipers swept their scopes across the building, searching for targets.

Salim sensed that something was wrong. He said, "I will speak later," and hung up. Constable Lock, his revolver still in its holster, beneath his uniform, had won a degree of confidence with Salim who addressed him respectfully as "Mr. Trevor." Lock, standing next to Salim, lifted the hotline telephone again, suggesting that the bus be brought without delay because "the people here expect an attack any moment." Salim snatched the telephone to complain, "There is suspicion. . . . Just a minute. I'll come back again." His men darted from room to room, guns ready. "No suspicious noises, Salim," soothed the negotiator. The attackers' radios sent the code "London Bridge." It was time to strike. "I'm going to check," Salim told the negotiator. Right on cue, the first explosive charge ripped apart a skylight in the roof. This had been reinforced on the advice of the SAS in the years before the Shah was overthrown. Red Team smashed their way into rooms on the upper floors while Blue saw to windows below, hurling CS riot gas grenades and stun grenades ahead of them as they entered. One of these devices, or the explosive charges on the windows, heard across half of London, set fire to curtains on one side of the building.

In a deadly coincidence, the leader of the Red assault team, a senior sergeant, was trapped in his abseil harness. A defective rope had jammed and he was now its prisoner at a point where flames from the curtains engulfed the lower half of his body. He tried to kick out, away from the building, only to swing back into the flames. Above him, as the second abseil team prepared to jump, one of them saw his predicament and cut the defective rope. The sergeant fell a long way before landing on a balcony. In spite of his injuries, he found a way into the building to join the fight.

In a first-floor office, Constable Lock pounced on Salim, put his revolver to the terrorist's head but "I could not bring myself to kill in anger." As the two men wrestled on the floor, an SAS corporal hauled Lock away with the order, "Trevor, leave off." A second or so later, the corporal and another rescuer poured sub-machine gunfire into the terrorist leader, hitting him with fifteen bullets.

Throughout the building, the rescuers hunted down one terrorist after another as smoke and CS gas swirled around them. In the telex room on the second floor, a terrorist armed with a submachine gun was covering fifteen terrified hostages. He threw a window open and hurled a grenade through it, having overlooked one detail. He had not extracted the pin that releases the detonator. As he glared out of the window, Sergeant S, one of the Hyde Park snipers, picked him off with a head shot at a range of around 300 meters. Other terrorists rushed into the telex room and began firing into the cowering hostages. SAS Corporal Tommy Palmer, a Scot, followed them into the same room and killed a terrorist holding a grenade with one pistol shot to the head. The surviving terrorists threw their guns from the window and tried to merge with the hostages. One was taken prisoner. Another, thrown unceremoniously with genuine survivors along a chain of SAS men down the stairs, was holding a grenade. Soldier I, as he is known, armed with an MP5 submachine gun, could not shoot the man without risk of hitting his own team, or hostages. He later wrote: "I raised the MP5 above my head and . . . brought the stock of the weapon down on the back of his neck. I hit him as hard as I could. His head snapped back . . . I caught sight of his tortured, hate-filled face. The sound of two magazines being emptied into him was deafening. As he twitched and vomited his life away, his hand opened and the grenade rolled away" . . . harmlessly, it should be said.[212] In the embassy garden, the hostages were ordered to lie face-down, their arms strapped to their bodies, until they were identified. The only surviving terrorist, Fowzi Nejad (aka Ali Abdullah), was given a life sentence. He was released on license in November 2008 and granted asylum in Britain as required by human rights law. Had he been deported to Iran, the British authorities concluded, he might have been tortured. Constable Lock was not impressed.

The SAS success at Princes Gate, London, echoed like the cheers for an Olympic victory around the world, politically empowering the right-wing Thatcher government. It was Britain's Entebbe. Ken Connor, with twenty-three years of frontline SAS service to his credit, was candid about the private feelings of the British establishment. He wrote: "The contrast between the Delta Force at Desert One and the Iranian Embassy could not have been more marked. Once more, while publicly sympathetic about the American misfortune, the SIS [Secret Intelligence Service] were ecstatic." SIS, perhaps, hoped that a military success in the war against terrorism might erase memories of its own disasters: the defections of Soviet spies including Kim Philby from the upper ranks of SIS after years of betrayal of NATO, Britain, and America. But there was more reason than schadenfreude for celebrations. Britain, like Israel, is a major exporter of military training. As Connor reminds us: "The Kennedy assassination had been the catalyst for the spread of British influence through SAS bodyguard training. . . . After the Iranian Embassy siege, SAS expertise became one of Britain's more successful exports in its own right. SAS troops would be hired out to friendly governments for training purposes *or even covert operations* [author's emphasis] at a rate that covered the actual costs many times over."[213] One of the "covert operations," in which regular SAS soldiers effectively became mercenaries hired by other, friendly governments, is discussed in chapter five.

The SAS had mixed feelings about the adulation that swamped it after Operation Pagoda. During the Second World War, it had achieved a golden reputation as a gung-ho raiding force operating behind enemy lines, either in four-man teams or at squadron strength with Resistance fighters in France. Suppressed by a Socialist government after the war, it had sinuously reinvented itself as a deep-jungle fighting force to take on Communist guerrillas in the jungles of Malaya and Borneo and the pitiless jebels of Aden. Its reserve regiments prepared to act as stay-behind forces in Europe, directing nuclear strikes in the event of a Soviet invasion. The regular, professional SAS shrank to one regiment of a few hundred brilliant individuals ("Misfits who happen to fit together"), an elite that ran a six-year war in Oman from 1970, exploring the possibilities of unconventional warfare to recruit yesterday's enemy by arming him with the latest assault rifle.

It was dangerous work. In the Battle of Mirbat on 18 July 1972, a training team of ten SAS men, isolated in a mud-walled town forty miles from the nearest military base, was attacked by 250 hand-picked Marxist guerrillas armed with Kalashnikovs, heavy machine-guns, 82-mm mortars, two 75-mm recoilless rifles, and an 84-mm rocket-launcher. The SAS had .50 caliber machine guns, smaller 7.62-mm machine guns, and mortars. The battle lasted all day as wave after wave of enemy tried to overrun the base, with its back to the sea. Two Fijian volunteers were part of the British team. One of them, under heavy fire, took possession of a Second World War artillery gun (a 25-pounder), loaded and fired it singlehanded over open sights at pointblank range. As the enemy closed in for the kill, two Strikemaster aircraft of the Sultan's Air Force, directed by the SAS, hit the position with 500-lb bombs. The SAS losses during the battle were two dead, two seriously wounded. This summary does not do justice to an epic, small-scale battle of a sort that had to await Afghanistan, more than thirty years later, to be understood. At the time, and for seven years later, the SAS said nothing. The British public were totally unaware of what had happened. In 1979, while this author was researching his first SAS history, *Who Dares Wins*, the story was revealed by a British officer who was not at Mirbat. Reluctantly, the SAS corrected my draft before it passed into Britain's military history.

By convention, the secret life and death of the SAS was carved on the regimental clock tower at Hereford. Not to be listed as killed-in-action on the tower was known, in the self-mocking culture of the SAS, as "beating the clock." But after Princes Gate, the Iranian Embassy job in 1980, the postwar SAS was a secret no more. Life in the public—and media—eye would prove very much more complicated.

The Oman War ended in victory in 1976 for the Ruler, Sultan Qaboos, a British ally who had been trained at the Royal Military Academy, Sandhurst. He had also served with a Scottish regiment in Germany. Oman was to become an invaluable asset for American as well as British forces in their operations in the Gulf and beyond. Back home in London, the U.K. government was struggling with the renewed Irish War. Seven years of violence and counterviolence by the IRA, Loyalist terrorists, and British security forces were in stalemate. In January 1976, a perplexed prime minister committed the SAS to Northern Ireland by way of a press release, without informing the Army. This was seen, and meant to be seen, as a major escalation of British armed force in Ulster. The SAS, sure enough, was opaque at that time. Such stories that did circulate, usually in the left-wing press, were the dirty end of fairyland as portrayed by the Brothers Grimm. The Nationalist Irish—mainly Catholics—were convinced that this mysterious entity, the SAS ("SAS=SS," republican graffiti proclaimed) was the source of all Britain's dirty operations. It was a pantechnicon into which Ulster's Catholic minority loaded their suspicions. At first, this impression was a useful psyops weapon against the IRA, but it also became counterproductive.

In fact, the British had been running undercover operations in

Ireland's renewed war for around six years when the SAS was committed by Prime Minister Harold Wilson to that conflict. Many of these misadventures were less than useful. Captain Fred Holroyd, an undercover military intelligence officer in Northern Ireland, described "how the rule of law and order was not what it seemed, and I would encounter illegalities on my own side which would severely dent my sense of purpose." He alleged that the SAS had a cupboard in its armory containing 9-mm Browning pistol barrels, extractors, and firing pins which had been officially declared unfit for use, and destroyed. In fact, "these parts could be placed in normal issue Brownings, fired, destroyed and replaced with the original 'official' parts. This would make it impossible to connect the weapon with any shooting: there would be no ballistic evidence." In 1973, Holroyd attended a lecture by Brigadier (later General) Frank Kitson, an innovator during the counter-insurgency war against the Kenyan resistance (including President Barack Obama's kin). Holroyd concluded, "The logic of the use of infiltration, pseudo-gangs and deep interrogation to defeat terrorist opposition, was . . . compelling." Holroyd would discover, the hard way, what that strategy implied.

Meanwhile, "on the evening of Kitson's lecture there was a party in the Officers' Mess. An American approached me dressed like a U.S. Cavalry Officer. . . . He quietly proceeded to try to recruit me, along with two other captains from the course, into the CIA." Holroyd believed that this was not real. It had to be an initiative test run by his instructors. "When I spoke to my Colonel, he assured me that the approach was genuine. At that moment I realised just how different my work would be from anything I once expected."[214]

The SAS, in fact, had made a brief foray into Northern Ireland before 1976, to look for Loyalist arms smugglers. The free-fire zone of Oman, out of media eyes, was more to its liking. When Prime Minister Wilson announced that the SAS was to join the Irish struggle, the regiment had just eleven men to spare. Several were recovering from wounds sustained in Oman. It was not just the IRA and its allies that believed in the regiment's mystique. So did the British government. It was not until the bloody theater of Princes Gate, 1980, that the myth was made real and public.

By then, the Irish War—in which the first British soldier was killed by the IRA in 1970—and the Munich Massacre of 1972 had triggered a mutation in the Army. The SAS responded to Munich by creating a Counter Revolutionary Warfare cell. In Ireland, influenced by Kitson and other Special Forces innovators, the conventional "Green Army" (so called because of its standard disruptive-pattern camouflage) invented the Military Reconnaissance Force. Operating in civilian clothes, employing ex-IRA informers, it followed suspects around Belfast by car with a photographer concealed in the luggage boot. In 1972 an MRF two-man patrol fired at two men at a bus stop in a drive-by shooting. The gun they used was a museum piece, a Thomson submachine gun favored by Al Capone's gang. "The rattle of a Thomson gun" was also celebrated in an Irish republican ballad. The soldiers were prosecuted but cleared of illegality after claiming they fired in self-defense. MRF was further exposed when a mobile laundry service it ran, disguised as the Four Square Laundry, was ambushed by the IRA, killing the driver. His woman assistant, a leg-endary Intelligence Corps NCO known as "Mags," escaped. Until then, the Four Square was a successful commercial enterprise, cleaning garments at bargain rates thanks to the military budget. All the clothes were forensically tested for the presence of explosives in a year when Ulster was racked by 10,268 shootings and 1,382 bomb-ings in which 468 people, most of them civilians, died violently. Another MRF front was a massage parlor, also compromised by an IRA double agent.

The MRF was rapidly replaced by a new team known by various

names. These included 14 Intelligence Company and/or "The Dets" (detachments). Its creator was Brigadier Bill Dodd, a former SAS officer who had served with the Secret Intelligence Service and returned to the army. After he retired he was in charge of the BBC's personnel department. Fourteen Int. Company was a covert intelligence agency that used women and men able to memorize faces, places, and details of suspects' homes, which they frequently burglarized, sometimes to plant bugs, hidden cameras, and tracing devices on weapons and explosives. They also had to be able to shoot their way out of trouble. Fourteen Int. Company had considerable success as well as one spectacular failure.

The failure was Robert Nairac, a handsome young boxing champion from Oxford University, by 1977 a captain in the elite Grenadier Guards. A Catholic, he identified with the underdog culture of Ulster, while collecting intelligence on the IRA. He acquired a Belfast accent, learned to sing rebel songs, and went on the road to the badlands of South Armagh, on the border with the Irish Republic. His Intelligence controller, Major (later Colonel) Clive Fairweather, warned Nairac that he had been targeted but "he did not seem to take it seriously. I showed him a report that the IRA were 'going to get the curly-haired little SAS man called Danny.' He laughed at me."

On 14 May 1977, a year after the SAS was publicly committed to the Irish War, Nairac walked into the Three Steps, an IRA bar in Dromintee (population around 300) in County Armagh. He did not trouble to let his headquarters know exactly where he was. When the time for his expected check call had passed, Fairweather shrugged. Nairac had failed to make check calls before, as a result of which SAS men were sent on a wild-goose chase to ensure his safety. Posing as an IRA man from the Ardoyne district of Belfast, Nairac entertained the locals with his big presence and seductive voice. He was still making fatal mistakes. He had left his pistol, in its shoulder holster, in the glove compartment of his car in case, as he raised his arms while responding to applause, the holster might be spotted. He also asked a local woman how he could cross the border without been spotted by British security forces. The local IRA were summoned to check him over. The pub band, scenting trouble, said they were leaving and suggested Nairac go with them. He said no, thanks.

Nairac walked out of the bar alone into the darkness of the car park. As he reached his car, he opened the door and leaned forward to retrieve his pistol. Several large hands snatched the scarf around his neck and pulled him backward. He was then set upon by a dozen men and fought back hard. Half conscious, he was hustled across the nearby Irish border into the republic and again savagely beaten. An IRA man impersonating a priest invited Nairac to make confession or be shot. Nairac replied: "Bless me, Father, for I have sinned." When he refused to give his captors any further information, a gun was brought. The first attempt to shoot him failed when the assassin's gun jammed. Finally, the deed was done. His body was never found. Rumors still circulate about its fate. One of his killers said, years later, "He never told us anything. He was a great soldier." He was posthumously awarded the George Cross for his bravery. Two of those involved in the attack were given sanctuary in the United States for decades afterward.

During the early years of SAS involvement in Northern Ireland, the IRA was on the back foot, thanks to ambiguous incidents that gave credence to the common belief that Special Forces were running black operations including extra-judicial executions. Jealousy of SAS luster by other agencies, including the Royal Ulster Constabulary and intelligence agencies, encouraged this view. On 15 April 1976, Peter Cleary, an IRA officer arrested by the SAS fifty yards from the Irish border, uttered his last, desolate words to a friend as he was escorted toward an Army helicopter. "I'm dead," he said. "What shall I do?"

Minutes later, he was killed by three bullets fired from an Army rifle. The soldiers claimed that he had tried to snatch the weapon from his escort and paid the price. Another IRA volunteer, Sean McKenna, was already in custody, having been woken in his bed in the Republic by a British officer holding a pistol to his head. An uppercrust English voice murmured in his ear: "I want to explain the case to you. Do you realize that I could have shot you? If you want to put up a struggle or if you don't want to come, say so. I will have no hesitation about shooting you now." McKenna agreed to go quietly and was marched 250 yards into Northern Ireland where he was allegedly found wandering and drunk, before being handed over to the police.

Over the following years, two major constraints emerged to limit the effectiveness of the SAS and other Special Forces in their wish to achieve a military victory. The SAS intention, expressed by one of its commanders, was that "We are in Northern Ireland to kill the IRA." Another spoke with relish of "an IRA cull." Successive British governments limited that ambition with "the yellow card procedure," requiring soldiers not to shoot unless they, or their comrades, or civilians, were at imminent risk of death. The rules specified: "You may only open fire against a person: (a) if he is committing or about to commit an act LIKELY TO ENDANGER LIFE, AND THERE IS NO OTHER WAY TO PREVENT THE DANGER" [sic].

Yellow card rules resulted in one British Red Beret soldier's being convicted of murder after he opened fire on a car driving at speed toward his checkpoint. All the signs pointed to an IRA attack. Private Lee Clegg's first three shots were strictly defensive and lawful. The fourth, fired after the vehicle—and the immediate danger—had passed him, was not. The fourth shot killed a woman passenger. The soldier was automatically sentenced to life imprisonment.

After the yellow card was imposed on military planners, all operations were subject to police primacy so as to maintain the fiction that the Irish problem was not an armed conflict but an internal security issue. The SAS took careful note of such limitations and made sure that its lethal capabilities met ambiguity with ambiguity. Whether by coincidence or not, an unofficial "clean kill" policy determined SAS ambushes, sometimes set up after weeks of close surveillance of IRA targets. The unwritten clean kill rules required that the enemy was armed and intent on murder at the moment the SAS intervened. Some informed sources paraphrased this alternative, unofficial policy as "Big Boys' Games, Big Boys' Rules."

When intelligence suggested that the risk was particularly high, the police were happy to receive SAS support in dealing with it. So it was that on the evening of 8 May 1987 an IRA team loaded a 200-pound bomb onto the shovel of a mechanical digger, covered it with a screen of bricks, and conveyed it nine miles along the back lanes of rural Tyrone to attack a police barracks at the village of Loughgall. An SAS team of more than forty men was waiting for the raid, some of its soldiers inside the targeted building with two heavy machine guns trained on approach roads, others in concealed sniper positions overlooking the area. The IRA convoy was led by a stolen blue Toyota van that drove cautiously into the killing zone, then out again. The SAS held their fire. The van halted in front of the barracks and Patrick Kelly, leading his hand-picked team of eight men, stepped out, rifle in hand, followed by two others. He pointed the gun at the building and started shooting. The attack was on. So was the turkey shoot. The machine guns cut down the men in the open and killed two still in the van, wearing flak jackets. That left two men who were the bomb team. One tried to ignite the bomb with a cigarette lighter, then ran for it, as did his companion. Both were shot dead before they had covered a few yards. There were also two civilian fatal casualties, brothers who drove into Loughgall before they realized that it was now a war zone.

A few months later, British intelligence officers stalked an IRA team that was clearly engaged in a reconnaissance of the U.K.'s Iberian colony, Gibraltar. Every week, a resident army parade would ceremoniously change the guard outside the governor's residence, complete with military band. It was a Ruritanian ritual watched by hundreds of tourists. The IRA saw it as a bombing opportunity, a lovely day for an auto-da-fe similar to its bloody attacks on a Remembrance Day service at Enniskillen and the Royal parks bombings in London. On 6 March 1988, four SAS marksmen in civilian clothes, Browning pistols tucked into the backs of their jeans, followed three IRA volunteers as they parked a car near the parade area, then strolled like tourists around the center of Gibraltar. The soldiers had been briefed on the dangers of a new IRA weapon. This, they were told, was a car bomb that could be radio-detonated by pressing a cordless button hundreds of yards away. Not surprisingly, the SAS men were also on a very short fuse. As one later told an official inquiry: "We were told that all three [IRA] members could be carrying a device to detonate the bomb."

Control of the situation was officially passed from local police to the SAS at 2:40 P.M. Two minutes later, the three terrorists—two men, one woman—were dead. Two were shot in the back. The total number of lethal shots fired in 120 seconds was twenty-seven. One of the dead was hit by sixteen bullets. A follow-up investigation established that there was no bomb in the terrorists' car. The IRA team was unarmed but this was, unquestionably, a reconnaissance for the operation that was to follow. An IRA car bomb was subsequently discovered in an underground car park at Marbella, Costa del Sol, thirty miles from Gibraltar. The bomb contained 143 pounds of Semtex high explosive, enough to flatten a building. There was also a timing device, not yet attached to the bomb, set to detonate the device at 11:20 A.M., when the guard-mounting ceremony would normally take place. Seven years later, an international court at Strasbourg ruled by a majority of one vote that the Gibraltar killings could have been avoided and that the IRA volunteers could have been arrested. The SAS, faithful to its "never confirm, never deny" philosophy, stayed silent. By then, the Irish War had moved on, in a sinister direction.

There is a story to be gleaned from the body count of IRA men and their families. Statistics are always dangerous, so the reasoning that follows has a clause that might read *caveat emptor*. During the first three years of SAS operations in Ireland, from 1976 to 1978, seven IRA men were killed by the regiment. From 1979 to 1982, no IRA deaths were attributed to the SAS. Only two IRA men were killed by the SAS by the end of 1983. But in the years following 1984, the year of the Brighton bomb (see below) until Gibraltar in 1988, the IRA "cull" rose dramatically. Between 1985 and February 1992, a total of twenty-seven (perhaps twenty-nine) IRA volunteers were killed by the SAS. But between 1992 and 1997, the SAS/Republican body count was down to one. The curve was in freefall.

Various reasons are advanced for the change. One is that after the IRA's attempt to wipe out most of the British government including Margaret Thatcher with a bomb at the Conservative Party's conference hotel in Brighton in 1984—an event used by President Reagan's Secretary of State George Shultz to legitimize a global war on terror—the increase in SAS kills over previous years was 300 per cent. With the departure of the Iron Lady and her replacement by the gentlemanly, cricket-loving John Major in 1990, the number fell back. But here's a strange coincidence. There was another trend on the graph, a rising curve representing the murder of IRA men, some of their dependents and legal advisers by Loyalist death squads. These doubled from eighteen in 1990 to almost fifty in 1993.

A British intelligence expert, Colonel Michael Mates MP, told the author: "A bunch of Loyalists came out of jail where they had been serving life sentences, during which time they had found out a helluva lot about how PIRA (the Provisional IRA) worked and they said to themselves, 'There must be a better way [of killing Republicans] than filling a [Catholic] bar with bullets. We need to knock off the major [IRA] players." The outcome was a selection committee that chose assassination targets. Between December 1993 and the IRA ceasefire of August 1994, "among those assassinated . . . were about fifteen top people. The IRA were taking a hell of a pasting. They said, 'We can't go on taking casualties at this rate.' . . ."[215]

There is evidence that some of the Loyalist assassins were assisted in their planning by elements within British military intelligence. In the late 1980s an Ulsterman named Brian Nelson, who had served in the British Army, was the intelligence chief of a Loyalist paramilitary group, the Ulster Defense Association. In 1985 he was recruited by an Intelligence Corps cell that specialized in running informers known as the Force (or Field) Reconnaissance Unit; the FRU. He later admitted charges including conspiracy to murder, having information of use to [Loyalist] terrorists and possessing a submachine gun. During his tenure at the UDA, at least sixteen murders were carried out by that organization, allegedly in spite of his efforts to warn the security authorities that these assassinations were imminent. Lieutenant-Colonel F, commanding the FRU, said Nelson was "a very courageous man whose mistakes were all very understandable." In January 1992, after a hearing lasting just one day, Nelson was sentenced to ten years. He served less than five and spent the rest of his life under a false identity. He died in Canada in 2003, apparently of a brain tumor. A veteran chronicler of the Irish War, David McKittrick, quoted Nelson's trial judge to claim that Nelson "acted with good motivation, not for gain and with the greatest courage" but that on five occasions, Nelson had "disobeyed Military Intelligence and crossed the line from lawful intelligence-gathering into criminal participation."[216]

After almost twenty years, the odor of collusion still hangs around the activities of Nelson and his handlers; and with it, a widespread belief that British military intelligence sources effectively supplied Nelson with a hit list of IRA suspects, leaving it to Loyalist assassins to act on that information. Sometimes they killed the wrong man, or woman. In 2003, after an investigation lasting fourteen years, a British police team headed by Sir John Stevens reported on "the allegation of widespread collusion between loyalist paramilitaries, the Royal Ulster Constabulary and the Army." Stevens found that there was collusion in two murders, one of them the killing of a solicitor, Pat Finucane, who was shot fourteen times by two masked gunmen in his home, in the presence of his wife and three children. "Collusion," Stevens concluded, "is evidenced in many ways. This ranges from the wilful failure to keep records . . . withholding of intelligence and evidence, through to the extreme of agents being involved in murder. . . . The unlawful involvement of agents in murder implies that the security forces sanction killings. . . . My inquiries have found all these elements of collusion. . . . Agents were allowed to operate without effective control and to participate in terrorist crimes. Nationalists were known to be targeted but were not properly warned or protected. . . ."[217]

Some reports suggested that responsibility went to the heart of "a shadowy unit in the Ministry of Defence with responsibility for special forces . . . the Home & Special Forces' Secretariat."[218] Finucane was one of many solicitors targeted by Loyalist terrorists. In March 1999 Rosemary Nelson, a lawyer who had testified to the U.S. Congress and the UN about threats to her life from police officers, was murdered by a bomb placed under her car. Ten years later, a panel of three judges, after a four-year inquiry, had not yet reported on its findings.[219]

In the murk of Ulster politics, it was not only Irish Nationalists who had reason to complain about dirty tricks. Ironically, the death of a British soldier, a sentry staked out like a tethered goat to be murdered by the IRA in South Armagh, was the last straw for the SAS. On 12 February 1997, a few months before the Belfast peace agreement and the formal end of IRA warlike operations, Lance Bombardier (corporal) Stephen Restorick was shot dead by an IRA sniper in a border region whose republican guerrillas were a law unto themselves, culturally insulated from the IRA's own high command. They even decorated local highways with a warning road sign, complete with logo, proclaiming: "Sniper at work!"

Restorick was a sentry at a checkpoint in the village of Bessbrook. The sniper team used a Mazda saloon car, fitted with a protective armored shield in the rear, in which a hole was cut to accommodate the barrel of a heavy, .50 Barrett rifle imported from the USA. The gun uses a three-inch bullet with an effective range of 1,800 meters. When the vehicle's rear luggage boot lid was lifted open, the Mazda was a perfect mobile sniper platform.

Following a series of sniper attacks in South Armagh in which a Barrett was used, the Royal Ulster Constabulary—controlling military operations according to its own rules—had been running an surveillance operation on the Mazda for almost a month when Restorick was killed. Four days before that, intelligence records examined by an inquiry into the death showed that "South Armagh PIRA [Provisional IRA] were at an advanced stage of an operation but the nature of the target or the attack were not known." An intelligence "action sheet" written the same day "was generated to locate the Mazda in the region of Crossmaglen. The document illustrates the police assessment that the Mazda was believed to be used in the advanced stages of a PIRA attack."[220] The Mazda was being tracked on behalf of RUC Intelligence by a covert military Special Forces team from 14 Intelligence Company, an organization that scored repeated successes in close surveillance operations. But the soldiers were denied permission by the police to get close enough to the Mazda to confirm that it was a sniper's nest. Their surveillance was limited to electronic tracking, standing so far out of sight from the target that they were not always sure of the vehicle's precise location. Shortly before Restorick was killed, the watchers established that "the Mazda was heading towards Bessbrook when it became static for approximately forty to sixty minutes." It is almost certain that at this point, the IRA sniper team were preparing their hit.

Soldier C, a senior operator with the watchers, recalled making requests to the police Tasking & Co-ordination Group, controlling the operation, "to mobilize his unit, which was refused on the basis that there was no intelligence to substantiate that the vehicle was planning an attack." He believed "the only means of establishing an accurate location [for the Mazda] was for his unit to be deployed on the ground." Restorick was shot dead soon afterward. In the early hours following Restorick's killing, the police controllers at last permitted Army intelligence to examine the vehicle at an unidentified location. Soldier B, the team's Regimental Sergeant Major, gave evidence that "evidence of the vehicle's adaptation for a sniper was video-recorded and shown to the TCG [police tasking group]." Soldier B said "members of the TCG still had to be convinced of the vehicle's connection" with the killing, while Soldier C believed "that the police took approximately seventy-two hours from the time of the murder to accept the link between the Mazda and the sniper." During that time, the IRA sniper team had made good their escape.

At their base a few miles away, the men of 14 Intelligence Company were outraged. Heavy-handed police control had prevented them from intervening in an IRA operation with a good chance of preventing the death of a young soldier now characterized as "a tethered goat" as he manned the checkpoint with no knowledge of the risk. To defuse the anger, a debrief was held at the unit's base addressed by a senior member of the police tasking group. Soldier B believed that "the debrief was held in response to ill feeling amongst soldiers in his unit caused by the frustration and anger of not performing closer and more intrusive form of surveillance." He added that an explanation from the police representative—that the Tasking Group feared that surveillance would be compromised if Army intelligence intervened—"satisfied the more mature members of the unit but the younger, less experienced members were not convinced."

They were not alone. One SF veteran told the author: "Earlier in the Troubles, the SAS would have expected that if IRA gangs could be caught in possession of weapons they would be intercepted and shot if they failed to surrender immediately. The rules were changed for political reasons. The emphasis was on restoring the IRA ceasefire without creating Republican martyrs." In a separate interview, an SAS colonel said: "We were disillusioned by what happened. Not long afterwards we arranged to be pulled out of Northern Ireland."

In this new political atmosphere, when an SAS team of sixteen struck at a remote farm in South Armagh to arrest five men including Restorick's alleged killer, Michael Caraher, the Special Forces soldiers used fists, rather than machine guns, to bring the IRA men to British justice. Though the IRA men were given long sentences (435 years in one case), the gang were released after sixteen months under the terms of the 1998 Belfast Agreement which brought peace, of a sort, in Northern Ireland. The IRA's leaders formally announced an end to their armed campaign in July 2005. As a gesture to Loyalist anxieties, the Irish government rewrote its constitution renouncing its claim to jurisdiction over the whole of Ireland.

The stalemate did not satisfy a handful of extremists on both sides. Twelve years after Restorick's death, two British soldiers on standby to serve in Afghanistan were gunned down by a splinter group called "the Real IRA." (As one Irish joke has it, when Republicans come together, the first item on the agenda is The Split.) Catholic civilians continued to be murdered by Loyalist gangs. They included a youth worker and a postman. A surprising postscript to the Irish War was a British Army analysis of its thirty-seven-year campaign in Ulster describing the IRA as "a professional, dedicated, highly skilled and resilient force" that had not been defeated. It added that the struggle had also shown the IRA that it could not win through violence.[221]

During their decades in Northern Ireland, elements of British Special Forces—the SAS and the Royal Marines' Special Boat Service—were also plunged into two exotic major conventional wars: one in the South Atlantic in 1982 after the Argentine invasion of the Falkland Islands, the other in the Iraqi desert in 1991 following Saddam Hussein's invasion of Kuwait in August 1990. In both cases, they demonstrated extreme endurance and bravery, but to what effect is debatable. The unique quality of Special Forces is their ability to achieve major strategic gains using small numbers of elite, intelligent soldiers supported by the latest technology. In the Falkands, the SAS suffered tactical reverses and a virtual mutiny by one squadron thanks to cowboy planning. But the regiment also tipped the balance of the conflict toward an unlikely British victory over an enemy of 11,000 men well dug in on a series of islands 9,000 miles from the U.K. This was one result of the regiment's unique capacity to run covert close observation of enemy dispositions for many weeks in a pitiless climate.

This was not a war in which black operations played a part. It saw the SAS back in its original role as a reconnaissance and sabotage force. Nevertheless, there were some novelties, two of which originated in the U.S. thanks to a friendship between the long-serving Ken Connor and a veteran of Delta Force, possibly its renowned first deputy commander, Lieutenant Colonel L. H. ("Bucky") Burruss, an ally of the SAS. Connor and another SAS NCO, Paddy O'Connor, were on a training job in America as the South Atlantic campaign started. They made contact with Delta and were offered the use of two of U.S. Special Forces' most secret new toys: an anti-aircraft, shoulder-fired missile named Stinger and satellite communications that gave SAS teams in their hides instant, secure voice links to their head-quarters in England as well as to their field commander, Lieutenant-Colonel Mike Rose. It is unclear whether the Pentagon or any other part of U.S. government ever approved of this release. What is certain is that it provided the outnumbered Brits with an edge they badly needed. The threat to the U.K.'s amphibious force by Argentine bombers equipped with sea-skimming Exocet missiles (supplied by France) was lethal. The SAS made repeated, unsuccessful attempts to strike at air bases on the Argentine mainland. In a daring raid on East Falkland island, however, they destroyed the greater part of Argentine air power. The Stinger was used more than once to intercept low-flying Argentine attackers.

The end of this campaign had much to do with Rose's use of psy-chology. In peacetime, the islanders used citizens' band (CB) radio to talk to one another. Rose employed a Marine captain who spoke fluent Argentine-Spanish to call up a doctor in Port Stanley to open negotiations with the Argentine high command. Eight days of nego-tiations followed during which Rose seduced his enemy with the proposition that Argentine honor was satisfied by its courageous resistance and that further slaughter of civilians as well as exhausted Argentine soldiers would serve no purpose. In truth, as a British admiral admitted later, the U.K. offensive was running out of steam. The jesuitical dialogue, the work of an Oxford graduate, worked. It was time to talk face to face. Rose, in a helicopter flying a white flag, was put down on the wrong landing zone in the capital, Port Stanley. He had to make his way through a series of enemy fortifications, on foot, accompanied by a signaler, to reach enemy HQ. There, two more hours of detailed negotiations led to the Argentine surrender. A seventy-four-day war, won after an opposed landing, requiring a forced march of around sixty miles across boggy West Falkland and a series of uphill assaults, ended with 649 Argentine dead, 1,068 wounded, and 11,313 taken prisoner. The respective British losses were 258 killed (including more than twenty SF personnel in a single helicopter crash), 777 wounded, and 115 taken prisoner.

Back home, the victory restored the fading popularity of Prime Minister Margaret Thatcher, propelling her to re-election in 1983. It also reinforced the personal alliance between Mrs. Thatcher and President Ronald Reagan. But soon after Saddam Hussein invaded Kuwait in August 1990, the political landscape had changed. Mrs. Thatcher was out of office and the SAS was out of favor with the architects of the war to liberate Kuwait. The allied commander, U.S. General H. Norman Schwarzkopf, known as "The Bear," had little faith in Special Forces operations thanks to his experience of Vietnam, and the escape route used by Vietcong into the sanctuary of Cambodia. Kicking the desert sand, he told journalists: "When you go to war, you're going to war all the way. . . . No more Cambodian border situations for me." During the five-month buildup known as Desert Shield, virtually no role was allotted to SF teams.

That changed on Scud Sunday, 2 December 1990. Saddam Hussein's army wheeled three Scuds into the desert, after dark, for a demonstration shoot, within Iraqi territory but toward Israel. The first missile was six minutes into a seven-minute flight before a U.S. satellite detected the flare from its rocket motor. A member of an allied headquarters staff in Riyadh that day witnessed "concern amounting to bewilderment that the high-tech solution to the Scud threat we had been assured was foolproof, had failed even before the fighting began." Not for the first time, when there is no alternative, the high command turned to Special Forces to salvage the situation, in this case to track and kill the Scuds before they could strike Israel or Saudi Arabia.

SAS patrols, with virtually no time for preparation, were hurled at the problem as the air offensive started in January 1991. A senior officer later told one of his men: "I would have sacrificed a squadron of men for a Scud." This was a desert war tailored for the SAS, yet it was to prove a turning point for the regiment, in the wrong direction. Lack of reliable radios, GPS satnav devices, rescue beacons, detailed maps, night vision goggles, weapons, and desert vehicles put the three SAS squadrons into the field to roam around almost randomly looking for targets of opportunity. Frontline reconnaissance was in the hands of U.S. Special Forces. The SAS was increasingly starved of resources while being maintained as a propaganda weapon by successive British governments. It was a pattern to be repeated after 2003 in Iraq and Afghanistan. In Texas, the syndrome is known as "all hat and no cattle."

In 1991, three eight-man patrols were to cover Iraqi movements in a "Scud box" of 340 square miles in Western Iraq. Around fourteen mobile missile launchers were thought to be in the area. RAF Chinooks attempted to place the three teams at twenty-mile intervals in the box, around 180 miles inside Iraqi territory, on a north-south axis. By this time, Scuds were hitting the suburbs of Tel Aviv and there was a real danger that Israel might hit back with nuclear weapons.

The SAS commander of the South road watch team did not release the Chinook before he had checked the ground in which he would operate. A wigwam parliament of the team concluded instantly that this was a potential death trap. There was no hope of concealment. The team returned to base. The Central Road Watch team called down an A-10 air attack by USAF on an Iraqi radar station. Flawed communications meant that the team was almost hit in the bombing that followed. After a journey through four freezing nights, this group turned up on the Saudi border, suffering, in some cases, from frostbite and exposure. Road Watch South, known by its call-sign as Bravo Two Zero, agreed to go into action in this wilderness on foot. It was an unwise decision if this was meant to be an offensive mission, rather than simply to maintain a road watch from a fixed position near the landing zone. Each man was carrying around 200 pounds of equipment which had to be hauled to the nearest viable laying-up position in a wadi. One of those involved, known as Chris Ryan, says that the purpose was to set up a ten-day observation post overlooking a main supply route.[222] "Mike (Kiwi) Coburn," a New Zealander on the team, recalls that there were no vehicles left, so, said Sergeant Vincent Phillips, "It's going to be a case of using the good old size nines" (boots). Staff Sergeant "Andy McNab," commanding the patrol, suggests that the decision to move on foot was a collective one because, "since our mission required us to stay in the same area for a long time, our best form of defense was going to be concealment and vehicles wouldn't help us with that at all." McNab also quotes a briefing given by Phillips (who died on the operation): "The options are to patrol in on foot, take vehicles, or have a heli drop-off."[223] There is nothing in his assertion to suggest that the SAS's favorite mode of transport in the desert, the long-wheelbase Land Rover, known as the "pinkie," was not available or that the choice of size nine boots was forced on the patrol as a result, yet again, of equipment shortages.

Once inserted, the patrol was soon spotted by local civilians and came under fire from an Iraqi unit armed with triple-A heavy machine guns. The SAS men fled north. Rescue contingency plans failed completely. As one of the survivors told the author: "The truth is, they [U.K. Special Forces] didn't have the resources to support the patrols they put on the ground." After thirty miles on foot, in a blizzard, the team lost its first man, Sergeant Vince Phillips. Disoriented, he collapsed and died of hypothermia. To reduce the risk of detection, the rest of the team split into units of four, two, and even one man. This individual, known as "Chris (Geordie) Ryan," was a reservist who covered 117 miles in seven nights' marching and seven days' concealment before reaching the sanctuary of Syria. Corporal Steven Lane died of exposure after swimming 400 yards across an icy River Euphrates. Trooper Robert Consiglio died of gunshot wounds while covering the escape of two of his comrades. The five others including Staff Sergeant "McNab" and "Coburn" were taken prisoner. "Ryan," "McNab," and "Coburn" were later to follow the example of the British commander in the Gulf, Lieutenant-General Sir Peter de la Billiere, in writing books about their service and SAS activities in this war.

The ripples from that would grow to become a shock wave that changed profoundly the nature of the SAS. A carefully worded legal judgment reported: "At the end of 1992 General Sir Peter de la Billiere, commanding officer of the British forces in the Gulf War and himself a former commanding officer of 22 SAS, wrote a book about the war which included a chapter on the Bravo Two Zero patrol. This appears to have been the first time that a member or former member of the SAS had published an account of one of its operations. Until then, the ethos of the regiment had been for its members to preserve total secrecy."[224] In fact, other retired SAS officers of earlier generations had written about operations in which they were involved, such as the Oman campaign. In 1996, the SAS introduced a service contract enforceable at civil law, in addition to Britain's already tight secrecy laws, to halt the flow of post-Iraq and other SAS memoirs. Under new management, the regiment's headquarters then tried to make the 1996 in-house rule retrospective, binding soldiers who had retired long before 1996.[225]

What made the case of De La Billiere (DLB to his friends) special was that his was the first inside account of an SAS operation after the Gulf War at a time when retired Special Forces veterans with a good story to tell could enter a ready market infested by literary agents waving checkbooks. The Iranian Embassy siege, and my own history of the postwar SAS, *Who Dares Wins*, had clearly signaled that change. Military history was no longer the preserve of the officer class. "McNab's" account of his disastrous patrol, *Bravo Two Zero*, became a runaway best seller and made him a media lion. It was a very British success.

The toxic controversy that resulted from profitable publication of some works followed by arbitrary suppression of others generated feuds that have damaged SAS morale ever since. As one informed account put it: "Up to fifty former members of the [SAS] regiment have been served with exclusion orders; they have been banned from all Special Forces property, which means they cannot attend reunions, Remembrance Day parades, wedding receptions or even funeral wakes on SAS bases."[226] In its attempts to suppress Coburn's book, *Soldier Five*, the U.K. government spent millions of dollars in courts around the world. It failed. Yet, as the Privy Council judgment cited above demonstrated, this was not an attempt to preserve essential military secrets. The court pointed out that the contract "was intended to prevent disclosures which would not necessarily be in themselves damaging to the public interest and might even be as to matters already in the public domain. *It had the broader object of preventing public controversy which might be damaging to the efficiency of the Special Forces*" [author's emphasis]. It seemed that after the exposure of the Iranian Embassy siege (a political plus for government) and the Irish War (less good PR) the SAS, under its new management, combining all U.K. Special Forces in one body along lines similar to U.S. Special Operations Command, was a sensitive flower to be sheltered from public controversy at all costs. This was a long way from the regiment's democratic roots as discovered by the American officer Charlie Beckwith in 1961 and Stirling's original idea of one company.

After its bad start with Bravo Two Zero in Iraq, the SAS tried again with four mobile fighting columns, each employing a dozen four-wheel-drive vehicles bristling with weapons. A frontal assault, launched on a Scud control complex identified as Victor Two, blew up a control tower while under a hail of enemy fire. After a month in the field, the squadrons were resupplied by a convoy of trucks ninety miles inside Iraq. On 24 February, Special Forces operations were stood down as the major ground offensive by conventional forces stormed across the frontiers of Saudi Arabia and occupied Kuwait. The Pentagon declared a ceasefire four days later.

The SAS claimed four confirmed Scud kills. It could also take credit for two strategic hits during this brief war. One was the capture of a detailed Iraqi army map, taken from a captured artillery officer. The map revealed the current deployment of an entire army division. This and the prisoner were sent back to allied lines by helicopter. American air power decimated the division. The other, less tangible victory was that the presence of Special Forces soldiers deep inside Iraq pressured the Iraqis to pull back their mobile Scuds from positions that endangered Israel.

Some of the lessons of this campaign were disagreeable and not discussed in public, with the exception of the long-serving Ken Connor, who wrote: "The Regiment's increasingly top-heavy administrative structure meant that, for the first time ever, SAS requests for equipment were subject to interpretation by staff officers who often had no experience whatsoever of special forces operations. If the officer decided that the equipment requested—Global Positioning Systems, claymore mines, .203 grenades, cold-weather gear and the rest—was excessive or unnecessary, it would not be supplied."[227] Connor's candor was not welcomed. The SAS regimental journal,

Mars and Minerva, barked: "This book should not have been published." It was an odd response from a regiment whose unusual tradition was to think laterally and learn from its mistakes.

In subsequent years, during the Iraq War and beyond, British Special Forces continued to suffer from lethal under-investment while saddled with the usual level of risk. The formula that worked best was a combination of American logistics and SAS knowhow, plus the effective alliance with Delta Force. In Iraq and Afghanistan, U.K. Special Forces (UKSF) became an organic part of America's Special Force structure. But an increasing number of SAS soldiers quit the army to join the profitable private security market, particularly during the Iraq bubble, 2003–2009. But some resignations reflected a deeper malaise, a loss of morale caused by lack of resources and consequent deaths. Here are some examples:

1. On 30 January 2005 a Royal Air Force Special Duties Hercules was brought down by small arms fire near the forward SAS base at Balad, Iraq. The British Defense Ministry (MoD) had chosen not to fit explosive suppressant foam around the plane's fuel tanks. One tank exploded, blowing off the plane's starboard wing. Nine airmen and a soldier died unnecessarily. A few hours earlier, the aircraft had delivered fifty SAS soldiers to Baghdad.

2. On 2 September 2006 an RAF Nimrod aircraft—an intelligence platform essential to effective special operations on the ground—caught fire soon after an air-to-air refueling operation 23,000 feet over Kandahar. Fuel is thought to have leaked into a bomb bay where it was ignited by a hot pipe. The Nimrod exploded with the loss of twelve airmen and two Special Forces soldiers. A

civilian coroner found that the Nimrod had never been airworthy.

3. At dusk on 20 November 2007, a "notoriously unreliable" radio system prevented the crews of four SAS helicopters from communicating with one another as they shadowed a terrorist team at low altitude. One of the machines crashed as it flew blind through a dust cloud. A valve to prevent fuel spillages did not work. The Puma helicopter—later described as "unairworthy"—went ablaze after hitting the ground. Two SAS men died. An inquest found that the immediate cause of the deaths was pilot error due to extreme stress, compounded by poor equipment.

4. In June 2008, an Intelligence Corps operator, Corporal Sarah Bryant, was on a mission in Helmand province, Afghanistan, escorted by three SAS Reservists, in vulnerable, thin-skinned "Snatch" Land Rovers when they were killed by a roadside mine. Their commander, Major Sebastian Morley, said that "chronic underinvestment" in military equipment was to blame for the deaths. The MoD, he said, "has blood on its hands." He resigned from the Army. Elsewhere in Helmand, many more conventional British soldiers, on foot and in vehicles, were killed by Improvised Explosive Devices (IEDs) laid by the Taliban.

5. In a false economy, the U.K. Foreign Office halted a $4 million helicopter support program, maintaining four Russian-made "Hip" helicopters that enabled the SBS to operate with Afghan commandos in raids on drug barons and Taliban guerrillas. The Foreign Office hoped Uncle Sam would pick up the tab to maintain

the helicopters and got it wrong. Simultaneously
Defense Chiefs were boosting Special Forces numbers
with a new Brigade Reconnaissance Force to be
attached to each of the army's front line fighting
brigades.

MoD incompetence in procuring military equipment was
becoming notorious. In August 2008 the *Sunday Times* revealed an
internal report suppressed by the Ministry, which asked: "How can it
be that it takes twenty years to buy a ship, or aircraft, or tank? Why
does it always seem to cost at least twice what was thought? Even
worse, at the end of the wait, why does it never quite seem to do what
it was supposed to?"[228]

Another procurement scandal arose from a decision to buy eight
Special Forces Chinook helicopters from Boeing in 1995. Reliable
reports suggest that the MoD and Royal Air Force insisted they knew
better when it came to designing avionics software for these aircraft.
Warnings from Boeing of incompatibility were ignored. In the fiasco
that followed, the machines were moth-balled in air-conditioned
hangars after delivery in 2001 until 2007. At that point, the MoD
decided to settle for a less sophisticated version capable of basic operations in good visibility. The cost of the new fleet had increased from
GBP 259 million to at least GBP 500 million. The first aircraft was
expected to enter service in 2010 after a fifteen-year delay. Meanwhile,
U.K. soldiers were being killed in Iraq and Afghanistan because their
mobility depended on road vehicles that were a soft target for IEDs.
The MoD tried to blame Boeing, alleging that the U.S. company had
deliberately withheld software codes needed to make the Chinooks
perform as contracted.[229]

In 2006, the U.K. Treasury capped the number of soldiers available
for an offensive against the Taliban around Musa Qala, where, at one

point, a favorite enemy target was guarded by just thirty men. Former SAS commander Brigadier Ed Butler, leading the operation, told members of parliament that he had just enough troops—3,300—to hold the line "but we couldn't sustain a higher tempo." Lack of helicopters meant that "the Taliban forced us off the road," using asymmetric tactics to ambush his men with roadside bombs.[230] By 2009, U.S. military planners were considering ceding Musa Qala and other areas of southern Helmand to the Taliban, more effectively to secure more densely populated areas of the province in line with General Stanley McChrystal's new doctrine.

There were other glaring shortages. British paratroopers in Afghanistan had to borrow .50 caliber ammunition for their Browning machine guns from American and Canadian allies. An officer involved said: "The ammo we had was rubbish. It just kept jamming. At one point we refused to go out [on patrol] because it was so bad. If we had not got that [Canadian] ammo we would certainly have lost a lot of people." The defective bullets were believed to come from the Czech Republic or Pakistan, at a cost of sixty U.S. cents, compared with $1.50 per round for British, Canadian, and American material. The Paras' complaints were rejected at first. "They [higher command] refused to believe it was all crap until Special Forces got involved," the anonymous officer told a journalist. "After that we had . . . new stuff within a week."[231]

In spite of this mess, the MoD enlarged the scale and scope of U.K. Special Forces on American lines. In 2004 what had started life in Northern Ireland as 14 Intelligence Company became the Special Reconnaissance Regiment, for which women as well as men were recruited for covert, close intelligence gathering. Initially, the SRR targeted Islamist fundamentalists in U.K. following the London bombing attacks of July 2005. Four years later, a British minister admitted that the government had overreacted to the threat of

Islamist bombs in Britain. In a febrile atmosphere, misidentification by the new team contributed to the killing of an innocent Brazilian on the London subway by police marksmen. At around the same time an SF group named 18th (UKSF) Signal Regiment, modeled on America's ISAF, was secretly set up.

U.K. Special Forces quick reaction teams now included personnel from the SAS, Special Boat Service, Special Reconnaissance Regiment, 18th Signals, and bomb disposal experts who were also trained as parachute-commandos. Sometimes dressed in civilian clothes, they responded to emergencies within the U.K., using two civilian executive jets and civilian helicopters, probably flown by aircrew from the RAF's Special Duties Flight (known as 7 Squadron) as a change from flying ageing Chinooks.

The U.K.'s reorganized Special Forces Group was enlarged even further in 2005 by a Joint Special Forces Support Group similar to the U.S. Army's Rangers, to give extra firepower in SAS snatch operations, hostage rescue, and backup for covert intelligence missions. The SFSG was constructed around 1 Parachute Regiment, the Red Berets, famous for their self-belief and aggressive approach to almost any situation. With other elements including Marine Commandos, the new group was expected to be a force of 1,200 men when it became fully operational. Its high-tech communications enabled it to receive instant intelligence from bases in the U.K.

UKSF was further enlarged in 2009 with the creation of new reconnaissance companies in a Brigade Reconnaissance Force. A company of 150 BRF soldiers would be used as a forward screen for conventional fighting units, possibly in an attempt to contain rising casualties from multiple IED booby traps. Total BRF strength was 900, augmenting the existing Special Forces Group. The manpower source of the new SF team, in an overstretched "Green Army," was not clear. Though the entity that now emerged bore an even stronger resemblance to America's Special Operations Command, Britain's lamentable failures to provide adequate equipment in Iraq and Afghanistan was a sad contrast with its efforts to upgrade and enlarge its Special Forces capability in line with U.S. developments.

The mismatch of military aspiration and reality sometimes provoked a breakdown in trust and a failure of the civil/military compact where it mattered, on the battlefield.

In 2007, the rancor resulted in the resignation of an unidentified SAS Commanding Officer, a lieutenant-colonel, in Iraq and Afghanistan. His habit of leading his men from the front provoked a smear that he had defied superior orders.[232] A year later, the resignation of Major Sebastian Morley following the loss of one of his teams was another protest that became public knowledge. In Afghanistan, the SAS depended increasingly upon reservists and retired officers, one of whom joked: "You can depend on me not to run from the enemy. I can't run very fast these days."

Given this background, the surprise is that UKSF continued to function as successfully as it did. In Iraq, the regular 22 SAS Regiment was praised by General David Petraeus as he stepped down from command there in 2008. He said: "They have helped immensely in the Baghdad area, in particular, to take down the al Qaeda car bomb networks and other al Qaeda operations in Iraq's capital city . . . a phenomenal job." He recalled how SAS soldiers rented a pink pickup truck, discarded body armor, and drove through traffic to catch a key target. "It was brilliant. They have exceptional courage and exceptional savvy. I can't say enough about how impressive they are in thinking on their feet."[233]

Working with the Iraqi special force trained by Delta, two SAS squadrons destroyed two Sunni car bomb groups in Baghdad, killed hundreds of key al Qaeda players, and rescued several hostages. Richard Williams, a former Commanding Officer of 22 SAS, claims:

"When we went into Iraq with the Delta Force in November 2006, more than 142 bombs per month were being detonated. By December 2007, that was down to two a month. We took out more than 3,000 bombers."[234]

For close-target reconnaissance operations, his soldiers dressed as locals, grew beards, dyed their skin brown and black if necessary, and used contact lenses to change the color of their eyes. They wore the fake gold watches favoured by Iraqi men and adopted their swaggering walk. Near the Syrian border, they intercepted foreign jihadis, killing twelve in one encounter. Inspired by the example of an earlier SAS generation and advised by Lieutenant-General Sir Graeme Lamb, they used jesuitical techniques to persuade some enemy personnel to defect. In 2009, Lamb retired from active service and was promptly hired by General Stanley McChrystal, U.S. commander in chief in Afghanistan, to run a program of reconciliation carefully targeted on Taliban leaders. Alongside the use of Special Forces to limit civilian casualties while killing the enemy, the new strategy employed covert negotiations with some of them, a pattern followed by the British in Northern Ireland.

Petraeus was not alone in praising the SAS in Iraq. General Sir Richard Dannatt, head of the British army at the time, said that coalition Special Forces, including the British elements, had confronted "al Qaeda and their mass-suicide tactics" and defeated them in Baghdad. "Al Qaeda didn't defeat itself in Baghdad," he said. "It was defeated, substantially defeated."[235] But the bombers returned just six weeks after the Iraqi government took control of its own internal security on 30 June 2009. By then, the SAS contingent was in Afghanistan, and U.S. forces still in Iraq were withdrawn to fixed bases outside Iraqi cities.

The regular 22 SAS Regiment was aware that Afghanistan was a tougher proposition than Iraq. The regiment's former commanding

officer, Richard Williams, had been among the first Special Forces soldiers to get his boots on Afghan soil six weeks after 9/11 in 2001. By
2009, the situation had not improved. Primitive, illiterate, insular, suspicious of strangers, its public institutions including the police generally corrupt, Afghanistan was not a place where friendship could be
bought, even if money changed hands. It was also a place of shifting
loyalties. In 2007 six key Taliban commanders were killed by British
Special Forces including the SBS. The bodies they discovered in one
compound in Helmand included that of a man whose identity documents revealed that he was also an officer in the Pakistani Army.
Britain's refusal to expose this case infuriated Afghan President Karzai,
who saw it as confirmation of covert Pakistani backing for the Taliban.
Lieutenant Colonel Chris Nash USMC confirmed that in June 2007,
Pakistani military forces flew repeated helicopter missions to resupply
Taliban fighters during a fierce battle against an American training
team embedded with Afghan Border Police. A raid into Pakistan by
U.S. Special Forces triggered a diplomatic row in which Pakistani offi-
cials denounced "a gross violation of Pakistan's territory."[236]

The raid was the first step in a radical new strategy pursued by the
newly elected President Obama and his choice of the Special Forces
expert, General Stanley McChrystal, to direct operations in a con-
tiguous battleground now known as "Af-Pak." In a parallel diplomatic offensive, Obama let loose Richard ("Bulldozer") Holbrooke as
his special envoy to the region. When Pakistan President Asif Ali
Zardari tried to buy off Islamists in the tribal areas on the North West
Frontier, permitting Sharia to replace state law, Zardari was left in no
doubt of Washington's displeasure. At this point, the Islamists over-
reached themselves and launched an offensive out of the Swat Valley
to a town only sixty miles from the capital, Islamabad. During the
preceding eighteen months, Taliban terrorists had murdered 2,500
civilians in Pakistan. Zardari at last identified the true threat to his

country and sent in the Army in another attempt to bring the region under control. Almost a million refugees fled from the war zone.

Zardari, by now, had turned a blind eye to CIA attacks, using remotely controlled drones to strike enemy hideouts. On the ground, local spies were used to place microchips near the targets as aids to missile navigation. The number of significant kills grew steadily. A dozen al Qaeda commanders were removed by this means in 2008. In August 2009 Baitullah Mehsud, the Taliban leader in Pakistan, was lying on the roof of a house owned by his father-in-law, an intravenous drip attached to his arm to relieve a kidney ailment, when a missile released from a drone demolished the building. In April, Sa'ad bin Laden, son of Osama, also fell victim to the intelligence+drone+missile weapon.

On the ground in Pakistan, U.S. and British Special Forces moved in to train the country's Frontier Force at camps in Baluchistan. The real battleground, however, was not in camps, or the urban areas of Lahore in which increasing numbers of Taliban tried to hide, but in the minds of ordinary Pakistanis, many of whom believe that 9/11 was an Israeli/ American plot to discredit a resurgent Islam. No surprise, then, that the new head of the British Army, General Sir David Richards, should predict that the U.K.'s involvement in Afghanistan might last for forty years, a prospect that daunted politicians both sides of the Atlantic.

Meanwhile, the campaign rolled on, turning up new surprises each day, particularly in the world of signals intelligence. In 2008, linguists flying with Nimrod aircraft of 51 Squadron RAF over Helmand, intercepting satcom telephones used by Taliban fighters, were astonished to eavesdrop on enemy warriors lost for words in Pashto, reverting to English. They then spoke with accents that were distinctive, nasal, Birmingham ("Brummy") voices planning attacks on British forces. It confirmed that U.K. Islamists, born and educated in Britain, had joined the jihad.

A NIMBLE, PRECISE STRATEGY

A s President Barack Obama celebrated his first year in the White House in that cool, intellectual style that had become his trademark, he knew that America faced a similar dilemma to that which confronted Richard Nixon almost exactly forty years before: how to resolve an apparently intractable conflict that had become a political and military quagmire. Nixon's solution in Vietnam was not exactly to cut and run but to march elegantly backward while handing over mission impossible to indigenous forces as if this were a plan ordained by God. Nixon had Henry Kissinger's word that, to paraphrase the secretary of state as well as Voltaire, all was for the best in the best of all possible worlds. In his version of the story of Candide, Leonard Bernstein even set the idea to music.

But when it came to Afghanistan 2009, there were discordant voices out there. Obama, as he prepared to receive his Nobel Peace

Prize, might have felt like Horatius defending Ancient Rome almost singlehanded on a narrow bridge in 507 B.C.E. in a scene described by the poet Macaulay:

> Was none who would be foremost
> To lead such dire attack;
> But those behind cried 'Forward!'
> And those before cried 'Back!'

Howard Hart, the CIA's Scarlet Pimpernel in the days when the Agency was supplying the mujahideen with weapons to fight the Soviets, told the BBC: "There is no one in the world more indefatigable, more courageous, meaner, nastier, looking for a fight than the tribals are. They love to fight. It almost doesn't matter who they are fighting. When the Soviets invaded Afghanistan back in '79 there was in existence a fairly large Soviet-trained Afghan army. They collapsed immediately as we turned on the insurgency. They deserted in large numbers. I think frankly if we were to raise an Afghan army that a great many of them would be providing the best trained and equipped insurgents that there were in the country."[237] Hart recalled that he had worked very closely with "many of these people who are fighting America now. . . . We invaded Afghanistan [in 2001] which meant going in after the Taliban first on the theory that was the only way we could destroy al Qaeda. We are forgetting that the Taliban had no quarrel with us, the West. I don't think it matters a bit—let's be hard boiled about this—if Afghanistan was to revert back to being a Taliban-controlled state, we managed to live with that for any number of years before 9/11 and then we went in after al Qaeda."

But wouldn't such a policy be a terrible betrayal of many Afghans who supported America during the war against the Taliban? "Yes, it would be. Those who really put their neck on the line, we have to take care of them. We have to bring 'em out, just as we did in Vietnam. But the truth of the matter is, most people who are on our side and happen to be Afghans, really their heart is not in this game. I have long had a rule in this neck of the woods and the rule is this, now in the minds of the locals. It doesn't matter who wins. What matters is that you are on the winning side when it's all over, and we can see already that much of the population either tacitly or actively supports the insurgents."

Did this mean it was time for the West to pull out, give up? "That is about right. Leave a few troops behind because we need some operating bases in country. The Taliban won't like it but we can cut a deal with them, I'm sure. I think it's time to say, 'Thank you very much but we're not going to pay in blood and in treasure for endless years to come.' There will never be an honest election in any number of generations in Afghanistan. Why don't we regard [the 2009 election] for what it is, just another example of why Afghanistan is not amenable to being fixed?"

Other clever, informed minds were pondering means by which deals might be cut with some of today's enemies. General Sir Graeme Lamb, who spent most of his thirty-eight years' soldiering with the SAS, turning enemies into allies in Iraq, retired in 2009 and was promptly invited by that other Special Forces veteran, General Stanley McChrystal, to attempt a repeat performance on the less tractable battlefield of Afghanistan. Like General McChrystal and Howard Hart, Lamb detected a failed strategy that combined drift with incoherence during the first eight years of war against the Taliban after 9/11. In spite of that, he was convinced that change, for the better, was possible. His doctrine was to convert swords into plowshares at the grass roots.

Speaking from Kabul, he said: "There are many young people out here who fight well for a bad cause. My view is if they could look at and reflect on the underlying reasons why they are fighting, then they may well question those. What we shouldn't be doing is to be so fixated in our minds we cannot negotiate across these divides." In Iraq, reconciling Shia militiamen and Sunnis running a major insurgency he had found "reasonably easy. . . . Actually the most difficult people to reconcile in many ways were the Americans; having Americans reconciled with the fact that at some point you have to talk to those you are fighting against. You know, Clausewitz didn't finish the sentence, that 'War is the continuation of politics.' The bit he missed out was 'To politics it must return.' . . . One of the comments in Iraq was why would you bring an alligator into your bedroom? Again one has to go back to [asking] who are these people? These are local people who need to understand why, and then they have a choice to have a better life. You know in Iraq I always said you can buy an insurgency if you have enough money. . . . But my view is the moment someone on the wrong side of the wire is inclined to come back, then we have to set the conditions whereby that young man comes back in and is not a pariah and is not, as he walks across the line, rearrested by somebody. Finding employment . . . is the reasonable basis for a more respectable and a better life. It's not simply a question of my going out and finding people who might be inclined to come across and say 'Right, pay you a dollar and stop fighting us for a month or two.'"[238]

Defense Secretary Gates seemed to share Lamb's position. "To truly achieve victory as Clausewitz defined it—to attain a political objective—the United States needs a military whose ability to kick down the door is matched by its ability to clean up the mess and even rebuild the house afterward." But this was easier said than done in Afghanistan, a loose federation of provinces where seventy per cent of the population was under twenty-five years old, only five per cent of them literate in the frontline province of Helmand; where corruption combined with drug rackets and kidnapping for ransom as the dominant economic activities. In Aghanistan, Lamb's nostrums appeared as idealistic as the West's worthy hopes of gender-equality and other dreams of human rights. Yet his concept of a Special Forces war-winning strategy that depended more on psychology than fire-power fitted well enough with the new doctrine unveiled by McChrystal and his team as Obama's first presidential anniversary approached.

The general's assessment of the campaign was bleak. The West had lost the initiative. Unless it was regained in twelve months, defeat was possible. "Preoccupied with protection of our own forces, we have operated in a manner that distances us—physically and psychologically—from the people we seek to protect. In addition, we run the risk of strategic defeat by pursuing tactical wins that cause civilian casualties or unnecessary collateral damage. The insurgents cannot defeat us militarily, but we can defeat ourselves. . . . Conventional wisdom is not sacred; security may not come from the barrel of a gun. Better force protection may be counterintuitive; it might come from less armor and less distance from the population. . . . Our conventional warfare culture is part of the problem. The Afghans must ultimately defeat the insurgency. . . . Protecting the people means shielding them from *all* threats."[239] The new doctrine also demanded a classic counterinsurgency campaign, yet more allied manpower and a drastic overhaul of ISAF.

Having thought the matter over for three months, President Obama descended from Olympus by helicopter to West Point in December 2009 and revealed his plan for the future. Actually there were two futures: one for Afghanistan, the second for wherever else in the world the threat of al Qaeda might appear. "As Commander-in-Chief, I have determined that it is our vital national interest to send an additional 30,000 U.S. troops to Afghanistan. After eighteen months, our troops will begin to come home. These are the resources that we need to seize the initiative, while building the Afghan capacity that can allow for a responsible transition of our forces out of Afghanistan." Integral to that timescale was the hope of training enough Afghan National Army and Afghan National Police to control a society that had rarely known public order though, as Major-General Nick Carter, the British general responsible for security in the unruly Helmand province, acknowledged: "When the Taliban were here, they did ensure security on the main highways. They did it very effectively. You could put your daughter on the bus in Kabul sure in the knowledge she would get to Kandahar in one piece."[240]

The other—unlimited—timescale mentioned by Obama passed almost unnoticed by most commentators. "The struggle against violent extremism will not be finished quickly, and it extends well beyond Afghanistan and Pakistan. It will be an enduring test of our free society and our leadership in the world. And unlike the great power conflicts and clear lines of division that defined the 20th century, our effort will involve disorderly regions and diffuse enemies. So as a result, America will have to show our strength in the way that we end wars and prevent conflict. We have to be nimble and precise in our use of military power. Where al Qaeda and its allies attempt to establish a foothold—whether in Somalia or Yemen or elsewhere—they must be confronted by growing pressure and strong partnerships."

America's oracle had spoken at last—and, like most oracular pronouncements, it lacked concrete detail. Yet there could be little doubt that Obama's nostrum of "nimble and precise" military power was his blessing on the emerging orchestra of Special Forces upon which, in this new kind of conflict, America's strategy and that of its allies would rest in the future.

APPENDIX 1

THE McCHRYSTAL REPORT ON AFGHANISTAN

30 AUGUST 2009

CONFIDENTIAL REL NATO/ISAF (UNCLASSIFIED WITH REMOVAL OF ENCLOSURE)

Headquarters
International Security Assistance Force
Kabul, Afghanistan

30 August 2009

The Honorable Robert M. Gates
Secretary of Defense
1400 Defense Pentagon
Washington, DC 20301 - 1400

SUBJECT: COMISAF'S INITIAL ASSESSMENT

REFERENCE: Secretary of Defense Memorandum 26 June 2009,
             Subject: Initial United States Forces – Afghanistan (USFOR-A) Assessment.

Dear Secretary Gates,

As directed by the Reference, my Initial Assessment is attached. A review of resources necessary to achieve the military campaign plan will be provided by separate correspondence at a later date.

Sincerely,

STANLEY A. McCHRYSTAL
General, U.S. Army
Commander,
United States Forces – Afghanistan/
International Security Assistance
Force, Afghanistan

Enclosure

cc: CDRUSCENTCOM
    SACEUR

CONFIDENTIAL REL NATO/ISAF (UNCLASSIFIED WITH REMOVAL OF ENCLOSURE)

Commander's Initial Assessment

30 August 2009

Commander
NATO International Security Assistance Force, Afghanistan
U.S. Forces, Afghanistan

Table of Contents

Purpose

On 26 June, 2009, the United States Secretary of Defense directed Commander, United States Central Command (CDRUSCENTCOM), to provide a multidisciplinary assessment of the situation in Afghanistan. On 02 July, 2009, Commander, NATO International Security Assistance Force (COMISAF) / U.S. Forces-Afghanistan (USFOR-A), received direction from CDRUSCENTCOM to complete the overall review.

On 01 July, 2009, the Supreme Allied Commander Europe and NATO Secretary General also issued a similar directive.

COMISAF subsequently issued an order to the ISAF staff and component commands to conduct a comprehensive review to assess the overall situation, review plans and ongoing efforts, and identify revisions to operational, tactical and strategic guidance.

The following assessment is a report of COMISAF's findings and conclusions. In summary, this assessment sought to answer the following questions:
- Can ISAF achieve the mission?
- If so, how should ISAF go about achieving the mission?
- What is required to achieve the mission?

The assessment draws on both internal ISAF components, to include Regional Commands, and external agencies such as GIRoA ministries, International Governmental Organizations and Nongovernmental Organizations. It also draws on existing ISAF and USFOR-A plans and policy guidance, relevant reports and studies, and the consultation of external experts and advisors.

i

Commander's Summary

The stakes in Afghanistan are high. NATO's Comprehensive Strategic Political Military Plan and President Obama's strategy to disrupt, dismantle, and eventually defeat al Qaeda and prevent their return to Afghanistan have laid out a clear path of what we must do. Stability in Afghanistan is an imperative; if the Afghan government falls to the Taliban – or has insufficient capability to counter transnational terrorists – Afghanistan could again become a base for terrorism, with obvious implications for regional stability.

The situation in Afghanistan is serious; neither success nor failure can be taken for granted. Although considerable effort and sacrifice have resulted in some progress, many indicators suggest the overall situation is deteriorating. We face not only a resilient and growing insurgency; there is also a crisis of confidence among Afghans -- in both their government and the international community – that undermines our credibility and emboldens the insurgents. Further, a perception that our resolve is uncertain makes Afghans reluctant to align with us against the insurgents.

Success is achievable, but it will not be attained simply by trying harder or "doubling down" on the previous strategy. Additional resources are required, but focusing on force or resource requirements misses the point entirely. The key take away from this assessment is the urgent need for a significant change to our strategy and the way that we think and operate.

NATO's International Security Assistance Force (ISAF) requires a new strategy that is credible to, and sustainable by, the Afghans. This new strategy must also be properly resourced and executed through an integrated civilian-military counterinsurgency campaign that earns the support of the Afghan people and provides them with a secure environment.

To execute the strategy, we must grow and improve the effectiveness of the Afghan National Security Forces (ANSF) and elevate the importance of governance. We must also prioritize resources to those areas where the population is threatened, gain the initiative from the insurgency, and signal unwavering commitment to see it through to success. Finally, we must redefine the nature of the fight, clearly understand the impacts and importance of time, and change our operational culture.

Redefining the Fight

This is a different kind of fight. We must conduct classic counterinsurgency operations in an environment that is uniquely complex. Three regional insurgencies have intersected with a dynamic blend of local power struggles in a country damaged by 30 years of conflict. This makes for a situation that defies simple solutions or quick fixes. Success demands a comprehensive counterinsurgency (COIN) campaign.

Our strategy cannot be focused on seizing terrain or destroying insurgent forces; our objective must be the population. In the struggle to gain the support of the people, every action we take must enable this effort. The population also represents a powerful actor that can and must be leveraged in this complex system. Gaining their support will require a better understanding of the people's choices and needs. However, progress is hindered by the dual threat of a resilient insurgency and a crisis of confidence in the government and the international coalition. To win their support, we must protect the people from both of these threats.

Many describe the conflict in Afghanistan as a war of ideas, which I believe to be true. However, this is a 'deeds-based' information environment where perceptions derive from actions, such as how we interact with the population and how quickly things improve. The key to changing perceptions lies in changing the underlying truths. We must never confuse the situation as it stands with the one we desire, lest we risk our credibility.

The Criticality of Time

The impact of time on our effort in Afghanistan has been underappreciated and we require a new way of thinking about it.

First, the fight is not an annual cyclical campaign of kinetics driven by an insurgent "fighting season." Rather, it is a year-round struggle, often conducted with little apparent violence, to win the support of the people. Protecting the population from insurgent coercion and intimidation demands a persistent presence and focus that cannot be interrupted without risking serious setback.

Second, and more importantly, we face both a short and long-term fight. The long-term fight will require patience and commitment, but I believe the short-term fight will be decisive. Failure to gain the initiative and reverse insurgent momentum in the near-term (next 12 months) -- while Afghan security capacity matures -- risks an outcome where defeating the insurgency is no longer possible.

Change the Operational Culture

As formidable as the threat may be, we make the problem harder. ISAF is a conventional force that is poorly configured for COIN, inexperienced in local languages and culture, and struggling with challenges inherent to coalition warfare. These intrinsic disadvantages are exacerbated by our current operational culture and how we operate.

Pre-occupied with protection of our own forces, we have operated in a manner that distances us -- physically and psychologically -- from the people we seek to protect. In addition, we run the risk of strategic defeat by pursuing tactical wins that cause civilian casualties or unnecessary collateral damage. The insurgents cannot defeat us militarily; but we can defeat ourselves.

Accomplishing the mission demands a renewed emphasis on the basics through a dramatic change in how we operate, with specific focus in two principle areas:

1. **Change the operational culture to connect with the people.** I believe we must interact more closely with the population and focus on operations that bring stability, while shielding them from insurgent violence, corruption, and coercion.

UNCLASSIFIED
1-2

2. **Improve unity of effort and command.** We must significantly modify organizational structures to achieve better unity of effort. We will continue to realign relationships to improve coordination within ISAF and the international community.

The New Strategy: Focus on the Population

Getting these basics right is necessary for success, but it is not enough. To accomplish the mission and defeat the insurgency we also require a properly resourced strategy built on four main pillars:

1. **Improve effectiveness through greater partnering with ANSF.** We will increase the size and accelerate the growth of the ANSF, with a radically improved partnership at every level, to improve effectiveness and prepare them to take the lead in security operations.

2. **Prioritize responsive and accountable governance.** We must assist in improving governance at all levels through both formal and traditional mechanisms.

3. **Gain the Initiative.** Our first imperative, in a series of operational stages, is to gain the initiative and reverse the insurgency's momentum.

4. **Focus Resources.** We will prioritize available resources to those critical areas where vulnerable populations are most threatened.

These concepts are not new. However, implemented aggressively, they will be revolutionary to our effectiveness. We must do things dramatically differently -- even uncomfortably differently -- to change how we operate, and also how we think. Our every action must reflect this change of mindset: how we traverse the country, how we use force, and how we partner with the Afghans. Conventional wisdom is not sacred; security may not come from the barrel of a gun. Better force protection may be counterintuitive; it might come from less armor and less distance from the population.

The Basis of Assessment: Analysis and Experience

My conclusions were informed through a rigorous multi-disciplinary assessment by a team of accomplished military personnel and civilians and my personal experience and core beliefs. Central to my analysis is a belief that we must respect the complexities of the operational environment and design our strategic approach accordingly. As we analyzed the situation, I became increasingly convinced of several themes; that the objective is the will of the people, our conventional warfare culture is part of the problem, the Afghans must ultimately defeat the insurgency, we cannot succeed without significantly improved unity of effort, and finally, that protecting the people means shielding them from *all* threats.

A Strategy for Success: Balancing Resources and Risk

Our campaign in Afghanistan has been historically under-resourced and remains so today. Almost every aspect of our collective effort and associated resourcing has lagged a growing insurgency – historically a recipe for failure in COIN. Success will require a discrete "jump" to gain the initiative, demonstrate progress in the short term, and secure long-term support.

UNCLASSIFIED
1-3

Resources will not win this war, but under-resourcing could lose it. Resourcing communicates commitment, but we must also balance force levels to enable effective ANSF partnering and provide population security, while avoiding perceptions of coalition dominance. Ideally, the ANSF must lead this fight, but they will not have enough capability in the near-term given the insurgency's growth rate. In the interim, coalition forces must provide a bridge capability to protect critical segments of the population. The status quo will lead to failure if we wait for the ANSF to grow.

The new strategy will improve effectiveness through better application of existing assets, but it also requires additional resources. Broadly speaking, we require more civilian and military resources, more ANSF, and more ISR and other enablers. At the same time, we will find offsets as we reprogram other assets and improve efficiency. Overall, ISAF requires an increase in the total coalition force capability and end-strength. This 'properly resourced' requirement will define the minimum force levels to accomplish the mission with an acceptable level of risk.

Unique Moment in Time

This is an important -- and likely decisive -- period of this war. Afghans are frustrated and weary after eight years without evidence of the progress they anticipated. Patience is understandably short, both in Afghanistan and in our own countries. Time matters; we must act now to reverse the negative trends and demonstrate progress.

I do not underestimate the enormous challenges in executing this new strategy; however, we have a key advantage: the majority of Afghans do not want a return of the Taliban. During consultations with Afghan Defense Minister Wardak, I found some of his writings insightful:

> "Victory is within our grasp, provided that we recommit ourselves based on lessons learned and provided that we fulfill the requirements needed to make success inevitable... I reject the myth advanced in the media that Afghanistan is a 'graveyard of empires' and that the U.S. and NATO effort is destined to fail. Afghans have never seen you as occupiers, even though this has been the major focus of the enemy's propaganda campaign. Unlike the Russians, who imposed a government with an alien ideology, you enabled us to write a democratic constitution and choose our own government. Unlike the Russians, who destroyed our country, you came to rebuild."

Given that this conflict and country are his to win -- not mine -- Minister Wardak's assessment was part of my calculus. While the situation is serious, success is still achievable. This starts with redefining both the fight itself and what we need for the fight. It is then sustained through a fundamentally new way of doing business. Finally, it will be realized when our new operational culture connects with the powerful will of the Afghan people.

Initial Assessment

The situation in Afghanistan is serious. The mission is achievable, but success demands a fundamentally new approach -- one that is properly resourced and supported by better unity of effort.

Important progress has been made, yet many indicators suggest the overall situation is deteriorating despite considerable effort by ISAF. The threat has grown steadily but subtly, and unchecked by commensurate counter-action, its severity now surpasses the capabilities of the current strategy. We cannot succeed simply by trying harder; ISAF must now adopt a fundamentally new approach. The entire culture -- how ISAF understands the environment and defines the fight, how it interacts with the Afghan people and government, and how it operates both on the ground and within the coalition[1] -- must change profoundly.

As announced by President Obama in his March 27, 2009 speech outlining the new U.S. Strategy for Afghanistan and Pakistan, the mission in Afghanistan has been historically under-resourced, resulting in a culture of poverty that has plagued ISAF's efforts to date. ISAF requires a properly-resourced force and capability level to correct this deficiency. Success is not ensured by additional forces alone, but continued under-resourcing will likely cause failure.

Nonetheless, it must be made clear: new resources are not the crux. To succeed, ISAF requires a new approach -- with a significant magnitude of change -- in addition to a proper level of resourcing. ISAF must restore confidence in the near-term through renewed commitment, intellectual energy, and visible progress.

This assessment prescribes two fundamental changes. First, ISAF must improve execution and the understanding of the basics of COIN -- those essential elements common to any counterinsurgency strategy. Second, ISAF requires a new strategy to counter a growing threat. Both of these reforms are required to reverse the negative trends in Afghanistan and achieve success.

ISAF is not adequately executing the basics of counterinsurgency warfare. In particular, there are two fundamental elements where ISAF must improve:

- change the operational culture of ISAF to focus on protecting the Afghan people, understanding their environment, and building relationships with them, and;

- transform ISAF processes to be more operationally efficient and effective, creating more coherent unity of command within ISAF, and fostering stronger unity of effort across the international community.

---

[1] "coalition" hereafter refers to ISAF's coalition of troop and resources contributing nations

Simultaneous to improving on these basic principles, ISAF must also adopt a profoundly new strategy with four fundamental pillars:

- develop a significantly more effective and larger ANSF with radically expanded coalition force partnering at every echelon;

- prioritize responsive and accountable governance -- that the Afghan people find acceptable -- to be on par with, and integral to, delivering security;

- gain the initiative and reverse the insurgency's momentum as the first imperative in a series of temporal stages, and;

- prioritize available resources to those critical areas where the population is most threatened.

There is nothing new about these principles of counterinsurgency and organizational efficacy. Rather, they represent profoundly renewed attention to pursuing the basic tenet of protecting the population, specifically adapted for this diverse force and unique conflict, and targeted to work through the most challenging obstacles that have hindered previous efforts.

ISAF's new strategy is consistent with the NATO Comprehensive Strategic Political Military Plan and supports the implementation of President Obama's strategy to disrupt, dismantle, and eventually defeat al Qaeda and prevent their return to Afghanistan. ISAF's new approach will be nested within an integrated and properly-resourced civilian-military counterinsurgency strategy.

This will be enormously difficult. To execute this strategy, ISAF must use existing assets in innovative and unconventional ways, but ISAF will also require additional resources, forces and possibly even new authorities. All steps are imperative and time is of the essence. Patience will see the mission through; but to have that chance, real progress must be demonstrated in the near future.

I. Describing the Mission

ISAF's mission statement is: "ISAF, in support of GIRoA, conducts operations in Afghanistan to reduce the capability and will of the insurgency, support the growth in capacity and capability of the Afghan National Security Forces (ANSF), and facilitate improvements in governance and socio-economic development, in order to provide a secure environment for sustainable stability that is observable to the population."

Accomplishing this mission requires defeating the insurgency, which this paper defines as a condition where the insurgency no longer threatens the viability of the state.

GIRoA must sufficiently control its territory to support regional stability and prevent its use for international terrorism. Accomplishing this mission also requires a better understanding of the nature of the conflict, a change in the basic operational culture, concepts and tactics, and a corresponding change in strategy.

NATO source documents[2] have been consulted and the new strategy remains consistent with the NATO comprehensive approach. Existing UN mandates will continue to provide a framework for ISAF's effort. The international military forces, their civilian counterparts, and international organizations are a key component of ISAF's shared mission to support the people of Afghanistan. It is crucial that ISAF preserve, bolster, and help focus this diverse partnership.

II. Nature of the Conflict

While not a war in the conventional sense, the conflict in Afghanistan demands a similar focus and an equal level of effort, and the consequences of failure are just as grave. The fight also demands an improved and evolved level of understanding.

The conflict in Afghanistan is often described as a war of ideas and perceptions; this is true and demands important consideration. However, perceptions are generally derived from actions and real conditions, for example by the provision or a lack of security, governance, and economic opportunity. Thus the key to changing perceptions is to change the fundamental underlying truths. To be effective, the counterinsurgent cannot risk credibility by substituting the situation they desire for reality.

Redefining the Fight

The conflict in Afghanistan can be viewed as a set of related insurgencies, each of which is a complex system with multiple actors and a vast set of interconnecting relationships among those actors. The most important implication of this view is that no element of the conflict can be viewed in isolation – a change anywhere will affect everything else. This view implies that the system must be understood holistically, and while such understanding is not predictive, it will help to recognize general causal relationships.

The new strategy redefines the nature of the fight. It is not a cyclical, kinetic campaign based on a set "fighting season." Rather it is a continuous, year-long effort to help GIRoA win the support of the people and counter insurgent coercion and intimidation.

There are five principal actors in this conflict: the Afghan population, GIRoA, ISAF, the insurgency, and the external 'players'. It is important to begin with an understanding of each of these actors, starting with the most important: the people.

---

[2] A list of references is included as Annex I.

UNCLASSIFIED
2-3

The people of Afghanistan represent many things in this conflict -- an audience, an actor, and a source of leverage -- but above all, they are the objective. The population can also be a source of strength and intelligence and provide resistance to the insurgency. Alternatively, they can often change sides and provide tacit or real support to the insurgents. Communities make deliberate choices to resist, support, or allow insurgent influence. The reasons for these choices must be better understood.

GIRoA and ISAF have both failed to focus on this objective. The weakness of state institutions, malign actions of power-brokers, widespread corruption and abuse of power by various officials, and ISAF's own errors, have given Afghans little reason to support their government. These problems have alienated large segments of the Afghan population. They do not trust GIRoA to provide their essential needs, such as security, justice, and basic services. This crisis of confidence, coupled with a distinct lack of economic and educational opportunity, has created fertile ground for the insurgency.

ISAF's center of gravity is the will and ability to provide for the needs of the population "by, with, and through" the Afghan government. A foreign army alone cannot beat an insurgency; the insurgency in Afghanistan requires an Afghan solution. This is their war and, in the end, ISAF's competency will prove less decisive than GIRoA's; eventual success requires capable Afghan governance capabilities and security forces. While these institutions are still developing, ISAF and the international community must provide substantial assistance to Afghanistan until the Afghan people make the decision to support their government and are capable of providing for their own security.

An isolating geography and a natural aversion to foreign intervention further works against ISAF. Historical grievances reinforce connections to tribal or ethnic identity and can diminish the appeal of a centralized state. All ethnicities, particularly the Pashtuns, have traditionally sought a degree of independence from the central government, particularly when it is not seen as acting in the best interests of the population. These and other factors result in elements of the population tolerating the insurgency and calling to push out foreigners.

Nonetheless, the Afghan people also expect appropriate governance, the delivery of basic services, and the provision of justice. The popular myth that Afghans do not want governance is overplayed – while Afghan society is rooted in tribal structures and ethnic identities, Afghans do have a sense of national identity.

However, these generalizations risk oversimplifying this uniquely complicated environment. The complex social landscape of Afghanistan is in many ways much more difficult to understand than Afghanistan's enemies. Insurgent groups have been the focus of U.S. and allied intelligence for many years; however, ISAF has not sufficiently studied Afghanistan's peoples whose needs, identities and grievances vary from province to province and from valley to valley. This complex environment is challenging to understand, particularly for foreigners. For this strategy to succeed, ISAF leaders must redouble efforts to understand the social and political dynamics of areas all regions of the country and take action that meets the needs of the people, and insist that GIRoA officials do the same.

Finally, either side can succeed in this conflict: GIRoA by securing the support of the people and the insurgents by controlling them. While this multi-faceted model of the fight is centered on the people, it is not symmetrical: the insurgents can also succeed more simply by preventing GIRoA from achieving their goals before the international community becomes exhausted.

Two Main Threats: Insurgency and Crisis in Confidence

The ISAF mission faces two principal threats and is also subject to the influence of external actors.

The first threat is the existence of organized and determined insurgent groups working to expel international forces, separate the Afghan people from GIRoA, and gain control of the population.

The second threat, of a very different kind, is the crisis of popular confidence that springs from the weakness of GIRoA institutions, the unpunished abuse of power by corrupt officials and power-brokers, a widespread sense of political disenfranchisement, and a longstanding lack of economic opportunity. ISAF errors have further compounded the problem. These factors generate recruits for the insurgent groups, elevate local conflicts and power-broker disputes to a national level, degrade the people's security and quality-of-life, and undermine international will.

Addressing the external actors will enable success; however, insufficiently addressing either principle threat will result in failure.

Insurgent Groups

Most insurgent fighters are Afghans. They are directed by a small number of Afghan senior leaders based in Pakistan that work through an alternative political infrastructure in Afghanistan. They are aided by foreign fighters, elements of some intelligence agencies, and international funding, resources, and training. Foreign fighters provide materiel, expertise, and ideological commitment.

The insurgents wage a "silent war" of fear, intimidation, and persuasion throughout the year—not just during the warmer weather "fighting season"—to gain control over the population. These efforts make possible, in many places, a Taliban "shadow government" that actively seeks to control the population and displace the national government and traditional power structures. Insurgent military operations attract more attention than this silent war but are only a supporting effort. Violent attacks are designed to weaken the government by demonstrating its inability to provide security, to fuel recruiting and financing efforts, to provoke reactions from ISAF that further alienate the population, and also to undermine public and political support for the ISAF mission in coalition capitals.

The major insurgent groups in order of their threat to the mission are: the Quetta Shura Taliban (QST), the Haqqani Network (HQN), and the Hezb-e Islami Gulbuddin (HiG). These groups coordinate activities loosely, often achieving significant unity of purpose and even some *unity of effort*, but they do not share a formal command-and-control structure. They also do not have a single overarching strategy or campaign plan. Each individual group, however, has a specific strategy, develops annual plans, and allocates resources accordingly. Each group has its own methods of developing and executing these plans and each has adapted over time. Despite the best efforts of GIRoA and ISAF, the insurgents currently have the initiative.

Insurgent Strategy and Campaign Design

The insurgents have two primary objectives: controlling the Afghan people and breaking the coalition's will. Their aim is to expel international forces and influences and to supplant GIRoA. At the operational level, the Quetta Shura conducts a formal campaign review each winter, after which Mullah Omar announces his guidance and intent for the coming year. ... **REDACTION.**

The key geographical objectives of the major insurgent groups are Kandahar City and Khowst Province. The QST has been working to control Kandahar and its approaches for several years and there are indications that their influence over the city and neighboring districts is significant and growing. HQN aims to regain eventually full control of its traditional base in Khowst, Paktia, and Paktika. HQN controls some of the key terrain around Khowst and can influence the population in the region. Gulbuddin Hekmatyar's HiG maintains militant bases in Nangarhar, Nuristan, and Kunar, as well as Pakistan, but he also sustains political connections through HiG networks and aims to negotiate a major role in a future Taliban government. He does not currently have geographical objectives as is the case with the other groups.

All three insurgent groups require resources – mainly money and manpower. The QST derives funding from the narcotics trade and external donors. HQN similarly draws resources principally from Pakistan, Gulf Arab networks, and from its close association with al Qaeda and other Pakistan-based insurgent groups. HiG seeks control of mineral wealth and smuggling routes in the east.

Insurgent Lines of Operation

The QST's main efforts focus on the governance line of operations. Security and information operations support these efforts. ISAF's tendency to measure the enemy predominantly by kinetic events masks the true extent of insurgent activity and prevents an accurate assessment of the insurgents' intentions, progress, and level of control of the population.

Governance. The QST has a governing structure in Afghanistan under the rubric of the Islamic Emirate of Afghanistan. They appoint shadow governors for most provinces, review their performance, and replace them periodically. They established a body to receive complaints against their own "officials" and to act on them. They install "shari'a" courts to deliver swift and enforced justice in contested and controlled areas. They levy taxes and conscript fighters and laborers. They claim to provide security against a corrupt government, ISAF forces, criminality, and local power brokers. They also claim to protect Afghan and Muslim identity against foreign encroachment. In short, the QST provides major elements of governance and a national and religious narrative. HQN and HiG co-exist with, but do not necessarily accept, the QST governing framework and have yet to develop competing governing structures.

Information. Major insurgent groups outperform GIRoA and ISAF at information operations. Information operations drive many insurgent operations as they work to shape the cultural and religious narrative. They have carefully analyzed their audience and target products accordingly. They use their Pashtun identity, physical proximity to the population, and violent intimidation to deliver immediate and enduring messages with which ISAF and GIRoA have been unable to compete. They leverage this advantage by projecting the inevitability of their victory, a key source of their strength.

Security. Major insurgent groups use violence, coercion and intimidation against civilians to control the population. They seek to inflict casualties on ISAF forces to break the will of individual ISAF countries and the coalition as a whole. They also use military activities to shape ISAF actions by denying freedom of movement, denying access to the population, and defending important terrain. The insurgents use the psychological effects of IEDs and the coalition force's preoccupation with force protection to reinforce the garrison posture and mentality. The major insurgent groups target GIRoA and ANSF to dissuade cooperation with the government and to show that GIRoA is ineffective. The insurgents control or contest a significant portion of the country, although it is difficult to assess precisely how much due to a lack of ISAF presence. ... **REDACTION.**

Social/Economic. The QST and other insurgent groups have deliberate social strategies that exacerbate the breakdown in Afghan social cohesion. They empower radical mullahs to replace local leaders, undermine or eliminate local elders and mullahs who do not support them, and consistently support weaker, disenfranchised, or threatened tribes or groups. They erode traditional social structures and capitalize on vast unemployment by empowering the young and disenfranchised through cash payments, weapons, and prestige.

Insurgent Enablers and Vulnerabilities

Criminal networks. Criminality creates a pool of manpower, resources, and capabilities for insurgents and contributes to a pervasive sense of insecurity among the people. Extensive smuggling diverts major revenue from GIRoA. Criminality exacerbates the fragmentation of Afghan society and increases its susceptibility to insurgent penetration. A number of Afghan Government officials, at all levels, are reported to be complicit in these activities, further undermining GIRoA credibility.

Narcotics and Financing. The most significant aspect of the production and sale of opium and other narcotics is the corrosive and destabilizing impact on corruption within GIRoA. Narcotics activity also funds insurgent groups, however the importance of this funding must be understood within the overall context of insurgent financing, some of which comes from other sources. Insurgent groups also receive substantial income from foreign donors as well as from other criminal activities within Afghanistan such as smuggling and kidnapping for ransom. Some insurgent groups 'tax' the local population through check points, demanding protection money, and other methods. Eliminating insurgent access to narco-profits -- even if possible, and while disruptive -- would not destroy their ability to operate so long as other funding sources remained intact.

Insurgent Vulnerabilities. The insurgents have important and exploitable shortcomings; they are not invulnerable. Command and control frictions and divergent goals hamper insurgent planning and restrict coordination of operations. ... **REDACTION**... Insurgent excesses can alienate the people. Moreover, the core elements of the insurgency have previously held power in Afghanistan and failed. Popular enthusiasm for them appears limited, as does their ability to spread viably beyond Pashtun areas. GIRoA and ISAF have an opportunity to exploit the insurgent's inability to mobilize public support.

In summary, ISAF confronts a loose federation of insurgent groups that are sophisticated, organized, adaptive, determined, and nuanced across all lines of operations, with many enablers, but not without vulnerability. These groups are dangerous and, if not effectively countered, could exhaust the coalition and prevent GIRoA from being able to govern the state of Afghanistan.

Crisis of Confidence in GIRoA and ISAF Actions

The Afghan government has made progress, yet serious problems remain. The people's lack of trust in their government results from two key factors. First, some GIRoA officials have given preferential treatment to certain individuals, tribes, and groups or worse, abused their power at the expense of the people. Second, the Afghan government has been unable to provide sufficient security, justice, and basic services to the people. Although the capacity and integrity of some Afghan institutions have improved and the number of competent officials has grown, this progress has been insufficient to counter the issues that undermine legitimacy. These problems contribute to the Afghan Government's inability to gain the support of the Afghan population. ISAF errors also compound the problem.

GIRoA State Weakness. There is little connection between the central government and the local populations, particularly in rural areas. The top-down approach to developing government capacity has failed to provide services that reach local communities. GIRoA has not developed the means to collect revenue and distribute resources. Sub-national officials vary in competency and capability and most provincial and district governments are seriously undermanned and under-resourced.

The Afghan Government has not integrated or supported traditional community governance structures -- historically an important component of Afghan civil society -- leaving communities vulnerable to being undermined by insurgent groups and power-brokers. The breakdown of social cohesion at the community level has increased instability, made Afghans feel unsafe, and fueled the insurgency.

Tolerance of Corruption and Abuse of Power. Widespread corruption and abuse of power exacerbate the popular crisis of confidence in the government and reinforce a culture of impunity. Local Afghan communities are unable to hold local officials accountable through either direct elections or judicial processes, especially when those individuals are protected by senior government officials. Further, the public perceives that ISAF is complicit in these matters, and that there is no appetite or capacity – either among the internationals or within GIRoA – to correct the situation. The resulting public anger and alienation undermine ISAF's ability to accomplish its mission. The QST's establishment of ombudsmen to investigate abuse of power in its own cadres and remove those found guilty capitalizes on this GIRoA weakness and attracts popular support for their shadow government.

Afghan power brokers and factional leaders. Some local and regional power brokers were allies early in the conflict and now help control their own areas. Many are current or former members of GIRoA whose financial independence and loyal armed followers give them autonomy from GIRoA, further hindering efforts to build a coherent Afghan state. In most cases. their interests are not aligned with either the interests of the Afghan people or GIRoA, leading to conflicts that offer opportunities for insurgent groups to exploit. Finally, some of these power brokers hold positions in the ANSF, particularly the ANP, and have been major agents of corruption and illicit trafficking. ISAF's relationship with these individuals can be problematic. Some are forces of stability in certain areas, but many others are polarizing and predatory.

There are no clear lines separating insurgent groups, criminal networks (including the narcotics networks), and corrupt GIRoA officials. Malign actors within GIRoA support insurgent groups directly, support criminal networks that are linked to insurgents, and support corruption that helps feed the insurgency.

ISAF Shortcomings. Afghan social, political, economic, and cultural affairs are complex and poorly understood. ISAF does not sufficiently appreciate the dynamics in local communities, nor how the insurgency, corruption, incompetent officials, power-brokers, and criminality all combine to affect the Afghan population. A focus by ISAF intelligence on kinetic targeting and a failure to bring together what is known about the political and social realm have hindered ISAF's comprehension of the critical aspects of Afghan society.

ISAF's attitudes and actions have reinforced the Afghan people's frustrations with the shortcomings of their government. Civilian casualties and collateral damage to homes and property resulting from an over-reliance on firepower and force protection have severely damaged ISAF's legitimacy in the eyes of the Afghan people. Further, poor unity of effort among ISAF, UNAMA, and the rest of the international community undermines their collective effectiveness, while failure to deliver on promises further alienates the people. Problematic contracting processes and insufficient oversight also reinforce the perception of corruption within ISAF and the international community.

In summary, the absence of personal and economic security, along with the erosion of public confidence in the government, and a perceived lack of respect for Afghan culture pose as great a challenge to ISAF's success as the insurgent threat. Protecting the population is more than preventing insurgent violence and intimidation. It also means that ISAF can no longer ignore or tacitly accept abuse of power, corruption, or marginalization.

External Influences

Pakistan. Afghanistan's insurgency is clearly supported from Pakistan. Senior leaders of the major Afghan insurgent groups are based in Pakistan, are linked with al Qaeda and other violent extremist groups, and are reportedly aided by some elements of Pakistan's ISI. Al Qaeda and associated movements (AQAM) based in Pakistan channel foreign fighters, suicide bombers, and technical assistance into Afghanistan, and offer ideological motivation, training, and financial support. Al Qaeda's links with HQN have grown, suggesting that expanded HQN control could create a favorable environment for AQAM to re-establish safe-havens in Afghanistan. Additionally, the ISAF mission in Afghanistan is reliant on ground supply routes through Pakistan that remain vulnerable to these threats.

Stability in Pakistan is essential, not only in its own right, but also to enable progress in Afghanistan. While the existence of safe havens in Pakistan does not guarantee ISAF failure, Afghanistan does require Pakistani cooperation and action against violent militancy, particularly against those groups active in Afghanistan. Nonetheless, the insurgency in Afghanistan is predominantly Afghan. By defending the population, improving sub-national governance, and giving disenfranchised rural communities a voice in their government, GIRoA – with support from ISAF – can strengthen Afghanistan against both domestic and foreign insurgent penetration. Reintegrating communities and individuals into the political system can help reduce the insurgency's virulence to a point where it is no longer an existential threat to GIRoA.

India. Indian political and economic influence is increasing in Afghanistan, including significant development efforts and financial investment. In addition, the current Afghan government is perceived by Islamabad to be pro-Indian. While Indian activities largely benefit the Afghan people, increasing Indian influence in Afghanistan is likely to exacerbate regional tensions and encourage Pakistani countermeasures in Afghanistan or India.

Iran. Iran plays an ambiguous role in Afghanistan, providing developmental assistance and political support to GIRoA while the Iranian Qods Force is reportedly training fighters for certain Taliban groups and providing other forms of military assistance to insurgents. Iran's current policies and actions do not pose a short-term threat to the mission, but Iran has the capability to threaten the mission in the future. Pakistan may see Iranian economic and political initiatives as threats to their strategic interests, and may continue to address these issues in ways that are counterproductive to the ISAF effort.

Russia/Central Asia. Afghanistan's northern neighbors have enduring interests in, and influence over, particular segments of Afghanistan. They pursue objectives that are not necessarily congruent to ISAF's mission. ISAF's Northern Distribution Network and logistical hubs are dependent upon support from Russian and Central Asian States, giving them the potential to act as either spoilers or positive influences.

III. Getting the Basics Right

ISAF is not adequately executing the basics of COIN doctrine. Thus the first major recommendation of this assessment is to change and focus on that which ISAF has the most control of: ISAF. The coalition must hold itself accountable before it can attempt to do so with others. Specifically, ISAF will focus on two major changes to improve execution of COIN fundamentals and enhance organizational alignment and efficacy:

- ISAF will change its operating culture to pursue a counterinsurgency approach that puts the Afghan people first. While the insurgency can afford to lose fighters and leaders, it cannot afford to lose control of the population.

- ISAF will change the way it does business to improve unity of command within ISAF, seek to improve unity of effort with the international community, and to use resources more effectively.

UNCLASSIFIED
2-11

New Operational Culture: Population-centric COIN.

ISAF must operate differently. Preoccupied with force protection, ISAF has operated in a manner that distances itself, both physically and psychologically, from the people they seek to protect. The Afghan people have paid the price, and the mission has been put at risk. ISAF, with the ANSF, must shift its approach to bring security and normalcy to the people and shield them from insurgent violence, corruption and coercion, ultimately enabling GIRoA to gain the trust and confidence of the people while reducing the influence of insurgents. Hard-earned credibility and face-to-face relationships, rather than close combat, will achieve success. This requires enabling Afghan counterparts to meet the needs of the people at the community level through dynamic partnership, engaged leadership, de-centralized decision making, and a fundamental shift in priorities.

Improve Understanding. ISAF – military and civilian personnel alike – must acquire a far better understanding of Afghanistan and its people. ISAF personnel must be seen as guests of the Afghan people and their government, not an occupying army. Key personnel in ISAF must receive training in local languages. Tour lengths should be long enough to build continuity and ownership of success. All ISAF personnel must show respect for local cultures and customs and demonstrate intellectual curiosity about the people of Afghanistan. The United States should fully implement – and encourage other nations to emulate – the "Afghan Hands" program that recruits and maintains a cadre of military and civilian practitioners and outside experts with deep knowledge of Afghanistan.

Build Relationships. In order to be successful as counterinsurgents, ISAF must alter its operational culture to focus on building personal relationships with its Afghan partners and the protected population. To gain accurate information and intelligence about the local environment, ISAF must spend as much time as possible with the people and as little time as possible in armored vehicles or behind the walls of forward operating bases. ISAF personnel must seek out, understand, and act to address the needs and grievances of the people in their local environment. Strong personal relationships forged between security forces and local populations will be a key to success.

Project Confidence. Creating a perception of security is imperative if the local population is to "buy-in" and invest in the institutions of governance and step forward with local solutions. When ISAF forces travel through even the most secure areas of Afghanistan firmly ensconced in armored vehicles with body armor and turrets manned, they convey a sense of high risk and fear to the population. ISAF cannot expect unarmed Afghans to feel secure before heavily armed ISAF forces do. ISAF cannot succeed if it is unwilling to share risk, at least equally, with the people.

UNCLASSIFIED
2-12

In fact, once the risk is shared, effective force protection will come from the people, and the overall risk can actually be reduced by operating differently. The more coalition forces are seen and known by the local population, the more their threat will be reduced. Adjusting force protection measures to local conditions sends a powerful message of confidence and normalcy to the population. Subordinate commanders must have greater freedom with respect to setting force protection measures they employ in order to help close the gap between security forces and the people they protect. Arguably, giving leaders greater flexibility to adjust force protection measures could expose military personnel and civilians to greater risk in the near term; however, historical experiences in counterinsurgency warfare, coupled with the above mitigation, suggests that accepting some risk in the short term will ultimately save lives in the long run.

Decentralize. To be effective, commanders and their civilian partners must have authorities to use resources flexibly -- and on their own initiative -- as opportunities arise, while maintaining appropriate accountability measures. ISAF must strike the right balance between control and initiative, but err on the side of initiative. Mistakes will inevitably be made, but a culture of excessive bureaucracy designed with the best of intentions will be far more costly in blood and treasure.

Re-integration and Reconciliation. Insurgencies of this nature typically conclude through military operations and political efforts driving some degree of host-nation reconciliation with elements of the insurgency. In the Afghan conflict, reconciliation may involve GIRoA-led, high-level political settlements. This is not within the domain of ISAF's responsibilities, but ISAF must be in a position to support appropriate Afghan reconciliation policies.

Reintegration is a normal component of counterinsurgency warfare. It is qualitatively different from reconciliation and is a critical part of the new strategy. As coalition operations proceed, insurgents will have three choices: fight, flee, or reintegrate. ISAF must identify opportunities to reintegrate former mid- to low-level insurgent fighters into normal society by offering them a way out. To do so, ISAF requires a credible program to offer eligible insurgents reasonable incentives to stop fighting and return to normalcy, possibly including the provision of employment and protection. Such a program will require resources and focus, as appropriate, on people's future rather than past behavior. ISAF's soldiers will be required to think about COIN operations differently, in that there are now three outcomes instead of two: enemy may be killed, captured, or reintegrated.

In executing a reintegration program ISAF will necessarily assume decentralized authorities, in coordination with GIRoA, for ISAF field commanders to support the reintegration of fighters and low-level leaders. Local leaders are critical figures in any reintegration efforts and must be free to make the decisions that bind their entire community.

UNCLASSIFIED
2-13

Economic Support to Counterinsurgency. ISAF has an important asymmetric advantage; it can aid the local economy, along with its civilian counterparts, in ways that the insurgents cannot. Local development can change incentive structures and increase stability in communities. Economic opportunity, especially job creation, is a critical part of reintegrating the foot-soldier into normal life. Economic support to counterinsurgency is distinct from and cannot substitute for longer-term development initiatives. With some coordination it can lay the groundwork for, and complement, those longer-term efforts and show that the Afghan government is active at the local level. ISAF must increase the flexibility and responsiveness of funding programs to enable commanders and their civilian partners to make immediate economic and quality of life improvements in accordance with Afghan priorities.

Improve Unity of Effort and Command

ISAF's subordinate headquarters must stop fighting separate campaigns. Under the existing structure, some components are not effectively organized and multiple headquarters fail to achieve either unity of command or unity of effort.

The establishment of an intermediate operational headquarters is the first step toward rectifying these problems. This new headquarters will enable the ISAF headquarters to focus on strategic and operational matters and enhance coordination with GIRoA, UNAMA, and the international community. The intermediate headquarters will synchronize operational activities and local civil-military coordination and ensure a shared understanding of the mission throughout the force. The intermediate headquarters must be supported with increased information collection and analysis capabilities to improve significantly ISAF's understanding of the political, cultural, social, and economic dynamics.

The intermediate headquarters will also provide command and control for all ANSF mentor teams, enabling CSTC-A and the new NATO Training Mission-Afghanistan (NTM-A) to focus on ANSF institution-building, force generation, force sustainment, and leader development. Command relationships must be clarified so that battle space owners at every echelon can synchronize operations in accordance with ISAF priorities, with effective control of all operations in their area of operations, to include theater wide forces, SOF, and mentoring teams. Mechanisms must be established at all echelons to integrate information from ISAF, ANSF, GIRoA, and other actors. Additional changes are required to address the myriad of other command and control challenges and parochial interests that have emerged over time. ISAF must continue to confront these challenges internally and in partnership with NATO and national capitals.

IV. A Strategy for Success

Success will be achieved when GIRoA has earned the support of the powerful Afghan people and effectively controls its own territory. This will not come easily or quickly. It is realistic to expect that Afghan and coalition casualties will increase until GIRoA and ISAF regain the initiative.

ISAF's strategy to defeat the insurgency and achieve this end state, based on an in-depth analysis of the nature of the conflict, includes four major pillars:

- ISAF will become radically more integrated and partnered with the ANSF to enable a more rapid expansion of their capacity and responsibility for security.

- ISAF will place support to responsive and accountable governance, including sub-national and community governance, on par with security.

- ISAF's operations will focus first on gaining the initiative and reversing the momentum of the insurgency.

- ISAF will prioritize available resources to those critical areas where the population is most threatened.

1. Increase partnership with the ANSF to increase size and capabilities

Radically Expanded and Embedded Partnering. Success will require trust-based, expanded partnering with the ANSF with assigned relationships at all echelons to improve effectiveness of the ANSF. Neither the ANA nor the ANP is sufficiently effective. ISAF must place far more emphasis on ANSF development in every aspect of daily operations. ISAF will integrate headquarters and enablers with ANA units to execute a full partnership, with the shared goal of working together to bring security to the Afghan people. ISAF units will physically co-locate with the ANSF, establish the same battle-rhythm, and plan and execute operations together. This initiative will increase ANSF force quality and accelerate their ownership of Afghanistan's security.

Accelerated Growth. The Afghan National Army (ANA) must accelerate growth to the present target strength of 134,000 by Fall 2010, with the institutional flexibility to continue that growth to a new target ceiling of 240,000. The target strength of the Afghan National Police (ANP) must be raised to 160,000. This will require additional mentors, trainers, partners and funds through an expanded participation by GIRoA, the support of ISAF, and the resources of troop contributing and donor nations.

The ANP suffers from a lack of training, leaders, resources, equipment, and mentoring. Effective policing is inhibited by the absence of a working system of justice or dispute resolution; poor pay has also encouraged corruption. Substantial reform with appropriate resources -- and possibly even new authorities -- are critically important and must not be delayed.

GIRoA and ISAF will evaluate the utility of using locally-based security initiatives such as the Afghan Public Protection Program (AP3), where appropriate conditions exist, to create village-level indigenous security in partnership with GIRoA and local shuras.

Detainee Operations. Effective detainee operations are essential to success. The ability to remove insurgents from the battlefield is critical to effective protection of the population. Further, the precision demanded in effective counterinsurgency operations must be intelligence-driven; detainee operations are a critical part of this. Getting the right information and evidence from those detained in military operations is also necessary to support rule of law and reintegration programs and help ensure that only insurgents are detained and civilians are not unduly affected.

Detainee operations are both complex and politically sensitive. There are strategic vulnerabilities in a non-Afghan system. By contrast, an Afghan system reinforces their sense of sovereignty and responsibility. As always, the detention process must be effective in providing key intelligence and avoid 'catch and release' approaches that endanger coalition and ANSF forces. It is therefore imperative to evolve to a more holistic model centered on an Afghan-run system. This will require a comprehensive system that addresses the entire "life-cycle" and extends from point of capture to eventual reintegration or prosecution.

ISAF has completed a full review of current detainee policies and practices with recommendations for substantial revisions to complement ISAF's revised strategy. Key elements of a new detention policy should include transferring responsibility for long-term detention of insurgents to GIRoA, establishing procedures with GIRoA for ISAF access to detainees for interrogation within the bounds of national caveats, application of counter-radicalization and disengagement practices, and training of ISAF forces to better collect intelligence for continued operations and evidence for prosecution in the Afghan judicial system. Afghanistan must develop detention capabilities and operations that respect the Afghan people. A failure to address GIRoA incapacity in this area presents a serious risk to the mission.

2. Facilitating Afghan governance and mitigating the effects of malign actors

Success requires a stronger Afghan government that is seen by the Afghan people as working in their interests. Success does not require perfection – an improvement in governance that addresses the worst of today's high level abuse of power, low-level corruption, and bureaucratic incapacity will suffice.

Learning from and leveraging the elections. The recent Presidential and Provincial Council elections were far from perfect. From a security standpoint, they were generally executed smoothly and without major physical disruption, although the credibility of the election results remains an open question. The country-wide spike in violence against ISAF and ANSF, with three to four times the average number of attacks, underscores the widespread reach of insurgent influence, particularly in the south and the east and in select areas of the north and west. However, the relatively low number of effective attacks against polling centers offers some evidence that insurgents were targeting ISAF and ANSF, not the voters. The Afghans' ability to plan and execute the elections, along with the close partnering between ISAF and ANSF, and the mass deployment of security forces were notable achievements nonetheless. The elections were also an opportunity, and a forcing function, that will help to improve future coordination within the ANSF and expand ISAF's partnership with GIRoA and the international community.

Supporting local governance. Elements of Afghan society, particularly rural populations, have been excluded from the political process. ISAF must support UNAMA and the international community in sub-national governance reform by working directly with local communities, starting by assessing Afghan civilian needs by population center and developing partnerships to act on them. By empowering local communities, GIRoA, supported by ISAF, can encourage them to support the political system. District elections and the civilian resources deployed to Provincial Reconstruction Teams, District Support Teams, and ISAF task forces will also help build legitimate governance structures at the sub-national levels.

Efforts are underway that may address some of these issues, including those that have been cultivated through the National Solidarity Program and the Afghan Social Outreach Program. These structures will enable improvements at the community level to link communities with the national government over time. In addition, GIRoA's proposed sub-national governance policy aims to give greater authority and responsibility to the elected councils and to clarify their relationships with governors and individual line ministries. The U.S. Government Integrated Civil-Military Campaign Plan also provides a basis for improving sub-national governance at every level – provided it is appropriately staffed and resourced. Similar coordinated action is also required from other partner governments. Similarly, the request for support from the Ministry of Finance for civilian technical assistance must be welcomed and met. Indeed, ISAF and the international community must support the acceleration of these efforts, while recognizing that additional legislative initiatives may be required.

Negative Influencers. ISAF must understand and address underlying factors that encourage malign behavior and undermine governance. The narco- and illicit economy and the extortion associated with large-scale developmental projects undermine the economy in Afghanistan. GIRoA cannot fund its operations because of its inability to raise revenue, a situation made worse by the illicit economy. Poorly paid officials may resort to petty corruption, contributing to the people's crisis in confidence. The international community must appropriately supplement revenues until these problems are addressed. ISAF must also change its concept of the "border fight" ... **REDACTION**...

to expanding GIRoA's revenue base through improved border control and customs collection.

Discerning Support. ISAF must develop a discerning approach that rewards competent Afghan governance and leadership, recognizes the distinction between incapacity and predatory behavior, and leverages ISAF's influence to address both challenges. ISAF and its partners must develop appropriate measures to reduce the incentives for corrupt actors that impede the mission, work around them if necessary, and develop actionable evidence of their malfeasance. Improving information collection and analysis will provide better understanding of the motivations, practices, and effects of corruption.

Transparency and Accountability. ISAF must work with UNAMA and the international community to build public finance mechanisms that enable GIRoA to create credible programs and allocate resources according to the needs of the Afghan people. The international community must address its own corrupt or counter-productive practices, including reducing the amount of development money that goes toward overhead and intermediaries rather than the Afghan people. A recent OXFAM report indicates that a significant percentage of such funding is diverted. ISAF must pay particular attention to how development projects are contracted and to whom. Too often these projects enrich power-brokers, corrupt officials, or international contractors and serve only limited segments of the population. Improving ISAF's knowledge of the environment and sharing this information with UNAMA and the international community will help mitigate such harmful practices.

ISAF will provide economic support to counterinsurgency operations to help provide a bridge to critical developmental projects in priority areas that UN agencies and the international community cannot reach, while working closely with UNAMA to help set conditions for NGOs to enter stabilized areas.

Rule of Law. Finally, ISAF must work with its civilian and international counterparts to enable justice sector reform and locate resources for formal and informal justice systems that offer swift and fair resolution of disputes, particularly at the local level. The provision of local justice, to include such initiatives as mobile courts, will be a critical enhancement of Afghan capacity in the eyes of the people. ISAF must work with GIRoA to develop a clear mandate and boundaries for local informal justice systems.

3. Gain the Initiative and Evolve in Stages

ISAF's new strategy will include three stages. These stages will unfold at different rates and times in different geographic areas of Afghanistan. Most importantly, they will be led increasingly by the Afghan people and their government.

Gain the Initiative. First, ISAF must re-focus its operations to gain the initiative in seriously threatened, populated areas by working directly with GIRoA institutions and people in local communities to gain their support and to diminish insurgent access and influence. This stage is clearly decisive to the overall effort. It will require sufficient resources to gain the initiative and definitively check the insurgency. A failure to reverse the momentum of the insurgency will not only preclude success in Afghanistan, it will result in a loss of public and political support outside Afghanistan.

In this stage, ISAF will take a new approach to integrate fully with the ANSF through extensive partnering. This will enable improved effectiveness and a more rapid growth of ANSF capability. Together with UNAMA and the international community, ISAF will work with all levels of GIRoA to expand substantially responsive and accountable governance that focuses on the needs of the people. Finally, there must be full international community support and commitment to the full range of civil-military capabilities concentrated in the priority areas.

Strategic Consolidation. As ISAF and ANSF capabilities grow over the next 12-24 months and the insurgency diminishes in critical areas, ISAF will begin a second stage – a strategic consolidation. As ANSF and GIRoA increasingly take the lead for security operations and as new civilian and military capacity arrives, security operations will expand to wider areas while consolidating initial gains. These efforts will increase the space in which the population feels protected and served by their government, and insulate them from a return of insurgent influence. Meanwhile, ANSF and ISAF must have the capability to respond flexibly to insurgent adaptation and retain the initiative.

Sustained Security. When the insurgent groups no longer pose an existential threat to GIRoA, ISAF will move into a third stage of sustained security to ensure achieved gains are durable as ISAF forces begin to draw down. As ANSF demonstrate the capability to defeat remaining pockets of insurgents on their own, ISAF will transition to a train, advise, and assist role. UNAMA and the international community will have increased freedom of action to continue to help develop the Afghan state and meet the needs of the Afghan people.

In all of these stages, the insurgents will adapt, possibly moving their operations to different areas. This risk is mitigated by the fact that the insurgents are weakened when forced to relocate from their traditional areas; the burden of migration, renewed recruiting, and re-establishing a stronghold will incur a cost to the insurgents. ISAF must have the capability to respond to these adaptations.

4. Prioritize Allocation of Resources to Threatened Populations.

In a country as large and complex as Afghanistan, ISAF cannot be strong everywhere. ISAF must focus its full range of civilian and military resources where they will have the greatest effect on the people. This will generally be in those specific geographical areas that represent key terrain. For the counterinsurgent, the key terrain is generally where the population lives and works. This is also where the insurgents are typically focused;

thus, it is here where the population is threatened by the enemy and that the two sides inevitably meet. ISAF will initially focus on critical high-population areas that are contested or controlled by insurgents, not because the enemy is present, but because it is here that the population is threatened by the insurgency.

The geographical deployment of forces may not be static; ISAF must retain the operational flexibility to adapt to changes in the environment. Based on current assessments, ISAF prioritizes the effort in Afghanistan into three categories to guide the allocation of resources. These priorities will evolve over time as conditions on the ground change:

REDACTION

V. Assessments: Measuring Progress

ISAF must develop effective assessment architectures, in concert with civilian partners and home nations, to measure the effects of the strategy, assess progress toward key objectives, and make necessary adjustments. ISAF must identify and refine appropriate indicators to assess progress, clarifying the difference between operational measures of effectiveness critical to practitioners on the ground and strategic measures more appropriate to national capitals. Because the mission depends on GIRoA, ISAF must also develop clear metrics to assess progress in governance.

VI. Resources and Risk

Proper resourcing will be critical. The campaign in Afghanistan has been historically under-resourced and remains so today – ISAF is operating in a culture of poverty.

Consequently, ISAF requires more forces. This increase partially reflects previously validated, yet un-sourced, requirements. This also stems from the new mix of capabilities essential to execute the new strategy. Some efficiency will be gained through better use of ISAF's existing resources, eliminating redundancy, and the leveraging of ANSF growth, increases in GIRoA capacity, international community resources, and the population itself. Nonetheless, ISAF requires capabilities and resources well in excess of these efficiency gains. The greater resources will not be sufficient to achieve success, but will enable implementation of the new strategy. Conversely, inadequate resources will likely result in failure. However, without a new strategy, the mission should not be resourced.

A 'properly-resourced' strategy provides the means deemed necessary to accomplish the mission with *appropriate and acceptable risk*. In the case of Afghanistan, this level of resourcing is less than the amount that is required to secure the whole country. By comparison, a 'fully-resourced' strategy could achieve *low risk*, but this would be excessive in the final analysis. Some areas are more consequential for the survival of GIRoA than others.

The determination of what constitutes 'properly-resourced' will be based on force-density doctrine applied with best military judgment of factors such as terrain, location and accessibility of the population, intensity of the threats, the effects of ISR capabilities and other enablers, logistical constraints, and historical experience. As always, assessment of risk will necessarily include subjective professional judgment. Under-resourcing COIN is perilous because the insurgent has the advantage of mobility whereas security forces become relatively fixed after securing an area. Force density doctrine is based in historical analysis and suggests that a certain presence of security forces is required to achieve a critical threshold that overmatches the insurgents ability to leverage their mobility. In short, a 'properly-resourced' strategy places enough things, in enough places, for enough time. All three are mandatory.

A 'properly-resourced' strategy is imperative. Resourcing coalition forces below this level will leave critical areas of Afghanistan open to insurgent influence while the ANSF grows. Thus, the first stage of the strategy will be unachievable, leaving GIRoA and ISAF unable to execute the decisive second stage. In addition, the international community is unlikely to have the access necessary to facilitate effective Afghan governance in contested areas. Failure to provide adequate resources also risks a longer conflict, greater casualties, higher overall costs, and ultimately, a critical loss of political support. Any of these risks, in turn, are likely to result in mission failure.

Civilian Capacity. ISAF cannot succeed without a corresponding cadre of civilian experts to support the change in strategy and capitalize on the expansion and acceleration of counterinsurgency efforts. Effective civilian capabilities and resourcing mechanisms are critical to achieving demonstrable progress. The relative level of civilian resources must be balanced with security forces, lest gains in security outpace civilian capacity for governance and economic improvements. In particular, ensuring alignment of resources for immediate and rapid expansion into newly secured areas will require integrated civil-military planning teams that establish mechanisms for rapid response. In addition, extensive work is required to ensure international and host nation partners are engaged and fully integrated.

ISAF's efforts in Afghanistan must be directed through its Afghan counterparts to enable them to succeed in the long-term. Working within Afghan constructs, fostering Afghan solutions, and building Afghan capacity is essential. Particular focus is required at the community level where the insurgency draws its strength through coercion and exploitation of the people's dissatisfaction with their government and local conditions. Focusing on the community can drive a wedge between the insurgents and the people, giving them the freedom and incentive to support the Afghan government.

Some of the additional civilian experts will partner with ISAF task forces or serve on Provincial Reconstruction Teams. Others will work with new District Support Teams as necessary to support this strategy. As necessary, ISAF must facilitate performance of civil-military functions wherever civilian capacity is lacking, the arrival of the civilians is delayed, or the authorities that the civilians bring prove insufficient. ISAF will welcome the introduction of any new civilian funding streams, but must be prepared to make up the difference using military funding as necessary.

Risks. No strategy can guarantee success. A number of risks outside of ISAF's control could undermine the mission, to include a loss of coalition political will, insufficient ability and political will on GIRoA's part to win the support of its people and to control its territory, failure to provide effective civilian capabilities by ISAF's partners, significant improvements or adaptations by insurgent groups, and actions of external actors such as Pakistan and Iran.

VII. Conclusion

The situation in Afghanistan is serious. The mission can be accomplished, but this will require two fundamental changes. First, ISAF must focus on getting the basics right to achieve a new, population-centric operational culture and better unity of effort. Second, ISAF must also adopt a new strategy, one that is properly resourced, to radically increase partnership with the ANSF, emphasize governance, prioritize resources where the population is threatened, and gain the initiative from the insurgency. This will entail significant near-term cost and risk; however, the long-term risk of not executing this strategy is greater. The U.S. Strategy and NATO mission for Afghanistan both call for a committed and comprehensive approach to the strategic threat of an unsecure and unstable Afghanistan. Through proper resourcing, rigorous implementation, and sustained political will, this refocused strategy offers ISAF the best prospect for success in this important mission.

UNCLASSIFIED

Background
ISAF CJ5, Plans and Strategy, conducted an analysis of the current campaign plan[1], supporting plans, and orders to determine whether the strategy and means provided are adequate to accomplish the desired endstate. Many elements ...**REDACTION**... are deemed to be adequate; however, there are gaps in the operational design.

Scope
A multidisciplinary Joint Operational Planning Group (JOPG) was formed to conduct a thorough assessment of the ISAF counterinsurgency campaign strategy. The JOPG conducted a detailed analysis of both the ISAF OPLAN[2] and OPORD[3]. Previous versions of these orders were also analyzed to ascertain the rationale for successive versions. Analysis was also conducted ... **REDACTION**... to confirm that the ISAF OPLAN and OPORD followed the guiding principles contained in the higher headquarters frameworks. The JOPG also reviewed the Afghanistan National Development Strategy and the UNAMA mandate. Other documents were also consulted and analyzed, including the draft U.S. Government Integrated Civilian-Military Campaign Plan for Support to Afghanistan. These efforts were complemented by an analysis of the seasonal, agricultural, and narcotic cycles as they relate to the historic operational cycle of insurgent forces to ensure that the subsequent recommendations were situated within a real world timeline. There was significant linkage to three other work efforts being conducted under the Initial Assessment:

1. The "Troops to Task" Working Group determining the resource requirements and allocation of forces and capabilities.
2. The Initial Assessment Working Group tasked with examining the overarching strategy.
3. The ANSF Expansion Working Group tasked with determining the feasibility for rapid growth of GIRoA security capacity.

Key Findings
a. **REDACTION**... This OPLAN explicitly states that it serves as the campaign plan for ISAF. Contained within this OPLAN is a clear mission and intent, supported by four Lines of Operation (LoO): Security (lead responsibility), Governance (supporting effort), Development (supporting effort), and Strategic Communications (supporting effort). Associated with these LoO are ten effects. These effects are broadly phrased and are not linked with Decisive Points (DP)/Decisive Conditions (DC). This missing element of operational design is crucial, as it should be used to generate associated actions (tasks and purposes) for the OPORD. Similarly, Measures of Effectiveness

---

[1]**REDACTION**
[2]**REDACTION**
[3]**REDACTION**

(MOE)/Measures of Performance (MOP) should inform assessments, demonstrating progress along the various LoO. Without this linkage, it is exceptionally difficult to provide accurate advice to the commander to inform optimal decisions on forces, resources, and tasks to continue on the projected path to achieve the desired endstate.

b. **REDACTION**... The OPORD contains much detail but does not explicitly link the Regional Commands (RC) operations under a coherent, single, nationwide strategy. This is one of the critical deficiencies of the existing OPORD. The following observations are provided:

    i. The mission and intent contained in the OPORD are broadly phrased, covering all lines of operation contained in the OPLAN, but it provides insufficient guidance for Regional Commanders to achieve unity of effort.

    ii. The Shape/Clear/Hold/Build construct **REDACTION**... provides the rudimentary elements of an operational framework that forms the basis for the tasks contained in the OPORD.

    iii. The OPORD is exceptionally detailed and complex. Within the Main Body alone, 47 tasks are directed toward the Regional Commands and ISAF Special Operations Forces (SOF). There are an additional 50 tasks found throughout the OPORD annexes. There is no clear prioritization of the tasks within the OPORD.

c. OPLAN and OPORD Development. Analysis of the successive versions of ...**REDACTION**...the OPORD indicate that each refinement sought to generate increased synchronization and clarity of tasks. The various staffs that generated these modifications were attempting to refine inherited products to produce improved linkages. Viewed independently, both the OPLAN and the OPORD are good products; however, the linkage from higher strategy down to specific tasks remains tenuous. Specifically, prioritization and synchronization have become unclear. Substance exists in both the OPLAN and the OPORD, however they are now overly complex, necessitating revision and alignment.

d. Prioritization. The lack of clear prioritization of tasks in the OPORD has allowed each of the five subordinate RCs to develop OPORDs with a slightly different emphasis. Some flexibility appears to be a key part of the OPORD design, allowing for sufficient variance between RCs to align toward the specific threats faced in their region. While minor variations were anticipated, a deeper examination shows a lack of coherence within the Security LoO between RCs. The OPORD allows RCs to determine their prioritization and focus within this "lead effort" LoO, with emphasis on protecting the population, growing security capacity, and/or combating insurgents (or other Enemies of Afghanistan). The diversity of Troop Contributing Nations (TCN) further increases variance and differences of interpretation across the force. The multiplicity of priorities (e.g. Focus Areas, Action Districts, Priority Action Districts, and Focused District Development) seemingly makes "everything" important.

e.   Synchronization. Although the OPORD attempts to generate synchronization, the variation in interpretation and prioritization of effort hinders development of the necessary synergy. Synchronization across the theater should provide a greater opportunity for the generation of collective effects across all LoO, but is not currently achieved. The lack of prioritization makes synchronization exceptionally difficult.

f.   Assessments. The campaign assessment construct uses a methodology to measure effectiveness of operations along the LoO described in the OPLAN. The current assessment provides a broad measure of progress that requires substantial interpretation to determine interrelationships among the various aspects within the LoO. The current campaign design does not utilize decisive points or milestones within the broad effects; accordingly, it is difficult to assess progress along a LoO. This does not assist the Commander in evaluating where changes in strategy or main effort may be required.

g.   Supporting Plans and Annexes.

i. Counternarcotics (CN). It is clear that CN efforts were not fully integrated into the counterinsurgency campaign; efforts were collaborative but not centrally coordinated. Substantial intelligence points directly at the Afghanistan narcotics industry as a significant economic enabler for the insurgency. The ISAF mandate, with its clear security focus and individual TCN caveats, coupled with the ubiquitous nature of the narcotics problem, clearly limited CN efforts by ISAF forces. CN engagement has increased significantly since the Budapest Summit which called upon NATO and TCN to grant sufficient legal authority to increase ISAF assistance to GIRoA to execute the Afghan National Drug Control Strategy. With the clarification of legal authorities, Annex RR – Counter Narcotics was integrated ...**REDACTION**. The RCs are currently developing supporting plans to address the 2010 opium poppy season. Though CN efforts are improving, they must be fully integrated into the overall plan.

ii. ISAF and ANSF Partnering and Mentoring. Partnering continues to evolve. Efforts to formalize the partnership between ISAF and ANSF can be traced to June 2008. It took until Nov 2008 to develop the framework for the plan and issue the fragmentary order[4] (FRAGO) directing this effort. The FRAGO sought to create a baseline for both partnering operations and reporting requirements; RCs continue to progress toward the objectives described in the FRAGO,

---

REDACTION

however they are hampered by the lack of clarity expressed in the operational design.

h. Operational Environment. Elements of the operational environment dictate the operational cycle of the insurgency. It is critical to consider the seasonal, agricultural, and narcotic cycles, as well as the religious calendar and external events like Pakistani military operations in the border area, in order to refine the campaign design. Traditionally, insurgents have used the winter months to reorganize and prepare for the "fighting" season which coincides with improving weather. Generally, ISAF forces have matched the insurgent's operational cycle each year. Without a significant change, ISAF will remain in consonance with this cycle. This winter, there is an opportunity to break our inadvertent operational synchronicity with the insurgents. The new operational design must be linked to 'real world' event cycles rather than being considered in abstract and place greater emphasis on non-kinetic operations, noting that the insurgency remains active within the population even when kinetic operations are greatly reduced during the winter.

i. Command Relationships. Although indirectly related to the analysis of the campaign design, command relationships are a key element to synchronization of efforts under the lines of operation provided in the ISAF OPORD and OPLAN. Within campaign design, the link between operational design and operational management is provided by operational command; accordingly a review of operational plans should also consider the relevant command relationships. The ISAF upper command and control arrangements are undergoing restructuring concurrently with the Initial Assessment. Clarification of the relationship between the evolving Four Star ISAF HQ and the new, Three Star ISAF Joint Command (IJC) will assist significantly in the synchronization of efforts across the campaign. The transition of CSTC-A/DATES to NATO Training Mission – Afghanistan (NTM-A) in the same timeframe as the formation of the IJC brings an opportunity to achieve a fully coordinated new operational level command structure with associated realignment of subordinate elements (e.g. Operational Mentoring and Liaison Teams (OMLTs) and Embedded Training Teams (ETTs). Realignment of these relationships necessitates an operational design that considers the new command lines provided to COMISAF. Efficient command and control alignment will enhance execution of the revised operational design.

Recommendations

a. OPLAN 38302. Retain major elements of the OPLAN as the base document that frames the ISAF Campaign Plan. The document is sufficient to complement the efforts of external agencies (e.g. GIRoA and UNAMA) along the supporting LoO of Governance and Development.   Significant change may be counterproductive in the short term; specifically, the Comprehensive and Integrated Approach described in Annex W of the OPLAN is procedurally understood by critical stakeholders. The OPLAN provides the framework for the "lead effort" Security LoO to guide development of the operational design. Within the OPLAN framework, the operational design should be revised substantially to provide the benchmarks of progress to guide prioritization and synchronization of subordinate efforts.

b.   Revise the OPORD. Given both the refined command relationships and anticipated direction to develop an operational design, the OPORD will require substantial revision to prioritize and synchronize the efforts across all COMISAF subordinates. The current OPORD contains elements that can be prioritized and synchronized in the short term through fragmentary orders until a new OPORD is developed and published.

c.   Command Relationships. The development of the operational design must incorporate the anticipated command relationships under which the order will be executed.

d.   Resourcing. Use the refined operational design as the basis to request additional resource capabilities that generate overmatch of insurgent forces prior to the historical operational tempo increase of insurgent operations.

Annex B: Command and Control, and Command Relationships

ISAF analysed the command relationships between military forces and civilian organizations operating in the Afghanistan Theater of Operations. To date, various initiatives have either been planned or are underway in order to improve unity of command and unity of effort within the Afghanistan Area of Operations (AoO).

Status Update

- On August 4th, NATO's North Atlantic Council officially approved the creation of an intermediate three-star command between COMISAF and the RCs. This new headquarters is on pace to reach Initial Operational Capability (IOC) by 12 October 09 and Full Operational Capability by 12 November 09.

- Along with the creation of the ISAF Joint Command (IJC), the decision was made to create NATO Training Mission-Afghanistan (NTM-A) to unify both NATO and U.S. forces previously operating under separate command relationship lines (Directorate for Afghan National Army Training and Equipment (NATO) and Combined Security Transition Command – Afghanistan (U.S.)) conducting advisory roles with the Afghan National Security Forces (ANSF) throughout Afghanistan. This new headquarters will reach IOC by 10 September 09.

- Related to the creation of NTM-A is a proposal to move all of the advisory elements that reside in the Afghanistan AOO—OMLTs, POMLTs, PMTs, ETTs, OCCs, etc.— under the operational control of the Regional Commands (RC) and battlespace owners (BSO). A portion of the ...**REDACTION**... staff will migrate to the IJC to manage various resourcing functions related to the support of these advisory elements.

- HQ ISAF issued FRAGO 408-2009 directing the establishment, in coordination with GIRoA, if a National Military Coordination Center (NMCC) for the coordination and planning of joint military operations.

- The RCs have been directed to partner with the ANSF at every level within their RC AOOs in order to gain synergy of operations and improve the capability and capacity of the ANSF.

- The RCs were also tasked with further developing Operations Coordination Centers at the Regional and Provincial level to enable a comprehensive approach to planning and operating down to the tactical level and to monitor and report partner ANSF unit readiness to COMISAF.

- USFOR-A has been tasked with the following:

UNCLASSIFIED

- o Direct CSTC-A to focus on force generation and institutional and ministerial development;
- o Transfer OEF units OPCON to COMISAF and place them on the ISAF Combined Joint Statement of Requirements;

- Draft C2 guidance for command and control of special operations forces will be issued soon. This FRAGO will direct the realignment of all SOF, ...**REDACTION**... OPCON to COMISAF. OEF and ISAF SOF will be directed to enhance the coordination of their operations through the provision of SOF operations and planning staff, SOF advisors, and liaison officers to the RC HQs.

- In cooperation with JFC-Brunssum, Allied Transformation Command (ATC), Joint Warfare Center, and the Joint Warfighting Center (USJFCOM), and V Corps, a training plan has been developed to support the stand up of the IJC.

Remaining Challenges

...**REDACTION**...

- Other challenges to unity of command lie in the variations of each troop contributing nation's Order of Battle Transfer of Authority (ORBATTOA) report. Since there is such variation in the ORBATTOA reports, it is difficult to achieve a common command authority structure throughout the theater.

- Another challenge comes from U.S. sponsored, non-NATO nations that deploy forces using U.S. Global-War-on-Terrorism (GWOT) funding under U.S. Code Title X. These nations include Georgia, Azerbaijan, Estonia, Mongolia, Bahrain, and others. The unique challenge created under this process specifies that Title X funding is tied to a direct command relationship with a U.S. commander.

- Even If unity of effort is achieved with all international military forces in full partnership with the ANSF, unity of command remains a significant challenge because of the many international community and nongovernmental organizations who make significant unilateral contributions in the Governance and Development Lines of Operation. In order to address this, the BSO must be fully engaged with GIRoA, UNAMA, ANSF and any civilian capacity building entities or International Organization. Engagement and coordination is critical; de-confliction by itself is insufficient. It is important that BSOs develop relationships with these organizations that help to achieve the desired end state.

- One issue to be resolved is whether COMISAF has the authority to move personnel assigned to ISAF HQ under CE 13.0 over to the new Intermediate HQ CE 1.0. Current planning is based on the assumption that he has this authority; however, this issue must be resolved in writing from SHAPE prior to any personnel migration.

The Integrated Civil-Military Campaign Plan (ICMCP) represents the collaborative planning efforts of United States Government (USG) operating in Afghanistan. It was signed by the United States Ambassador to Afghanistan Karl Eikenberry and General Stanley McChrystal, Commander, United States Forces Afghanistan, on 15 August 2009 and forwarded to Ambassador Richard Holbrooke, United States Special Representative for Afghanistan and Pakistan and General David Petraeus, Commander, United States Central Command. The USG will execute this plan from a 'whole-of-government' approach in coordination with the International Security Assistance Force (ISAF), United Nations Mission in Afghanistan (UNAMA), and the Government of the Islamic Republic of Afghanistan (GIRoA).

The ICMCP aligns USG efforts on a single objective: the people of Afghanistan. It specifies that every action must focus on securing and enabling the Afghan people to resist the insurgents and engage with GIRoA and the international community to develop effective governance. Shifting focus to deliver results for the population requires comprehensive integration and synchronization of USG and ISAF civilian-military teams working across the Security, Development, and Governance Lines of Operation. The ICMCP details how this new integrated approach will be applied across 11 Counter-insurgency (COIN) Transformative Effects (see table opposite). These effects will enable tangible progress in fighting the insurgency and building stability at the local community, provincial, and national level.

> **11 Transformative Effects:**
> - Population Security
> - Claim the Information Initiative
> - Access to Justice
> - Expansion of Accountable and Transparent Governance
> - Elections and Continuity of Governance
> - Action Against Irreconcilables
> - Creating Sustainable Jobs
> - Agricultural Opportunity and Market Access
> - Countering the Nexus of Narcotics, Corruption, Insurgency and Criminality
> - Community and Government led Reintegration
> - Cross-Border Access for Commerce Not Insurgents

ICMCP implementation is supported by two significant civilian initiatives. First, U.S. Senior Civilian Representative positions have been established in RC(E) and RC(S) at each sub-regional U.S. Brigade Task Force, and in each province and district support team to coordinate activities of civilians operating under Chief of Mission authority to execute US policy and guidance, serve as the civilian counterpart to the military commander, and integrate and coordinate civ-mil efforts. The second civilian initiative, the USG Civilian Uplift, will deploy additional USG civilians throughout Afghanistan at the regional, brigade task force, provincial, and district levels.

In summary, the ICMCP describes target activities and initiatives for our personnel on the ground. By mandating an integrated, multi-level civilian chain of command for the best partnership possible with military forces, U.S. personnel will have a sound construct within which to determine what areas of the plan to implement in their respective areas.

UNCLASSIFIED
C-1

Background

The information domain is a battlespace, and it is one in which ISAF must take aggressive actions to win the important battle of perception. Strategic Communication (StratCom) makes a vital contribution to the overall effort, and more specifically, to the operational center of gravity: the continued support of the Afghan population. In order to achieve success we must make better use of existing assets and bolster these with new capabilities to meet the challenges ahead. To date, the Insurgents (INS) have undermined the credibility of ISAF, the International Community (IC), and Government of the Islamic Republic of Afghanistan (GIRoA) through effective use of the information environment, albeit without a commensurate increase in their own credibility. Whilst this is a critical problem for ISAF, the consequences for GIRoA are even starker. GIRoA and the IC need to wrest the information initiative from the INS.

Scope

ISAF has undertaken a comprehensive assessment of StratCom objectives, policies, and capability requirements which has resulted in several key recommendations in order to achieve the mission. The command also developed a StratCom Action Plan which details those tasks and activities which must be implemented in order to put the recommendations into effect. This plan is not focused on ISAF in isolation but has been derived from a variety of other planning efforts which have set the framework for this assessment. While the primary focus was on the Afghan environment, some of the actions outlined may have a wider effect in the regional context. The planning process benefitted from the participation of StratCom experts in the 'community of interest', including HQ NATO, SHAPE, and JFC-B as well as the visiting Initial Assessment Team.

Key Findings

DEVELOPING CAPACITY

Apart from improving its own performance, ISAF needs to help ensure that GIRoA receives the necessary partnering, assistance, training and equipment to further develop their own capacity and improve performance. In so doing, we need to be careful that we do not continue to over promise and under deliver across the lines of operation. ISAF needs to be able to support both the NATO strategic centre of gravity, (the maintenance of Alliance cohesion as specified in the ISAF OPLAN), as well as ensure that GIRoA is placed at the forefront of all possible endeavors with its credibility enhanced. Over the years a consistent set of problems have been identified but not adequately addressed, primarily as a result of insufficient coordination and a lack of resources. The key for StratCom is to implement a plan based on these lessons learned. ISAF is not the sole player in the StratCom area. Success also depends on improving the currently inadequate capabilities of other non-military critical players, especially in areas outside security such as the governance, reconstruction, and development arenas.

UNCLASSIFIED

NEW OBJECTIVES

For success, the following StratCom objectives need to be accomplished in partnership with other key stakeholders:

- Discredit and diminish insurgents and their extremist allies' capability to influence attitudes and behaviour in AFG.

- In partnership, assist GIRoA and the populace in developing a sense of ownership and responsibility for countering violent extremism in order to advance their own security, stability, and development.

- Increase effectiveness of international and GIRoA communications with the Afghan people and the IC.

- Increase AFG political and popular will to counter violent extremism and protect the operational centre of gravity, namely the support of the Afghan people.

- Enhance StratCom coordination with Higher Headquarters (HHQ) and, through them, the troop contributing nations (TCN) in order to support SACEUR's strategic center of gravity which is the maintenance of Alliance cohesion.

- Promote the capability of, and confidence in, the Afghan National Security Forces as a force for good in the country.

- Maintain and increase international and public support for ISAF goals and policies in AFG.

MAIN EFFORT

The StratCom main effort is to maintain and strengthen the Afghan population's positive perception of, and support for, GIRoA institutions and the constructive supporting role played by ISAF and the IC.

Recommendations

Change of Culture

There must be a fundamental change of culture in how ISAF approaches operations. StratCom should not be a separate Line of Operation, but rather an integral and fully embedded part of policy development, planning processes, and the execution of operations. Analyzing and maximizing StratCom effects must be central to the formulation of schemes of maneuver and during the execution of operations. In order to affect this paradigm shift, ISAF HQ must synchronize all StratCom stakeholders. Implicit in this change of culture is the clear recognition that modern strategic communication is about credible dialogue, not a monologue where we design our systems and resources to deliver messages to target audiences in the most effective manner. This is now a population centric campaign and no effort should be spared to ensure that the Afghan people are part of the conversation. Receiving, understanding, and amending behavior as a result of messages received from audiences can be an effective method of gaining genuine trust and credibility. This would improve the likelihood of the population accepting ISAF messages and changing their behavior as a result.

Win the battle of perceptions

ISAF must act to assist GIRoA in the battle of perceptions through gaining and maintaining the Afghan population's trust and confidence in GIRoA institutions. This will help establish GIRoA as a credible government. For GIRoA and ISAF to win the battle of perceptions we must demonstrably change behavior and actions on the ground - our policies and actions must reflect this reality. StratCom should take every opportunity to highlight the protection of civilians in accordance with the revised Tactical Directive dated 1 July 2009, which is a key StratCom tool.

Build AFG capacity and capability

Additional emphasis must be placed on assisting and building AFG capacity and capability so that they are better able to take the lead in StratCom related issues. Better linkages and a robust partnership must be forged with MOD and MOI spokespersons, allowing a supportive and complementary network to be developed. Increasing capacity requires an improved understanding of the environment, better procedures, and additional required equipment and training. The Government Media and Information Centre needs to be expanded to include regional nodes able to disseminate government briefings and releases throughout the region.

Post election engagement

ISAF's engagement with senior GIRoA members should be reassessed following the Presidential Elections, in order to promote the effective coordination of messaging.

Expand reach of messaging

ISAF must extend both the reach and propagation of its message delivery, together with determining the effectiveness of that message. Focus should be on identifying the optimum medium for propagation rather than just on the message alone. The following means will be evaluated:

UNCLASSIFIED
D-3

- Commercial communications systems and systems operated by ISAF and GIRoA must be further developed with the necessary protection for communications infrastructure. ISAF should partner more effectively with the Afghan commercial sector to enhance COIN effects by empowering the population through access to telecommunications and information via TV and radio.
- The use of traditional communications to disseminate messages must be better exploited using both modern technology and more orthodox methods such as word of mouth. These messages should be delivered by authoritative figures within the AFG community, both rural and urban, so that they are credible. This will include religious leaders, maliks, and tribal elders.
- There must be development and use of indigenous narratives to tap into the wider cultural pulse of Afghanistan.
- Increased cultural expertise is required in order to enhance the development and use of StratCom messaging.
- A more comprehensive and reliable system of developing metrics for Communication Measurement of Effectiveness must be developed, to inform ISAF of the perceptions and atmospherics within AFG communities.

Offensive Information Operations (IO)

Offensive IO must be used to target INS networks in order to disrupt and degrade their operational effectiveness, while also offering opportunities for lower level insurgent re-integration. ISAF should continue to develop and implement a robust and proactive capability to counter hostile information activities and propaganda. A more forceful and offensive StratCom approach must be devised whereby INS are exposed continually for their cultural and religious violations, anti-Islamic and indiscriminate use of violence and terror, and by concentrating on their vulnerabilities. These include their causing of the majority of civilian casualties, attacks on education, development projects, and government institutions, and flagrant contravention of the principles of the Koran. These vulnerabilities must be expressed in a manner that exploits the cultural and ideological separation of the INS from the vast majority of the Afghan population.

Agile response to incidents

ISAF, in conjunction with GIRoA, must enhance its responsiveness to incidents. Subordinate echelons must have the authority and freedom to act within an agile, transparent, and unified environment. Information must be widely shared, horizontally and vertically, including with GIRoA and the IC. New Tactics, Techniques and Procedures (TTPs) must be produced to reflect a flatter command philosophy whereby subordinates are expected to act in accordance with the Commander's Intent to ensure a swift, effective response to achieve the information initiative against the enemy. In particular, risk mitigation measures in the event of CIVCAS must be widely understood and practiced before the incident and accomplished in a timely manner so that we are 'first with the truth.'

Counter-IED IO focus

The C-IED IO efforts must be fully integrated into the overall StratCom strategy and structures. StratCom must focus on encouraging the population to assist in countering the scourge of IEDs. Effective messaging and offensive Information Operations (IO) are critical to this effort.

StratCom capacity

Throughout the ISAF chain of command StratCom elements must be structured and resourced appropriately, and manned at the requisite levels of expertise to achieve the desired effects. Some of these elements are known to be relatively weak in RC(N), RC(W) and RC(C) and will need augmenting. The inclusion of the critical capabilities provided by Information Operation Task Force (IOTF), Information Operation Advisory Task Force(IOATF), Media Monitoring, STRATCOM Information Fusion Network and CAPSTONE contracts within the StratCom structure should be supported as these will significantly enhance the Directorate's enabling, monitoring, and assessment efforts.

Unity of Command – Unity of Effort

ISAF and USFOR-A StratCom IO and Public Affairs (PA) components must be fully integrated in order to provide unity of command and effort and enable coherent and rapid messaging. It will be necessary to promote the single ISAF "brand" to multiple internal and external stakeholders.

Refocus Media efforts

ISAF must re-focus its media efforts in the following specific areas:

- Migrate to a 24/7 StratCom operation
- Delegate Public Affairs (PA) release authority to the appropriate level
- Create opportunities for Afghans to communicate as opposed to attempting to always control the message
- Link regional stories back to national Afghan ones
- Concentrate on the youth and those pursuing further education[1]
- Orientate the message from a struggle for the 'hearts and minds' of the Afghan population to one of giving them 'trust and confidence'
- Seek ways to reach the INS in Pakistan

---

[1] 70% of the Afghan population are under 22 years old.

- Focus media operations and subsequent analysis on context, characterization and accuracy
- Re-prioritize the policies governing practical support for media in terms of military airlift, credentialing, and embeds

Declassification Authority for ISR/WSV

There has been consistent recognition of problems in using visual imagery, particularly ISR and weapons' system video, and other operational information for StratCom purposes. Every effort must be made to identify, declassify, and exploit such material in a timely manner.

StratCom links

StratCom links to intelligence organizations must be strengthened. This will enable more effective counter-measures to hostile propaganda and provide more detailed network analysis in support of IO targeting.

New Media

HQ ISAF must understand and adapt to the immediacy of the contemporary information environment through the employment of new/social media as well as cell phones, TV, and radio in order to promote interactive communication between Afghan and international audiences. This will involve a significant investment in technical architecture.

StratCom messengers and partners

ISAF must develop a more widely understood internal communication strategy that enables every member of ISAF to be able to clearly articulate a short narrative of what ISAF wants to achieve in Afghanistan and how it is going to do it. Every soldier must be empowered to be a StratCom messenger for ISAF.

ISAF must strengthen its partnership with relevant IC stakeholders, both within the NATO system and internationally, to improve the flow of information and cooperation both horizontally and vertically. Specifically, in theater communication efforts to coordinate between TCNs must involve the office of the Senior Civilian Representative and HHQs in order to maximize the propagation of COMISAF's intent and help protect NATO/SHAPE's strategic center of gravity in national capitals.

NATO has had consistent problems producing trained personnel in all information disciplines. Significant investment is required to solve both a short-term problem and generate a longer term solution to producing the necessary fully-qualified personnel.

Annex E: Civilian Casualties, Collateral Damage, and Escalation of Force

Background

Civilian casualties (CIVCAS) and damage to public and private property (collateral damage), no matter how they are caused, undermine support for GIRoA, ISAF, and the international community in the eyes of the Afghan population. Although the majority of CIVCAS incidents are caused by insurgents, the Afghan people hold ISAF to a higher standard. Strict comparisons of amount of damage caused by either side are unhelpful. To protect the population from harm, ISAF must take every practical precaution to avoid CIVCAS and collateral damage.

ISAF established a CIVCAS Tracking Cell in August 2008. This step was reinforced by a revised Tactical Directive (TD) issued to all troops in theatre on 1 July 2009, which, inter alia, clearly described how and when lethal force should be used. All subordinate commanders were explicitly instructed to brief their troops (to include civilian contractors) on the TD. Further, a thorough review of ISAF and USFOR-A operating procedures and processes has been ordered.

Scope

The TD, in conjunction with COMISAF's COIN guidance and other supporting directives, describes how ISAF will both mitigate CIVCAS incidents, and change its approach to COIN and stability operations. These measures will improve the ability of ISAF to protect the population from harm.

This paper proposes recommendations to enhance the direction given in the TD.

Key Findings
Training

Though it is not possible to prescribe the appropriate use of force for every situation on a complex battlefield, all troops must know, understand, comply, and train with the direction outlined in the TD. This implies a change in culture across the force. ISAF units and soldiers must be fully prepared to operate within the guidelines of the TD and other directives prior to deployment. Home-station training events must be nested within these directives. Training must continue in theater to ensure the guidance is being implemented correctly.

Recommendation: ISAF must utilize expertise resident at the Counter Insurgency Training Center-Afghanistan ("COIN Academy") and within ISAF organizations to ensure all units in theater understand and are able to apply the TD, COIN Guidance, and standing ROE. ISAF must also work together with home-station training centers and professional development schools to ensure units are properly prepared through education and pre-deployment training.

UNCLASSIFIED

The TD and COIN Guidance will be disseminated rapidly to U.S. Combat Training Centers and to NATO and ISAF Troop Contributing Nations (TCNs) for inclusion in scenario development and programs of instruction.

Troops in Contact (TIC)

The TD stresses the necessity to avoid winning tactical victories while suffering strategic defeats. Ground commanders must fully understand the delicate balance between strategic intent and tactical necessity. Commanders must prioritize operational effectiveness within their operating areas by considering the effects of their actions on the Afghan population at every stage.

Recommendation: Under the direction of Task Force Commanders, sub-unit ground commanders must plan for and rehearse a full range of tactical options to include application of force in unpopulated areas, de-escalation of force within populated ones, or even breaking contact as appropriate to accomplish the mission.

Proportionality

In order to minimize the risk of alienating the Afghan population, and in accordance with International Law, ISAF operations must be conducted in a manner that is both proportionate and reasonable.

Recommendation: When requesting Close Air Support (CAS) ground commanders and Joint Tactical Air Controllers (JTAC) must use appropriate munitions or capabilities to achieve desired effects while minimizing the risk to the Afghan people and their property. Ground commanders must exercise similar judgment in the employment of indirect fires.

Shaping the Environment and Preconditions

The importance of cultural awareness during the conduct of operations is highlighted in the TD. Specifically, it notes that a significant amount of CIVCAS occur during Escalation of Force (EoF) procedures (14% of people killed and 22% of those wounded during the last recorded 6 months). These incidents tend to occur in units with less training experience and lower unit cohesion. Fear and uncertainty among ISAF soldiers contributes to escalation of force incidents. Furthermore, although ISAF has refined and enhanced the warnings that are issued, many Afghans do not understand them and consequently fail to comply. Low literacy levels and cultural differences may explain a misunderstanding of EoF procedures and the actions that ISAF troop expect them to take.

UNCLASSIFIED

E-2

Recommendation: Effective pre-deployment training and the development of unit cohesion are essential in honing the tactical judgment of soldiers and small unit leaders. Training scenarios at home station and combat training centers must improve. As ISAF reviews and modifies its escalation of force procedures to better fit the Afghan context, ISAF, and GIRoA must communicate those procedures more effectively to the Afghan people in appropriate media.

Press Release / Public Information

The TD also stresses the requirement to acknowledge any CIVCAS incident in the media expeditiously and accurately; timely engagement with key leaders is also a critical element. The aim is to be 'first with the known truth', based on the information available at the time. ISAF competes with insurgents (INS) information operations (IO), and the INS IO is not hampered by the need to be truthful; moreover, any statements made by the INS are rapidly disseminated, and can be persuasive to the Afghan population. As the TD notes, it is far more effective to release a factual statement with the known details early, and then a follow-on statement with additional clarification at a later stage. This procedure is more effective than simply issuing a rebuttal of an INS version of the account. Furthermore, debating the number of people killed or injured misses the point. The fact that civilians were harmed or property was damaged needs to be acknowledged and investigated, and measures must be taken for redress.

Recommendation: First, ISAF and GIRoA must aim for a consistent rather than conflicting message through appropriate media, to include word of mouth in affected local communities. Be first with the known truth; be transparent in the investigation. Second, ISAF and GIRoA should follow-up on any incident with periodic press updates regarding the progress of the investigation, procedures for redress, and measures taken to ensure appropriate accountability.

Aircraft Video Release Procedures

The advantage of photographic imagery to support any Battle Damage Assessment (BDA) is covered in the TD. This can be expanded to include aircraft weapon system imagery. The NATO Comprehensive Strategic Political Military Plan (CSPMP) for Afghanistan requires nations to establish agreed procedures for declassifying and making use of national operational imagery to reinforce NATO messages. Presently, national caveats apply to the release of aircraft BDA and weapon release imagery, and these caveats have different procedures and timelines for release. Some nations do not comply with the CSPMP.

Recommendation: Establish a standard procedure for all nations and services to attain the necessary release approval and delivery of the footage.

UNCLASSIFIED

E-3

Honor and "Assistance"

Under the terms of the Military Technical Agreement between ISAF and GIRoA (dated 4 Jan 02), ISAF is not required to make compensation payments for any damage to civilian or governmental property. Contributing nations are responsible for damages caused by their soldiers. Some nations contribute to individual or collective compensation, a number do not, whilst others contribute in different ways. This creates an extremely unhelpful imbalance and undermines COIN Strategy. To address this, the NATO CSPMP for Afghanistan, encourages nations to fund the NATO Post Operations Emergency Relief Fund (POERF) to compensate or assist individuals and communities.

CIVCAS payments and compensation must be carefully considered against a large number of different factors. Whilst being sensitive to the affected families and communities, improper procedures and poor investigations and accountability may encourage subsequent exaggerated claims.

Recommendation: Develop and implement an equitable system of compensation for damages, whether individual or community based. ISAF TCNs must develop a common policy for compensation and redress due to injury, loss of life, and damage to property. Although compensation can never make up for such loss, appropriate measures to ensure accountability and recognition of the importance of Afghan life and property can help mitigate public anger over the incident.

UNCLASSIFIED

E-4

Annex F: Detainee Operations, Rule of Law, and Afghan Corrections

Background

Detention operations, while critical to successful counterinsurgency operations, also have the potential to become a strategic liability for the U.S. and ISAF. With the drawdown in Iraq and the closing of Guantanamo Bay, the focus on U.S. detention operations will turn to the U.S. Bagram Theater Internment Facility (BTIF). Because of the classification level of the BTIF and the lack of public transparency, the Afghan people see U.S. detention operations as secretive and lacking in due process. It is critical that we continue to develop and build capacity to empower the Afghan government to conduct all detentions operations in this country in accordance with international and national law. The desired endstate must be the eventual turnover of all detention operations in Afghanistan, to include the BTIF, to the Afghan government once they have developed the requisite sustainable capacity to run those systems properly.

Currently, Taliban and Al Qaeda insurgents represent more than 2,500 of the 14,500 inmates in the increasingly overcrowded Afghan Corrections System (ACS). These detainees are currently radicalizing non-insurgent inmates and worsening an already over-crowded prison system. Hardened, committed Islamists are indiscriminately mixed with petty criminals and sex offenders, and they are using the opportunity to radicalize and indoctrinate them. In effect, insurgents use the ACS as a sanctuary and base to conduct lethal operations against GIRoA and coalition forces (e.g., Serena Hotel bombing, GIRoA assassinations, governmental facility bombings).

The U.S. came to Afghanistan vowing to deny these same enemies safe haven in 2001. They have gone from inaccessible mountain hideouts to recruiting and indoctrinating hiding in the open, in the ACS. There are more insurgents per square foot in corrections facilities than anywhere else in Afghanistan. Unchecked, Taliban/Al Qaeda leaders patiently coordinate and plan, unconcerned with interference from prison personnel or the military.

Multiple national facilities are firmly under the control of the Taliban. The Central Prisons Directorate (CPD) accepts a lack of offensive violence there as a half-win. Within the U.S. Bagram Theater Internment Facility (BTIF), due to a lack of capacity and capability, productive interrogations and detainee intelligence collection have been reduced. As a result, hundreds are held without charge or without a defined way-ahead. This allows the enemy to radicalize them far beyond their pre-capture orientation. This problem can no longer be ignored.

Scope

In order to transform detention and corrections operations in theater, U.S. Forces-Afghanistan (USFOR-A) proposes the formation of a new Combined Joint Interagency Task Force, CJIATF ...**REDACTION**... to work toward the long-term goal of getting the U.S. out of the detention business. The priority for the CJIATF ... **REDACTION**... in cooperation with the U.S. Embassy and our interagency and international partners, will be to build the capacity of the Afghan government to take over responsibility for detention in its own country as soon as possible, to include the BTIF. The CJIATF will provide two primary functions:

- Assume oversight responsibilities and Title 10 support for detention and interrogation operations of all U.S.-held detainees in Afghanistan; and

- Conduct Rule of Law (Corrections) operations, in coordination with the U.S. Embassy, working with and advising the Ministry of Defense, the Afghan Central Prison Directorate (CPD), and associated Afghan Ministries.

The CJIATF will train and apply sound corrections management techniques and Rule of Law principles in all detention systems in Afghanistan, whether currently run by the U.S. government or the Afghan government. These sound corrections management techniques ("best practices") and Rule of Law principles, applicable to all detention facilities, include: adherence to international humanitarian law; due process; vocational and technical training; de-radicalization; rehabilitation; education; and classifying and segregating detainee populations (segregating hard-core insurgents from low level fighters, juveniles from adults, women from men, common criminals from insurgents, etc.).

Systemic Challenges in Detention and Corrections
The CJIATF ...**REDACTION**... will address 10 systemic challenges in the current U.S., Afghan military, and CPD detention and prison systems. These include:

- Need for a country wide, coalition supported, corrections and detention plan to help establish unity of effort.

- Need for all detainees and prisoners to be correctly classified and separated accordingly.

- Need for a GIRoA and International community supported Rule of Law program which allows for and codifies alternatives to incarceration.

- Within U.S. Detention and Afghanistan Prison systems alike, take immediate measures to counter insurgent actions and minimize the religious radicalization process of inmates.

- Need to plan and provide for Afghanistan corrections infrastructure multi-year sustainment.

- Need to ensure meaningful corrections reform in both U.S. and Afghanistan detention/prison systems. These reforms include changing punishment from retribution to rehabilitation, purposeful and effective staff training, equity of pay, and improved alignment with law enforcement and legal systems, both formal and informal.

- Need to review and ensure the intelligence policy and procedures match the exigencies of the Government of Afghanistan and Coalition counter-insurgent activity.

- Need to address the current and projected over-crowding situation.

- Need to address the current shortage of knowledgeable, competent, and committed leadership within both U.S. and Afghanistan corrections systems and advisory groups.

- Need to address the command and control, and unity of command over both U.S. detention and Afghan advisory efforts.

Recommendations
Establish a CJIATF

Establish a CJIATF commanded by a General Officer, with a civilian deputy at the Ambassador level, to lead an organization of approximately 120 personnel (70 civilian, 50 military). The CJIATF will be a Major Subordinate Command under USFOR-A with a coordination relationship reporting to the U.S. Ambassador Afghanistan. The CJIATF will have a Command/Control Headquarters Element and the following six Lines of Operation:

- The U.S. Detention Operations Brigade will provide safe, secure, legal and humane custody, care, and control of detainees at the BTIF.

- The Intelligence Group will support the Task Force's mission to identify and defeat the insurgency through intelligence collection and analysis, and improve interrogations intelligence collection though operations at the Joint Interrogation Debriefing Center and Strategic Debriefing Center, including input from field detention sites after capture.

- The Detention and Prisons Common Program Support Group will establish and conduct a series of programs designed to move detention/corrections operations from retribution to rehabilitation. A de-radicalization process will attack the

UNCLASSIFIED

enemy ethos center of gravity and enable successful reintegration of inmates back to the Afghan (or home origin) population.

- The Engagement and Outreach Group will formulate and implement strategic communication and outreach as a proactive tool to protect and defend the truth of U.S. detention and interrogation practices, to further assist in the development of the Rule of Law within Afghanistan.

- The Legal Group will identify gaps in the Rule of Law framework that are inhibiting U.S. and Afghan detention/corrections operations from completing their mission and will develop solutions through consistent engagement with GIRoA elements and the International Community.

- The Afghanistan Prison Engagement Group will assist GIRoA in reforming the Central Prisons Directorate (CPD) so it can defeat the insurgency within its walls. The reformed CPD National Prison System will meet international standards, employ best correctional practices, comply with Afghan laws, and be capable of sustaining de-radicalization, rehabilitation, and reintegration programs.

Capabilities
The CJIATF Concept will be developed based on three capabilities (or phases):

- Capability 1 - Assume the U.S. detention oversight and support responsibilities ...**REDACTION**... to include the operation and management of the BTIF, to allow ...**REDACTION**... focus on the operational fight. Once the JTF stands up, and the commander and his staff are on the ground in Afghanistan, they can begin planning and further developing Capabilities 2 and 3.

- Capability 2 - Conduct corrections and Rule of Law development within the Afghan National Defense Force (ANDF) detention facilities.

- Capability 3 - In close coordination and cooperation with the U.S. Embassy, conduct corrections and Rule of Law development within the Afghan CPD system of prisons.

Endstate
The desired endstate is the turnover of all detention operations in Afghanistan, to include the BTIF, to the Afghan government once they have developed the requisite sustainable capacity to run those detention systems in accordance with international and national law. This will empower the Afghan government, enable counterinsurgency operations, and restore the faith of the Afghan people in their government's ability to

apply good governance and Rule of Law with respect to corrections, detention, and justice.

Background

The ANSF is currently not large enough to cope with the demands of fighting the resilient insurgency in Afghanistan. Accelerating the growth and development of both the Afghan National Army (ANA) and Afghan National Police (ANP) is a vital part of the strategy to create the conditions for sustainable security and stability in Afghanistan. Demonstrable progress by the Afghan government and its security forces in countering the insurgency over the next 12 to 18 months is critical in order to preserve the sustained commitment and support of the international community. A key component of success will be the ability of the ANSF to assume progressively greater responsibility for security operations from the deployed international forces. The requirement to expand the ANSF (both ANA and ANP) rapidly to address the challenges of the insurgency will require ISAF to provide enhanced partnering, mentoring, and enabling capabilities until parallel capabilities are developed within the ANSF.

Key Findings

ANA

The ANA has a force structure of nearly 92k and, while still nascent and dependent on enablers provided by international forces, is increasingly capable of leading or conducting independent operations; however, more COIN capable Afghan Army forces are required in order to conduct sustained COIN operations in key areas of the country.

Over the past several years, the ANA has grown in capacity and capability. Late last year a decision to increase the size of the ANA to 134k was followed by a plan from the Afghan Ministry of Defense (supported by CSTC-A) to accelerate the training of 8 Kandaks in order to enhance security in key areas, mainly in Southern Afghanistan. That acceleration is currently ongoing.

The growth of the ANA to 134k needs to be brought forward from December 2011 to October 2010 in order to create sufficient ANA capacity to create conditions for rapid and sustainable progress in the current campaign; however, there is a requirement for further substantial growth (to an estimated endstrength of 240k) of COIN capable ANA troops in order to increase pressure on the insurgency in all threatened areas in the country. Current plans provide for a start date of Oct 2009 to commence an acceleration in growth through a combination of over manning and rapid force generation of ANA infantry and combat service support units. In order to generate the required numbers of "boots on the ground," the emphasis will be on the development of maneuver units rather than enabler capabilities. The generation of previously planned and programmed enablers such as corps engineers, artillery, motorized quick

UNCLASSIFIED

G-1

reaction forces, and large support battalions will be deferred to enable a more rapid generation of maneuver forces that provide the operational capabilities required now. The forces generated during this phase will have sufficient training, capability and equipment to conduct effective COIN operations and to generate momentum. Tighter, restructured training programs will deliver an infantry-based, COIN capable, force in a shorter period of time with the capability of conducting "hold" operations with some "clear" capability while closely partnered with coalition forces. These forces will be equipped at a "minimally combat essential" level as determined by the Ministry of Defense, ISAF's operational requirements, and CSTC-A's ability to generate forces. Initially, facilities will be austere and temporary (including tented camps at the outset) in order to reduce construction timelines and cost.

Risks inherent in this approach such as inadequate training and a lack of organic enablers will be mitigated through close partnering and mentoring by Regional Commanders delivered through the ISAF Joint Command. More inexperienced leaders will be accepted into the junior officer and NCO ranks and the risk will be balanced by close partnering ANSF with coalition forces. In time, a "rebalancing" and generation of enabling capabilities must occur as part of subsequent ANA growth to ensure that the ANA can achieve a degree of self-sufficiency, sustainable capability, and capacity. The growth of the ANA beyond 134k will be tailored to meet operational conditions on the ground and to create the required effects desired in the regions.

Finally, the Afghan National Army Air Corps will continue to grow and develop at a measured pace, given the long lead times required for the acquisition of aircraft and development of technical skills to operate and maintain the aircraft in the inventory. In the short term, the accelerated acquisition of additional Mi-17 airframes will enable greater lift capacity for the ANSF. In parallel, dedicated training of Mi-35 aircrews will add a rotary wing attack capability in the fall of 2009. Deliveries of the first C-27 aircraft in November 2009 will dramatically increase operational capability as the first crews are trained in March 2010.

ANP

The Afghan National Police has grown to a current force structure of approximately 84k and is several years behind the ANA in its development. Due to a lack of overall strategic coherence and insufficient resources, the ANP has not been organized, trained, and equipped to operate effectively as a counter-insurgency force. Promising programs to reform and train police have proceeded too slowly due to a lack of training teams. To enhance the ANP's capacity and capabilities, the Focused District Development (FDD) program must be accelerated to organize, train, equip, and reform police that have not yet completed a formal program of instruction, and new police forces such as the elite Afghan National Civil Order Police (ANCOP) must be generated to prepare the ANP properly to operate in this challenging COIN environment.

UNCLASSIFIED

G-2

The ANP must increase in size in order to provide sufficient police needed to hold areas that have been cleared of insurgents, and to increase the capacity to secure the population. This assessment recommends further growth of the ANP to a total of 160k as soon as practicable with the right mix of capabilities that better satisfies the requirements of a counter-insurgency effort. This larger number of policemen also needs to be trained more quickly in order to "thicken" security forces in the districts, provinces, and regions. The numbers of Afghan Border Police (ABP) and Afghan National Civil Order Police (ANCOP) should also be considerably increased, and consideration should be given to expanding the Afghan Public Protection Force or other similar initiatives where appropriate.

In April 2009, a decision was made to grow the ANP by 4.8K to provide security for Kabul in advance of the Afghan National elections. This action was followed by second decision to further grow the police by 10K in order to enhance security in 14 key provinces for the upcoming elections. This 14.8K police growth is proceeding and will increase the ANP authorized strength to 96.8K while improving accountability of "non and above tashkiel" police.

Subsequent ANP growth to 160k will include doubling ANP strength at the District and Provincial levels, significantly increasing the police-to- population ratio. The growth of ANCOP will be accelerated by generating 5 national battalions in FY '10 followed by the generation of 34 new provincial battalions and 6 new regional battalions. While the number of ABP companies will remain the same, each ABP company will increase in strength by 65% to 150 men per company. Finally, the Afghan Public Protection Force (APPF) personnel will be absorbed into the ANP as it expands.

Over the 4 year program, special police growth will provide important niche capabilities. The national Crisis Response Unit (CRU) will provide Assault, Surveillance, and Support squadrons. Counter-Narcotics Aviation is projected to grow by over 100%. Afghan Special Narcotics forces grow by 25%. Security forces will also be provided to ensure international and non-governmental organizations' freedom of movement.

NATO Training Mission – Afghanistan (NTM-A)

On 12 June, 2009 the North Atlantic Council endorsed the creation of NATO Training Mission – Afghanistan (NTM-A) to oversee higher level training for the ANA and for development of the ANP. CSTC-A and NTM-A will co-exist as a single HQ with fully integrated staff sections under a dual-hatted commander. As approved by the North Atlantic Council, the NTM-A will stand up in mid-September to generate forces and provide institutional training for the ANA and ANP. Once the IJC is operational, the three NATO tasks assigned to NTM-A associated directly with providing NATO OMLTs and POMLTs to the ANA and ANP will migrate to the IJC. At that time, NATO/ISAF will

UNCLASSIFIED

redirect responsibilities for developing fielded ANSF to the IJC. NTM-A will retain responsibility for ANSF institutional training, education, and professional development activities. CJTF Phoenix and its two subordinate Brigades will be transferred to the IJC when it establishes Initial Operating Capability.

Key Stakeholder Engagement

This assessment recommends that the United States Government develop an engagement strategy to garner the international support and the multi-lateral approval required for the continued growth of the ANSF to the 400k target (240K ANA, 160K ANP). This includes the actions necessary to secure greater international funding to pay a fair share of the growth and sustainment costs of the ANSF, as well as generating the training teams required to support ANSF development. As a point of reference, the international community contributed $25M (~7%) of the cost of the expansion of the ANP by 14.8k earlier this summer. Furthermore, the European Commission requested a parallel study to recommend the character and end strength of ANP. When the EC study is completed, the findings will be reconciled to gain consensus in the international community about the way ahead.

A more cost effective way to procure capabilities for the ANSF

This initial assessment recommends that the OSD Comptroller fund CSTC-A directly, and allow CSTC-A to work directly with the appropriate contracting agency to procure required capabilities for the ANSF. The current system of executing Afghan Security Forces Funding (ASFF) must become more agile in the face of the requirement to adapt this program quickly. All procurement actions for the ANSF are handled as "pseudo" Foreign Military Sales Cases by the Defense Security Cooperation Agency (DSCA) and the United States Army Security Assistance Command (USASAC), each of which charge considerable fees for an "Above Standard Level of Service." These fees and the direct involvement of the DSCA apply to the procurement of most capabilities, including those that are executed by local contracting authorities as well as other actions not directly related to Foreign Military Sales such as construction. Direct authority to obligate ASFF without passing actions through the DSCA or USASAC will shorten timelines and preserve more money for the specific purpose of supporting the growth and sustainment of the ANSF.

Strengthen ANSF development through realigned C2

CSTC-A is responsible for three lines of operation: ministerial and institutional development; generation of the force; and develop the fielded force. This assessment concludes that the IJC should assume responsibility for developing the fielded force. The transfer of this mission will require the reassignment of CJTF Phoenix and its subordinate elements to the IJC. CSTC-A will retain the responsibility to train, advise,

UNCLASSIFIED

and educate personnel in the Afghan Ministries of Defense and Interior, as well as those in the institutional elements of the Army and Police (national logistics, medical, facilities management, detainee operations, etc.). CSTC-A will also retain responsibility to resource the fielded ANSF.

Unity of effort and coherence in police development

In an effort to streamline police development efforts and to create greater unity of effort in the development of COIN capable police, the responsibility and authority for all police training should be placed under the commander CSTC-A/NTM-A. The Department of State's Bureau of International Narcotics and Law Enforcement (INL) should transfer responsibility for police training to CSTC-A. Since 2005, OSD has transferred funding to INL for developmental efforts of the ANP. CSTC-A will execute this mission and contract as appropriate for trainers with law enforcement experience to augment efforts by the IJC to develop fielded police, and to assist CSTC-A's actions for ministerial and institutional training.

Build and leverage Afghan ministerial capacity

CSTC-A should take every opportunity to build and leverage ministerial capacity to shift the responsibility for the long term sustainability of a larger ANSF to the Afghan Government. One opportunity is to find an appropriate legal and accountable way to allow the Afghan Ministries of Defense and Interior to contract for the construction of their own facilities. Today, more than 70% of all major construction projects in support of the ANA are at least 10% behind schedule. In response to this situation, CSTC-A and the Army Corps of Engineers have already standardized and reduced the scope of future projects to mitigate costs and delays. Additionally, CSTC-A will investigate the feasibility and practicality of providing discreet funding for Afghan Ministries to contract for the construction of their own facilities to drive lower costs and improve project timeliness. This process will also provide an opportunity to develop Afghan ministerial capacity. There are inherent risks in this approach but CSTC-A will develop a construct for this proposal with CENTCOM and OSD to ensure proper program management and the required oversight of funding provided to the Afghan ministries.

Recommendations

1. Grow the ANA to a target authorization of 240k. Accelerate the growth of the currently approved COIN focused infantry force of 134K by late 2010 and generate more counter-insurgency forces consistent with operational requirements.

2. Grow and develop the ANP to a total of 160k as soon as practicable to "thicken and harden" security in the districts, provinces, regions. This total will also more than

UNCLASSIFIED

G-5

double the size of Afghan Border Police, considerably grow ANCOP and allow for expansion of the Afghan Public Protection Force where appropriate.

3. Realign and streamline the responsibilities for ANSF generation and development:

    a. CSTC-A/NATO Training Mission-Afghanistan (NTM-A) focuses on ANSF force generation consistent with operational requirements, develops Afghan ministerial and institutional capabilities, and resources the fielded forces.
    b. Shift responsibility for development of fielded ANSF to the IJC.
    c. Employ enhanced partnering and mentoring to more rapidly develop Afghan forces.

4. Provide CSTC-A direct authority to obligate Afghan Security Forces Funding (ASFF) without passing actions through the Defense Security Cooperation Agency to shorten capabilities procurement timelines and avoid unnecessary fees.

5. Shift the responsibility and authority for execution of all police training from the Department of State's Bureau of International Narcotics and Law Enforcement (INL) to CSTC-A to enhance unity of effort in police development. CSTC-A will assume operational control of INL contracted trainers as soon as possible until January 2010 when a new contract managed by CSTC-A can begin.

UNCLASSIFIED

A

ABP	Afghan Border Police
ACS	Afghan Corrections System
AFCENT	Air Forces Central Command
ANA	Afghan National Army
ANCOP	Afghan National Civil Order Police
ANP	Afghan National Police
ANSF	Afghan National Security Forces
AOO	Area of Operations
AP3	Afghan Public Protection Program
APPF	Afghan Public Protection Force
AQAM	Al Qaeda and associated movements
ASFF	Afghan Security Forces Funding
ATC	Allied Transformation Command

B

BDA	Battle Damage Assessment
BSO	Battlespace owner
BTIF	Bagram Theater Internment Facility

C

C2	Command and Control
CAS	Close Air Support
CE	Crisis Establishment
CENTCOM	Central Command
CFACC	Combined Forces Air Component Commander
CFSOCC-A	Combined Forces Special Operations Component Command – Afghanistan
CIS	Communications Infrastructure
CIVCAS	Civilian Casualties
CJIATF	Combined Joint Interagency Task Force
CJOC	Coalition Joint Operations Center
CN	Counternarcotics
COIN	Counterinsurgency
COIN TE	Counterinsurgency Transformative Effects
COMISAF	Commander ISAF
CPD	Central Prisons Directorate
CRU	Crisis Response Unit
CSPMP	Comprehensive Strategic Political Military Plan
CSTC-A	Combined Security Transition Command - Afghanistan

D

DC	Decisive Conditions
DCOS	Deputy Chief of Staff
DoD	Department of Defense (US)

UNCLASSIFIED

H-1

DP	Decisive Points
DSCA	Defense Security Cooperation Agency

E

EoF	Escalation of Force
ETT	Embedded Training Team

F

FDD	Focused District Development
FID	Foreign Internal Defense
FOC	Fully Operational Capability
FRAGO	Fragmentary Order

G

GIRoA	Government of the Islamic Republic of Afghanistan

H

HiG	Hezb-e Islami Gulbuddin
HHQ	Higher Headquarters
HQN	Haqqani Network

I

IC	International Community
ICMCP	Integrated Civil-Military Campaign Plan
IED	Improvised Explosive Device
IJC	ISAF Joint Command
INL	International Narcotics and Law Enforcement Affairs (US Dept. of State)
INS	Insurgents
IO	Information Operations
IOATF	Information Operation Advisory Task Force
IOTF	Information Operations Task Force
ISAF	International Security Assistance Force
ISI	Inter-Services Intelligence
ISR	Intelligence, Surveillance, and Reconnaissance

J

JFC-B	Joint Force Command - Brunssum
JIDC	Joint Interrogation Detention Center
JOPG	Joint Operational Planning Group
JOPS	Joint Operations
JTAC	Joint Tactical Air Controllers

K

KAIA	Kabul International Airport

L

LoO	Lines of Operation

M

MARCENT	Marine Corps Central Command
MOE	Measures of Effectiveness

UNCLASSIFIED

MOP	Measures of Performance
N	
NAC	North Atlantic Council
NATO	North Atlantic Treaty Organization
NCO	Non-Commissioned Officer
NGO	Non-governmental organization
NSC	National Security Council (US)
NSE	National Support Element
NTM-A	NATO Training Mission - Afghanistan
O	
OEF	Operation Enduring Freedom
OMLT	Operational Mentoring and Liaison Team
OPCOM	Operational Command
OPCON	Operational Control
OPLAN	Operational Plan
OPORD	Operational Order
OSD	Office of the Secretary of Defense (US)
P	
PA	Public Affairs
POERF	Post Operations Emergency Fund Relief
POMLT	Police Operational Mentoring Liaison Team
PRT	Provincial Reconstruction Team
Q	
QST	Quetta Shura Taliban
R	
RC	Regional Command
RLS	Real life support
ROE	Rules of Engagement
S	
S/CRS	State Department Coordinator for Reconstruction and Stabilization (US)
SACEUR	Supreme Allied Commander Europe
SDC	Strategic Debriefing Center
SHAPE	Supreme Headquarters Allied Powers Europe
SOCCENT	Special Operations Command – Central Command
SOF	Special Operations Forces
SOP	Standard Operating Procedures
StratCom	Strategic Communications
T	
TACOM	Tactical Command
TACON	Tactical Control
TCN	Troop Contributing Nation
TD	Tactical Directive

UNCLASSIFIED

H-3

TTPs	Tactics, Techniques, Procedures

U

UNAMA	United Nations Assistance Mission in Afghanistan
USASAC	United States Army Security Assistance Command
USFOR-A	US Forces - Afghanistan
USG	United States Government
USMC	US Marine Corps

W

WSV	Weapons Systems Video

UNCLASSIFIED

Annex I: References

1. Agreement on Provisional Arrangements in Afghanistan Pending the Reestablishment of Permanent Government Institutions (Bonn Agreement), 5 Dec 01.
2. Military Technical Agreement (MTA) Between the International Security Assistance Force (ISAF) and the Interim Administration of Afghanistan (31 Dec 01), 4 Jan 02; Amendment 2, 14 Mar 03.
3. **REDACTION**
4. The Bonn Agreement 2004
5. The Afghan Compact 2006
6. **REDACTION**
7. **REDACTION**
8. **REDACTION**
9. **REDACTION**
10. COMISAF Commander's Initial Guidance dated 13 June 2009
11. COMISAF Tactical Directive dated 01 July 2009
12. **REDACTION**
13. Bucharest Summit Declaration Apr 08
14. United Nations Security Council Resolutions

   a. Resolution 1383 (2001) of 6 December – endorses the Bonn Agreement as a first step towards the establishment of a broad-based, gender sensitive, multiethnic and fully representative government in Afghanistan.

   b. Resolution 1386 (2001) of 20 December – authorizes the deployment for six months of an International Security Assistance Force for Afghanistan (ISAF).

   c. Resolution 1401 (2002) of 28 March – establishes for an initial period of 12 months a United Nations Assistance Mission In Afghanistan (UNAMA).

   d. Resolution 1413 (2002) of 23 May – extends the authorization of ISAF for an additional 6 months.

   e. Resolution 1419 (2002) of 26 June – welcomes the results of the Emergency Loya Jirga and commends the role of UNAMA and ISAF.

   f. Resolution 1444 (2002) of 27 November – extends the authorization of ISAF for one year beyond 20 Dec 02.

   g. Resolution 1453 (2002) of 24 December – recognizes the Transitional Administration (TA) as the sole legitimate government of Afghanistan and welcomes the Kabul Declaration on Good-Neighbourly Relations signed by the TA and the States neighbouring Afghanistan.

h. Resolution 1471 (2003) of 28 March – extends UNAMA for another 12 months.

i. Resolution 1510 (2003) of 13 October – authorising expansion of the ISAF mandate outside of Kabul and its environs.

j. Resolution 1776 (2007) of 19 September - extends the mandate of ISAF for 12 months beyond 13 Oct 07.

k. Resolution 1806 (2008) of 20 March- extends UNAMA for another 12 months and designates it as the IC lead in AFG.

l. Resolution 1817 (2008) of 11 June adopts a declaration on the global effort to combat drug trafficking

m. Resolution 1833 (2008) of 22 September- extends the mandate of ISAF for 12 months beyond 13 Oct 08.

APPENDIX 2

AFGHANISTAN'S NARCO WAR: BREAKING THE LINK BETWEEN DRUG TRAFFICKERS AND INSURGENTS

10 AUGUST 2009

11th Congress
1st Session

COMMITTEE PRINT

S. PRT.

AFGHANISTAN'S NARCO WAR:
BREAKING THE LINK BETWEEN
DRUG TRAFFICKERS AND INSURGENTS

A REPORT

TO THE

COMMITTEE ON FOREIGN RELATIONS
UNITED STATES SENATE

ONE HUNDRED ELEVENTH CONGRESS

FIRST SESSION

AUGUST 10, 2009

Printed for the use of the Committee on Foreign Relations

Available via World Wide Web: http://www.gpoaccess.gov/congress/index.html

U.S. GOVERNMENT PRINTING OFFICE

WASHINGTON: 2009

For sale by the Superintendent of Documents, U.S. Government Printing Office
Internet: bookstore.gpo.gov
Phone: toll free (866) 512–1800; DC area (202) 512–1800; Fax: (202) 512-2104
Mail: Stop IDCC, Washington, DC 20402–0001

323

COMMITTEE ON FOREIGN RELATIONS

JOHN F. KERRY, Massachusetts, *Chairman*

CHRISTOPHER J. DODD, Connecticut

RUSSELL D. FEINGOLD, Wisconsin

BARBARA BOXER, California

ROBERT MENENDEZ, New Jersey

BENJAMIN L. CARDIN, Maryland

ROBERT P. CASEY, JR., Pennsylvania

JIM WEBB, Virginia

JEANNE SHAHEEN, New Hampshire

EDWARD E. KAUFMAN, Delaware

KIRSTEN E. GILLIBRAND, New York

RICHARD G. LUGAR, Indiana

BOB CORKER, Tennessee

JOHNNY ISAKSON, Georgia

JAMES E. RISCH, Idaho

JIM DEMINT, South Carolina

JOHN BARRASSO, Wyoming

ROGER F. WICKER, Mississippi

JAMES M. INHOFE, Oklahoma

DAVID MCKEAN, *Staff Director*
KENNETH A. MYERS, JR., *Republican Staff Director*

CONTENTS

LETTER OF TRANSMITTAL

United States Senate,
Committee On Foreign Relations,
Washington, DC, August 10, 2009.

Dear colleague: The administration is several months into its ambitious new strategy in Afghanistan, and we are seeing the first effects of the increases in military and civilian resources. One of the emerging changes is on counter-narcotics policy. In the past, our emphasis was on eradication. Today, we are focused for the first time on breaking the link between the narcotics trade and the Taliban and other militant groups. To accomplish that important goal, the administration and our military commanders have made targeting major drug traffickers who help finance the Taliban a priority for U.S. troops. In addition, a new intelligence center to analyze the flow of drug money to the Taliban and corrupt Afghan officials is beginning operations and plans are under way to create an interagency task force to pursue drug networks. The attached report represents the findings of research conducted by the committee staff in Afghanistan, the United Arab Emirates and the United States. The report describes the implementation of the new counter-narcotics strategy and offers recommendations. We also hope that the report will provide new impetus for a national debate on the risks and rewards associated with our increasing commitment to the war in Afghanistan.

Sincerely,

John F. Kerry,
Chairman.

AFGHANISTAN'S NARCO WAR:
BREAKING THE LINK BETWEEN
DRUG TRAFFICKERS AND INSURGENTS

EXECUTIVE SUMMARY

At the end of March when President Obama fulfilled his pledge to make the war in Afghanistan a higher priority, he cast the U.S. mission more narrowly than the previous administration: Defeat Al Qaeda and eliminate its safe havens in Afghanistan and Pakistan. To accomplish these twin tasks, however, the President is making a practical commitment to Afghanistan that is far greater than that of his predecessor—more troops, more civilians, and more money. As the American footprint grows, so do the costs. July was the deadliest month yet for American and coalition troops in Afghanistan, and military experts predict more of the same sad trajectory in the coming months.

As part of the military expansion, the administration has assigned U.S. troops a lead role in trying to stop the flow of illicit drug profits that are bankrolling the Taliban and fueling the corruption that undermines the Afghan Government. Tens of millions of drug dollars are helping the Taliban and other insurgent groups buy arms, build deadlier roadside bombs and pay fighters. The emerging consensus among senior military and civilian officials from the United States, Britain, Canada and other countries operating in Afghanistan is that the broad new counter-insurgency mission is tied inextricably with the new counter-narcotics strategy. Simply put, they believe the Taliban cannot be defeated and good government cannot be established without cutting off the money generated by Afghanistan's opium industry, which supplies more than 90 percent of the world's heroin and generates an estimated $3 billion a year in profits.

The change is dramatic for a military that once ignored the drug trade flourishing in front of its eyes. No longer are U.S. commanders arguing that going after the drug lords is not part of their mandate. In a dramatic illustration of the new policy, major drug traffickers who help finance the insurgency are likely to find themselves in the crosshairs of the military. Some 50 of them are now officially on the target list to be killed or captured. Simultaneously, the U.S. has set up an intelligence center to analyze the flow of drug money to the Taliban and corrupt Afghan officials, and a task force combining military, intelligence and law enforcement resources from several countries to pursue drug networks linked to the Taliban in southern Afghanistan awaits formal approval.

An equally fundamental change is under way on the civilian side of the counter-narcotics equation. The administration has declared that eradication of poppies, the mainstay of the former administration, is a failure and that the emphasis will shift to promoting alternative crops and building a legal agricultural economy in a country without one for 30 years. This marks the first time the United States has had an agriculture strategy for Afghanistan.

The attempt to cut off the drug money represents a central pillar of counter-insurgency strategy—deny financing to the enemy. This shift is an overdue move that recognizes the central role played by drug traffickers and drug money in the deteriorating situation in Afghanistan. While it is too early to judge whether this will be a watershed, it is not too early to raise questions about whether the goals of the counter-narcotics strategy can be achieved. Is it possible to slow the flow of drug money to the insurgency, particularly in a country where most transactions are conducted in cash and hidden behind an ancient and secretive money transfer system? Does the U.S. Government have the capacity and the will to provide the hundreds more civilians required to carry out the second step in the counter-narcotics program and transform a poppy-dominated economy into one where legitimate agriculture can thrive? Can our NATO allies be counted on to step up their contributions on the military and civilian sides at a time when support for the war is waning in most European countries and Canada?

The ability to stop—or at least slow—the money going to the insurgency will play a critical role in determining whether we can carve out the space required to provide the security and economic development necessary to bring a level of stability to Afghanistan that will prevent it from once again being a safe haven for those who plot attacks against the United States and our allies. But counter-narcotics alone will not win the war. The new strategy is one aspect, albeit an important one, of the administration's decision to move troops into Afghan villages and shift more resources to building a functioning and legal economy.

The scope of development needed to create jobs, promote alternatives to growing poppy and train Afghan security forces is enormous. Unlike Iraq, Afghanistan is not a reconstruction project—it is a construction project, starting almost from scratch in a country that will probably remain poverty-stricken no matter how much the U.S. and the international community accomplish in the coming years.

The administration has raised the stakes by transforming the Afghan war from a limited intervention into a more ambitious and potentially risky counter-insurgency. This transformation raises its own set of questions. How much can any amount of effort by the United States and its allies transform the politics and society of Afghanistan? Why is the United States becoming more deeply involved in Afghanistan nearly eight years after the invasion? Does the American public understand and support the sacrifices that will be required to finish the job? Even defining success remains elusive: Is it to build a nation or just to keep the jihadists from using a nation as a sanctuary?

These core questions about commitment and sacrifice can be answered only through a rigorous and informed national debate, sparked by Congress with the support of the administration. The American people need to understand the extent of our country's involvement in Afghanistan and neighboring Pakistan and try to reach a consensus to help guide policymakers and the President and his team.

The Senate Foreign Relations Committee has held a series of public hearings in recent months focusing on the evolving policies toward Afghanistan and Pakistan. In an effort to stimulate a larger debate, the committee plans another round of hearings, beginning soon after Congress returns from the Labor Day recess. As part of that effort, the committee staff prepared this report examining the new counter-narcotics strategy as a way of evaluating the overall policy being put in place by the administration in Afghanistan. The report examines the counter-narcotics policy and addresses these questions in six chapters, followed by a set of recommendations.

1. The Fruits of Neglect—Recent Rise of the Drug Trade
2. Why Eradication Failed —2001 to 2008
3. How the Taliban Exploits the Drug Trade
4. Implementing New Strategies for Afghanistan
5. A Metaphor for War—the Battle of Marjah
6. The Missing Civilian Component
7. Recommendations for Afghanistan

1. The Fruits of Neglect—Recent Rise of the Drug Trade

Beyond the tragic fact that Afghan opium is flooding Europe, the real problem for U.S. and coalition forces is the amount of drug profits being paid in taxes and protection money to the Taliban and other insurgents.

Stemming this flow requires an understanding of the evolution of the drug trade in Afghanistan over the past three decades. It also requires the overdue acknowledgement that the drug situation has deteriorated sharply under the stewardship of the Government of President Hamid Karzai, the United States and NATO-led International Security Assistance Force (ISAF).

Opium poppies have been grown in Afghanistan throughout its history. Hearty plants that thrive even under harsh conditions, they are cultivated for their gummy sap, which is converted into opium paste. Some paste is processed into heroin at dozens of crude labs in Afghanistan and the rest is smuggled out along with the processed heroin via three principal routes: Pakistan in the west, Iran in the east and Tajikistan in the north.

The United Nations Office on Drugs and Crime (UNODC) estimates that Afghanistan now produces more than 90 percent of the world's opium. While the agency says that acreage under cultivation dropped this year and more provinces are "poppy free," opium yield and the resulting profits in 2009 are expected to remain about the same as in the last two years.

While opium poppies have a long history in Afghanistan, the country was not always the world's biggest opium supplier. At the time of Afghanistan's pro-Communist coup in 1978, Afghan farmers were producing an estimated 300 tons of opium annually. It was enough to satisfy local and regional demand and supply a handful of heroin production labs that sold their product to Western Europe. Most of the poppies were grown in the less fertile areas of the northern part of the country because the productive land in Helmand and other southern provinces was the country's bread basket, producing enough wheat, fruit and vegetables to make Afghanistan self-sufficient and account for some exports.

In the period that followed the Soviet invasion of 1979, Afghanistan was dragged through a decade of brutal warfare. Livestock was killed, American-built irrigation systems from the 1950s and 1960s were destroyed and roads were ruined. The country's ability to grow food and get it to market plunged. Desperate to earn money to pay for imported food, Afghan farmers turned to the one product that grew with little water and was relatively easy to transport—opium. Like a seesaw, opium production rose as food production dropped.

Poppy remained the crop of choice under the warlords who replaced the Soviets and the Taliban who took power in 1995. Afghanistan produced 4,500 tons of opium in 1999, roughly 15 times the output of 20 years earlier. The huge increase sent heroin cascading across Europe and the former Soviet Union, leading to pressure on the Taliban to reduce production. Eager to end its virtual isolation by the international community and profit from its own stockpiles of opium, the Taliban announced a ban on poppy cultivation in late 2000. The fundamentalists in their black turbans enforced the fragile ban through a complex process of persuasion, negotiation and coercion, resulting in a sharp reduction in output to 185 tons in 2001. The shift was praised by the United States and other countries, but it was soon undone.

Unintended Consequences of the Invasion

Events in the fall of 2001 changed the equation, laying the groundwork for the nexus between the drug trade, the insurgency and government corruption that defines Afghanistan today. The U.S. ouster of the Taliban had the unintended consequence of eliminating the ban on cultivation. Poppy farmers were eager to plant more crops to recoup losses incurred when the Taliban stopped most production. According to the UNODC, production jumped more than 16 fold to 3,400 tons for the harvest in the fall of 2002. Afghanistan was back in the opium business. The dramatic rebound in just a year demonstrated the resilience of poppy farmers who had few other ways to feed their families.

Another factor influenced the escalation of opium production. After the invasion, the Central Intelligence Agency and U.S. Special Forces put regional and local warlords and militia commanders on their payroll to undermine the Taliban regime and go after Al Qaeda operatives. Despite alliances with the opium trade, many of these warlords later traded on their stature as U.S. allies to take senior positions in the new Afghan Government, laying the groundwork for the corrupt nexus between drugs and authority that pervades the power structure today.

Barnett R. Rubin, a scholar of Afghanistan at New York University and now a senior advisor to Ambassador Richard C. Holbrooke, the administration's envoy to Afghanistan and Pakistan, saw this transition as a defining moment in the evolution of the drug trade and governance in Afghanistan. "The empowerment and enrichment of the warlords who allied with the

United States in the anti-Taliban efforts, and whose weapons and authority now enabled them to tax and protect opium traffickers, provided the trade with powerful new protectors," he wrote in a 2004 paper, Road to Ruin: Afghanistan's Booming Opium Industry. "Opium production immediately resumed the growth path it was on before the Taliban ban."

Total income from producing, processing and trafficking in opium in 2003 had soared to $2.3 billion, roughly half of the country's legal and illegal gross domestic product. By the following year, some U.S. leaders recognized that drugs were propelling the country down the wrong path. Zalmay Khalilzad, the previous administration's special envoy and ambassador to Afghanistan, acknowledged at the time that "rather than getting better, it's gotten worse. There is a potential for drugs overwhelming the institutions—a sort of narco-state."

Despite the warning signals, the U.S. military and CIA did not consider counter-narcotics part of their mission and failed to recognize the early signs linking the drug traffickers to the insurgents. Little Afghan heroin makes it to the United States, but Afghan heroin floods British streets, so the British took the lead on developing a counter-narcotics strategy for Afghanistan. But their effort suffered from chronic personnel shortages and contradictory policies among ISAF members. For example, some countries prohibited their troops from carrying out operations against the drug trade.

See No Evil

American troops had the option of destroying drug shipments and supplies encountered in the larger context of patrols and fighting, but there were no direct orders compelling them to do so—and it is clear that many commanders and others saw drugs as a distraction. In the best-selling book *State of War*, author James Risen described an Army Green Beret who said he was "specifically ordered to ignore heroin and opium when he and his unit discovered them on patrol." On a broader level, congressional committees received reports that U.S. forces were refusing to disrupt drug sales and shipments and rebuffing requests from the Drug Enforcement Administration for reinforcements to go after major drug kingpins.

Efforts by officials outside the military to move narcotics up the priority list fell on deaf ears. In late 2004, Assistant Secretary of State Bobby Charles, who ran the department's Bureau for International Narcotics and Law Enforcement, was growing increasingly concerned over the worsening drug crisis in Afghanistan. "We needed to be pro-active," he recalled in an interview with the committee staff. "If we let it go for even one year, I knew we would lose it."

At one point, Charles argued to Secretary of Defense Donald Rumsfeld that stopping the drug trade should be made an explicit part of the military mission in Afghanistan. Charles remembers that Rumsfeld initially seemed to agree, but the Pentagon's senior generals, already suffering from a drain on resources for the Iraq war, resisted strongly. Charles said Rumsfeld turned him down. It was, Charles says, a monumental error that opened the door for the steadily rising opium production and deepening ties between the drug traffickers and the insurgency.

The difficulty of persuading the U.S. military to play a role in counter-narcotics persisted throughout the previous administration. Even after NATO agreed that drug labs could be attacked in late 2008, the Pentagon resisted and no effort was approved until early 2009, according to a former senior U.S. general involved in the discussion. Instead the focus was on eradicating poppy cultivation, a half-step that had little chance of success from the outset in part because of circumstances unique to Afghanistan and in part because of a lack of resources.

---

2. WHY ERADICATION FAILED—2001 TO 2008

The resurgence of Afghanistan's poppy culture in the years after the U.S. invasion forced U.S. civilian agencies to get more deeply involved in the counter-narcotics effort even as the military ignored the problem. The effort failed and has been rejected by the new administration.

Eradication in particular was seen as a silver bullet or at least the centerpiece of counter-narcotics efforts by many in the previous administration, including former U.S. Ambassador to Afghanistan William Wood, who largely based his assessment on U.S. success in Colombia where he was ambassador from 2003 to 2007.

The State Department's counter-narcotics strategy for Afghanistan, which was developed in 2004 and retooled in 2007, focused on five pillars: Poppy elimination and eradication; interdiction and law enforcement; justice reform and prosecution; public information; and alternative crop development. Each pillar, however, was not weighted equally in terms of attention and resources, with alternative livelihoods receiving the short end of the stick and eradication becoming the primary focus. Perhaps more important, success was measured primarily on levels of cultivation in a given year and few resources were devoted to incorporating a counter-narcotics strategy into a broader state-building and economic development policy.

Early signs of progress were misunderstood. Eradication's supporters argued that they were winning the war against drugs when the 2005 poppy harvest turned out to be smaller than the previous year. Unfortunately, the reduction was primarily because of poor weather and the harvest was back up the following year. The fact is that U.S. counter-narcotics efforts—with eradication in the driver's seat—were artificially separated from broader efforts to defeat the insurgency and even drove some farmers and landowners into the arms of the Taliban because it failed to provide alternative livelihood options.

Grounding Eradication

The Afghan Government agreed to the concept of eradication, but it insisted that eradication be delivered only by manual or mechanical ground-based means. The effect was to reduce efforts to men dragging metal bars across poppy fields behind all-terrain vehicles to knock down plants. It was inefficient, slow and dangerous. Crews often came under fire from the Taliban and gunmen working directly for the traffickers and growers. In 2007, the latest year for complete statistics, the UNODC reported that 15 Afghan police officers were killed and 31 were injured during eradication campaigns.

The most effective method for widespread eradication is widely understood to be aerial spraying, the technique used to eliminate huge portions of Colombia's coca crop. Crop dusters can drop herbicides on vast fields in a short time, outside the range of insurgent fire. But the Afghan Government, Britain and other countries opposed aerial spraying for a variety of reasons. Explaining the benefits and safety of spraying would be difficult in a country with a literacy rate of only 28 percent. More significantly, the tactic would give the Taliban a dynamic propaganda victory. "If we began aerial spraying of poppy crops, every birth defect in Afghanistan would be blamed on the United States," said Ronald Neumann, a former U.S. ambassador to Afghanistan. "Afghans also still remember that the Russians dropped small bombs disguised as toys. Every time a child picked one up, death and destruction resulted. The general belief is that bad things come from planes."

Others offer a more sinister interpretation of the refusal of Afghan officials to allow aerial spraying. In 2004 and 2005, Charles and other State

Department counter-narcotics officials thought that they had reached an agreement among a large number of influential clerics and tribal leaders in southern Afghanistan to support aerial spraying. President Karzai agreed tentatively to a pilot project. But the Aghan cabinet rejected the idea outright, banning all forms of aerial spraying. "Some of them were protecting the source of their own wealth," said Charles in the recent interview.

Gone Today, Here Tomorrow

Without access to aerial spraying, eradication does not work without the sort of massive show of force and persuasion demonstrated by the Taliban in 2000. Research shows that without alternative crops, farmers invariably return to poppy once the eradication teams are gone. Half the villages where the U.S. eradicated poppy in 2007 simply planted the crop again in the fall of 2008. In some cases, farmers increased the land under poppy cultivation to make up for losses from crops destroyed the previous year. Eradication also has the added disadvantage of imposing the hardship on the people at the bottom of the pyramid—farmers who have to harvest crops to feed their families and pay debts—rather than targeting the traffickers and their protectors.

Conventional wisdom holds that most opium farmers likely would stop opium poppy cultivation if they had access to an alternate livelihood, but few have realistic substitutes available to test the theory. Moreover, the lack of roads, irrigation systems, and storage facilities makes growing wheat, fruits, vegetables and other perishables extremely difficult. Many peasant farmers find themselves trapped by debt and feel they are left with no alternative but to grow opium poppy, which can be stored for long periods and is more easily transported. Others grow poppy simply because it pays well (see Appendix 1).

The Taliban and its associates in the drug trade make the poppy business as easy as possible by offering "one-stop shopping." At the start of planting season in the fall, they provide farmers with loans to buy poppy seeds and feed their families over the winter. When the growers cultivate and harvest the poppy in the spring, the Taliban provides security and workers to help in the fields. At the end of the harvest, the traffickers return to collect the poppy and pay the farmers the remainder of their money. The Taliban and traffickers conduct all of their business at the farm gate, so the farmers never have to worry about transporting or selling their crop.

There has been some success. The number of poppy-free provinces has dramatically increased from 0 in 2004 to 18 in 2008 to an expected 22 or 23 later this year. But David Mansfield and Adam Pain, counter-narcotics and rural livelihood experts with the Afghanistan Research and Evaluation Unit, argue that measuring success based on the number of poppy-free provinces confuses correlation with causality and "reflects a fundamental failure to understand the different determinants of cultivation and how these vary by location and socioeconomic group."

Officials with the UNODC in Kabul and American experts said the opium yield for 2008 was about the same as the previous year because farmers had been using high-quality fertilizer smuggled in from Pakistan to produce more poppies per acre. They predict a similar high yield this year once the harvest estimate is completed, particularly in the volatile south. In a report issued in June, the UNODC highlighted the link between drug-producing areas and the insurgency, saying: "Opium poppy cultivation continued to be associated with insecurity. Almost the entire opium poppy-cultivating area was located in regions characterized by high levels of insecurity."

A Dramatic Change of Strategy

In late June, Ambassador Holbrooke announced that the administration was abandoning wide-scale eradication at the G-8 conference in Trieste, Italy. He said that the United States would shift from its strategy from destroying poppy fields to interdicting drug supplies, destroying processing labs that turn opium into heroin, and promoting alternative crops. He also said the State Department would phase out funding for eradication, transferring the money to agriculture assistance efforts.

Eradication has proven an expensive failure. DynCorp International, a major U.S. Government contractor, has been paid $35 million to $45 million a year to supervise manual eradication efforts most often carried out by Afghans paid a few dollars a day. In addition, the State Department has been spending around $100 million annually on aircraft used in eradication and counter-narcotics programs.

But complete elimination of eradication programs is regarded by most military commanders and civilian officials as a step too far. They said that Afghan governors should retain the authority to continue to conduct poppy eradication. Ample evidence shows that the credible threat of eradication can persuade farmers to cultivate legal crops in areas where there is good security and at least fair governance.

"Eradication should be part of a comprehensive counter-narcotics strategy," said a senior U.S. military officer who works in Helmand Province, the biggest poppy-producing part of Afghanistan and the place where the governor has used the threat effectively in his campaign to replace poppies with legitimate crops.

––––––––

3. How the Taliban Exploits the Drug Trade

As it reconstituted from a defeated government to an insurgency force, the Taliban developed a sophisticated multi-pronged scheme for raising money from the opium trade. The money has played a critical role in financing the resurgence of the militants.

The adoption of the new financing strategy coincided roughly with the increase in attacks on U.S. and coalition forces in 2006. Some, like journalist Gretchen Peters, the author of the recent book *Seeds of Terror*, say the Taliban has transformed itself into something closer to the Mafia than a traditional insurgency, particularly in its stronghold of southern Afghanistan. "The Sopranos are the real model for the Taliban," Peters told the committee staff. "They are driven by economic factors. Remember, the Mafia started out as an insurgency in Sicily."

Like the Mafia, the Taliban is not a monolith, but a collection of insurgent groups—"families" in mob parlance—operating with varying degrees of autonomy in Afghanistan and Pakistan. Central figures in the fallen Taliban government like Mullah Omar control the insurgency in Pashtun-dominated southern Afghanistan and pockets in the north and east. Factions like the network of warlord Jalaluddin Haqqani operate in eastern Afghanistan and western Pakistan. These insurgent groups formed alliances with drug traffickers that are opportunistic and tactical, rather than strategic. For the insurgents, the cooperation with the traffickers is chiefly to raise money to finance operations, though there are reports that insurgent leaders have grown rich off the drug trade. For the traffickers, they pay for protection and intimidation if it is required.

To raise money, the Taliban runs a sophisticated protection racket for poppy farmers and drug traffickers, collecting taxes from the farmers and payoffs from the traffickers for transporting the drugs through insurgent-controlled areas. They also demand large payments to the group's exiled leadership. The payment system can be broken down this way:

- Taliban commanders charge poppy farmers a 10 percent tax, called an *ushr*, on the product at the farm gate.
- Taliban fighters augment their pay by working in the poppy fields during harvest.
- Small traders who collect opium paste from the farmers pay the Taliban a tax, and truckers pay them a transit tariff for each kilo of opium paste or heroin smuggled out of the country.
- The Taliban is paid for protecting the labs where the paste is turned into heroin.
- Finally, the biggest source of drug money for the Taliban is the regular payments made by large drug trafficking organizations to the Quetta shura, the governing body of the Taliban whose leaders live in Quetta, the Pakistani border city.

Where Does the Money Go?

No one knows how much money the Taliban collects from the drug trade. The UNODC estimates that the total value of Afghan drugs last year was in the range of $3 billion, which would be the equivalent of 25 percent of the country's current gross domestic product if all the money returned to Afghanistan. But there is no effective mechanism for monitoring how much of that money finds its way back, how much goes to the Taliban and how much is siphoned off by corrupt officials and stashed outside the country. Afghanistan is a still a predominantly cash economy in which most transactions are executed by hawala dealers, who operate an age-old informal money transfer system that moves money around the country and throughout the world cheaply and quickly, leaving little paper trail (see Appendix 2).

The result is that estimates of drug money going to the insurgency vary wildly. U.S. officials in Afghanistan said the CIA and the Pentagon's Defense Intelligence Agency estimate annual Taliban revenue from drugs at about $70 million a year. Outsiders like Peters have put the figure as high as $500 million a year. In 2008, the UNODC estimated that the Taliban and militant off-shoots collected $400 million in taxes and protection payments from the drug trade.

But doubts crept in among senior UNODC analysts, so this year they revised the way they calculated the drug proceeds. Later this summer, the agency plans to release a new estimate that will put the amount of drug payments in taxes and protection money to the Taliban at around $125 million. In explaining the sharp disparity, officials at the agency's Kabul office said they had miscalculated by extrapolating figures from the opium-producing, Taliban-controlled provinces of Kandahar and Helmand to cover the entire country.

The insurgency is a relatively cheap war for the Taliban to fight, and $125 million a year buys a lot of rifles, explosives and rocket-propelled grenade launchers and pays a lot of foot soldiers. American commanders dub the fighters "$10 Taliban" because that is what they are paid for a day's fighting—more than most policemen earn. They can collect double or triple pay for planting an improvised explosive device.

Surprisingly, there is no evidence that any significant amount of the drug proceeds go to Al Qaeda. Contrary to conventional wisdom, numerous money laundering and counter-narcotics experts with the United States Government in Afghanistan and Washington said flatly that they have seen no indication of the Taliban or traffickers paying off Al Qaeda forces left inside the country. "A lot of people have been looking for an Al Qaeda role in drug trafficking and it's not really there," said a senior State Department official involved in the region.

Instead, officials in Afghanistan and Washington said the remnants of Osama bin Laden's organization in Afghanistan, like the elements of the terrorist group inside Pakistan, are financed primarily by contributions from wealthy individuals and charities from the Persian Gulf countries and some nongovernmental organizations working inside Afghanistan.

The Scope of Corruption

Just as getting a handle on the amount of drug money flowing to insurgents is proving difficult, so is building cases against major traffickers and corrupt government officials. The United States and the United Kingdom have trained specially vetted Afghans to prosecute and preside over trials in a special drug court. In the year that ended in March, the court convicted 259 people on drug charges, which carry a minimum sentence of 10 years in prison. But those convicted were low-level to medium-level figures; no major traffickers have even been arrested in Afghanistan since 2006. The court itself ran into some trouble recently when the chief judge was dismissed after he failed the polygraph test administered every 90 days to the vetted personnel.

Afghanistan has long had a reputation for low-level corruption, what many people call "functional corruption." Local political leaders required small payments for services, but people tended to benefit because the locals returned something of greater value to them. In recent years, however, corruption has become more systematic and greedy leaders at the district, provincial and national levels have taken payoffs without returning anything to the people.

American officials told committee staff about several Afghan officials suspected of corruption—a governor who is expected to be fired after the August 20 election, two police chiefs on whom the U.S. military has accumulated extensive dossiers outlining collaboration with drug traffickers and a handful of senior officials at ministries in Kabul. A senior State Department official involved in Afghanistan told the committee staff that police chiefs in poppy-dominated districts pay as much as $100,000 to get appointed to a job that pays $150 a month, with the knowledge that they will recoup far more in bribes and kickbacks. Yet efforts to track down illicit assets have gone nowhere, according to U.S. and United Nations officials.

Nowhere is the corruption worse than in the huge payoffs from drug traffickers. In a country where the drug business is so pervasive and laws so difficult to enforce, accusing someone of drug dealing is easy—proving or disproving the charges is tough. A frequent target of such accusations is Ahmed Wali Karzai, the powerful head of the Kandahar Provincial Council and one of the President's brothers. Stories about him are legendary—how Afghan police and military commanders who seize drugs in southern Afghanistan are told by Ahmed Wali to return them to the traffickers, how he arranged the imprisonment of a DEA informant who had tipped the Americans to a drug-laden truck near Kabul, how his accusers often turn up dead. No proof has surfaced, and he and President Karzai have denied the accusations.

Ahmed Wali Karzai's reputation came up not long ago when a senior U.S. diplomat, his British counterpart and the country chiefs of their two intelligence services met with President Karzai. The U.S. diplomat told the committee staff that he suggested to the President that his brother was involved in drugs and that perhaps he should be sent out of the country as an ambassador.

"Is there hard evidence that my brother has drug links?" asked President Karzai, according to the diplomat.

"There is no evidence in a judicial sense," said the diplomat. "There is rumor and circumstantial evidence."

Last year, the Afghan President offered a sweeping denial to the German magazine *Der Spiegel*. "This is really a lot of rubbish," he said. "I have thoroughly investigated all of these allegations and of course none of them are true."

Questions have been raised in the past about whether the United States has the political will to go after influential members of the Government. Officials in Afghanistan said they have adopted a tougher line and expressed a willingness to pursue senior government officials, provided the evidence is available. At a recent interagency meeting to discuss the new initiative, a British official asked at what level the investigators would stop. "We said, if you have evidence, it doesn't matter," a U.S. official told the committee staff. "The new political leadership in the U.S. embassy has told us there is no red line on anybody for corruption."

New Tactics in the Field

The new consensus among U.S. military commanders in Afghanistan that the war cannot be won without severing the links between the drug traffickers, insurgents and corrupt government officials began to get traction as the administration increased resources for the war. When U.S. Marines descended upon the volatile Helmand River Valley in early July, the operation represented the first major test of the new counter-insurgency strategy and counter-narcotics efforts.

The 4,000 troops from the 2nd Marine Expeditionary Brigade, part of the first wave of 21,000 additional troops arriving this year, have pushed into areas where the U.S. and NATO have had little presence in the previous 8 years. Rather than killing Taliban fighters, the Marines are focused on implementing a counter-insurgency strategy by protecting civilians from the Taliban and staying long enough to restore government services and promote alternatives to poppy production. They will be, in effect, sitting amidst the most fertile poppy fields and hoping to hold their ground and force the growers into marginal areas where it is harder to cultivate poppies and riskier to get the opium to market.

In a more dramatic example of the new counter-narcotics strategy in Helmand, the U.S. military bombed an estimated 300 tons of poppy seeds in a dusty field in late July. The aircraft dropped a series of 1,000-pound bombs on the mounds of seeds and followed with strikes from helicopters, according to a CNN reporter who watched the destruction.

The Taliban has retreated and regrouped in response to the increase in

U.S. troops, but it is not on the run. By providing a sustained presence in pockets that have been controlled by the Taliban and adopting a tough approach on narcotics, however, the Marines will open the door to civilian workers who can concentrate on developing alternatives to poppy. The new security should also permit the first permanent DEA presence in Helmand Province. Up until now, security conditions have kept the drug agency from maintaining a post within the province that produces half the country's opium. DEA officials say they hope to get four or five agents up and running in Helmand Province as part of a major increase in resources. By the end of 2009, DEA officials said the number of investigators in Afghanistan will rise to 55 from 5 in addition to rotating DEA paramilitary teams already at work in the country.

If the operation in Helmand Province displaces the Taliban and disconnects the insurgency from one of its prime sources of drugs, it will represent a critical step in implementing the broad counter-insurgency strategy advocated by the administration. But it is only a start. The United States and its allies must develop lasting alternatives to poppy cultivation that will provide an income to farmers, a challenge that requires a big increase in agricultural assistance, road building and water for irrigation—and the people to oversee those projects.

"If we're going to bleed this summer to secure these areas, if soldiers and Marines are going to die, we need a plan to come in behind and build long-term security through development," said Army Brig. Gen. John W. Nicholson Jr., the deputy commander for the six tough provinces that comprise Regional Command South.

———————

4. Implementing New Strategies for Afghanistan

Fighting the drug traffickers who help finance the Taliban and similar groups is one of the priorities of the new strategy in Afghanistan. Military officers now regard it as part of the mission.

It was not too long ago that American commanders were convinced that the drug problem in Afghanistan was not a military issue. With limited resources, they were understandably worried about what they called "mission creep." Current U.S. Ambassador to Afghanistan Karl Eikenberry, a retired lieutenant general, was wary of engaging troops in counter-narcotics efforts when he was the top military commander in Afghanistan as recently as 2007. Now he says the strategy has evolved, and he embraces the plan to break the links between traffickers and the insurgency. "The narcotics trade is not only a significant source of funding for the insurgency, but also undermines legitimate political and economic development by promoting a culture of corruption and squeezing out licit agricultural growth," Eikenberry said in an email to the committee staff.

Commanders on the ground and the Pentagon now view the war on Afghan drugs as an integral part of the mission, and it is being played out at several locations.

Bagram Air Base lies between mountains and desert 25 miles northeast of Kabul. During the 1980s, it was the main staging area for the Soviets. After the U.S. invasion, Bagram was updated with new buildings, runways and barracks to serve as the bustling U.S. operations center. Tucked away in one of the nondescript buildings is the Afghan Threat Finance Cell (ATFC), a key weapon in the new phase of the war.

The ATFC is modeled after an operation set up in 2005 in Iraq to choke off funds going to Al Qaeda and militias like the Mahdi army of anti-American cleric Moqtada al-Sadr. The Afghan version was established with a skeleton crew earlier this year with the dual mission of disrupting the trafficking networks supporting the insurgents and collecting information on senior Afghan Government officials suspected of corruption. So far, only about 15 people are in place, but the eventual staff of 60 is expected to reflect an interagency approach—they will come from the Treasury Department, DEA, the FBI and the Defense Intelligence Agency. By the end of 2009, the unit expects to have analysts and investigators poring over evidence gathered by the military, Afghan police and U.S. and international law enforcement and intelligence agencies.

"There is a growing realization that the way to attack the Taliban is to go at the financial network behind the insurgency," one of the financial experts setting up the ATFC told the committee staff. "This is largely a self-financed insurgency, and the number one source of money is drug money."

The unit is part of ramping up to gather intelligence on the nexus between the drug traffickers and insurgents. Another element operates inside an Afghan army compound in Kabul, where the DEA and private contractors have spent months vetting and training Afghan police to join the counternarcotics police. Training the Afghan army and police is a core goal for the United States and its NATO allies. A key part of the program is developing

345

enough counter-narcotics officers to station the specialized units within police departments in every district across the country. So far 2,000 policemen have passed through the training and been dispatched.

In addition, DEA has worked with the Afghan Ministry of Interior to select and train members of three elite forces—the special investigative unit, which so far has 56 officers who have submitted to polygraphs and trained at the DEA academy in Quantico, Virginia, to investigate drug networks; the national interdiction unit, which is comprised of about 300 paramilitary police officers who mount raids by air and ground on suspected drug centers and traffickers; and the technical investigative unit, whose members are trained to intercept telephone calls involving suspected illicit transactions.

"The top priority is the drug trafficking organizations linked to the insurgency," said Michael Marsac, the DEA country attaché as he guided the committee staff through the training facilities in late June. "There are two types of drug organizations. There are drug traffickers who are supporting the insurgency and there are insurgents who use drugs to fund their operations. We are targeting both."

Gathering hard evidence is difficult in Afghanistan. The police are only beginning to develop the skills for the painstaking investigations required to collect and analyze information. Bribes and intimidation of police, from commanders on down to rank and file cops, are stock in trade for drug traffickers and their protectors. Still, Marsac said he is optimistic and pointed to the new telephone monitoring capability as an important tool.

Last December 18, the switch was flipped to allow the monitoring of cellular phones, the preferred method of communication in a country where landlines are rare. The eavesdropping is sanctioned under Afghan law so long as it is approved by a special court. By mid-summer, 100 Afghan nationals fluent in the many languages and dialects used in the country were monitoring telephone calls involving suspected drug and insurgent activity. The start has been rocky, with the eavesdropping going fairly well in Kabul but suffering from equipment difficulties and lack of electricity in other major cities like Heart, Kandahar and Jalalabad.

Marsac described one notable success. Last February, Taliban suicide bombers and gunmen attacked government buildings at three sites in Kabul, killing 20 people and wounding nearly 60. The attack was a complex and well-coordinated operation that symbolized the country's deteriorating security situation on the eve of a visit from Ambassador Holbrooke.

A few days later, a special Afghan police unit working with British troops to monitor cell phones in southern Afghanistan picked up chatter about a second attack. The information was relayed to the DEA-trained investigators in Kabul who tracked the phone calls to an apartment in Kabul. Police kicked down the door and arrested six additional suicide bombers.

"Remove Them from the Battlefield"

Soon a new task force targeting drug traffickers, insurgents and corrupt officials is expected to begin formal operations out of Kandahar Air Field in southern Afghanistan. The unit will link the U.S. and British military with the DEA, Britain's Serious Organized Crime Agency (SOCA) and police and intelligence agencies from other countries. While the ATFC at Bagram will primarily gather intelligence and build legal cases, the Joint Interagency Task Force (JIATF) will go after drug networks linked to the insurgency, interdict drug shipments, destroy heroin labs and identify and arrest their protectors in government.

The JIATF is awaiting formal approval in Washington and London, but operations have been coordinated informally through what officers involved call "goodwill" among British, U.S. and Australian personnel. An investigator with SOCA involved in the JIATF described the approach as a critical opportunity to blend military and law enforcement expertise. "In the past, the military would have hit and evidence would not have been collected," he explained. "Now, with law enforcement present, we are seizing the ledgers and other information to develop an intelligence profile of the networks and the drug kingpins."

An American military officer with the project was blunter, telling the committee staff, "Our long-term approach is to identify the regional drug figures and corrupt government officials and persuade them to choose legitimacy or remove them from the battlefield."

The Rules of Engagement, known as ROE, govern the conduct of the U.S. military in Afghanistan, spelling out when and how much force can be used on the battlefield. The precise rules are classified, but two U.S. generals in Afghanistan said that the ROE and the internationally recognized Law of War have been interpreted to allow them to put drug traffickers with proven links to the insurgency on a kill list, called the joint integrated prioritized target list. The military places no restrictions on the use of force with these selected targets, which means they can be killed or captured on the battlefield; it does not, however, authorize targeted assassinations away from the battlefield. The generals said standards for getting on the list require two verifiable human sources and substantial additional evidence. Currently, there are roughly 50 major traffickers who contribute funds to the insurgency on the target list.

"We have a list of 367 'kill or capture' targets, including 50 nexus targets who link drugs and insurgency," one of the officers explained to the committee staff.

The authorization for using lethal force on traffickers caused a stir at NATO earlier this year when some countries questioned whether the killing traffickers and destroying drug labs complied with international law. Jaap de Hoop Scheffer, secretary general of NATO at the time, said filters had been put in place to make sure the alliance remains within the bounds of the law.

Not every investigation will land someone on the hit list. More often, information will be used to develop cases for prosecution. American officials would like to put Afghanistan's drug kingpins on trial in the United States, where they have more confidence in the judicial system. But those efforts have been largely blocked by the absence of an extradition treaty that would allow Afghans to be transferred to the U.S., a technique employed effectively against Colombian and Mexican cartel bosses. Treaty negotiations have been stalled by Afghanistan's insistence on reciprocity, which would allow Kabul to seek extradition of Americans.

Responding to the Stalemate

The inaction has led to some creative responses by U.S. law enforcement. In October 2008, agents from the DEA and Britain's SOCA tricked Haji Juma Khan, a major kingpin linked to the Taliban who ran his empire out of Quetta, into flying to Indonesia. He was arrested upon arrival in Jakarta and, by prearrangement, deported the next day to New York City, where he is awaiting trial on charges of conspiracy to distribute narcotics and supporting a terrorist organization. American prosecutors say that he moved up to $1 billion worth of opium a year, paying protection to the Taliban and bribes to officials in Afghanistan, Pakistan and Iran. In a similar ruse, Haji Bashi Noorzai, a big-time trafficker with ties to fugitive Taliban leader Mullah Mohammad Omar, was lured to New York and arrested on the pretense of meeting with U.S. officials to discuss curbing poppy cultivation. Noorzai was convicted of heroin smuggling and sentenced to life in prison on April 30.

Had either man been arrested in Afghanistan, they would have wound up in a narcotics court system that is still being developed, under the guidance of prosecutors and other advisers from the U.S. and Britain. So far, the special drug court has convicted low-level and mid-level dealers, but it has not handled any cases against major figures because none has been arrested. In addition to continuing to improve the court's Afghan personnel, officials at the U.S. embassy said they need a team of 10 to 15 experienced prosecutors and investigators to build financial and drug cases against big traffickers.

No one from ATFC or JIATF said disrupting the drug networks and their allies would be fast or easy. Along with the normal difficulties of building a solid case, the investigators and troops face the added obstacles of working in a place where the courts are suspect, witnesses can be killed with impunity and investigators face the threats associated with working in a war zone.

Though the CIA has hundreds of employees in Afghanistan, the new interagency groups are working to fill a gap left by the absence of any concerted effort on the part of the intelligence agency to monitor the money movement between traffickers and insurgents, according to U.S. officials. "I have to ring their neck to get anything out of them," said a senior official at the U.S. embassy in Kabul. "If we don't get a handle on the money, we will lose this war to corruption."

The Regional Spillover—Problems in Pakistan

Afghanistan and Pakistan are separated by a 1,600-mile border known as the Durand Line. The border is isolated, rugged and crisscrossed by thousands of trails; it is well known that militants cross with ease. Less publicized is the freedom of movement enjoyed by drug smugglers, particularly along the 745-mile stretch in the south. Afghanistan's virtually invisible border with the Pakistani province of Baluchistan runs through some of the most desolate and rugged wastelands on the planet, making it ideal for transporting drugs out of Afghanistan and bringing in the precursor chemicals used to process opium paste into heroin. UN officials estimate that about a third of Afghanistan's drug production exits through Pakistan, with most moving from Helmand and Kandahar provinces via land to the Makran Coast on the Arabian Sea for shipment throughout the region by boat.

A recent Defense Department assessment found that the Pakistani Government has a limited capability to conduct counter-narcotics operations on the Makran Coast and in Baluchistan because of the inhospitable terrain, limited resources and lack of political will. The June 18 report was sharply critical of Pakistan's primary Anti-Narcotics Force (ANF), which is under the Ministry of Narcotics Control. "Even though the ANF is the premier counter-narcotics agency in Pakistan, it currently does not have the manpower, nor willing leadership, to effectively counteract the enormity of the narcotics issues throughout the country," said the report. "At this time, Pakistan counter-narcotics capabilities are weak."

A senior U.S. law enforcement official in the region told the committee staff that cooperation between the United States and the ANF is poor. He said major traffickers cross the border from Afghanistan and operate with impunity in Quetta and other Pakistani cities. "They pick up the low-lying fruit," said the official in describing the ANF tactics. "We give them leads on targets. We give them phone numbers of traffickers that they should be interested in. We are constantly doing that. We get smiles, a decent cup of tea, occasional reheated sandwiches and assertions of progress, and we all leave with smiles on our faces."

The lack of cooperation is one reason that the leadership of the exiled Taliban government resides safely in Quetta, the capital of Baluchistan, outside the reach of U.S. forces and flush with cash from the major drug traffickers in Kandahar and Helmand provinces.

Beyond the Pakistan Border

The American focus on the southern border dates back to the mujahideen connections and it is now reinforced by the arrival of 4,000 new troops. But the border on the north with Tajikistan and Turkmenistan is equally porous and United Nations and American officials estimate that another third of Afghanistan's opium and heroin production goes out through the northern route.

In Tajikistan, the biggest exit point, the United States and the European Union have divided responsibility for working with local authorities to train police and patrol the 835-mile border with Afghanistan. But the mountainous terrain and network of established smuggling trails makes stopping more than a fraction of the drugs impossible, according to U.S. officials in the region.

Poverty also encourages smuggling in Tajikistan, the poorest of the former Soviet states, and it underscores the need for economic development to avoid a failed state on the northern border of Afghanistan. "The current counter-narcotics programs aren't well geared to tackle questions of development, governance and corruption," said a senior U.S. official in Tajikistan.

On Afghanistan's western border lies Iran, which the UNODC says suffers from the highest per capita drug use in the world. The UN agency estimates that another third or so of Afghanistan's drug production is smuggled into

Iran on its way to Turkey and on to Europe, despite a lengthy wall extending along part of the 945-mile border and efforts by the Iranian army to stop the smugglers. The drugs enter Iran along trails used by smugglers for centuries, carried by truck, car, motorbikes, on foot and in caravans of camels. Iran has lost an estimated 4,000 soldiers in battles with smugglers in the last decade and its jails are filled with buyers, sellers and users of opium, hashish and heroin.

---

5. A Metaphor for War—The Battle of Marjah

A war is neither won nor lost in a single battle. But three days of intense fighting in mid-May can be seen as a demonstration of the new counter-narcotics strategy and a metaphor for the larger war in Afghanistan.

An analysis of the battle of Marjah early this summer crystallizes the dilemma embodied in the administration's new strategy: The operational tactics were extremely effective in disrupting both the Taliban and drug traffickers, but the results demonstrated that the U.S. and ISAF forces face a formidable enemy that will not be defeated without a substantial increase in military and civilian resources.

The village of Marjah in southern Afghanistan has long been an insurgent stronghold and bustling hub of drug smuggling about 15 miles southwest of Lashkar Gah, the capital of poppy-rich Helmand Province. The Taliban felt safe gathering and training there, and they often stored weapons and explosives in the village bazaars.

In late April 2009, U.S. military intelligence picked up information that a spectacular attack on Lashkar Gah had been ordered by the Taliban's leadership in exile, safely ensconced across the border in Quetta, Pakistan. The target appeared to be Gulab Mangal, the new governor who was having some success persuading farmers to turn away from poppy to other crops.

Marjah was designated by the Taliban leadership as the staging ground for the attack, and fighters from across Afghanistan and as far away as Waziristan in Pakistan began filtering into the village. Along with the usual arsenal of AK-47s, grenade launchers and explosives, they towed in four Soviet-era anti-aircraft guns, a sign the operation was going to be big.

As the contingent grew, the Taliban bosses in Quetta pressed to launch the attack. But the local commanders insisted on delaying because many of their fighters were working in the fields, harvesting the last of the poppy crop. "We still have poppies in the field," one commander said in a conversation picked up by military intelligence. "We do it when we come out."

A Surprise Attack

As Afghan and U.S. troops prepared for their surprise assault on Lashkar Gah, an opportune distraction occurred. British forces killed a local tribal leader in an unrelated skirmish, causing the Taliban to postpone the attack for three days of funeral services for the leader, who had ties to the insurgency. The Taliban fighters were in the midst of the second night of mourning on May 19 when they heard the prodigious thumping of a fleet of military helicopters approaching. Within minutes, the night sky was ablaze with the first shots in what would become a fierce three-day firefight on a deadly piece of ground not far from the border with Pakistan.

The composition of the coalition force that attacked Marjah says a lot about how far we have come in Afghanistan. Eighty percent of the 216 troops were American-trained commandos from the Afghan National Army. They were augmented by U.S. Special Forces and NATO soldiers. The presence of a 12-man DEA paramilitary team also reflected a new level of cooperation between the military and law enforcement; the DEA was there to identify the drugs and processing chemicals that intelligence had said were hidden in the local bazaars.

After three days of intense fighting, about 60 militants lay dead and coalition forces had seized roughly 100 tons of heroin, hashish, opium paste, poppy seeds and precursor chemicals used to turn opium into heroin. The troops also uncovered a cache of weapons, suicide belts and explosives as well as sophisticated communications equipment inside the opium bazaar, indicating that the Taliban had used it as a command center.

The haul was dragged into a huge pile on the outskirts of the town and plans were made to have a jet fly over and bomb the material. But a senior U.S. military officer said a targeting officer determined that the resulting explosion would be the equivalent of an 80,000-pound bomb, which would have wiped out everything in a wide swath. So the cache was divided into smaller piles and blown up from the ground.

A potentially bigger prize eluded the troops. The Taliban had defended a second bazaar deeper within Marjah with ferocity. The American general who commanded the attack told the committee staff that he sought air support and reinforcements from coalition command in Kabul and the U.S. military in Kandahar to go after the second bazaar, but he was told that there was no help available. So the coalition troops pulled back and their commanders watched the next day via aerial surveillance as trucks left the untouched bazaar, carrying away whatever weapons and drugs the Taliban had fought so hard to defend.

The Pluses and Minuses of Marjah

There is much to praise in the battle of Marjah, not least the performance of Afghan commandos. Creating a credible national army and police force is central to any exit strategy. In addition, the DEA agents helped identify vast quantities of drugs and chemicals, an example of overdue cooperation between the military and law enforcement. Finally, along with stopping a Taliban attack, the outcome hit the insurgency in the pocket book—the supply of opium and heroin dropped noticeably in the weeks that followed, which meant less money for the militants.

"Marjah was a nexus target," said David Wright, a senior European Union official training Afghan counter-narcotics police in Helmand Province. "A year ago, they wouldn't have done that operation."

There is reason for concern, too. The inability to muster the resources to complete the attack is troubling, both with regard to the specific battle and to the larger war. The Taliban and its various offshoots have proven to be a resourceful enemy, capable of retreating and regrouping. In fact, a 700-strong contingent of British, Danish and Afghan troops had executed a similar attack on Marjah just two months earlier and the Taliban had returned almost overnight.

Plus, there is plenty more heroin in the pipeline—while eradication efforts have reduced the planted acreage in the poppy centers of southern Afghanistan, yields there are up sharply because farmers have used fertilizer smuggled in from Pakistan. Then there is the matter of who owns the drugs destroyed in Marjah. In a different place, the DEA would be unraveling a trail to the owner. But the DEA does not have a single agent in Helmand Province and investigative efforts are nonexistent so far, though U.S. military and law enforcement officials say there is strong evidence the drugs belonged to a former police chief now living in Kabul.

At least as serious in the long term, there are not enough civilian resources yet in Helmand and Kandahar provinces to come in behind the troops to provide the economic development required to consolidate any future military gains and achieve something resembling a lasting victory.

Despite commitments, the State Department and U.S. Agency for International Development have not added the new staff that was promised since the Marines arrived earlier this summer, according to interviews and published accounts.

Similarly, while Canadian, Dutch and British soldiers have shouldered a heavy burden and sustained substantial casualties in southern Afghanistan, many European Union countries have failed to fulfill pledges to provide staff for non-military functions. For example, the EU committed to provide 400 people to train Afghan police last year, but the actual number is under 200, according to the European Council on Foreign Relations. Now there are concerns that troops and civilians may be reduced in the future because the war is unpopular in most European countries as well as Canada.

---

6. The Missing Civilian Component

The counter-insurgency doctrine laid out in the Army and Marine Corps Counterinsurgency Field Manual specifies that the military can provide 20 percent of the solution, but the civilian side must provide the remaining 80 percent.

President Obama implicitly recognized the importance of the civilian contribution when he divided his plan for Afghanistan into four tasks: (1) disrupt the insurgent networks capable of planning attacks against the U.S. and its allies; (2) promote a more accountable and effective Afghan Government; (3) build the Afghan military and police to a level of self sufficiency; and (4) persuade NATO allies and other countries to contribute under the auspices of the United Nations. This course of action recognizes that the surge in military force needs to be synthesized with a strategic program that protects the Afghan population and provides an alternative not just to poppy cultivation but to the Taliban and its insurgent allies.

None of these tasks can be accomplished easily, and none without the support of the Afghan people. Most Afghans welcomed U.S. troops when they arrived and few want a return of the Taliban's harsh rule. But polls show a sharp drop in support for the United States as civilian casualties and violence have increased, the foreigners have stayed longer than expected and economic development has lagged. Similarly, the faith of Afghans in their own government has plunged, primarily because of what they see as its

354

inability to provide security and the unprecedented spread of corruption. A poll earlier this year by ABC-TV and the BBC found that 85 percent of Afghans call government corruption a problem; 63 percent say it is a big problem.

A Verdict on Kabul and Washington

On August 20, Afghans will go to the polls for presidential and provincial elections. Many people see the vote as a referendum on the legitimacy of the Karzai Government, which has been so thoroughly penetrated by the drug economy that Secretary of State Hillary Clinton referred to Afghanistan as a "narco-state" in her confirmation testimony in January, a tough assessment echoed by some and disputed by others. For many voters, their decision to vote for Karzai will rest in good part on whether they blame or credit Karzai and the international community for levels of poppy cultivation.

But the vote is also a referendum on the failure of the United States and its allies to provide the security and economic development required to build a stable country. Only now are the necessary resources being discussed in Washington and other capitals of NATO nations—and the answers are not all positive yet.

The administration is dramatically shifting gears on counter-narcotics by phasing out eradication in favor of promoting alternative crops and agriculture development. For the first time, the United States will have an agriculture strategy for Afghanistan. While this strategy is still being finalized by Ambassador Holbrooke's team and Secretary of Agriculture Tom Vilsack and his experts, it will focus on increasing agricultural productivity, regenerating the agribusiness sector, rehabilitating watersheds and irrigation systems, and building capacity in the Afghan agriculture ministry. The U.S. Department of Agriculture plans to increase its staffing to 64 by early 2010, up from the 3 in 2003 and 14 in 2009.

The new agriculture officers will be part of an additional 450 civilians being deployed to Afghanistan in the coming months. But already there are questions about whether the new people will have the right skills to carry out the development strategy and whether they will be dispatched to the often-unsafe rural areas where the work must be done—and whether 450 more will be even close to enough. In late June, the U.S. embassy in Kabul asked the State Department to authorize another 350 civilian slots for Afghanistan. While there is recognition among policymakers that the war effort in Afghanistan has been under-resourced for years and will require intensive resources over the next few years to achieve the President's goals, scaling up the commitment without changing the fundamentals of how the money is spent will achieve little beyond expanding the U.S. presence and creating new vulnerabilities.

"The mission is 20 percent military, 80 percent civilian, and the civilian side is behind," said John Nagl, a retired army lieutenant colonel and a co-author of the counter-insurgency field manual who is now president of the Center for New American Security in Washington, D.C.

Two Bright Spots

There are some bright spots on the development landscape. In Helmand Province, Governor Mangal has proven to be among a new breed of inde-pendent-minded governors, praised for his efforts to eradicate poppy fields and persuade farmers to grow other crops. Last planting season, he handed out free wheat seeds to promote the kinds of alternative crops that once made the province the bread basket of Afghanistan. This fall, he plans to add more crops to his giveaway list.

Improving access to crops like wheat, grapes, pomegranates and apples and developing a legitimate rural economy are part of the civilian-led effort to push poppy farming out of the prime growing area along the Helmand River Valley and similar fertile areas across the country. Most experts said that poppy cultivation will never be eradicated completely in Afghanistan. A more realistic goal is to force poppy fields into the marginal areas.

In another positive development, the Afghan Government's National Sol-idarity Program has helped villages across the country identify, plan and manage development projects, from digging wells to educating farmers. Despite the poor security environment, the program even operates in Hel-mand Province, where its well-regarded leader, Mohammed Ehsan Zia, the minister of Rural Rehabilitation and Development, said the early success "is testimony to the honesty and courage of the rural people of Afghanistan."

There are no easy answers to ridding Afghanistan of drug trafficking, and none but the most optimistic believe the country will ever be free of poppy cultivation. The goal is to build an agricultural economy for the long term that will weaken the power of the drug lords and halt or at least reduce the flow of money to insurgents. Much work remains to integrate these approaches into the broader security and development framework so that counter-narcotics efforts and economic development are not artificially sep-arated. Fundamentally, this means rethinking how we measure success on counter-narcotics efforts, shifting away from the sole goal of reducing opium poppy cultivation to avoid the risk of undermining longer-term development and security in Afghanistan.

_____

7. RECOMMENDATIONS FOR AFGHANISTAN

Accepting that Afghanistan requires a greater commitment of U.S. troops and civilians means that the public should understand the sacrifices that will be required in the coming years.

The deterioration of the security situation in Afghanistan is conspicuous. Forty-two American soldiers and Marines died in July, the highest since the start of the war, and the casualties were not just associated with the Marine push into Helmand Province. Coalition troops from Britain, Canada and other NATO allies also suffered their highest death toll since 2001. More powerful improvised explosive devices are appearing and in some cases the Taliban has demonstrated a new ability to launch complex attacks.

The coming months will test the administration's deepening involvement, its new strategy on counter-narcotics specifically and its counter-insurgency effort in general. Some observers fear that the moment for reversing the tide in Afghanistan has passed and even a narrow victory will remain out of reach, despite the larger American footprint. Others see promise in the commitment of additional resources and the recognition that success requires providing Afghans with the security and assistance that will allow them to find their own way to the future. None of the civilian officials or military officers interviewed in Afghanistan and elsewhere expected substantial progress in the short term. They talked in terms of years—two, five and 10.

Recommendations:

1. Congress and the administration should join in efforts to promote a national debate that will provide the public with a clear understanding of the commitment required in Afghanistan and Pakistan. The debate should articulate the administration's goals, the costs of meeting these goals and the consequences for failing to do so.

2. Given the significance of the new counter-narcotics strategy, the administration should provide Congress with a written

description of that policy and a clear road map for how it will be integrated with the other components of the counter-insurgency, including the development of alternative crops for Afghan farmers.

3. As requested by Congress two years ago, the administration should develop a clear system of metrics to assess progress in Afghanistan on counter-narcotics, corruption, security and economic development. These metrics should reflect both quantitative and qualitative indicators and both near-term and long-term goals.

4. The Department of State should pursue enhanced cooperation with Afghanistan's neighbors to identify and support regional counter-narcotics efforts and better understand the important linkages and flows of drugs, money, and people from Afghanistan to Pakistan, Tajikistan, Kyrgyzstan, Uzbekistan, Turkmenistan, and Iran. In particular, Ambassador Holbrooke should lead efforts to travel to Central Asia to strengthen cooperation on Afghanistan and better link U.S. policy towards Central Asia with our strategy in Afghanistan.

5. Sending more civilians to Afghanistan should be part of the national debate. But as the administration prepares to deploy the additional 450 civilians already committed to going, serious efforts should be made to match civilian expertise in key districts across the country and not just staff up Embassy Kabul or forward operating bases. Efforts should be made to recruit civilians with expertise in agriculture, development, and other technical skills that can be adapted to needs in Afghanistan, including recruiting civilian expertise from Afghanistan's neighbors, which would be more cost-effective and bring people who know the region, climate, language, and soil.

APPENDIX

1. A Discussion of Alternative Crops—Poppy v. Wheat

A realistic goal for the coalition and Afghan forces is to push poppy cultivation out of the fertile areas along the Helmand River into the periphery, into the desert. It won't stop cultivation completely, but it will make the job much harder and costlier because those who still want to grow poppies will be restricted to arid areas where they will have to dig wells 90 to 100 feet for water. The key here is not to reduce cultivation levels in absolute terms, but to focus on delivering security, governance, and development to major population centers. But that policy will only work in the long term if farmers have access to substitute crops and sufficient security to grow them and get them to market. "Farmers need to earn a living," said a U.S. Army officer in Kandahar. "We don't want them putting out IEDs or shooting at us."

One alternative that has not been widely used in Afghanistan is the concept of cultivating various crops with short growing seasons. For example, if a farmer rotates crops with different harvest times on the same plot of land, the farmer will make more money than he otherwise would have with poppy, and he will not mortgage his future to the Taliban. Onions, tomatoes, and cucumbers are examples of crops with short growing seasons. Growing these crops while planting tree fruits for the long term can produce current income to replace poppy revenue.

Wheat, touted as the best way to transition poppy farmers away from opium, is neither a panacea nor good predictor for whether farmers will make a permanent shift. Wheat prices are volatile and farmers are likely to switch back to poppy when wheat prices fall or when prolonged droughts damage wheat crops. With prices high, farmers cultivate wheat to eat and sell. But when prices fall, farmers grow poppy and buy higher-quality Pakistani wheat to eat, defeating the purpose of transitioning to wheat. Furthermore, the lack of security on Afghanistan's roads keeps transportation costs artificially high, making wheat more expensive than poppy to get to market.

Despite the fact that the current balance is tipped in favor of poppy, Afghanistan will be a net exporter of wheat in 2009 for the first time in 30 years. While Afghan and U.S. officials justifiably tout the success, some experts caution that it may be an anomaly more attributable to environmental and economic factors than to eradication efforts. "As soon as wheat prices fall again—and they will—wheat farmers will revert to poppy," said David Mansfield of the Afghanistan Research and Evaluation Unit, who has spent 12 consecutive years working in Afghanistan.

WHY POPPY?

Why would Afghan farmers risk legal consequences and eradication of their crops by growing poppy?

- Poppy is 40 percent more profitable than wheat, on average.
- Poppy has a shorter cultivation time than wheat and is harvested earlier in the season. The shorter growing time allows farmers to grow maize after the poppy crop is finished.
- Poppy is nearly weather-resistant. It can withstand drought and poor soil, and few insects can destroy a season's harvest.
- Once refined, opium does not need refrigeration, it does not expire, it does not require safe handling or specialized transportation, and it sells quickly.
- The Taliban provide loans to farmers to buy poppy seeds in the marketplace.
- The Taliban provide capital for poppy farmers by pre-paying for a portion of the crop. The Taliban also provides farmers with security to guard their investment.

That is precisely why alternative crops are so necessary. Many tribal elders remember when Afghans could feed themselves. To do so again, they need roads, power, and water. The first step toward that goal, now that the Marines have taken up what their commander says is long-term residence in Helmand Province, is to bring in teams from the U.S. Department of Agriculture to help identify what crops to grow and where. The United States should be prepared to provide assistance to farmers for several years until pomegranate orchards and vineyards mature into cash-producing alternatives to poppy. In addition, the administration needs to push hard to reach agreement in negotiations between Pakistan and Afghanistan that would open a route for Afghan farmers to get their products to the growing middle-class market in India.

Faced with a dangerous and costly problem, it is human nature to look for a panacea. Some have advocated using Afghanistan's flourishing poppy fields to produce medicines such as morphine and codeine, which are high-demand painkillers in a growing global market. Legal opium production is permitted under the United Nations Single Convention on Narcotic Drugs and other international drug treaties. Turkey produces 50 percent of the world's legal opium and India produces another 30 percent. The governments process all opium into paste; the paste is then either refined or sold to international pharmaceutical companies. Violators who divert poppy to illegal drugs face harsh penalties in both countries. But these two legal opium poppy production regimes work only because they are built on trust and on the rule of law, important tenets which are missing in Afghanistan.

U.S. officials say that the Afghan opium industry would be impossible to monitor because of the country's harsh landscape, the absence of the rule of law, and pervasive corruption. In addition, the country lacks the type of clean facilities required to produce medical-grade opiates. Finally, any new Afghan opium on the legal market would have a negative impact on prices in an industry where there is already little profit.

Besides squeezing existing producers like Turkey and India, the cultivation of medical opium in Afghanistan would have a negative impact on prices of illicit opium, with opium farmers competing against each other to produce enough opium poppy to supply both the legal and illegal industries. The incentive would be for farmers to grow as much poppy as possible on whatever land was available.

―――――――――

2. The Intricacies of Hawala—The Road to Nowhere

Following the money is a time-tested means of assembling criminal cases against drug traffickers and corrupt government officials, but that task is probably harder in Afghanistan than anywhere in the world because of the ancient and secretive system called hawala.

The Arabic term for "transfer," hawala at its most basic interpretation means transferring value and money from one place to another through money exchangers known as hawaladars. Typically, a hawaladar receives money, say $5,000, from a customer who wants to transfer the funds to someone in another location. The customer pays a small fee and receives a numerical code written on a hawala slip. The hawaladar contacts his counterpart in the other location and instructs him to pay $5,000 to someone who will come in with the numerical code. After receiving the code from the original customer, the recipient goes to the hawaladar, presents the code and gets the $5,000. The hawala dealer who took the initial $5,000 owes that amount to his counterpart. Accounts are settled through additional transactions, commodity exchanges and normal banking services.

Hawala networks span countries and continents and are used by millions of people for legitimate transactions. The most common involve workers in foreign countries like Saudi Arabia or the United Arab Emirates sending money home to families in Afghanistan, India, Pakistan or the Philippines. Dealers charge a small commission on each transaction and often profit from currency exchange rates.

The system is most often associated in the Western public's mind with more notorious customers like Osama bin Laden, who used the hawala networks in Pakistan, Dubai and throughout the Middle East to transfer funds and store money, according to the 9/11 Commission Report.

Afghanistan is a natural place for hawala. A majority of business is conducted in cash and the State Department estimates that 80 to 90 percent of all financial transfers are made through hawala. In Kabul, the hawaladars congregate in a specific neighborhood along the banks of the Kabul River, not far from the gold and gem dealers. During the Soviet and Taliban eras, the hawaladars fully replaced the formal banking system. Today, the country has only 15 commercial banks and few people have bank accounts because of illiteracy, the cost of bank transactions and the small footprint of traditional banking. As a result, hawaladars are still used by humanitarian and development organizations to move money to rural areas outside the reach of the country's fledgling banking system.

Convenience, security and secrecy make hawala the method of choice for Afghanistan's drug traffickers to move and disguise profits with little or no paper trail. In the basic transaction, the traffickers receive payments for drugs from middlemen and buyers in other countries and turnaround and launder the money by transferring it to hawaladars in places like Dubai, where the drug lords and their nominees use the cash to buy real estate and commodities.

United Nations Office on Drugs and Crime (UNODC) officials in Kabul said they have inspected records of drug-related transactions involving $1 million and recently saw evidence of a $15 million transfer using hawala. In some cases, the officials described seeing major transactions in which heroin or opium were used as collateral for payments.

The existence of the written records contradicts the widespread misconception that hawala is paperless. While recordkeeping is far from formalized, most hawaladars maintain carefully coded logs of transactions as part of the settlement process. Those handling dirty money tend to be more secretive, destroying even rudimentary records once transactions are completed or avoiding any record of the criminal deals. "Not surprisingly, transfers made on behalf of drug traffickers tend to be kept more discreet, either by maintaining very simple notes locked in a safe, or by not keeping a record at all," scholar Edwina A. Thompson wrote in her study, *The Nexus of Drug Trafficking and Hawala in Afghanistan*. One dealer told Thompson that he kept the records of his shop's drug-related transfers on his son's computer at home.

Family and tribal ties guarantee that the process works smoothly and provide another layer of secrecy. Intermarriages among hawaladar families in Afghanistan are common because they cement trust between dealers. Brothers and cousins also tend to operate in the same system to provide broader coverage of financial centers in the Mideast, Europe and the United States. A report by Samuel Maimbo of the World Bank described a dealer in the Afghan city of Jalalabad, which lies on a major smuggling route for drugs, who operated with a brother in Kabul, a cousin in the western Afghan commercial hub of Herat and another brother who ran a hawala in Melbourne, Australia. The Jalalabad hawaladar also worked with affiliated dealers in Tokyo, London, Peshawar and Dubai.

Close Knit and Close Mouthed

The close-knit nature of the system, the absence of effective regulation and the ingrained secrecy combine to make transactions conducted through hawala almost impossible to track. Officials in Afghanistan and the United Arab Emirates, which include Dubai, repeatedly said they had no idea how much money moves through the informal exchange system. A U.S. intelligence official in the region said it was almost impossible to penetrate hawala networks, explaining that the family nature of the businesses made it difficult to get inside cooperation. He said records seized from the occasional raid were usually too fragmentary to provide clues to the beneficiaries of transactions.

No one knows how many hawaladars exist in Afghanistan. Thompson estimated in 2005 that there were 900 significant hawaladars in the entire country and others have estimated that 50 or so dealers in Kabul and Kandahar account for the bulk of the drug transactions. There are countless smaller operators in cities and villages across the country and most of them mix drug money with legitimate transactions.

The Afghan Government has registered about 125 of Kabul's hawala dealers, but many in the capital are unregistered and progress has been slow elsewhere. A diplomat described a conversation in which he urged an official of the Afghan Central Bank to register dealers outside Kabul. "They're everywhere," the official replied. "I can't do that."

The Central Bank official's attitude reflects the difficulty in developing a system of banking supervision and money controls in Afghanistan. An antimoney laundering law was adopted in 2004 and followed with a statute allowing for the seizure of assets in criminal cases. Prosecutors and bank examiners have been trained by the U.S. and others to spot suspicious transactions and investigate money laundering cases. But efforts have been plagued by inadequate staffing and a sense that drug lords and their accomplices are outside the reach of the law, according to U.S. and foreign officials.

Statistics tell the sorry story: In a country awash with drug money, no one was prosecuted for money laundering or terrorist financing in 2008 in Afghanistan and no attempts were made to seize or freeze assets. "While efforts continue to strengthen police and customs forces, there remain few resources, limited capacity, little expertise and insufficient political will to seriously combat financial crimes," the State Department said in a blunt report issued in February.

A Regional Perspective on the Money Flow

The lack of progress has caused some financial-crimes experts in the region to suggest focusing outside Afghanistan to try to stop the flow of illicit proceeds both into and out of the country. The first place mentioned by almost everyone in the know is Dubai, the city-state on the Persian Gulf in the United Arab Emirates, just a three-hour flight from Kabul.

"It's quite open among the diaspora of Afghans and hawaladars that the favorite hidey hole for money is Dubai," said a senior UN official in Kabul. "It would be better to target Dubai because it cares more about its financial system."

Dubai has worked hard to polish its image as the Middle East's leading financial center. Its star exhibit is the Dubai International Finance Center, a free-trade zone open to foreign-owned banks and financial firms. The center resembles an offshore banking haven in the midst of a freewheeling city-state. It sits on 110 acres amidst Dubai's seemingly endless parade of skyscrapers and malls and runs its own regulatory and judicial system. Most of the auditors and regulators are drawn from the U.K., Australia and the United

States and transactions are governed by British and U.S. law. Some of the world's biggest financial institutions, like HSBC and Goldman Sachs, have set up shop in the zone to take advantage of its tax-free status and ready access to the Middle East.

Outside the free-trade zone, however, regulations are more haphazard and efforts to restrict the flow of drug money from Afghanistan and elsewhere are hit and miss, according to American and foreign officials. After the attacks of September 11, 2001, Dubai and others of the seven city-states that comprise the UAE were criticized because terrorists had moved money through the banks and hawala dealers. The Government responded with new financial laws, including one in 2003 requiring hawala dealers to register, and its Central Bank insists that the country has made great strides in instituting tough controls on money and trade.

But there are signs that Dubai—and to a lesser extent the city-state of Sharjah—remains a destination spot for hot money. Earlier this year, the State Department said that narcotics traffickers were increasingly attracted to Dubai and other trade and financial centers in the UAE. The International Monetary Fund also raised concerns, recommending that UAE laws be amended to block loopholes and match international standards and that it should increase the resources devoted to enforcing financial laws.

In addition, the Financial Action Task Force, a Paris-based intergovernmental body that develops and promotes policies to combat money laundering and terrorist financing, criticized the UAE for failing to exercise regulatory controls over hawala dealers despite its law. Registration is voluntary and there are no penalties for dealers who refuse to register.

Abdulrahim Moammed Al Awadi, the head of the anti-money laundering at the Central Bank in Abu Dhabi, told the committee staff that the UAE has instituted tough measures throughout its financial sector. In a power-point presentation, he listed dozens of international agreements and UAE laws implemented to clean up the country's financial system.

One of the laws that Awadi touts was the first-ever law to register and regulate hawala dealers. So far, he said, the country has more than 300 licensed hawaladars who are required to keep complete records, including official identification documents for customers, and alert the authorities to suspicious transactions. Hawala is particularly popular in Dubai and other Gulf states because of the high percentage of low-paid, foreign workers who use the system to send remittances home; in Dubai, for instance, 85 percent of the population is foreign workers.

Awadi said that registration and reporting are voluntary for the dealers and he declined to provide the committee staff with a list of registered hawaladars. He defended the registration system and said the Central Bank had been stung by the criticism by the Financial Action Task Force. As a result, Awadi said the Government was debating whether to abandon its efforts to regulate the informal sector.

Hawala is not the only way to move cash quietly to and from Dubai. UAE law enforcement authorities have intercepted couriers arriving at Dubai's huge international airport from Afghanistan with millions of dollars in suitcases. But U.S. officials said the general rule is that couriers are simply required to declare the cash and allowed to move on, without seizing suspected illicit cash or creating a database of couriers for intelligence purposes. U.S. law enforcement agencies proposed a training program to teach inspectors at Dubai airport to spot suspicious couriers, but the effort was blocked by the Central Bank.

"We don't know, once the money comes into Dubai, where it goes," said an official at the U.S. embassy.

The United States has plans to increase its resources in the UAE. The DEA is considering bumping up the number of agents in Dubai from two to 10 as part of a new regional approach to drug trafficking and money laundering. As in Afghanistan, however, the CIA is not playing an active role investigating the money trail. "Ninety percent of our intelligence resources are devoted to counter-terrorism, counter-intelligence and counter-proliferation," complained an official at the U.S. embassy in Abu Dhabi.

Regulating the movement of money throughout the region, from Afghanistan and the UAE to Pakistan and Europe, should be a critical element of the strategy to choke off the funds going to the insurgency in Afghanistan and to corrupt officials there who undermine the efforts of international agencies, governments and good Afghans to build a stable and secure country. The harder it is to make money from drugs in Afghanistan, the more likely the ties can be broken to the Taliban and other militant organizations.

TORA BORA REVISITED: HOW WE FAILED TO GET BIN LADEN AND WHY IT MATTERS

30 NOVEMBER 2009

TORA BORA REVISITED: HOW WE FAILED TO GET BIN LADEN AND WHY IT MATTERS TODAY

A Report To Members

OF THE

COMMITTEE ON FOREIGN RELATIONS

UNITED STATES SENATE

John F. Kerry, Chairman

ONE HUNDRED ELEVENTH CONGRESS

FIRST SESSION

NOVEMBER 30, 2009

Printed for the use of the Committee on Foreign Relations

Available via World Wide Web: http://www.gpoaccess.gov/congress/
index.html

U.S. GOVERNMENT PRINTING OFFICE

??–??? PDF   WASHINGTON : 2009

For sale by the Superintendent of Documents, U.S. Government Printing Office
Internet: bookstore.gpo.gov   Phone: toll free (866) 512–1800; DC area (202) 512–1800
Fax: (202) 512–2104   Mail: Stop IDCC, Washington, DC 20402–0001

COMMITTEE ON FOREIGN RELATIONS

JOHN F. KERRY, Massachusetts, *Chairman*

CHRISTOPHER J. DODD, Connecticut
RUSSELL D. FEINGOLD, Wisconsin
BARBARA BOXER, California
ROBERT MENENDEZ, New Jersey
BENJAMIN L. CARDIN, Maryland
ROBERT P. CASEY, JR., Pennsylvania
JIM WEBB, Virginia
JEANNE SHAHEEN, New Hampshire
EDWARD E. KAUFMAN, Delaware
KIRSTEN E. GILLIBRAND, New York

RICHARD G. LUGAR, Indiana
BOB CORKER, Tennessee
JOHNNY ISAKSON, Georgia
JAMES E. RISCH, Idaho
JIM DeMINT, South Carolina
JOHN BARRASSO, Wyoming
ROGER F. WICKER, Mississippi
JAMES M. INHOF, Oklahoma

DAVID McKean, *Staff Director*
KENNETH A. MYERS, JR., *Republican Staff Director*

CONTENTS

APPENDIXES

LETTER OF TRANSMITTAL

UNITED STATES SENATE,
COMMITTEE ON FOREIGN RELATIONS,
Washington, DC, November 30, 2009.

DEAR COLLEAGUE: This report by the Committee majority staff is part of our continuing examination of the conflict in Afghanistan. When we went to war less than a month after the attacks of September 11, the objective was to destroy Al Qaeda and kill or capture its leader, Osama bin Laden, and other senior figures in the terrorist group and the Taliban, which had hosted them. Today, more than eight years later, we find ourselves fighting an increasingly lethal insurgency in Afghanistan and neighboring Pakistan that is led by many of those same extremists. Our inability to finish the job in late 2001 has contributed to a conflict today that endangers not just our troops and those of our allies, but the stability of a volatile and vital region. This report relies on new and existing information to explore the consequences of the failure to eliminate bin Laden and other extremist leaders in the hope that we can learn from the mistakes of the past.

Sincerely,

JOHN F. KERRY,
Chairman.

TORA BORA REVISITED: HOW WE FAILED TO GET BIN LADEN AND WHY IT MATTERS TODAY

EXECUTIVE SUMMARY

On October 7, 2001, U.S. aircraft began bombing the training bases and strongholds of Al Qaeda and the ruling Taliban across Afghanistan. The leaders who sent murderers to attack the World Trade Center and the Pentagon less than a month earlier and the rogue government that provided them sanctuary were running for their lives. President George W. Bush's expression of America's desire to get Osama bin Laden "dead or alive" seemed about to come true.

Two months later, American civilian and military leaders celebrated what they viewed as a lasting victory with the selection of Hamid Karzai as the country's new hand-picked leader. The war had been conceived as a swift campaign with a single objective: defeat the Taliban and destroy Al Qaeda by capturing or killing bin Laden and other key leaders. A unique combination of airpower, Central Intelligence Agency and special operations forces teams and indigenous allies had swept the Taliban from power and ousted Al Qaeda from its safe haven while keeping American deaths to a minimum. But even in the initial glow, there were concerns: The mission had failed to capture or kill bin Laden.

Removing the Al Qaeda leader from the battlefield eight years ago would not have eliminated the worldwide extremist threat. But the decisions that opened the door for his escape to Pakistan allowed bin Laden to emerge as a potent symbolic figure who continues to attract a steady flow of money and inspire fanatics worldwide. The failure to finish the job represents a lost opportunity that forever altered the course of the conflict in Afghanistan and the future of international terrorism, leaving the American people more vulnerable to terrorism, laying the foundation for today's protracted Afghan insurgency and inflaming the internal strife now endangering Pakistan. Al Qaeda shifted its locus across the border into Pakistan, where it has trained extremists linked to numerous plots, including the July 2005 transit bombings in London and two recent aborted attacks involving people living in the United States. The terrorist group's resurgence in Pakistan has coincided with the rising violence orchestrated in Afghanistan by the Taliban, whose leaders also escaped only to re-emerge to direct today's increasingly lethal Afghan insurgency.

This failure and its enormous consequences were not inevitable. By early December 2001, Bin Laden's world had shrunk to a complex of caves and tunnels carved into a mountainous section of eastern Afghanistan known as Tora Bora. Cornered in some of the most forbidding terrain on earth, he and several hundred of his men, the largest concentration of Al Qaeda fighters of the war, endured relentless pounding by American aircraft, as many as 100 air strikes a day. One 15,000-pound bomb, so huge it had to be rolled out the back of a C-130 cargo plane, shook the mountains for miles. It seemed only a matter of time before U.S. troops and their Afghan allies overran the remnants of Al Qaeda hunkered down in the thin, cold air at 14,000 feet.

Bin Laden expected to die. His last will and testament, written on December 14, reflected his fatalism. "Allah commended to us that when death approaches any of us that we make a bequest to parents and next of kin and to Muslims as a whole," he wrote, according to a copy of the will that surfaced later and is regarded as authentic. "Allah bears witness that the love of jihad and death in the cause of Allah has dominated my life and the verses of the sword permeated every cell in my heart, 'and fight the pagans all together as they fight you all together.' How many times did I wake up to find myself reciting this holy verse!" He instructed his wives not to remarry and apologized to his children for devoting himself to jihad.

But the Al Qaeda leader would live to fight another day. Fewer than 100 American commandos were on the scene with their Afghan allies and calls for reinforcements to launch an assault were rejected. Requests were also turned down for U.S. troops to block the mountain paths leading to sanctuary a few miles away in Pakistan. The vast array of American military power, from sniper teams to the most mobile divisions of the Marine Corps and the Army, was kept on the sidelines. Instead, the U.S. command chose to rely on airstrikes and untrained Afghan militias to attack bin Laden and on Pakistan's loosely organized Frontier Corps to seal his escape routes. On or around December 16, two days after writing his will, bin Laden and an entourage of bodyguards walked unmolested out of Tora Bora and disappeared into Pakistan's unregulated tribal area. Most analysts say he is still there today.

The decision not to deploy American forces to go after bin Laden or block his escape was made by Secretary of Defense Donald Rumsfeld and his top commander, Gen. Tommy Franks, the architects of the unconventional Afghan battle plan known as Operation Enduring Freedom. Rumsfeld said at the time that he was concerned that too many U.S. troops in Afghanistan would create an anti-American backlash and fuel a widespread insurgency. Reversing the recent American military orthodoxy known as the Powell doctrine, the Afghan model emphasized minimizing the U.S. presence by relying on small, highly mobile teams of special operations troops and CIA paramilitary operatives working with the Afghan opposition. Even when his own commanders and senior intelligence officials in Afghanistan and Washington argued for dispatching more U.S. troops, Franks refused to deviate from the plan.

There were enough U.S. troops in or near Afghanistan to execute the classic sweep-and-block maneuver required to attack bin Laden and try to prevent his escape. It would have been a dangerous fight across treacherous terrain, and the injection of more U.S. troops and the resulting casualties would have contradicted the risk-averse, "light footprint" model formulated by Rumsfeld and Franks. But commanders on the scene and elsewhere in Afghanistan argued that the risks were worth the reward.

After bin Laden's escape, some military and intelligence analysts and the press criticized the Pentagon's failure to mount a full-scale attack despite the tough rhetoric by President Bush. Franks, Vice President Dick Cheney and others defended the decision, arguing that the intelligence was inconclusive about the Al Qaeda leader's location. But the review of existing literature, unclassified government records and interviews with central participants underlying this report removes any lingering doubts and makes it clear that Osama bin Laden was within our grasp at Tora Bora.

For example, the CIA and Delta Force commanders who spent three weeks at Tora Bora as well as other intelligence and military sources are certain he was there. Franks' second-in-command during the war, retired Lt. Gen. Michael DeLong, wrote in his autobiography that bin Laden was "definitely there when we hit the caves"—a statement he retracted when the failure became a political issue. Most authoritatively, the official history of the U.S. Special Operations Command determined that bin Laden was at Tora Bora. "All source reporting corroborated his presence on several days from 9-14 December," said a declassified version of the history, which was based on accounts of commanders and intelligence officials and published without fanfare two years ago.

The reasons behind the failure to capture or kill Osama bin Laden and its lasting consequences are examined over three sections in this report. The first section traces bin Laden's path from southern Afghanistan to the mountains of Tora Bora and lays out new and previous evidence that he was there. The second explores new information behind the decision not to launch an assault. The final section examines the military options that might have led to his capture or death at Tora Bora and the ongoing impact of the failure to bring him back "dead or alive."

1. FLIGHT TO TORA BORA

Whether Osama bin Laden was at Tora Bora in late 2001 has been the topic of heated debate since he escaped Afghanistan to the tribal belt of Pakistan. The evidence is convincing that the Al Qaeda leader was in the mountains of eastern Afghanistan in that critical period. The information comes from U.S. military officers at Tora Bora, from detainees who were in the camps with bin Laden, from the senior CIA officer in Afghanistan at the time, and from the official history of the special operations forces. Based on that evidence, it is clear that the Al Qaeda leader was within reach of U.S. troops three months after the attacks on New York and Washington.

In the middle of August 2001, two Pakistani nuclear scientists sat down in a mud-walled compound on the outskirts of Kandahar in southern Afghanistan, the spiritual and tactical headquarters of Taliban fundamentalists who controlled most of the country. Seated with them were bin Laden and Ayman al-Zawahiri, the Egyptian surgeon who was his chief deputy and strategist. The four men spent two days discussing Al Qaeda's determination to obtain nuclear weapons before bin Laden and Zawahiri abruptly excused themselves and left the compound. Before departing, bin Laden promised the Pakistanis that something momentous was going to happen soon.

American intelligence had already picked up indications that something momentous was coming. George Tenet, who was director of central intelligence at the time, later testified before the 9/11 Commission that the "system was blinking red" from July 2001 until the actual attacks. The first reports of possible attacks on the United States had been picked up in June and the warnings increased steadily from then on. On July 12, Tenet went to Capitol Hill to provide a top-secret briefing for senators about the rising threat of an imminent attack. Only a handful of senators turned up in S-407, the secure conference room in the Capitol, to hear the CIA director warn that he was extremely worried that bin Laden and Al Qaeda were preparing an attack on U.S. soil. Tenet told them the attack was not a question of *if,* but *when.*

Less than a month later, on August 6, President Bush's daily briefing repeated the warning under the ominous headline "Bin Ladin Determined To Strike in US." The text described previous plots carried out by Al Qaeda against American targets overseas and said the FBI had uncovered "patterns of suspicious activity in this country consistent with preparations for hijackings or other types of attacks, including recent surveillance of federal buildings in New York." At the time, President Bush later told the 9/11 Commission that he regarded the warning as historical in nature. The commission's voluminous report said its investigators "found no indication of any further discussion before September 11 among the president and his top advisers of the possibility of a threat of an Al Qaeda attack in the United States."

Bin Laden's movements in the days surrounding September 11 remain sketchy. Some facts have emerged from reputable journalists, U.S. military and intelligence sources and Afghans who said they saw the Al Qaeda leader at various points along his path to Tora Bora. He was spotted in Khost in eastern Afghanistan around September 11. On November 8, he and Zawahiri met in Kabul with Hamid Mir, a respected Pakistani journalist. By then, U.S. special operations forces and Northern Alliance troops were closing in on the Afghan capital. The Al Qaeda leaders had risked the trip to attend a memorial service honoring the Uzbek militant leader Juma Khan Namangani, who had been killed in a U.S. airstrike. Before Kabul fell, bin Laden and Zawahiri traveled five hours east to the ancient trading center of Jalalabad. From there, by all reliable accounts, they went to ground at Tora Bora, one of bin Laden's old haunts from the days of fighting the Soviets in the 1980s.

Tora Bora is a district about 30 miles southeast of Jalalabad. Rather than a single place, the name covers a fortress-like section of the White Mountains that stretches about six miles long and six miles wide across a collection of narrow valleys, snow-covered ridgelines and jagged peaks reaching 14,000 feet. During the 1980s, when he was fighting the Soviets in Afghanistan, bin Laden turned the site into a formidable stronghold. He built a rough road from Jalalabad and brought in heavy equipment to fortify the natural caves and dig new ones. He supervised the excavation of connecting tunnels so fighters could move unseen between locations in the fights against Soviet troops.

After the defeat of the Soviet Union in 1989, bin Laden left Afghanistan and eventually set up the operations of his fledgling terrorist organization in the northeastern African nation of Sudan. After pressure from the United States, Sudan expelled bin Laden in 1996 and he flew with his wives and children to Jalalabad on a chartered jet. Upon his return to Afghanistan, bin Laden began expanding the fortress at Tora Bora, building base camps at higher elevations for himself, his wives and numerous children, and other senior Al Qaeda figures. Some rooms were reported to be concealed 350 feet inside the granite peaks. The mountainsides leading to those upper reaches were steep and pitted with well-built bunkers cloaked in camouflage. In the years that followed, Bin Laden got to know the surrounding geography well from spending hours on long hikes with his children. His familiarity with the worn trails used over the centuries by traders and smugglers to traverse the few miles into Pakistan would serve him well.

The United States rightly anticipated that bin Laden would make his last stand at Tora Bora. The precise dates of his arrival and departure are hard to pin down, but it's clear that U.S. intelligence picked up his trail well before he got there. The CIA had evidence that bin Laden was headed for the mountain redoubt by early November, according to Tenet, the former CIA director. Outside experts like Peter Bergen, the last American to interview bin Laden, estimate that he arrived by the end of November, along with 1,000 to 1,500 hardened fighters and bodyguards. In a television interview on November 29, 2001, Vice President Cheney said he believed the Al Qaeda leader was in the general area of Tora Bora. "He's got a large number of fighters with him probably, a fairly secure personal security force that he has some degree of confidence in, and he'll have to try to leave, that is, he may depart for other territory, but that's not quite as easy as it would have been a few months ago," Cheney said.

The Sheikh Arrives

Bin Laden's presence was more than conjecture. A major with the Army's Delta Force, who is now retired and uses the pen name Dalton Fury, was the senior U.S. military officer at Tora Bora, commanding about 90 special operations troops and support personnel. He and his fellow commandos from the elite and secretive Delta Force arrived in early December, setting up headquarters in a former schoolhouse near the mountains alongside a handful of CIA operatives who were already there. The Americans were there to direct airstrikes on Tora Bora and work with Afghan militias assembled by two local warlords who had been paid by the CIA to help flush out bin Laden and the Al Qaeda contingent. The Delta Force soldiers were disguised to blend in with the Afghan militia, wearing local clothing, growing bushy beards and sometimes carrying the same types of weapons.

Fury recounted his experiences in a book, Kill Bin Laden, which was published in 2008. He expanded on them in interviews with Committee staff. Both the book and the interviews left no doubt that Fury's team knew bin Laden was holed up at Tora Bora and that he was eager to go get him. In the interviews, he explained that Al Qaeda fighters arrayed in the mountains used unsecure radios, which meant their communications were easily intercepted by his team and by a sophisticated listening post a few miles from the mountain. As a result, the Delta Force and CIA operatives had real-time eavesdropping capabilities on Al Qaeda almost from their arrival, allowing them to track movements and gauge the effectiveness of the bombing. Even more valuable, a few days after arriving, one of the CIA operatives picked up a radio from a dead Al Qaeda fighter. The radio gave the Americans a clear channel into the group's communications on the mountain. Bin Laden's voice was often picked up, along with frequent comments about the presence of the man referred to by his followers as "the sheikh."

Fury, who still uses his pen name to protect his identity, said there was no doubt the voice on the radios was bin Laden. "The CIA had a guy with them called Jalal and he was the foremost expert on bin Laden's voice," he said. "He worked on bin Laden's voice for seven years and he knew him better than anyone else in the West. To him, it was very clear that bin Laden was there on the mountain."

Another special operations expert who speaks fluent Arabic and heard the intercepted communications in real time in Afghanistan told the Committee staff that it was clearly bin Laden's voice. He had studied the Al Qaeda leader's speech pattern and word choices before the war and he said he considered the communications a perfect match.

Afghan villagers who were providing food and other supplies for the Al Qaeda fighters at Tora Bora also confirmed bin Laden's presence. Fury said some of the villagers were paid by the CIA for information about precise locations of clusters of fighters that could be targeted for bombing runs. The locals also provided fragmentary information on bin Laden's movements within the Al Qaeda compound, though the outsiders never got near the sheikh. The cooperating villagers were given rudimentary global positioning devices and told to push a button at any spot where they saw significant numbers of fighters or arms caches. When the locals turned in the devices to collect their payments, the GPS coordinates recorded by pushing the buttons were immediately passed along to targeting officers, who programmed the coordinates into bombing runs.

For several days in early December, Fury's special ops troops moved up the mountains in pairs with fighters from the Afghan militias. The Americans used GPS devices and laser range finders to pinpoint caves and pockets of enemy fighters for the bombers. The Delta Force units were unable to hold any high ground because the Afghans insisted on retreating to their base at the bottom of the mountains each night, leaving the Americans alone inside Al Qaeda territory. Still, it was clear from what they could see and what they were hearing in the intercepted conversations that relentless bombing was taking its toll.

On December 9, a C-130 cargo plane dropped a 15,000-pound bomb, known as a Daisy Cutter, on the Tora Bora complex. The weapon had not been used since Vietnam and there were early fears that its impact had not been as great as expected. But later reports confirmed that the bomb struck with massive force. A captured Al Qaeda fighter who was there later told American interrogators that men deep in caves had been vaporized in what he called "a hideous explosion." That day and others, Fury described intercepting radio communications in which Al Qaeda fighters called for the "red truck to move wounded" and frantic pleas from a fighter to his commander, saying "cave too hot, can't reach others."

At one point, the Americans listened on the radio as bin Laden exhorted his men to keep fighting, though he apologized "for getting them trapped . and pounded by American airstrikes." On December 11, Fury said bin Laden was heard on the radio telling his men that he had let them down and it was okay to surrender. Fury hoped the battle was over, but he would soon determine that it was part of an elaborate ruse to allow Al Qaeda fighters to slip out of Tora Bora for Pakistan.

Fury is adamant that bin Laden was at Tora Bora until mid-December. "There is no doubt that bin Laden was in Tora Bora during the fighting," he wrote in Kill Bin Laden. "From alleged sightings to the radio intercepts to news reports from various countries, it was repeatedly confirmed that he was there."

Other Voices, Same Conclusion

Fury was not alone in his conviction. In some cases, confirmation that bin Laden was at Tora Bora has come from detainees at Guantanamo Bay. A "summary of evidence" prepared by the Pentagon for the trial of an unnamed detainee says flatly that the man "assisted in the escape of Osama bin Laden from Tora Bora." The detainee was described as one of bin Laden's commanders in the fight against the Soviets. The document, which was released to the Associated Press in 2005 through a Freedom of Information request, was the first definitive statement by the Pentagon that the master mind of 9/11 was at Tora Bora during the American bombing before slipping away into Pakistan.

Another confirmation came from the senior CIA paramilitary commander in Afghanistan at the time. Gary Berntsen was working at the CIA's counterterrorist center in October 2001 when his boss summoned him to the front office and told him, "Gary, I want you killing the enemy immediately." Berntsen left the next day for Afghanistan, where he assumed leadership of the CIA's paramilitary operation against the Taliban and Al Qaeda. His primary target was bin Laden and he was confident that the Al Qaeda leader would make his last stand at Tora Bora. His suspicions were confirmed when he learned bin Laden's voice had been intercepted there.

From the outset, Berntsen says he was skeptical about relying on Afghan militias "cobbled together at the last minute" to capture or kill the man who ordered the 9/11 attacks. "I'd made it clear in my reports that our Afghan allies were hardly anxious to get at al Qaeda in Tora Bora," he wrote in his own book, Jawbreaker, which was published in late 2005. He also knew that the special operations troops and CIA operatives on the scene were not enough to stop bin Laden from escaping across the mountain passes. In the book, Berntsen uses exclamation points to vent his fears that the most wanted man in the world was about to slip out of our grasp.

"We needed U.S. soldiers on the ground!" he wrote. "I'd sent my request for 800 U.S. Army Rangers and was still waiting for a response. I repeated to anyone at headquarters who would listen: We need Rangers now! The opportunity to get bin Laden and his men is slipping away!!"

At one point, Berntsen recalled an argument at a CIA guesthouse in Kabul with Maj. Gen. Dell Dailey, the commander of U.S. special operations forces in Afghanistan at the time. Berntsen said he renewed his demand that American troops be dispatched to Tora Bora immediately. Following orders from Franks at U.S. Central Command (CentCom) headquarters at MacDill Air Force Base in Tampa, Florida, Dailey refused to deploy U.S. troops, explaining that he feared alienating Afghan allies.

"I don't give a damn about offending our allies!" Berntsen shouted. "I only care about eliminating al Qaeda and delivering bin Laden's head in a box!"

Dailey said the military's position was firm and Berntsen replied, "Screw that!"

For those like Franks, who later maintained that bin Laden might not have been at Tora Bora, Berntsen is respectfully scornful. "We could have ended it all there," he said in an interview.

Berntsen's views were generally shared by Gary Schroen, another senior CIA operative in Afghanistan. Schroen, who had spent years cultivating ties to Afghanistan's opposition elements, bemoaned the reliance on local tribal leaders to go after bin Laden and guard escape routes. "Unfortunately, many of those people proved to be loyal to bin Laden and sympathizers with the Taliban and they allowed the key guys to escape," Schroen, who retired from the CIA, said in a television interview in May 2005. He added that he had no doubt that bin Laden was at Tora Bora.

Franks' second-in-command during the war, General DeLong, was convinced that bin Laden was at Tora Bora. In his memoir, Inside CentCom, DeLong described the massive, three-week bombing campaign aimed at killing Al Qaeda fighters in their caves at Tora Bora. "We were hot on Osama bin Laden's trail," he wrote. "He was definitely there when we hit the caves. Every day during the bombing, Rumsfeld asked me, 'Did we get him? Did we get him?' I would have to answer that we didn't know." The retired general said that intelligence suggested bin Laden had been wounded during the bombings before he escaped to Pakistan, a conclusion reached by numerous journalists, too.

DeLong argued that large numbers of U.S. troops could not be dispatched because the area surrounding Tora Bora was controlled by tribes hostile to the United States and other outsiders. But he recognized that the Pakistani Frontier Corps, asked to block any escape attempt by bin Laden, was ill-equipped for the job. "To make matters worse, this tribal area was sympathetic to bin Laden," he wrote. "He was the richest man in the area, and he had funded these people for years."

The book was published in September 2004, a year after DeLong retired from the Army. That fall, the failure to capture or kill bin Laden had become an issue in the presidential campaign. Franks had retired from the Army in 2003 and he often defended the events at Tora Bora. On October 19, 2004, he wrote an opinion article in The New York Times saying that intelligence on the Al Qaeda leader's location had been inconclusive. "We don't know to this day whether Mr. bin Laden was at Tora Bora in December 2001," he wrote. "Some intelligence sources said he was; others indicated he was in Pakistan at the time; still others suggested he was in Kashmir. Tora Bora was teeming with Taliban and Qaeda operatives, many of whom were killed or captured, but Mr. bin Laden was never within our grasp."

Two weeks after the Franks article was published and barely two months after publication of his own book, DeLong reversed the conclusion from his autobiography and echoed his former boss in an opinion article on November 1 in The Wall Street Journal. After defending the decision to rely heavily on local militia and the Pakistani Frontier Corps, DeLong wrote: "Finally, most people fail to realize that it is quite possible that bin Laden was never in Tora Bora to begin with. There exists no concrete intel to prove that he was there at the time."

DeLong said in an interview with Committee staff that the contradiction between his book and the opinion article was the result of murky intelligence. "What I put in the book was what the intel said at the time," he said. "The intel is not always right. I read it that he was there. We even heard that he was injured. Later intel was that he may or may not have been there. Did anybody have eyeballs on him? No. The intel stated that he was there at the time, but we got shot in the face by bad intel many times."

DeLong amplified the reasons for not sending American troops after bin Laden. "The real reason we didn't go in with U.S. troops was that we hadn't had the election yet," he said in the staff interview, a reference to the installation of Hamid Karzai as the interim leader of Afghanistan. "We didn't want to have U.S. forces fighting before Karzai was in power. We wanted to create a stable country and that was more important than going after bin Laden at the time."

"A Controversial Fight"

Military and intelligence officers at Tora Bora have provided ample evidence that bin Laden was there. Al Qaeda detainees have maintained that he was there. And the Pentagon's own summary of evidence in the case against a former senior jihadi commander at Guantanamo Bay concluded the detainee helped bin Laden escape. But the most authoritative and definitive unclassified government document on bin Laden's location in December 2001 is the official history of the United States Special Operations Command.

The Special Operations Command, based alongside CentCom at MacDill Air Force Base, oversees the special forces of the Army, Air Force, Navy and Marine Corps. The heavy reliance on special operations forces during the first stages of the Afghan campaign meant that the command played a central role in executing the war plan. Its units included the Delta Force team on the scene at Tora Bora. In preparing the official history of the command, a team of historians working for the command interviewed military and intelligence officials from every branch of the armed forces. The unclassified version of the history was published in 2007 and includes a lengthy section on the operations at Tora Bora.

The section opens by saying that bin Laden and a large contingent of Al Qaeda troops had fled the area around Kabul for Nangahar Province and its provincial capital, Jalalabad, in early November. "Analysts within both the CIA and CentCom correctly speculated that UBL would make a stand along the northern peaks of the Spin Ghar Mountains at a place then called Tora Gora," says the history. "Tora Bora, as it was redubbed in December, had been a major stronghold of AQ for years and provided routes into Pakistan." The history said bin Laden had "undoubtedly" chosen to make his last stand there prior to the onset of winter, along with between 500 and 2,000 others, before escaping into Pakistan.

In the concluding passage assessing the battle of Tora Bora, the historians from the Special Operations Command wrote: "What has since been determined with reasonable certainty was that UBL was indeed at Tora Bora in December 2001. All source reporting corroborated his presence on several days from 9-14 December. The fact that SOF (special operations forces) came as close to capture or killing UBL as U.S. forces have to date makes Tora Bora a controversial fight. Given the commitment of fewer than 100 American personnel, U.S. forces provide unable to block egress routes from Tora Bora south into Pakistan, the route that UBL most likely took."

Franks declined to respond to any questions about the discrepancies about bin Laden's location or the conclusion of the Special Operations Command historians. "We really don't have time for this," one of his aides, retired Col. Michael T. Hayes, wrote in an email to the Committee staff. "Focused on the future, not the past. Gen Franks made his decisions, based on the intel at the time."

2. THE AFGHAN MODEL: A FLAWED MASTERPIECE OR JUST FLAWED?

Writing in Foreign Affairs in the spring of 2002, the military analyst Michael O'Hanlon declared Operation Enduring Freedom "a masterpiece of military creativity and finesse." The operation had been designed on the fly and O'Hanlon praised Rumsfeld, Franks and CIA Director George Tenet for devising a war plan that combined limited American power and the Afghan opposition to defeat the Taliban and Al Qaeda with only 30 U.S. casualties in the first five months. But O'Hanlon tempered his praise, calling the plan "a flawed masterpiece" because of the failure to capture or kill bin Laden and other enemy leaders. The resurgence of the Taliban and Al Qaeda in recent years, and the turmoil they have wrought in Afghanistan and Pakistan, raise the question of whether the plan was a flawed masterpiece—or simply flawed.

The Afghan model required elite teams of American commandos and CIA paramilitary operatives to form alliances with Afghans who opposed the Taliban and had the militias to help topple the religious fundamentalists. Some of these Afghans were legitimate ethnic and tribal leaders who chafed at the restrictions of the

Taliban and the sanctuary it provided to Al Qaeda. Others were allies of convenience, Taliban rivals who held power by force and paid their men by collecting tolls and taxes on legitimate commerce and trafficking in heroin. By providing money and weapons, the U.S. forces helped the warlords destroy their rivals and expand their personal power. Many later entered the Afghan government and remain influential figures. The strategy was a short cut to victory that would have consequences for long-term stability in Afghanistan.

When it came to bin Laden, the special operations forces relied on two relatively minor warlords from the Jalalabad area. Haji Hazarat Ali had a fourth-grade education and a reputation as a bully. He had fought the Soviets as a teenager in the 1980s and later joined the Taliban for a time. The other, Haji Zaman Ghamsharik, was a wealthy drug smuggler who had been persuaded by the United States to return from France. Ghamsharik also had fought the Soviets, but when the Taliban came to power, he had gone into exile in France. Together, they fielded a force of about 2,000 men, but there were questions from the outset about the competence and loyalties of the fighters. The two warlords and their men distrusted each other and both groups appeared to distrust their American allies.

The Delta Force commandos had doubts about the willingness and ability of the Afghan militias to wage a genuine assault on Tora Bora almost from the outset. Those concerns were underscored each time the Afghans insisted on retreating from the mountains as darkness fell. But the suspicions were confirmed by events that started on the afternoon of December 11.

Haji Ghamsharik approached Fury and told him that Al Qaeda fighters wanted to surrender. He said all they needed to end the siege was a 12-hour ceasefire to allow the fighters to climb down the mountains and turn in their weapons. Intercepted radio chatter seemed to confirm that the fighters had lost their resolve under the relentless bombing and wanted to give up, but Fury remained suspicious.

"This is the greatest day in the history of Afghanistan," Ghamsharik told Fury.

"Why is that?" asked the dubious American officer.

"Because al Qaeda is no more," he said. "Bin Laden is finished."

The Special Operations Command history records that CentCom refused to back the ceasefire, suspecting a ruse, but it said the special ops forces agreed reluctantly to an overnight pause in the bombing to avoid killing the surrendering Al Qaeda fighters. Ghamsharik negotiated by radio with representatives of Al Qaeda. He initially told Fury that a large number of Algerians wanted to surrender. Then he said that he could turn over the entire Al Qaeda leadership. Fury's suspicions increased at such a bold promise. By the morning of December 12, no Al Qaeda fighters had appeared and the Delta Force commander concluded that the whole episode was a hoax. Intelligence estimates are that as many as 800 Al Qaeda fighters escaped that night, but bin Laden stuck it out.

Despite the unreliability of his Afghan allies, Fury refused to give up. He plotted ways to use his 40 Delta Force soldiers and the handful of other special ops troops under his command to go after bin Laden on their own. One of the plans was to go at bin Laden from the one direction he would never anticipate, the southern side of the mountains. "We want to come in on the back door," Fury explained later, pointing on a map to the side of the Tora Bora enclave facing Pakistan. The peaks there rose to 14,000 feet and the valleys and precipitous mountain passes were already deep in snow. "The original plan that we sent up through our higher headquarters, Delta Force wants to come in over the mountain with oxygen, coming from the Pakistan side, over the mountains and come in and get a drop on bin Laden from behind." The audacious assault was nixed somewhere up the chain of command. Undeterred, Fury suggested dropping hundreds of landmines along the passes leading to Pakistan to block bin Laden's escape. "First guy blows his leg off, everybody else stops," he said. "That allows aircraft overhead to find them. They see all these heat sources out there. Okay, there is a big large group of Al Qaeda moving south. They can engage that." That proposal was rejected, too.

About the time Fury was desperately concocting scenarios for going after bin Laden and getting rejections from up the chain of command, Franks was well into planning for the next war—the invasion of Iraq.

A Shift in Attention and Resources

On November 21, 2001, President Bush put his arm on Defense Secretary Rumsfeld as they were leaving a National Security Council meeting at the White House. "I need to see you," the president said. It was 72 days after the 9/11 attacks and just a week after the fall of Kabul. But Bush already had new plans.

According to Bob Woodward's book, *Plan of Attack,* the president said to Rumsfeld: "What kind of a war plan do you have for Iraq? How do you feel about the war plan for Iraq?" Then the president told Woodward he recalled saying: "Let's get started on this. And get Tommy Franks looking at what it would take to protect America by removing Saddam Hussein if we have to." Back at the Pentagon, Rumsfeld convened a meeting of the Joint Chiefs of Staff to draft a message for Franks asking for a new assessment of a war with Iraq. The existing operations plan had been created in 1998 and it hinged on assembling the kind of massive international coalition used in Desert Storm in 1991.

In his memoir, *American General,* Franks later described getting the November 21 telephone call from Rumsfeld relaying the president's orders while he was sitting in his office at MacDill Air Force Base in Florida. Franks and one of his aides were working on air support for the Afghan units being assembled to push into the mountains surrounding Tora Bora. Rumsfeld said the president wanted options for war with Iraq. Franks said the existing plan was out of date and that a new one should include lessons about precision weapons and the use of special operations forces learned in Afghanistan.

"Okay, Tom," Rumsfeld said, according to Franks. "Please dust it off and get back to me next week."

Franks described his reaction to Rumsfeld's orders this way: "Son of a bitch. No rest for the weary."

For critics of the Bush administration's commitment to Afghanistan, the shift in focus just as Franks and his senior aides were literally working on plans for the attacks on Tora Bora represents a dramatic turning point that allowed a sustained victory in Afghanistan to slip through our fingers. Almost immediately, intelligence and military planning resources were transferred to begin planning on the next war in Iraq. Though Fury, Berntsen and others in the field did not know what was happening back at CentCom, the drain in resources and shift in attention would affect them and the future course of the U.S. campaign in Afghanistan.

"We're Going to Lose Our Prey"

In his memoir, *At the Center of the Storm,* former CIA Director Tenet said it was evident from the start that aerial bombing would not be enough to get bin Laden at Tora Bora. Troops needed to be in the caves themselves, he wrote, but the Afghan militiamen were "distinctly reluctant" to put themselves in harm's way and there were not enough Americans on the scene. He said that senior CIA officials lobbied hard for inserting U.S. troops. Henry Crumpton, the head of special operations for the CIA's counterterrorism operation and chief of its Afghan strategy, made direct requests to Franks. Crumpton had told him that the back door to Pakistan was open and urged Franks to move more than 1,000 Marines who had set up a base near Kandahar to Tora Bora to block escape routes. But the CentCom commander rejected the idea, saying it would take weeks to get a large enough U.S. contingent on the scene and bin Laden might disappear in the meantime.

At the end of November, Crumpton went to the White House to brief President Bush and Vice President Cheney and repeated the message that he had delivered to Franks. Crumpton warned the president that the Afghan campaign's primary goal of capturing bin Laden was in jeopardy because of the military's reliance on Afghan militias at Tora Bora. Crumpton showed the president where Tora Bora was located in the White Mountains and described the caves and tunnels that riddled the region. Crumpton questioned whether the Pakistani forces would be able to seal off the escape routes and pointed out that the promised Pakistani troops had not arrived yet. In addition, the CIA officer told the president that the Afghan forces at Tora Bora were "tired and cold" and "they're just not invested in getting bin Laden."

According to author Ron Suskind in *The One Percent Solution,* Crumpton sensed that his earlier warnings to Franks and others at the Pentagon had not been relayed the president. So Crumpton went further, telling Bush that "we're going to lose our prey if we're not careful." He recommended that the Marines or other U.S. troops be rushed to Tora Bora.

"How bad off are these Afghani forces, really?" asked Bush. "Are they up to the job?

"Definitely not, Mr. President," Crumpton replied. "Definitely not."

Flight from Tora Bora

On December 14, the day bin Laden finished his will, Dalton Fury finally convinced Ali and his men to stay overnight in one of the canyons that they had captured during daylight. Over the next three days, the Afghan militia and their American advisers moved steadily through the canyons, calling in airstrikes and taking out lingering pockets of fighters. The resistance seemed to have vanished, prompting Ali to declare victory on December 17. Most of the Tora Bora complex was abandoned and many of the caves and tunnels were buried in debris. Only about 20 stragglers were taken prisoner. The consensus was that Al Qaeda fighters who had survived the fierce bombing had escaped into Pakistan or melted into the local population. Bin Laden was nowhere to be found. Two days later, Fury and his Delta Force colleagues left Tora Bora, hoping that someone would eventually find bin Laden buried in one of the caves.

There was no body because bin Laden did not die at Tora Bora. Later U.S. intelligence reports and accounts by journalists and others said that he and a contingent of bodyguards departed Tora Bora on December 16. With help from Afghans and Pakistanis who had been paid in advance, the group made its way on foot and horseback across the mountain passes and into Pakistan without encountering any resistance.

The Special Operations Command history noted that there were not enough U.S. troops to prevent the escape, acknowledging that the failure to capture or killing bin Laden made Tora Bora a controversial battle. But Franks argued that Tora was a success and he praised both the Afghan militias and the Pakistanis who were supposed to have protected the border. "I think it was a good operation," he said in an interview for the PBS show Frontline on the first anniversary of the Afghan war. "Many people have said, 'Well, gosh, you know bin Laden got away.' I have yet to see anything that proves bin Laden or whomever was there. That's not to say they weren't, but I've not seen proof that they were there."

Bin Laden himself later acknowledged that he was at Tora Bora, boasting about how he and Zawahiri survived the heavy bombing along with 300 fighters before escaping. "The bombardment was round-the-clock and the warplanes continued to fly over us day and night," he said in an audio tape released on February 11, 2003. "Planes poured their lava on us, particularly after accomplishing their main missions in Afghanistan."

In the aftermath of bin Laden's escape, there were accusations that militiamen working for the two warlords hired by the CIA to get him had helped the Al Qaeda leader cross into Pakistan. Michael Scheuer, who spent 15 years working on Afghanistan at the CIA and at one point headed the agency's bin Laden task force, was sharply critical of the war plan from the start because of its reliance on Afghan allies of dubious loyalty. "Everyone who was cognizant of how Afghan operations worked would have told Mr. Tenet that he was nuts," Scheuer said later. "And as it turned out, he was. ... The people we bought, the people Mr. Tenet said we would own, let Osama bin Laden escape from Tora Bora in eastern Afghanistan into Pakistan."

The American forces never had a clear idea how many Al Qaeda fighters were arrayed against them. Estimates ranged as high as 3,000 and as low as 500, but the consensus put the figure around 1,000—at least until so many escaped during the fake surrender.

Regardless of the exact number of enemy fighters, assaulting Tora Bora would have been difficult and probably would have cost many American and Afghan lives. The Special Operations Command's history offered this tightly worded assessment: "With large numbers of well-supplied, fanatical AQ troops dug into extensive fortified positions, Tora Bora appeared to be an extremely tough target."

For Dalton Fury, the reward would have been worth the risk. "In general, I definitely think it was worth the risk to the force to assault Tora Bora for Osama bin Laden," he told the Committee staff. "What other target out there, then or now, could be more important to our nation's struggle in the global war on terror?"

3. AN ALTERNATIVE BATTLE PLAN

Rather than allowing bin Laden to escape, Franks and Rumsfeld could have deployed American troops already in Afghanistan on or near the border with Pakistan to block the exits while simultaneously sending special operations forces and their Afghan allies up the mountains to Tora Bora. The complex mission would have been risky, but analysis shows that it was well within the reach and capability of the American military.

In the years following the Vietnam War, the U.S. military developed a doctrine intended to place new constraints on when the country went to war and to avoid a repeat of the disastrous and prolonged conflict in Southeast Asia. In its most simplistic form, the doctrine focused on applying overwhelming and disproportionate military force to achieve concrete political goals. It called for mobilizing the military and political resources necessary for ending conflicts quickly and leaving no loose ends. The concept was known informally as the Powell doctrine, named for General Colin Powell, who outlined his vision at the end of the Persian Gulf War in 1991.

The Afghan model constructed by Rumsfeld and Franks in response to the attacks on September 11 stood the Powell doctrine on its head. The new template was designed to deliver a swift and economical knockout blow through airpower and the limited application of troops on the ground. Instead of overwhelming force, the Afghan model depended on airpower and on highly mobile special operations forces and CIA paramilitary teams, working in concert with opposition warlords and tribal leaders. It was designed as unconventional warfare led by indigenous forces, and Franks put a ceiling of 10,000 on the number of U.S. troops in Afghanistan. Despite the valor of the limited American forces, the doctrine failed to achieve one of its most concrete political goals—eliminating the leadership of Al Qaeda and the Taliban. The result has turned out to be nothing close to decisive victory followed by quick withdrawal.

Assembling the size force required to apply overwhelming force across a country as large and rugged as Afghanistan would have taken many weeks. The only country in the region likely to provide the major bases required to prepare an invasion by tens of thousands of troops was Pakistan, and political sensitivities there would have made full cooperation both doubtful and risky for its leadership. The Pakistanis provided limited bases for U.S. operations in the early stages of planning and the invasion; the footprint was kept small to avoid a public outcry. But soldiers and scholars alike have argued that there were sufficient troops available in Afghanistan and nearby Uzbekistan to mount a genuine assault on Osama bin Laden's position at Tora Bora. And they could have been augmented within about a week by reinforcements from the Persian Gulf and the United States.

The most detailed description of the assault option was laid out in an article in the journal *Security Studies* by Peter John Paul Krause of Massachusetts Institute of Technology. Entitled "The Last Good Chance: A Reassessment of U.S. Operations at Tora Bora," the article described a large-scale operation called a block and sweep. The plan is simple enough: One group of American forces would block the likely exit avenues to Pakistan on the south side of Tora Bora while a second contingent moved against Al Qaeda's positions from the north. Simplicity should not be mistaken for sure success: Variables like weather conditions, the effectiveness of the remaining Al Qaeda fighters and the ability to close the escape routes would have made the mission risky. The dangers of attacking fortified positions manned by hardened fighters would likely have resulted in significant U.S. casualties.

The assault would not have required thousands of conventional forces. A large number of troops would have taken too long to deploy and alerted Al Qaeda to the approaching attack. "My opinion is that bin Laden would have left even earlier as soon as he received word that the U.S. troops were surrounding him," Fury told the Committee staff. "I think he only stayed as long as he did because he thought the mujahedin would not aggressively pursue him."

The preferred choice would have been a small, agile force capable of deploying quickly and quietly and trained to operate in difficult terrain against unconventional enemies. The U.S. military has large numbers of soldiers and Marines who meet those criteria— Delta Force, Green Berets, Navy Seals, Marine special operations units and Army Rangers and paratroopers. The effectiveness of U.S. special operations commandos, even in small numbers, was demonstrated on December 10. Two U.S. soldiers were able to get close enough to the Al Qaeda positions to call in air strikes for 17 straight hours, forcing enemy fighters to retreat and enabling the Afghan militia to capture key terrain near bin Laden's suspected location. It was an example of what a larger U.S. force could have accomplished, with support from available air power.

The CIA's Berntsen had requested a battalion of Rangers, about 800 soldiers, and been turned down by CentCom. A battalion would have been a substantial increase in the U.S. presence, but it probably would not have been enough to both assault the stronghold from the north and block the exits on the south. Krause estimated that as few as 500 troops could have carried out the initial northern assault, with reinforcements arriving over the course of the battle. At least twice as many troops would have been required to execute the blocking mission on the southern, eastern and western reaches of Tora Bora. Krause proposed spreading about 1,500 troops to capture or kill anyone trying to flee. O'Hanlon estimated that closing off escape routes to Pakistan would have required 1,000 to 3,000 American troops. In all, an initial force of roughly 2,000 to 3,000 troops would have been sufficient to begin the block-and-sweep mission, with reinforcements following as time and circumstances allowed.

Troops Were Ready to Go

Assembling the troops to augment the handful of special ops commandos under Fury's leadership at Tora Bora would have been a manageable task. Franks had set the ceiling of 10,000 U.S. troops to maintain a light footprint. Still, within that number there were enough ready and willing to go after bin Laden. In late November, about the time U.S. intelligence placed bin Laden squarely at Tora Bora, more than 1,000 members of the 15th and 26th Marine Expeditionary Units, among the military's most mobile arms, established a base southwest of Kandahar, only a few hours flight away. They were primarily interdicting traffic and supporting the special operations teams working with Afghan militias. Another 1,000 troops from the Army's 10th Mountain Division were split between a base in southern Uzbekistan and Bagram Air Base, a short helicopter flight from Tora Bora. The Army troops were engaged mainly in military police functions, according to reports at the time.

Both forces are trained in unconventional warfare and could have been redeployed rapidly for an assault. Lt. Col. Paul Lacamera, commander of a 10th Mountain battalion, later said that his men had been prepared to deploy anywhere in Afghanistan since mid-November. "We weren't just sitting there digging holes and looking out," said Lacamera, whose actions in a later assault on Al Qaeda forces won him a Silver Star. "We were training for potential fights because eventually it was going to come to that."

The commander of the Marines outside Kandahar, Brig. Gen. James N. Mattis, told a journalist that his troops could seal off Tora Bora, but his superiors rejected the plan. Everyone knew that such an operation would have conflicted with the Afghan model laid down by Franks and Rumsfeld. But there were other reasons to hesitate. One former officer told the Committee staff that the inability to get sufficient medical-evacuation helicopters into the rough terrain was a major stumbling block for those who considered trying to push for the assault. He also said there were worries that bad weather would ground transport helicopters or, worse, knock them out of the sky.

In addition to the troops in country, a battalion of Army Rangers was stationed in the Persian Gulf country of Oman, and 200 of them had demonstrated their abilities by parachuting into an airfield near Kandahar at night in October. In Krause's analysis, a battalion of about 800 soldiers from the 82nd Airborne Division at Fort Bragg, North Carolina, could have been deployed to Tora Bora in less than a week, covering the 7,000 miles in C-17 transport aircraft.

No one should underestimate the logistical difficulty and danger of deploying even specially trained troops into hostile territory at altitudes of 7,000 to 10,000 feet. Landing zones for helicopters would likely have come under fire from Al Qaeda positions and drop zones for paratroopers were few and far between in the jagged terrain. But Chinook helicopters, the work horse for rapid deployments, proved capable of carrying combat troops above 11,000-foot mountain ranges as part of Operation Anaconda, a similar block-and-sweep mission carried out in February 2002 in eastern Afghanistan.

Former U.S. military officers said that sending American troops into Tora Bora was discussed at various times in late November and early December of 2001. The CIA's Afghan chief, Hank Crumpton, made specific requests to Franks for U.S. troops and urged President Bush not to rely on Afghan militias and Pakistani paramilitary troops to do the job. CentCom went so far as to develop a plan to put several thousand U.S. troops into Tora Bora. Commanders estimated that deploying 1,000 to 3,000 American troops would have required several hundred airlift flights by helicopters over a week or more.

DeLong defended the decision not to deploy large numbers of American troops. "We didn't have the lift," he told the Committee staff. "We didn't have the medical capabilities. The further we went down the road, the easier the decision got. We wanted Afghanistan to be peaceful for Karzai to take over. Right or not, that was the thinking behind what we did."

The Afghan model proved effective in some instances, particularly when Afghan opposition forces working with American advisers were arrayed against poorly trained Taliban foot soldiers. The precision bombs and overwhelming airpower also played a major role in dispersing the Taliban forces and opening the way for the rapid takeover of the country, though critics now say scattering the Taliban simply allowed them to regroup later. In the early days at Tora Bora, the light footprint allowed a handful of CIA and special operations operatives to guide bombs that killed dozens, if not hundreds, of Al Qaeda fighters. But the model was ineffective when it came to motivating opposition militiamen of questionable skills and doubtful resolve to carry the fight to the biggest concentration of Al Qaeda fighters of the war, particularly when the jihadis were battling to protect their leader. Fewer than 100 special operations force soldiers and CIA operatives were unable to turn the tide against those odds.

Some critics said bin Laden escaped because the United States relied too heavily on Afghan militias to carry the fight forward at Tora Bora and on Pakistan's paramilitary Frontier Corps to block any escape. As Michael O'Hanlon pointed out, our allies did not have the same incentives to stop bin Laden and his associates as American troops. Nor did they have the technology and training to carry out such a difficult mission. The responsibility for allowing the most wanted man in the world to virtually disappear into thin air lies with the American commanders who refused to commit the necessary U.S. soldiers and Marines to finish the job.

The same shortage of U.S. troops allowed Mullah Mohammed Omar and other Taliban leaders to escape. A semi-literate leader who fled Kandahar on a motorbike, Mullah Omar has re-emerged at the helm of the Taliban-led insurgency, which has grown more sophisticated and lethal in recent years and now controls swaths of Afghanistan. The Taliban, which is aligned with a loose network of other militant groups and maintains ties to Al Qaeda, has established shadow governments in many of Afghanistan's provinces and is capable of mounting increasingly complex attacks on American and NATO forces. Bruce Riedel, a former CIA officer who helped develop the Obama administration's Afghan policy, recently referred to the mullah's return to power "one of the most remarkable military comebacks in modern history."

Ironically, one of the guiding principles of the Afghan model was to avoid immersing the United States in a protracted insurgency by sending in too many troops and stirring up anti-American sentiment. In the end, the unwillingness to bend the operational plan to deploy the troops required to take advantage of solid intelligence and unique circumstances to kill or capture bin Laden paved the way for exactly what we had hoped to avoid—a protracted insurgency that has cost more lives than anyone estimates would have been lost in a full-blown assault on Tora Bora. Further, the dangerous contagion of rising violence and instability in Afghanistan has spread to Pakistan, a nuclear-armed ally of the United States which is now wracked by deadly terrorist bombings as it conducts its own costly military campaign against a domestic, Taliban-related insurgency.

The Price of Failure

Osama bin Laden's demise would not have erased the worldwide threat from extremists. But the failure to kill or capture him has allowed bin Laden to exert a malign influence over events in the region and nearly 60 countries where his followers have established extremist groups. History shows that terrorist groups are invariably much stronger with their charismatic leaders than without them, and the ability of bin Laden and his terrorist organization to recover from the loss of their Afghan sanctuary reinforces the lesson.

Eight years after its expulsion from Afghanistan, Al Qaeda has reconstituted itself and bin Laden has survived to inspire a new generation of extremists who have adopted and adapted the Al Qaeda doctrine and are now capable of attacking from any number of places. The impact of this threat is greatest in Pakistan, where Al Qaeda's continued presence and resources have emboldened domestic extremists waging an increasingly bloody insurrection that threatens the stability of the government and the region. Its training camps also have spawned new attacks outside the region—militants trained in Pakistan were tied to the July 2005 transit system bombings in London and several aborted plots elsewhere in Europe.

Closer to home, the Federal Bureau of Investigation says two recent suspected plots disrupted by U.S. authorities involved long-time residents of the United States who had traveled to Pakistan and trained at bases affiliated with Al Qaeda. One of the plots involved two Chicago men accused in late October of planning to attack the Danish newspaper that published cartoons of the Prophet Mohammad. In the other, an Afghan-born man who drove a shuttle bus in Denver was arrested on suspicion of plans to detonate improvised explosives in the United States. Court papers said the man had been trained in weapons and explosives in Pakistan and had made nine pages of handwritten notes on how to make and handle bombs.

For American taxpayers, the financial costs of the conflict have been staggering. The first eight years cost an estimated $243 billion and about $70 billion has been appropriated for the current fiscal year—a figure that does not include any increase in troops. But the highest price is being paid on a daily basis in Afghanistan and Pakistan, where 68,000 American troops and hundreds of U.S. civilians are engaged in the ninth year of a protracted conflict and the Afghan people endure a third decade of violence. So far, about 950 U.S. troops and nearly 600 allied soldiers have lost their lives in Operation Enduring Freedom, a conflict in which the outcome remains in grave doubt in large part because the extremists behind the violence were not eliminated in 2001.

NOTES

EXECUTIVE SUMMARY

1. **One 15,000-pound bomb:** "Daisy Cutter bomb produced flurry of intel," United Press International, December 12, 2001; Benjamin Lambeth, *Air Power Against Terror: America's Conduct of Operation Enduring Freedom,* p 149 (RAND, Santa Monica, 2005).

2. **Bin Laden expected to die:** *"Al-Majallah* Obtains Bin Laden's Will," *Al-Majallah,* October 27, 2002.

3. **Fewer than 100:** Accounts of the small American troop presence and Tora Bora and the requests for reinforcements are plentiful. The CIA commander in Afghanistan at the time, Gary Berntsen, wrote in his book *Jawbreaker: The Attack on Bin Laden and Al Qaeda* (Crown, New York, 2005) about his requests for 800 Army Rangers and his disputes with the military over its refusal to provide the troops. In his book, *Kill Bin Laden: A Delta Force Commander's Account of the Hunt for the World's Most Wanted Man,* (St. Martin's Press, New York, 2008) Dalton Fury said one of the key mistakes by U.S. commanders was not committing enough conventional troops to the battle at Tora Bora and not using U.S. forces to seal the escape routes. Writing an article, entitled "Lost at Tora Bora," in The *New York Times Magazine* on September 11, 2005, Mary Anne Weaver said that Brig. Gen. James Mattis, the commander of at least 1,200 Marines at a base outside Kandahar in November 2001, was convinced his troops could seal off Tora Bora. Michael E. O'Hanlon said the U.S. Central Command made preparations for sending several thousand troops to Tora Bora but rejected the plan in "A Flawed Masterpiece," *Foreign Affairs,* Volume 81 No. 3 (March/April 2002) p.57–58.

4. **On December 16:** Berntsen, pp 307–308. The date of bin Laden's escape remains imprecise. In his book, Fury concluded that bin Laden had fled Tora Bora by December 17, when U.S. troops entered the complex. Peter Bergen, the last American to interview bin Laden and highly regarded authority on Al Qaeda, told the Committee staff that bin Laden left around December 14. Other accounts put the date on or around December 16, the end of Ramadan.

5. **Rumsfeld said at the time:** O'Hanlon, p 57. For a thorough discussion of the Afghan model and its reliance on the CIA and special operations forces, see Henry A. Crumpton, "Intelligence and War 2001–2002," *Transforming U.S. Intelligence* (Georgetown University Press, 2005).

6. **There were enough:** Peter John Paul Krause, "The Last Good Chance: A Reassessment of U.S. Operations at Tora Bora," Security Studies, pp 644–684, Volume 17, 2008. Krause's well-documented article is the most thorough examination of the alternatives available to military commanders at Tora Bora. For a broader overview of the Afghan model, see Stephen Biddle, *Afghanistan and the Future of Warfare: Implications for Army and Defense Policy* (Carlisle Barracks, PA: Strategic Studies Institute, U.S. Army War College, 2003).

7. **For example, CIA:** Committee staff interview with Fury, October 2009; Berntsen, pp 314–315.

8. **Franks' second-in-command:** Michael DeLong, *Inside CentCom: The Unvarnished Truth About the Wars in Afghanistan and Iraq,* pp 57–58 (Regnery Publishing, Chicago, 2004).

9. **"All source reporting:** U.S. Special Operations Command History, p 101, sixth edition, March 2008 (www.socom.mil/SOCOMHome/Documents/history6thedition.pdf). The history was first published in 2007, but the internet link here is to the most recent edition; the section on Tora Bora is unchanged from the 2007 version.

10. **In the middle of August:** Douglas Frantz and Catherine Collins, *The Man From Pakistan: The True Story of the World's Most Dangerous Nuclear Smuggler,* pp 263–264 (Twelve Books, New York, 2007). George Tenet, *At the Center of the Storm: My Years at the CIA,* p 266 (HarperCollins, New York, 2007).

1. FLIGHT TO TORA BORA

11. **The first reports:** The 9/11 Commission Report, *Final Report of the National Commission on Terrorist Attacks Upon the United States,* pp 259–260.

12. **Only a handful of senators:** U.S. Senate records and Committee staff interview.

13. **Less than a month:** The 9/11 Commission Report, pp 261–263.

14. **Bin Laden's movements:** Hamid Mir, "Osama claims he has nukes: If US uses N-arms it will get same response," Dawn, November 10, 2001.The article included a photo of Mir with bin Laden. Hamid Mir, "How Osama bin Laden escaped death four times after 9/11," *The News*, September 11, 2007. Philip Smucker, "A day-by-day account of how Osama bin Laden eluded the world's most powerful military machine," *The Christian Science Monitor*, March 4, 2002.

15. **After pressure:** Steve Coll, *The Bin Ladens: An Arabian Family in the American Century*, pp 461–462 (The Penguin Press, New York, 2008).

16. **U.S. intelligence had:** Tenet, p 225.

17. **Outside experts like:** Committee staff interview with Peter Bergen, October 2009.

18. **"He's got a large:** *ABC News Prime Time*, Diane Sawyer interview with Vice President Dick Cheney, November 29, 2001.

19. **Bin Laden's presence:** Fury; staff interviews with Fury and one of his colleagues who requested anonymity because he is not authorized to speak about classified matters, October and November 2009.

20. **Fury, who still uses:** Staff interview with Fury.

21. **Another special:** Staff interview with the Delta Force participant referenced in Note 19.

22. **Afghan villagers:** Staff interview with Fury. In another staff interview, a former CIA counter-terrorism officer confirmed elements of the information, including the agency's use of push-button GPS devices.

23. **On December 9:** "Daisy Cutter bomb produced flurry of intel;" Lambeth, p 149; Fury, p 153, p 225; Berntsen, p 295.

24. **But later reports:** Staff interview with the former CIA counter-terrorism officer who described the interrogation report of a detainee from Tora Bora.

25. **At one point:** Staff interview with Fury; various press reports.

26. **"There is no doubt:** Fury, p 281, a view he repeated in his staff interview.

27. **A "summary of:** "U.S. holding man who allegedly helped terror leader flee Tora Bora," Associated Press, March 23, 2005.

28. **Another confirmation:** Berntsen, p 86.

29. **"We needed U.S. soldiers:** Ibid., pp 306–307.

30. **"We could have:** Richard Leiby, "Knocking on Osama's Cave Door," *The Washington Post*, February 16, 2006.

31. **"Unfortunately, many:** NBC News *Meet the Press*, Tim Russert interview with Gary Schroen, May 10, 2005.

32. **In his memoir:** DeLong, pp 56–59.

33. **"To make matters:** Ibid.

34. **On October 19:** Tommy Franks, "War of Words", *The New York Times*, October 19, 2004.

35. **Two weeks after:** Michael DeLong, "Setting the Record Straight on Tora Bora," *The Wall Street Journal*, November 1, 2004.

36. **DeLong said:** Committee staff interview with DeLong, October 2009.

37. **The section opens:** U.S. Special Operations Command History, p 97.

38. **In the concluding:** Ibid., p 101.

39. **Franks declined:** E-mail response from Michael T. Hayes, admin@tommy franks.com, October 27, 2009.

40. **Writing in Foreign Affairs:** O'Hanlon, pp 47–63.

41. **When it came:** Weaver, "Lost at Tora Bora;" Smucker, "A day-by-day account of how Osama bin Laden eluded the world's most powerful military machine."

42. **Haji Ghamsharik:** Fury, pp 217–218.

43. **The Special Operations:** U.S. Special Operations Command History, p 100; staff interview with Fury.

44. **Despite the unreliability:** Staff interview with Fury; CBS New 60 Minutes, "Elite Officers Recalls Bin Laden Hunt," October 5, 2008.

45. **According to Bob:** Bob Woodward, *Plan of Attack,* p 8 (Simon & Shuster, New York, 2008).

46. **In his memoir:** Tommy Franks, *American Soldier,* p 315 (Regan Books, New York, 2004).

47. **In his memoir:** Tenet, pp 226–227.

48. **According to author:** Ron Suskind, *The One Percent Doctrine: Deep Inside America's Pursuit of Its Enemies Since 9/11,* pp 58–59 (Simon & Shuster, New York, 2006).

49. **On December 14:** Fury, pp 270–275.

50. **"I think it was:** PBS *Frontline,* "Campaign Against Terror," October 2, 2002.

51. **Bin Laden himself:** Bin Laden audio and translation provided by the Intel Center at http://www.intelcenter.com.

52. **"Everyone who was:** PBS *Frontline,* "Campaign Against Terror."

53. **The Special Operations:** U.S. Special Operations Command History, p 97.

54. **"In general:** Staff interview with Fury.

3. AN ALTERNATIVE PLAN

55. **In the years following:** Michael A. Cohen, "The Powell Doctrine's Enduring Relevance," *World Politics Review,* July 22, 2009.

56. **The most detailed:** Krause, "The Last Good Chance: A Reassessment of U.S. Operations at Tora Bora."

57. **"My opinion:** Staff interview with Fury.

58. **The effectiveness of U.S. special:** U.S. Special Operations Command History, p 100.

59. **Krause proposed:** Krause, pp 657–661.

60. **O'Hanlon estimated:** O'Hanlon, p 57.

61. **Assembling the troops:** *Ibid.,* p 53, 58; Krause, pp 655–657; various press accounts.

62. **Lt. Col. Paul Lacamera:** Philip Smucker, *Al Qaeda's Great Escape,* p 83 (Potomac Books, Washington DC, 2004).

63. **The commander of the Marines:** Weaver, "Lost at Tora Bora." The Pentagon declined to make General Mattis, who remains on active duty, available to the Committee for an interview.

64. **One former officer:** Staff interview with DeLong.

65. **Former U.S. military:** Committee staff interviews with former intelligence and military officers who requested anonymity because the matter remains classified, October and November 2009.

66. **DeLong defended:** Staff interview with DeLong.

67. **Bruce Riedel:** Scott Shane, "A Dogged Taliban Chief Rebounds, Vexing U.S.," *The New York Times,* October 11, 2009.

68. **Closer to home:** David Johnston and Eric Schmitt, "Small Terrorism Plots Pose Threat, Officials Say," *The New York Times,* November 1, 2009.

APPENDIXES

APPENDIX I.—"A Flawed Masterpiece," Michael E. O'Hanlon, *Foreign Affairs,* March/April 2002

A FLAWED MASTERPIECE[1]

Michael E. O'Hanlon

ASSESSING THE AFGHAN CAMPAIGN

Throughout most of the twentieth century, the U.S. armed forces were seen as an overmuscled giant, able to win wars through brute strength but often lacking in daring and cleverness. This basic strategy worked during the two world wars, making the United States relatively tough to challenge. But it failed in Vietnam, produced mediocre results in Korea, and worked in the Persian Gulf War largely because the terrain was ideally suited to American strengths.

What a difference a new century makes. Operation Enduring Freedom has been, for the most part, a masterpiece of military creativity and finesse. Secretary of Defense Donald Rumsfeld, U.S. Central Command (centcom) head General Tommy Franks, and Director of Central Intelligence George Tenet devised a plan for using limited but well-chosen types of American power in conjunction with the Afghan opposition to defeat the Taliban and al Qaeda. Secretary of State Colin Powell helped persuade Pakistan to sever its ties with the Taliban, work with Afghanistan's Northern Alliance, provide the bases and overflight rights needed by U.S. forces, and contribute to the general war effort. Besides pushing his national security team to develop an innovative and decisive war-fighting strategy, President George W. Bush rallied the American people behind the war effort and established a close relationship with Russian President Vladimir Putin, making it far easier for the United States to work militarily in Central Asia. The U.S. effort to overthrow the Taliban deprived al Qaeda of its sanctuary within Afghanistan and left its surviving leaders running for their lives.[2]

At their peak, the U.S. forces involved in the war effort numbered no more than 60,000 (about half of which were in the Persian Gulf), and Western allies added no more than 15,000. But the U.S.-led military campaign has hardly been small in scale. By the end of January, the United States had flown about 25,000 sorties in the air campaign and dropped 18,000 bombs, including 10,000 precision munitions. The number of U.S. sorties exceeded the number of U.S. sorties flown in the 1999 Kosovo war, and the United States dropped more smart bombs on Afghanistan than NATO dropped on Serbia in 1999. In fact, the total number of precision munitions expended in Afghanistan amounted to more than half the number used in Operation Desert Storm. (In addition, more than 3,000 U.S. and French bombs were dropped on surviving enemy forces in March during Operation Anaconda, in which some 1,500 Western forces and 2,000 Afghans launched a major offensive against about 1,000 enemy troops in the mountainous region of eastern Afghanistan.)

If the U.S. strategy has had many virtues, however, it has also had flaws. Most important, it has apparently failed to achieve a key war goal: capturing or killing Osama bin Laden and other top enemy leaders. Such hunts are inherently difficult,

---

[1] This article originally appeared in FOREIGN AFFAIRS magazine, May/June 2002, Volume 81, Number 3. It is reproduced here with permission. Michael E. O'Hanlon is Senior Fellow in Foreign Policy Studies at the Brookings Institution. His most recent book is *Defense Policy Choices for the Bush Administration, 2001–2005.*

[2] Bob Woodward and Dan Balz, "At Camp David, Advise and Dissent," *The Washington Post,* January 31, 2002, p. A1; Bill Keller, "The World According to Powell," THE NEW YORK TIMES MAGAZINE, November 25, 2001, pp. 61–62.

but the prospects for success in this case were reduced considerably by U.S. reliance on Pakistani forces and Afghan militias for sealing off enemy escape routes and conducting cave-to-cave searches during critical periods. If most al Qaeda leaders stay at large, the United States and other countries will remain more vulnerable to terrorism than they would be otherwise—perhaps significantly so.

But on balance, Operation Enduring Freedom has been very impressive. It may wind up being more notable in the annals of American military history than anything since Douglas MacArthur's invasion at Inchon in Korea half a century ago. Even Norman Schwarzkopf's famous "left hook" around Iraqi forces in Operation Desert Storm was less bold; had it been detected, U.S. airpower still could have protected coalition flanks, and American forces could have outrun Iraqi troops toward most objectives on the ground. By contrast, Operation Enduring Freedom's impressive outcome was far from preordained. Too much American force (e.g., a protracted and punishing strategic air campaign or an outright ground invasion) risked uniting Afghan tribes and militias to fight the outside power, angering the Arab world, destabilizing Pakistan, and spawning more terrorists. Too little force, or the wrong kind of force, risked outright military failure and a worsening of Afghanistan's humanitarian crisis—especially given the limited capabilities of the small militias that made up the anti-Taliban coalition.

ZEROING IN

Beginning on October 7, Afghans, Americans, and coalition partners cooperated to produce a remarkable military victory in Afghanistan. The winning elements included 15,000 Northern Alliance fighters (primarily from the Tajik and Uzbek ethnic groups), 100 combat sorties a day by U.S. planes, 300-500 Western special operations forces and intelligence operatives, a few thousand Western ground forces, and thousands of Pashtun soldiers in southern Afghanistan who came over to the winning side in November. Together they defeated the Taliban forces, estimated at 50,000 to 60,000 strong, as well as a few thousand al Qaeda fighters.

Various Western countries, particularly several NATO allies and Australia, played important roles as well. A formal NATO role in the war was neither necessary nor desirable, given the location of the conflict and the need for a supple and secretive military strategy. Still, NATO allies stood squarely by America's side, invoking the alliance's Article V mutual-defense clause after September 11, and demonstrated that commitment by sending five awacs aircraft to help patrol U.S. airspace. Forces from the United Kingdom, Australia, France, and Canada appear to have frequently contributed to the effort in Afghanistan; forces from Denmark, Norway, and Germany also participated in Operation Anaconda in March. Allied aircraft flew a total of some 3,000 sorties on relief, reconnaissance, and other missions. As noted, France dropped bombs during Operation Anaconda, and the United Kingdom fired several cruise missiles on the first day of battle as well. Numerous countries, including the Netherlands, Italy, and Japan, deployed ships to the Arabian Sea. The cooperation continues today, as major Western allies constitute the backbone of the un-authorized stability force in Kabul.

The short war has had several phases. The first began on October 7 and lasted a month; the second ran through November and saw the Taliban lose control of the country; the third was characterized by intensive bombing of suspected al Qaeda strongholds in the Tora Bora mountain and cave complex in December; the fourth began with the inauguration of Hamid Karzai as interim prime minister and continues to date.

During the first part of the war, Taliban forces lost their large physical assets such as radar, aircraft, and command-and-control systems, but they hung on to power in most regions. Most al Qaeda training camps and headquarters were also destroyed. Although Taliban forces did not quickly collapse, they were increasingly isolated in pockets near the major cities. Cut off from each other physically, they were unable to resupply or reinforce very well and had problems communicating effectively.

In the first week of the war, U.S. aircraft averaged only 25 combat sorties a day, but they soon upped that total to around 100. (Some 70 Tomahawk cruise missiles were fired in the early going; a total of about 100 had been used by December.) The United States comparably increased the number of airlift, refueling, and other support missions. U.S. air strikes by b-52 and b-1 bombers operating out of Diego Garcia typically involved six sorties a day; other land-based aircraft, primarily f-15es and ac-130 gunships from Oman, flew about as much. Planes from the three U.S. aircraft carriers based in the Arabian Sea provided the rest of the combat punch. Reconnaissance and refueling flights originated from the Persian Gulf region and Diego Garcia. Some air support and relief missions also came from, or flew over,

400

Central Asia, where U.S. Army soldiers from the Tenth Mountain Division helped protect airfields.

Most air attacks occurred around Afghanistan's perimeter, because the rugged central highlands were not a major operating area for the Taliban or al Qaeda. By the middle of October, most fixed assets worth striking had already been hit, so combat sorties turned to targeting Taliban and al Qaeda forces in the field. Aircraft continued to fly at an altitude of at least 10,000 feet, because the Pentagon was fearful of antiaircraft artillery, Soviet sa-7 and sa-13 portable antiaircraft missiles, and some 200-300 Stinger antiaircraft missiles presumed to be in Taliban or al Qaeda possession. But most precision-guided weapons are equally effective regardless of their altitude of origin, provided that good targeting information is available—as it was in this case, thanks to U.S. troops on the ground.

The first month of the war produced only limited results and had many defense and strategic analysts worried about the basic course of the campaign. Some of those critics began, rather intemperately and unrealistically, to call for a ground invasion; others opposed an invasion but thought that a substantial intensification of efforts would prove necessary.

In phase two, beginning in early November, that intensification occurred. But it was due not so much to an increased number of airplanes as to an increase in their effectiveness. By then, 80 percent of U.S. combat sorties could be devoted to directly supporting opposition forces in the field; by late November, the tally was 90 percent. In addition, the deployment of more unmanned aerial vehicles and Joint Surveillance and Target Attack Radar System (jstars) aircraft to the region helped the United States maintain continuous reconnaissance of enemy forces in many places. Most important, the number of U.S. special operations forces and CIA teams working with various opposition elements increased greatly. In mid-October, only three special operations "A teams," each consisting of a dozen personnel, were in Afghanistan; in mid-November, the tally was 10; by December 8, it was 17. This change meant the United States could increasingly call in supplies for the opposition, help it with tactics, and designate Taliban and al Qaeda targets for U.S. air strikes using global positioning system (gps) technology and laser range finders. The Marine Corps also began to provide logistical support for these teams as the war advanced.

As a result, enemy forces collapsed in northern cities such as Mazar-i-Sharif and Taloqan over the weekend of November 9-11. Taliban fighters ran for their lives, provoking their leader, Mullah Muhammad Omar, to broadcast a demand that his troops stop "behaving like chickens." Kabul fell soon afterward. By November 16, Pentagon officials were estimating that the Taliban controlled less than one-third of the country, in contrast to 85 percent just a week before. Reports also suggested that Muhammad Atef, a key al Qaeda operative, was killed by U.S. bombs in mid-November. Kunduz, the last northern stronghold of enemy forces where several thousand Taliban and al Qaeda troops apparently remained, fell on November 24-25.

In late November, more than 1,000 U.S. marines of the 15th and 26th Marine Expeditionary Units established a base about 60 miles southwest of Kandahar, which the Taliban continued to hold. They deployed there directly from ships in the Arabian Sea, leapfrogging over Pakistani territory at night (to minimize political difficulties for the government of President Pervez Musharraf) and flying 400 miles inland to what became known as Camp Rhino. Their subsequent resupply needs were largely met using Pakistani bases. Once deployed, they began to interdict some road traffic and carry out support missions for special operations forces.

Meanwhile, Pashtun tribes had begun to oppose the Taliban openly. By November, they were accepting the help of U.S. special forces, who had previously been active principally in the north of the country. Two groups in particular—one led by Hamid Karzai, the other by another tribal leader, Gul Agha Shirzai—closed in on Kandahar. Mullah Omar offered to surrender in early December but in the end fled with most of his fighters, leaving the city open by December 8-9. Pockets of Taliban and al Qaeda resistance, each with hundreds of fighters or more, remained in areas near Mazar-i-Sharif, Kabul, Kandahar, and possibly elsewhere, but the Taliban no longer held cities or major transportation routes.

Why this part of the campaign achieved such a rapid and radical victory remains unclear. Taliban forces presumably could have held out longer if they had hunkered down in the cities and put weapons near mosques, hospitals, and homes, making their arsenal hard to attack from the air. Opposition fighters were too few to defeat them in street-to-street fighting in most places, and starving out the Taliban would have required the unthinkable tactic of starving local civilian populations as well.

Most likely, the Taliban got caught in positions outside major cities that they could neither easily escape nor defend. Once the Afghan opposition began to engage the enemy seriously in November and Taliban forces returned fire, they revealed

401

their positions to American special operations personnel who could call in devastating air strikes. Sometimes they were tricked into revealing their locations over the radio. Even trench lines were poor defenses against 2-ton bombs delivered within 10 to 15 meters of their targets. Just what Taliban fighters could have done differently, once stranded in that open terrain, is unclear. They might have been better advised either to go on the offensive or to try to escape back into urban settings under cover of night or poor weather, although many U.S. reconnaissance assets work well under such conditions. But both approaches would have been difficult and dangerous, especially for a relatively unsophisticated military force such as the Taliban.

The third main phase of the war began in early December. By this time, U.S. intelligence had finally pinpointed much of al Qaeda's strength near Jalalabad, in eastern Afghanistan. In particular, al Qaeda forces, including Osama bin Laden, were supposedly holed up in the mountain redoubts of Tora Bora. Traveling with perhaps 1,000 to 2,000 foreign fighters, most of them fellow Arabs, bin Laden could not easily evade detection from curious eyes even if he might elude U.S. overhead reconnaissance. Thus, once Afghan opposition fighters, together with CIA and special operations forces, were deployed in the vicinity, U.S. air strikes against the caves could become quite effective. By mid-December, the fight for Tora Bora was over. Most significant cave openings were destroyed and virtually all signs of live al Qaeda fighters disappeared. Sporadic bombing continued in the area, and it was not until mid-January that a major al Qaeda training base, Zawar Kili, was destroyed. But most bombing ended by late 2001.

So why did bin Laden and other top al Qaeda leaders apparently get away? The United States relied too much on Pakistan and its Afghan allies to close off possible escape routes from the Tora Bora region. It is not clear that these allies had the same incentives as the United States to conduct the effort with dogged persistence. Moreover, the mission was inherently difficult. By mid-December, the Pentagon felt considerably less sure than it had been of the likely whereabouts of bin Laden, even though it suspected that he and most of his top lieutenants were still alive.

Although estimates remain rough, Taliban losses in the war were considerable. According to New York Times correspondent Nicholas Kristof, as many as 8,000 to 12,000 were killed—roughly 20 percent of the Taliban's initial fighting capability. Assuming conservatively at least two wounded for every person killed, Taliban losses could have represented half their initial fighting strength, a point at which most armies have traditionally started to crumble. Another 7,000 or more were taken prisoner. Kristof's tally also suggests that Afghan civilian casualties totaled only about 1,000, a mercifully low number despite several wrongly targeted U.S. bombings and raids during the war. Although a couple of those U.S. mistakes probably should have been prevented, they do not change the basic conclusion that the war caused relatively modest harm to innocents.

U.S. forces had lost about 30 personnel by the middle of March: about a dozen on the battlefield (8 during Operation Anaconda) and the rest in and around Afghanistan through accidents. Most were Marine Corps and Army troops, but other personnel were lost as well, including a CIA operative. The casualty total was 50 percent greater than those of the invasions of Grenada and Haiti in the 1980s but less than the number of troops killed in Somalia in 1992-93.

FOLLOW THE LEADER

On the whole, Operation Enduring Freedom has been masterful in both design and execution. Using specially equipped CIA teams and special operations forces in tandem with precision-strike aircraft allowed for accurate and effective bombing of Taliban and al Qaeda positions. U.S. personnel also contributed immensely to helping the Northern Alliance tactically and logistically. By early November, the strategy had produced mass Taliban retreats in the north of the country; it had probably caused many Taliban casualties as well.

More notably, the U.S. effort helped quickly galvanize Pashtun forces to organize and fight effectively against the Taliban in the south, which many analysts had considered a highly risky proposition and centcom had itself considered far from certain. Had these Pashtun forces decided that they feared the Northern Alliance and the United States more than the Taliban, Afghanistan might have become effectively partitioned, with al Qaeda taking refuge exclusively in the south and the war effort rendered largely futile. Convincing these Pashtun to change sides and fight against the Taliban required just the right mix of diplomacy, military momentum and finesse, and battlefield assistance from CIA and special operations teams.

Yet despite the overall accomplishments, mistakes were made. The Pentagon's handling of the al Qaeda and Taliban detainees at Guantanamo Bay, Cuba, was one

of them. Whether these men should have been designated as prisoners of war can be debated. Neither group fought for a recognized government, and al Qaeda fighters satisfied virtually none of the standard criteria associated with soldiers. The Bush administration's decision not to designate the detainees as pows is thus understandable, particularly since it did not want to be forced to repatriate them once hostilities in Afghanistan ended. But it probably would have been wiser to accord the detainees pow rights initially, until a military tribunal could determine them ineligible for pow status, as the Geneva Conventions stipulate.

The pow issue aside, the administration's initial reluctance to guarantee the basic protections of the Geneva Conventions to Taliban soldiers and its continued refusal to apply them to al Qaeda were unwise. These decisions fostered the impression that the detainees were not being treated humanely. This perception was wrong, but it became prevalent. Rumsfeld had to go on the defensive after photos circulated around the world showing shackled prisoners kneeling before their open-air cells; Joint Chiefs of Staff Chairman General Richard Myers talked somewhat hyperbolically about how the detainees might gnaw through hydraulic cables on airplanes if not forcibly restrained; and some Pentagon officials even suggested that the detainees did not necessarily deserve Geneva treatment, given the crimes of al Qaeda on September 11. But Rumsfeld's comments came too late, and America's image in the Arab world in particular took another hit.

The big U.S. mistake, however, concerned the hunt for top al Qaeda leaders. If Osama bin Laden, Ayman al-Zawahiri, Abu Zubaydah, and other top al Qaeda officials are found to have survived, the war will have failed to achieve a top objective. Rather than relying on Afghan and Pakistani forces to do the job in December near Tora Bora, Rumsfeld and Franks should have tried to prevent al Qaeda fighters from fleeing into Pakistan by deploying American forces on or near the border. U.S. troops should also have been used in the pursuit of Mullah Omar and remnants of the Taliban, even though this mission was less important than the one against al Qaeda leaders.

Admittedly, there were good reasons not to put many Americans in Afghanistan. First, Washington feared a possible anti-American backlash, as Rumsfeld made clear in public comments. Complicating matters, the United States would have had a hard time getting many tens of thousands of troops into Afghanistan, since no neighboring country except Pakistan would have been a viable staging base—and Pakistan was not willing to play that role.

But even though Rumsfeld's reasoning was correct in general, it was wrong for Tora Bora. Putting several thousand U.S. forces in that mountainous, inland region would have been difficult and dangerous. Yet given the enormity of the stakes in this war, it would have been appropriate. Indeed, centcom made preparations for doing so. But in the end, partly because of logistical challenges but perhaps partly because of the Pentagon's aversion to casualties, the idea was dropped. It is supremely ironic that a tough-on-defense Republican administration fighting for vital national security interests appeared almost as reluctant to risk American lives in combat as the Clinton administration had been in humanitarian missions—at least until Operation Anaconda, when it may have been largely too late.

Furthermore, local U.S. allies were just not up to the job in Tora Bora. Pakistan deployed about 4,000 regular army forces along the border itself. But they were not always fully committed to the mission, and there were too few well-equipped troops to prevent al Qaeda and Taliban fighters from outflanking them, as many hundreds of enemy personnel appear to have done. Afghan opposition forces were also less than fully committed, and they were not very proficient in fighting at night.

What would have been needed for the United States to perform this mission? To close off the 100 to 150 escape routes along the 25-mile stretch of the Afghan-Pakistani border closest to Tora Bora would have required perhaps 1,000 to 3,000 American troops. Deploying such a force from the United States would have required several hundred airlift flights, followed by ferrying the troops and supplies to frontline positions via helicopter. According to centcom, a new airfield might have had to be created, largely for delivering fuel. Such an operation would have taken a week or more. But two Marine Corps units with more than 1,000 personnel were already in the country in December and were somewhat idle at that time. If redeployed to Tora Bora, they could have helped prevent al Qaeda's escape themselves. They also could have been reinforced over subsequent days and weeks by Army light forces or more marines, who could have closed off possible escape routes into the interior of Afghanistan. Such an effort would not have assured success, but the odds would have favored the United States.

How much does it matter if bin Laden, al-Zawahiri, and their cohorts go free? Even with its top leaders presumably alive, al Qaeda is weaker without its Afghan sanctuary. It has lost training bases, secure meeting sites, weapons production and storage facilities, and protection from the host-country government. But as terrorism expert Paul Pillar has pointed out, the history of violent organizations with charismatic leaders, such as the Shining Path in Peru and the Kurdistan Workers' Party (pkk) in Turkey, suggests that they are far stronger with their leaders than without them. The imprisonment of Abimael Guzmán in 1992 and Abdullah Ocalan in 1999 did much to hurt those organizations, just as the 1995 assassination of Fathi Shikaki of the Palestinian Islamic Jihad weakened that group significantly. Some groups may survive the loss of an important leader or become more violent as a result—for example, Hamas flourished after the Israelis killed "the Engineer" Yahya Ayyash in 1996. But even then they may have a hard time coming up with new tactics and concepts of operations after such a loss.

If bin Laden, al-Zawahiri, and other top al Qaeda leaders continue to evade capture, they may have to spend the rest of their lives on the run. And their access to finances may be sharply curtailed. But they could still inspire followers and design future terrorist attacks. If successful, their escape would be a major setback.

EVOLUTION IN MILITARY AFFAIRS

Even though advocates of the famous "revolution in military affairs" have generally felt frustrated over the past decade, a number of important military innovations appeared in Operation Enduring Freedom. They may not be as revolutionary as blitzkrieg, aircraft-carrier war, and nuclear weapons, but they are impressive nonetheless. Advocates of radical change have tended to underestimate the degree to which the U.S. military can and does innovate even without dramatic transformation.

Several developments were particularly notable. First, there was the widespread deployment of special operations forces with laser rangefinders and gps devices to call in extremely precise air strikes. Ground spotters have appeared in the annals of warfare for as long as airplanes themselves, but this was the first time they were frequently able to provide targeting information accurate to within several meters and do so quickly.

Second, U.S. reconnaissance capabilities showed real improvement. Unmanned aerial vehicles (uavs), together with imaging satellites and jstars, maintained frequent surveillance of much of the battlefield and continuous coverage of certain specific sites—providing a capability that General Myers described as "persistence."

Also notable were advances in battlefield communications. The networks established between uavs, satellites, combat aircraft, and command centers were faster than in any previous war, making "persistence" even more valuable. The networks were not always fast enough, especially when the political leadership needed to intercede in specific targeting decisions. Nor were they available for all combat aircraft in the theater; for example, the Air Force's "Link 16" data links are not yet installed on many strike aircraft. But they did often reduce the time between detecting a target and destroying it to less than 20 minutes.

Perhaps most historic was the use of CIA-owned Predator uavs to drop weapons on ground targets. Aside from cruise missiles, this was the first time in warfare that an unmanned aircraft had dropped bombs in combat, in the form of "Hellfire" air-to-ground missiles. There were also further milestones in the realm of precision weapons, which for the first time in major warfare constituted the majority of bombs dropped. They were dropped from a wide range of aircraft, including carrier-based jets, ground-based attack aircraft, and b-52 as well as b-1 bombers. The bombers were used effectively as close-air support platforms, loitering over the battlefield for hours until targets could be identified. They delivered about 70 percent of the war's total ordnance.

In addition to the laser-guided bomb, the weapon of choice for the United States quickly became the joint direct attack munition (jdam). First used in Kosovo, it is a one-ton iron bomb furnished with a $20,000 kit that helps steer it to within 10 to 15 meters of its target using gps and inertial guidance. It is not quite as accurate as a laser-guided bomb but is much more resistant to the effects of weather. In the Kosovo war, only the b-2 could deliver it, but now the jdam can be dropped by most U.S. attack aircraft. By the end of January, the United States had dropped more than 4,000 laser-guided bombs and more than 4,000 jdams as well.

Other ordnance was also important. Up to 1,000 cluster bombs were used, with accuracy of about 30 meters once outfitted with a wind-correcting mechanism. Although controversial because of their dud rate, cluster bombs were devastating against Taliban and al Qaeda troops unlucky enough to be caught in the open. A number of special-purpose munitions were used in smaller numbers, including cave-busting munitions equipped with nickel-cobalt steel-alloy tips and special software; these could penetrate up to 10 feet of rock or 100 feet of soil.

The ability to deliver most U.S. combat punch from the air kept the costs of war relatively modest. Through January 8, the total had reached $3.8 billion, while the military costs of homeland security efforts in the United States had reached $2.6 billion. The bills in Afghanistan included $1.9 billion for deploying troops, $400 million for munitions, $400 million for replacing damaged or destroyed equipment, and about $1 billion for fuel and other operating costs.

LESSONS FOR THE FUTURE

What broad lessons emerge from this conflict? First, military progress does not always depend on highly expensive weapons platforms. Many important contemporary trends in military technology and tactics concern information networks and munitions more than aircraft, ships, and ground vehicles. To take an extreme example, b-52 bombers with jdam were more useful in Operation Enduring Freedom than were the stealthy b-2s. Second, human skills remain important in war, as demonstrated best by the performance of special operations forces and CIA personnel. The basic infantry skills, foreign language abilities, competence and care in using and maintaining equipment, and physical and mental toughness of U.S. troops contributed to victory every bit as much as did high-tech weaponry.

Third, military mobility and deployability should continue to be improved. The Marine Corps did execute an impressive ship-to-objective maneuver, forgoing the usual ship-to-shore operation and moving 400 miles inland directly. But most parts of the Army still cannot move so quickly and smoothly. Part of the solution may be the Army's long-term plans for new and lighter combat equipment. (The Marine Corps' v-22 Osprey tilt-rotor aircraft may be useful, too, at least in modest numbers and once proven safe.) But the Army could also emulate the Marine Corps' organization, training, and logistics where possible—and soon. The task is hardly hopeless; Army forces were tactically quite mobile and impressive in Operation Anaconda.

Finally, the war showed that more joint-service experimentation and innovation are highly desirable, given that the synergies between special operations forces on the ground and Air Force and Navy aircraft in the skies were perhaps the most important keys to victory.

How do these lessons match up with the Bush administration's Quadrennial Defense Review of September 30, 2001, and its long-term budget plan of February 4, 2002? The administration has basically preserved the force structure and weapons modernization plan that it inherited from the Clinton administration, added missile defense and one or two other priorities—and threw very large sums of money into the budget. The Bush administration envisions a national security budget (Pentagon spending plus nuclear weapons budgets for the Department of Energy) that will grow to $396 billion in 2003 and $470 billion in 2007. (It was $300 billion when Bush took office and is $350 billion in 2002.) The war on terrorism cannot explain this growth; its annual costs are currently expected to be less than $10 billion after 2003. That $470 billion figure for 2007 is a whopping $100 billion more than the Clinton administration envisioned for the same year in its last budget plan.

For many critics who tend to focus on weapons procurement, the problem with Bush's plan is that it protects the traditional weapons priorities of the military services without seeking a radical enough transformation of the U.S. armed forces. But this common criticism is only half right. The Bush administration has an aggressive program for so-called defense transformation, principally in research, development, and experimentation, where it envisions spending an additional $100 billion between 2002 and 2007. If anything, these plans are slightly too generous and ambitious.

In fact, the problem is the traditional one: the unwillingness to set priorities and to challenge the military services to do so as well, especially in the procurement accounts. Despite the lack of a superpower rival, the administration proposes replacing most major combat systems with systems often costing twice as much, and doing so throughout the force structure. This plan would drive up the procurement budget to $99 billion by 2007 from its present level of $60 billion.

A more prudent modernization agenda would begin by canceling at least one or two major weapons, such as the Army's Crusader artillery system. But the more important change in philosophy would be to modernize more selectively in general. Only a modest fraction of the armed forces need to be equipped with the most sophisticated and expensive weaponry. That high-end or "silver bullet" force would be a hedge against possible developments such as a rapidly modernizing Chinese military. The rest of the force should be equipped primarily with relatively inexpensive, but highly capable, existing weaponry carrying better sensors, munitions, computers, and communications systems. For example, rather than purchase 3,000 joint-strike fighters, the military would buy only 1,000 of those and then add aircraft such as new f-16 Block 60 fighters to fill out its force structure.

Other parts of the proposed Bush plan deserve scrutiny, too. After several successive years of increases, military pay is now in fairly good shape. In most cases, compensation is no longer poor by comparison with private-sector employment; as such, the administration's plans for further large increases go too far. The proposed research and development budgets, meanwhile, exceed the already hefty increases promised by Bush during his presidential campaign; given that research and development were not severely cut during the 1990s, such growth seems excessive now. Finally, the Pentagon needs to reform the way it provides basic services such as military health care, housing, and various base operations. Unfortunately, if budgets get too big, the Pentagon's incentives to look for efficiencies often weaken. On balance, the planned increases in defense spending are roughly twice as much as necessary for the years ahead.

A final assessment of Operation Enduring Freedom depends on whether bin Laden and his top lieutenants have escaped Afghanistan. It could be a while before anyone knows; indeed, Rumsfeld has speculated that U.S. troops could remain in Afghanistan into 2003. A verdict will also have to await a better sense of where Afghanistan is headed. Whatever the stability of the post-Taliban government, it is doubtful that the Taliban and al Qaeda will ever control large swaths of the country again. But if pockets of terrorists remain in the country, or if Afghanistan again descends into civil war, the victory will be incomplete. In the former case, Afghanistan could still be an important if diminished asset for al Qaeda; in the latter, the U.S. image throughout the Islamic world may take another blow as critics find more fuel for their claims that Americans care little about the fate of Muslim peoples.

To prevent such outcomes, Washington needs to work hard with other donors to make reconstruction and aid programs succeed in Afghanistan. The Bush administration also needs to rethink its policy on peacekeeping. Its current unwillingness to contribute to a stability force for Afghanistan is a major mistake that U.S. allies may not be able to redress entirely on their own. A force of 20,000 to 30,000 troops is clearly needed for the country as a whole; several thousand troops in Kabul will probably not suffice.

That said, the situation in Afghanistan has improved enormously since October 7—and so has U.S. security. The Afghan resistance, the Bush administration, its international coalition partners, the U.S. armed forces, and the CIA have accomplished what will likely be remembered as one of the greater military successes of the twenty-first century.

GLOBAL WAR ON TERRORISM
Operation ENDURING FREEDOM
Afghanistan

In the aftermath of the 9/11 terrorist attacks, the U.S. Government determined that Usama bin Laden (UBL) and his al Qaeda (AQ) terrorist network were responsible. The Taliban regime in Afghanistan harbored UBL and his supporters, and President Bush demanded that the Taliban hand them over to U.S. authorities. When the Taliban refused, the President ordered U.S. Central Command (CENTCOM) to eliminate Afghanistan as a sponsor and safe haven for international terrorists. The primary objective was to destroy the al Qaeda terrorist network and capture or kill UBL.

Afghanistan is a land-locked country about the size of Texas with a population of around 24 million. The massive mountain ranges and remote valleys in the north and east contrasted with the near desert-like conditions of the plains to the south and west. Road and rail networks were minimal and in disrepair. The rough terrain would challenge any U.S. military effort, especially moving large numbers of conventional troops. Because bombing and cruise-missile attacks, which could be launched quite soon, would probably not be decisive, and because a ground invasion might be decisive, but could not begin for some time, even conventional staff officers realized that an unconventional option could fill the gap between the conventional courses of action.

In September 2001, CENTCOM did not have an unconventional warfare (UW) plan for Afghanistan. Initially, CENTCOM only tasked the Special Operations Command, Central (SOCCENT) with Combat Search and Rescue (CSAR), but SOCCENT planners, nonetheless, developed a plan for a UW campaign for Afghanistan in September. Late that month, after SOCCENT briefed its UW campaign plan, the CENTCOM Commander, General Tommy Franks, said, "Okay. Do it." Thus, SOF would be his main effort against the Taliban.

> The Taliban (taken from "Tulaba," referring to students of Islam) was a Sunni Islamic, pro-Pashtun movement that ruled most of the country from 1996 until 2001, except for some small areas held by Northern Alliance forces northeast of Kabul and in the northwest of the country.

U.S. Army Special Forces doctrine described seven phases of a U.S. sponsored insurgency: psychological preparation, initial contact, infiltration, organization, buildup, combat operations, and demobilization. Other government agencies, such as the State Department or the Central Intelligence Agency (CIA), took the lead role in the first three phases. U.S. SOF and DOD would typically take the leading role in the next three phases: organizing the insurgent forces; buildup (training and equipping the insurgent forces); and conducting combat operations with the insurgents. The final phase would be demobilization, which would involve a variety of U.S. agencies and the newly-installed

Operation RESOLUTE EAGLE

After 9/11, the first SOF counterterrorism operations were not conducted in Afghanistan or even in the Middle East, but in Europe. Islamic extremists had transited the Balkans for years and had been involved in ethnic warfare in Bosnia-Herzegovina. In late September 2001, U.S. SOF learned that Islamic extremists with connections to Usama bin Laden were in Bosnia. SOCEUR forces quickly put together Operation RESOLUTE EAGLE to capture them. U.S. SOF surveilled the terrorists, detained one of the groups, and facilitated the capture of another group by coalition forces. These raids resulted in the capture of all the suspected terrorists and incriminating evidence for prosecution and intelligence exploitation.

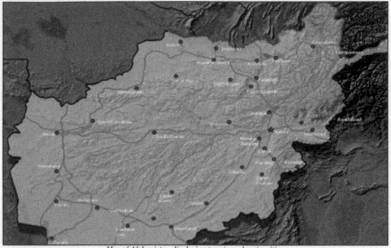
Map of Afghanistan displaying terrain and major cities.

government, so the "lead agency" for demobilization would vary depending on the situation.

The use of indigenous Islamic, anti-Taliban forces (ATF) would undermine Taliban legitimacy and reinforce that the fight was between Afghans, and not a U.S.-led war against Afghanistan or Islam. In September 2001, the only insurgency opposing the Taliban was the beleaguered Northern Alliance (NA), which controlled about ten percent of Afghanistan.

To execute the plan, SOCCENT would stand up Joint Special Operations Task Forces (JSOTFs), the first of which would be established in Uzbekistan and would focus on CSAR and then UW. Beginning on 5 October, Joint Special Operations Task Force-North (JSOTF-N) stood up CSAR operations (under command of Col Frank Kisner) at Karshi-Kanabad (K2), Uzbekistan, and the bombing of Afghanistan began on 7 October. The 5th SFG (A), under the command of COL John Mulholland, deployed to K2 and formed the core of this JSOTF, more commonly known as Task Force (TF) DAGGER. UW became DAGGER's principal mission. This task force included aviators from the 160th SOAR (A) and Special Tactics personnel from AFSOC.

Operations in Northern Afghanistan—Mazar-e Sharif

The UW plan called for SF Operational Detachments Alpha (ODAs), augmented with tactical air control party (TACP) members, to land deep in hostile territory, contact members of the NA, coordinate their activities in a series of offensive operations, call U.S. airpower to bear against Taliban and AQ forces, and help

> **Unconventional Warfare**: A broad spectrum of military and paramilitary operations, normally of long duration, predominately conducted by indigenous or surrogate forces who are organized, trained, equipped, supported, and directed in varying degrees by an external source. It includes guerrilla warfare and other direct offensive, low visibility, covert, or clandestine operations, as well as the indirect activities of subversion, sabotage, intelligence activities, and evasion and escape. . . . Special operations Forces (SOF) provide advice, training, and assistance to existing indigenous resistance organizations.
>
> *Joint Doctrine Encyclopedia*
> *16 July 1997*

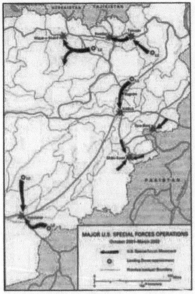

MAJOR U.S. SPECIAL FORCES OPERATIONS
October 2001–March 2002

overthrow the government of Afghanistan (GOA). Bad weather in Uzbekistan and northern Afghanistan delayed the infiltration of the first ODAs in Afghanistan until the night of 19 October 2001. This insertion, and the ones that followed, required a hazardous, two and a half hour flight, at night, through high mountains, and in extremely dicey weather.

After the first 12-man detachment, ODA 595, reached its LZ south of Mazar-e Sharif, it linked up with General Abdul Rashid Dostum, a warlord with a strong power base in this area. ODA 595 split into two elements to better assist Dostum's scattered forces.

Team Alpha began calling in close air support (CAS) from U.S. aircraft, but Dostum initially forbade the team from moving close to the

Taliban lines. He told the SF soldiers, "500 of my men can be killed, but not one American can even be injured or you will leave." Soon, the team chose their own observation posts (OPs), and their calls for fire became more effective.

The massive CAS, brought down by the team, had a huge adverse psychological effect on the Taliban and a correspondingly positive effect on General Dostum's men. Starting on 22 October, Team Alpha rode on horses with Dostum's cavalry, and from OPs, team members called in CAS missions. In one 18-hour period, they destroyed over 20 armored and 20 support vehicles. At first, the Taliban sent in reinforcements, but all that did was provide more targets for the SOF in the OPs. Numerous key command posts, armored vehicles, troop concentrations, and AAA pieces were destroyed by air strikes.

Meanwhile, Team Bravo, also mounted on horseback, moved south and interdicted Taliban forces in the Alma Tak Mountain Range, destroying over 65 enemy vehicles, 12 command positions, and a large enemy ammunition storage bunker. ODA 534, which was inserted in early November to assist Mohammed Atta's forces, also directed CAS to similar effect.

Mazar-e Sharif fell to Dostum and the ODA on 10 November. The capture of Mazar-e Sharif was the first major victory for the U.S.-led coalition in the war in Afghanistan, giving it a strategic foothold and an airfield in northern Afghanistan. The victory once again validated SF's UW role as a combat multiplier. This template was used elsewhere in Afghanistan.

Objectives Rhino and Gecko

On the night of 19-20 October 2001, U.S. SOF airdropped into Afghanistan, seizing two objectives and demonstrating America's ability to assault into Taliban strongholds. The plan called for pre-assault fires and then a Ranger airborne insertion on Objective Rhino and a helicopter insertion/assault on Objective Gecko.

> "Right off the bat," Rear Admiral Albert Calland, SOCCENT Commander, recalled, "we knew that the Northern Alliance was working, we knew the history that the Soviets had, and that bringing a large land force into Afghanistan was not the way to do business. So, it became quickly apparent that the way to do this was to get 5th Group and put them in place to start a UW campaign."

Objective Rhino, a desert landing strip southwest of Kandahar, was divided into four objectives, TIN, IRON, COPPER, and COBALT (a walled compound). Before the Rangers parachuted in, B-2 Stealth bombers dropped 2,000-pound bombs on Objective TIN. Then, AC-130 gunships fired on buildings and guard towers within Objective COBALT, and identified no targets in Objective IRON. The gunships placed heavy fire on Objective TIN, reporting 11 enemy KIAs and 9 "squirters."

After the pre-assault fires, four MC-130s dropped 199 Army Rangers, from 800 feet and under zero illumination, onto Objective RHINO. A Company(-), 3rd Battalion, 75th Rangers, with an attached sniper team, assaulted Objective TIN. They next cleared Objective IRON and established blocking positions to repel counterattacks. C Company assaulted Objective COBALT, with PSYOP loudspeaker teams broadcasting messages encouraging the enemy to surrender. The compound was unoccupied.

A Combat Talon landed 14 minutes after clearing operations began, and six minutes later, a flight of helicopters landed at the RHINO forward arming and refueling point (FARP). Air Force Special Tactics Squadron (STS) personnel also surveyed the desert landing strip, and overhead AC-130s fired upon enemy reinforcements. After more than five hours on the ground, the Rangers boarded MC-130s and departed, leaving behind PSYOP leaflets.

Objective GECKO was the compound belonging to Taliban leader Mullah Mohammed Omar. SOF's mission was to disrupt Taliban leadership and AQ communications, gather intelligence, and detain select personnel. AC-130s and MH-60s delivered pre-assault fires on the objective. Four MH-47s infiltrated 91 SOF troopers onto the compound. Security positions were established, and the buildings on the objective were cleared. While the ground forces were clearing the buildings, the MH-60s provided CAS, and the MH-47s loitered waiting to pick up the force. The ground force spent one hour on the objective.

While Objectives RHINO and GECKO were being assaulted, four MH-60K helicopters inserted 26 Rangers and two STS at a desert air strip, to establish a support site for contingency operations. One MH-60K crashed while landing in "brown-out" conditions, killing two Rangers and injuring others.

Securing Kabul and northeastern Afghanistan

On 19 October, TF DAGGER also infiltrated a second detachment, ODA 555, into northeastern Afghanistan to contact the Northern Alliance forces dug in on the Shomali Plains, where they controlled an old Soviet airbase at Bagram. The Special Forces team met with warlords General Fahim Khan and General Bismullah Khan on 21 October at Bagram Airfield (BAF) to establish a plan to retake the Shomali Plains between Bagram and Kabul. Upon surveying the airfield, the detachment discovered that the air traffic control tower was an ideal position for an OP. The control tower provided observation of Taliban forces across the plains, and ODA 555 began calling in air strikes. The calls for fire lasted through mid-November, and "Triple Nickel" was assisted by ODA 594, which inserted on 8 November.

The bombings so weakened the Taliban and its defenses that the Afghan Generals decided to attack south, well ahead of schedule. When the NA soldiers attacked on 13 November, the enemy defenses crumbled, and on the next day, to the surprise of the world press, General Fahim Khan's ground forces liberated Kabul without incident. The Taliban and AQ forces had fled in disarray toward Kandahar in the south and into the sanctuary of the Tora Bora Mountains to the east near Jalalabad.

While prosecuting the fight for Mazar-e Sharif and the Shomali Plains, TF DAGGER simultaneously focused on the central northern area around Taloqan-Konduz, to the east of Mazar-e Sharif. ODA 585 had infiltrated into the area on 23 October to support Burillah Khan. On 8 November, ODA 586 inserted and moved quickly to link up with General Daoud Khan, a warlord who had gained fame fighting the Soviet invaders. By 11 November, SF soldiers had established OPs overlooking the defensive positions around Taloqan and were prepared to call in CAS. Daoud launched his offensive that day, and by midnight Taloqan had fallen, a major victory for the NA. Daoud and his SF began moving west toward the city of Konduz.

On 13 November, Daoud met his first heavy resistance, and after receiving both heavy direct and indirect fire, the SF element repositioned to a different OP, called in air strikes, and helped to repel a Taliban counterattack. Daoud relied on U.S. air attacks to weaken the Taliban, and for the next ten days, the ODAs and their TACPs called in air support to pound Taliban forces near Khanabad and Konduz. Daoud initiated talks with the enemy in Konduz, and the Taliban leaders agreed to surrender on 23 November.

Qala-i Jangi
The Trojan Horse

As part of the terms, the Taliban and foreign fighters would capitulate on 25 November, and the Northern Alliance would incarcerate them in Qala-i Jangi fortress, Dostum's former headquarters. But on 24 November, at a checkpoint near the Mazar-e Sharif airport, NA forces stopped an armed enemy convoy and accepted the surrender of the enemy force, a day early and 100 miles west of the agreed upon capitulation site. Despite warnings by the American Special Forces soldiers, the NA did not search the prisoners and, instead, only simply told them to lay down their arms. The prisoners were taken to the Qala-i Jangi fortress, meaning "house of war." This huge, nineteenth century fortress on the western outskirts of Mazar-e Sharif was divided in half by a 20-foot high mud-brick wall. The enemy prisoners were housed in the southern compound, which contained a storage area for ammunition and weapons and an underground bunker.

As the prisoners were unloaded at the fortress, NA guards attempted to search them, and one prisoner exploded a grenade in a suicide attack, killing himself, two other prisoners, and two NA officers. Later

An Aerial View of Qala-i Jangi.

the same evening, prisoners carried out a second grenade suicide attack against the guards, whom they outnumbered four to one. The next day, two CIA agents went to the fortress to question the prisoners. While they questioned prisoners, the enemy attacked and overpowered their guards, seizing control of the southern compound along with its stockpile of ammunitions and weapons. They killed one of the Americans, Mike Spann, and the second American narrowly escaped but remained pinned down inside the fortress.

The Battle of Qala-i Jangi lasted from 25 to 29 November, and U.S. SOF assisted the NA forces in quelling this revolt. The ad hoc reaction force—consisting of American and British troops, Defense Intelligence Agency (DIA) linguists, and local interpreters—established overwatch positions, set up radio communications, and had a maneuver element search for the trapped CIA agent. The agent escaped on the 25th. The next day, as the SOF reaction force called in air strikes, one bomb landed on a parapet and injured five Americans, four British, and killed several Afghan troops. The pilots had inadvertently entered friendly coordinates

U.S. SOF and NA on the northwest parapet of the Qala-i Jangi Fortress.

411

rather than target coordinates into the Joint Direct Attack Munition (JDAM) guidance system. Later during the battle, AC-130s were used to contain the enemy. Ultimately, the NA forces, supported by tank fire, fought their way into the southern compound. An American team recovered the body of the dead American. On 29 November, the last of the enemy fighters surrendered.

The timing of the enemy uprising suggested that the Taliban planned to use the "Trojan Horse" attack to slip armed enemy soldiers into a lightly defended position near Mazar-e Sharif. Had the gambit succeeded, the Taliban could have controlled the main approach to Mazar-e Sharif and the massive munitions stockpile at Qala-i Jangi, and would likely be reinforced by armed enemy forces pre-positioned nearby. U.S. SOF and NA efforts at Qala-i Jangi prevented that from taking place.

The U.S. SOF officer who commanded the ground force, MAJ Mark Mitchell, received the first Distinguished Service Cross awarded since the Vietnam War for his leadership. A Navy SEAL, BMCS Stephen Bass, received the Navy Cross for his actions and leadership during this battle.

During the Mazar-e Sharif and Taloqan-Konduz campaigns, the NA forces, accompanied by SOF ODAs and joint tactical air controllers (JTACs) directing air strikes, liberated six provinces of Afghanistan. To accomplish this feat, SF and JTAC personnel had traveled by horse, all-terrain vehicle, pickup truck, and on foot along hazardous mountain trails, often at night and in extremes of weather and terrain. They did all of this in about a month with only a few U.S. casualties, while inflicting thousands of casualties on the enemy and completing the destruction of Taliban and AQ defensive positions in the north.

Beside SF and AFSOC, other SOF combat multipliers made significant contributions to the liberation of northern and central Afghanistan. PSYOP leaflets offered rewards for fugitive Taliban and AQ leaders, informed the Afghan people about their pending liberation, and warned them of the dangers of unexploded ordnance and mines. Civil Affairs teams with TF DAGGER began assessing humanitarian needs

Two SOF operators identify targets.

even as the fighting was winding down in northern Afghanistan.

Two Approaches to Kandahar

Following the tactical successes in northern Afghanistan, Kandahar, far to the south, was the next U.S. objective. The populous city was of a different ethnic makeup—Pashtuns, not Tajiks—and was the spiritual and political center of the Taliban movement.

Two separate SF elements infiltrated into the region on 14 November, linked up with anti-Taliban forces, and approached the city from the north and the south, with the host nation commanders picking up support along the way. ODA 574 inserted into Tarin Khowt to support and protect the emerging choice as Afghanistan's future leader, Hamid Karzai. Only two days later, ODA 574 had to act quickly to save Karzai's resistance group from destruction. Fearing Karzai's potential power, Taliban leaders sent 500 soldiers north to crush him. In response, Karzai deployed his handful of men and relied on his SF team for CAS. U.S. planes pounded the Taliban convoy, and the Afghan opposition fighters repulsed the attack.

On 5 December, the U.S. effort suffered a setback. While the Special Forces were calling in CAS, a 2,000-pound JDAM bomb landed in the middle of their position. The soldiers were literally blown off their feet. Three Americans were killed and dozens wounded, along with many of their Afghan allies.

As the SF teams were recovering from the bomb accident, Karzai's negotiators finalized an agreement for the surrender of the Taliban forces and the city of Kandahar. On 6 December, the force began moving again toward the now open city.

Meanwhile, to the southeast of Kandahar near the Pakistan border, on the night of 18 November, another SF element from TF DAGGER, ODA 583, infiltrated and joined the local anti-Taliban leader, Gul Agha Sherzai, the former governor of Kandahar. His force was heavily outnumbered by the local Taliban and in a vulnerable position. The SF team moved quickly to provide weapons and food to support his army of close to 800 tribesmen.

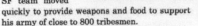
Hamid Karzai (middle row, third from left) and Special Forces.

In late November, the ODA's CAS calls drove the Taliban out of the Takrit-e Pol area, and Sherzai's forces seized the town and the main highway from Spin Boldak to Kandahar. These successes allowed Sherzai's forces to man an OP overlooking Kandahar Airfield, and for the next week, ODA 583 directed CAS on Taliban positions. On 7 December, as his forces moved to attack the airfield, Sherzai learned of the surrender terms Karzai had negotiated. Sherzai gathered his personal security detail and, along with members of 583, sped into the city toward the governor's mansion, his former home. The city had fallen without a shot, and Karzai subsequently confirmed Sherzai as the governor of the city.

Tora Bora

In mid-November 2001, the CIA began receiving reports that a large contingent of AQ, to include UBL, had fled from the area around Kabul to Nangahar Province. Subsequent reporting corroborated AQ presence in the vicinity of Jalalabad and to its south along the Spin Ghar Mountain Range. Analysts within both the CIA and CENTCOM correctly speculated that UBL would make a stand along the northern peaks of the Spin Ghar Mountains at a place then called Tora Gora. Tora Bora, as it was redubbed in December, had been a major stronghold of AQ for years and provided routes into Pakistan. The mountainous complex sat between the Wazir and Agam valleys and amidst 12,000-foot peaks, roughly 15 kilometers north of the Pakistan border. AQ had developed fortifications, stockpiled with weapon systems, ammunition and food within the jagged, steep terrain. The terrorists had improved their positions over many years, digging hundreds of caves and refuges and establishing training camps. UBL knew the terrain from the time of the Soviet invasion and chose it, undoubtedly, as a place to make a stand prior to the onset of winter and to defeat American attempts both to capture senior leaders and destroy the organization. Estimates of AQ troop strength ranged widely from 250 to 2,000 personnel. With large numbers of well-supplied, fanatical AQ troops dug into extensive fortified positions, Tora Bora appeared to be an extremely tough target.

Moreover, the local ATF of the Eastern Alliance [also dubbed Opposition Group (OG) forces], under the command of Generals Hazarat Ali and Haji Zaman, were even more disorganized than those of the NA. Not only were OG forces divided into mutually hostile factions competing for control of Nangahar Province, but each group was also deeply distrustful of American aims. Ali was especially reluctant to ally himself overtly to U.S. forces, given his fears that he would be blamed for introducing foreign occupying troops into eastern Afghanistan. Based on estimates, Ali and Zaman may have had up to 2,000 men, but whether this force would prove adequate to both assault fortifications and encircle the enemy remained to be seen. Given AQ's orientation, surrounding and cutting off the terrorists' egress routes would also prove a tremendous challenge, especially given uncertain force ratios. Added to these challenges were the advent of Ramadan in December and the fact that AQ was known to have a sympathetic following in Nangahar Province, particularly in the vicinity of Tora Bora. The likelihood of successfully repeating combined operations that had worked so well in the Shomali Plains, Konduz, and Mazar-e Sharif seemed remote.

American troop levels in Afghanistan were far from robust in late November 2001. In mid-November, the CIA had deployed one of its "Jawbreaker" teams to Jalalabad to encourage General Ali's pursuit of UBL and to call air strikes against the AQ forces. The Jawbreaker element, however, was very small, and the operatives needed assistance. Few conventional forces were available. At the time, the U.S. Marines had established a small forward base at Rhino, south of Kandahar, and only a reinforced company of the 10th Mountain Division was at Bagram and Mazar-e Sharif.

TF DAGGER had already committed most of its forces elsewhere in Afghanistan. When approached by the CIA, the Dagger commander, COL John F. Mulholland, agreed to commit an ODA and potentially a few others once the "Jawbreaker" team had established a presence and developed a feasible plan. Even if TF DAGGER—or even CENTCOM—had the forces to commit, the existing logistics infrastructure would likely have proven insufficient to sustain a long fight. Few MEDEVAC and resupply platforms were currently in country.

Thus, a general consensus emerged within CENTCOM that despite its obvious limitations, the only feasible option remained the existing template: employment of small SOF teams to coordinate airpower in support of Afghan militia. On 2 December, ODA 572, using the codename COBRA 25, convoyed to Jalalabad both to prod General Ali to attack and coordinate air support.

The forces of Hazarat Ali were a heterogeneous mixture of Eastern Alliance soldiers whose fighting qualities proved remarkably poor. Given its resource constraints, TF DAGGER would permit COBRA 25 only to provide the Afghans advice and assistance with air support, not to lead them into battle or venture toward the forward lines. The plan was to send the Afghan forces into the Tora Bora Mountains to assault AQ positions located in well-protected canyons, with the ODA in OPs. The latest intelligence placed senior AQ leaders, including UBL, squarely in Tora Bora. Directing joint fires and various groups of Afghans toward AQ positions, COBRA 25 hoped to either capture or destroy UBL and his AQ followers.

The detachment moved south out of Jalalabad to General Ali's headquarters near Pachir Agam on 6 December and completed plans to establish OPs along the high ground northwest and northeast of the canyon. The ODA established an OP on the canyon's eastern ridgeline on 7 December with seven personnel and immediately began directing air support. The detachment called the position COBRA 25A. The detachment then established a second OP, COBRA 25B, with six personnel on the northwestern side of the canyon. Small Afghan security elements accompanied each split team to protect them while they called air strikes. COBRA 25B relieved a "Jawbreaker" element that had been in position calling air strikes for five days. The split teams then coordinated air strikes, bottling AQ into its defensive positions and preventing it from moving north.

As COBRA 25 established its surveillance positions, CENTCOM committed an additional SOF Task Force (SOTF), to the fight at Tora Bora. On 8 December, the SOTF assumed command and control of the battle. Lacking the restrictions imposed upon the ODA, the SOTF planned to move its elements farther south in concert with Ali's troop movements and along his front line trace. The SOTF could commit a larger number of U.S. SOF personnel, and even employ a small British contingent. Still, the SOTF force package would total only 50 SOF personnel, and added to the 13 personnel from COBRA 25, the SOF contingent would be up against a much larger force in a mountainous area about nine and a half kilometers wide and ten kilometers long.

Along with General Ali, the SOTF's ground force commander conducted his initial reconnaissance of the Tora Bora area on 8 December. He caught a glimpse of just how well-defended the AQ fortifications were during this reconnaissance. After entering the northeastern portion of the main battle area, the reconnaissance party received accurate small arms and mortar fire. Fortunately, the party took no casualties. The SOTF commander also discovered that General Ali's forces maintained no real front line trace, but rather clusters of troops in the Agam Valley that were scattered willy-nilly.

The restrictions placed on COBRA 25 prevented them from observing activity in the center and south of the battle area. The SOTF commander planned on inserting several OPs forward of OPs 25A and 25B during hours of darkness on 10 December, and augment both 25A and 25B OPs with two SOTF operators each.

In the late afternoon on 10 December, however, General Ali requested that several SOF personnel accompany him to the front to direct CAS in support of a planned frontal assault. With only a five-minute notice, the SOF commander sent two SOF and one translator to support the general

Air Strikes in the Tora Bora Mountains.

and show that Americans would face the same dangers his men did. At about 1600 local, Afghan troops reported that they had not only spotted UBL but had him surrounded, and asked for additional help. Changing mission from planning to execution, the SOTF commander directed his task force (33 soldiers) to move quickly to the front to support Ali. With darkness rapidly approaching, the SOF element spent at least a half-hour convincing Ali's rear echelon to provide guides to the front. Guides secured, the SOF element loaded into six Toyota pickups to begin its ten kilometer trek at 1730 local. Midway en route while traversing a steep,

one vehicle trail, the Americans ran into a convoy of Ali and his men departing the battlespace. As the Afghan forces passed by, Ali promised the TF commander that he would turn his convoy around at the bottom of the hill to continue the pursuit of UBL. Neither Ali nor his forces would return that night.

In the meantime, the two SOF operators who had accompanied Ali began receiving effective fire from multiple AQ positions in the northeast quadrant of the battlespace. Upon receiving fire, the remaining Afghan soldiers fled the battlefield, leaving the two special operators and their translator both stranded and potentially surrounded. These SOF personnel radioed their evasion codeword and began moving under enemy fire toward friendly positions. Fortunately, the SOF evaders had communications with the SOTF soldiers in 25A OP; they sent word to the task force, now mounted and roughly two-thirds of its way to the front.

As the evaders attempted to clear the danger areas, the men of the SOTF tried to locate any Afghan OP with eyes on the AQ front line and UBL specifically. No such position existed. The Afghan guides who accompanied the SOF personnel grew extremely nervous as the party approached known AQ positions and refused to go farther. Faced with the improbable circumstance of Ali's return, much less pinpointing UBL's position at night, the quick reaction force (QRF) turned its attention to recovering the evaders. After moving several kilometers under cover of darkness, attempting to ascertain friend from foe, and negotiating through "friendly" checkpoints without requisite dollars for the required levy to pass, the evaders finally linked up with their parent element. All returned to base to reassess the situation and plan for subsequent insertion the following day.

Despite what, in retrospect, may have seemed a comedy of errors, the events of 10 December proved to be the decisive ones of the operation at Tora Bora. The decision to augment COBRA 25A with two SOTF personnel proved very beneficial. Having observed and recorded the events unfolding at the AQ strongpoint, to include Ali's retreat and the SOF evasion, the SOTF soldiers successfully identified AQ mortar positions and heavy machine-guns. Upon the departure of friendly personnel on the night of 10 December, these two soldiers, along with the COBRA 25A JTAC, called air strikes for 17 continual hours on 10-11 December, knocking out principal AQ positions. The decisive point in the battle for Tora Bora, the actions on 10-11 December, caused AQ elements to retreat to alternate positions and enabled the Afghan militia to capture key terrain in the vicinity of UBL's potential location the following day.

Events of 10 December also led the SOTF to revise its plan. It had originally intended to employ several small OPs while keeping the bulk of its forces at General Ali's headquarters to provide a QRF. The purpose of the QRF was to respond either to sightings of UBL or to employ forces to assist Ali in exploiting an advance. After his experiences of 9-10 December, the task force commander determined that he needed more forces forward to establish a front and thus entice Ali to hold terrain. Additionally, he and his men believed that there would be nothing "quick" about any response from a rearward position, given the difficulties they had encountered and their lack of any rotary wing lift.

Thus, on the afternoon of 11 December, the SOTF elements began their treks into the Tora Bora Mountains. The task force planned to insert at least four OPs in a northern arc and move them gradually forward as they directed joint fires onto AQ posi-

tions. Two mission support sites (MSSs) would deploy just behind the OPs to provide local, dismounted QRF and logistics support and to liaise with General Ali's forces. For the most part, the movements proved slow and hazardous. After a short trip in the ubiquitous pickup trucks, the various SOTF teams unloaded and moved forward on foot with burros carrying their packs. Moving into mountains where the altitude varied from 10,000 to 12,000 feet, they progressed slowly over rocky and narrow paths.

From 11 to 14 December, the SOTF teams continually rained fire onto enemy positions as the Afghan forces of Hazarat Ali began moving into the canyons. The teams hit targets of opportunity, to include the suspected locations of UBL, all the while attempting to avoid fratricide in the absence of any semblance of a front line trace. On the afternoon of 11 December, in a Byzantine twist, Ali's erstwhile compatriot turned rival, General Zaman, engaged in negotiations with AQ elements for a conditional surrender. CENTCOM refused to support the action, but the negotiation caused the SOTF to pause bombing for several hours to avoid fratricide. For each evening through the 14 December, Ali's and Zaman's forces departed from the terrain that they had seized to seek shelter and eat. Ramadan had commenced, and Eastern Alliance forces observed religious requirements to fast during daylight hours. The U.S. SOF were frequently the only individuals

Battle of Tora Bora
6-18 Dec 2001
Final Coalition Troop Disposition

12/16/2001

An SF Soldier assists Eastern Alliance Soldiers in supervising al Qaeda Prisoners.

occupying terrain from the combined effort, save nominal Afghan security details.

Despite the challenges, each day the various SOTF OPs would also move forward to call for more accurate fire and support the movement of Ali's forces. Each night, as the enemy forces would light their campfires to keep warm, the teams used their thermal imagers and optics to bring in bombs and fire missions from a variety of aircraft, including AC-130 gunships. Having obviated the need for OPs 25B and 25A, the task force commander pulled both elements on the early mornings of 13 and 14 December, respectively. By 14 December, the task force commander convinced Ali and his men to occupy overnight the terrain that they had captured. The noose around AQ tightened consistently through 17 December, and the enemy pocket shrank accordingly. By 17 December, Ali declared victory. The general consensus remained that the surviving AQ forces had either fled to Pakistan or melted into the local population. SOTF forces departed the battlefield on 19 December, but without knowing whether they had killed UBL and destroyed AQ in Afghanistan.

The enemy had fought stubbornly; yet, their fortifications proved no match for the tons of ordnance, coordinated by SOF in OPs. Estimates of AQ dead from the battle were hard to determine. the SOTF's ground force commander estimated about 250. What has since been determined with reasonable certainty was that UBL was indeed in Tora Bora in December 2001. All source reporting corroborated his presence on several days from 9-14 December. The fact that SOF came as close to capturing or killing UBL as U.S. forces have to date makes Tora Bora a controversial fight. Given the commitment of fewer than 100 American personnel, U.S. forces proved unable to block egress routes from Tora Bora south into Pakistan, the route that UBL most likely took. Regardless, the defeat for AQ at Tora Bora, coupled with the later defeat during Operation ANACONDA, ensured that neither AQ, nor the Taliban would mass forces to challenge American troops in the field until 2006. SOF elements proved once again that combining airpower in support of a surrogate force could result in a decisive defeat of a well-fortified and numerically superior enemy force, no matter how disciplined.

With the capture of Kabul and Kandahar and the destruction of organized resistance in Tora Bora, Afghanistan was now in effect liberated. It had taken fewer than 60 days of concentrated military operations and only a few hundred soldiers to seize the country from the Taliban and its terrorist allies. On 11 December 2001 Hamid Karzai was sworn in as Prime Minister of the interim government.

ENDNOTES

1. Tony Geraghty: *BRIXMIS—The Untold Exploits of Britain's Most Daring Cold War Spy Mission*—HarperCollins London 1996.
2. Ibid.
3. Colonel Roger M. Prezzelle U.S. Army (Retd) former chief, Special Operations Division, Joint Chiefs of Staff Organization: *Military Capabilities and Special Operations in the 1980s*—in *Special Operations in US Strategy* edited by Frank R. Barnett; B. Hugh Tover; Richard H. Schultz—National Defense University Press & National Strategy Information Center Inc 1984.
4. Gordon L. Rottman: *US Army Special Forces 1952–84*—Osprey London 1985.
5. *The Times* Archive 21 April 2009.
6. U.S. Senator Mike Gravel et al.: *The Pentagon Papers* Vol. 2 p. 439.
7. Winston Churchill: Letter to Japanese Ambassador to London, 8 December.
8. See Alfred H. Paddock: *Psychological Operations, Special Operations and US Strategy* in Barnett, Tover, Schultz, op. cit.
9. Prezzelle op. cit.
10. Fitzroy MacLean: *Eastern Approaches*—Jonathan Cape 1949.
11. Max Hastings: Churchill's War—Daily Mail (London) 22 August 2009.
12. Alan Hoe: *David Stirling—the Authorized Biography of the Creator of the SAS*—Warner Books 1999.
13. Ian Traynor: *UK arranged transfer of Nazi scientists to Australia—The Guardian* 17 August 1999.
14. Robert Gates: *Speech to National Defense University* 29 September 2008.
15. Colonel Charlie A. Beckwith (Retd) and Donald Knox: *Delta Force: The Inside Story of America's Super-secret Counterterrorist Unit*—Fontana Paperbacks 1985.
16. Colonel John T. Carney Jr. and Benjamin F. Schemmer: *No Room For Error—The Covert Operations of America's Special Tactics Units from Iran to Afghanistan*—Ballantine Books 2002.
17. James Bamford: *Body of Secrets: Anatomy of the Ultra-Secret National Security Agency*—Anchor Books 2002.
18. President Franklin D. Roosevelt: *Memorandum to Secretary of State Hull, 24 January 1944*—Retrieved 15 September 2009 from Roosevelt's Trusteeship Concept, U.S. Federal Government.
19. *Pentagon Papers* op. cit. p. 104.

20. Ibid.
21. Ibid.
22. Ibid.
23. Ibid.
24. Air Force General Edward G. Lansdale (OSS & CIA): *Lansdale Team's Report on Covert Saigon Mission in 1954 and 1955*—quoted in *Pentagon Papers* op. cit.
25. Colonel Francis John Kelly: *Vietnam Studies: US Army Special Forces 1961–1971*—CMH Publication 90-23 Department of the Army Washington 1973.
26. Henry Kissinger: *Lessons of Vietnam*—12 May 1975.
27. Joint Research and Test Activity APO San Francisco 96243: *Test of Armalite Rifle, AR-15.*
28. Ken Connor, quoted by David Leppard: *SAS Men get GBP 100,000 To Bribe Iraqi Fighters*—*Sunday Times* 21 August 2005.
29. Kelly op. cit.
30. Ibid.
31. Ibid.
32. Paris D. Davis, Major, U.S. Army: *Report of Action at Camp Bong Son*—Cited in Vietnam Studies, Kelly op. cit.
33. *Pentagon Papers* op. cit.
34. Ibid.
35. Dr. Edwin E. Moise: *Tonkin Gulf and the Escalation of the Vietnam War*—Chapel Hill: University of North Carolina Press 1996.
36. Robert J. Hanyok: *Skunks, Bogies, Silent Hounds and the Flying Fish: The Gulf of Tonkin Mystery*—Cryptology Quarterly Vol. 19 No. 4/Vol. 20 No. 1, Winter 2000/Spring 2001 declassified November 2005. The quarterly is described by Weiner, op. cit., as "a highly classified NSA publication."
37. Hanyok op. cit.
38. Alexander M. Haig Jr.: *Caveat*—Macmillan, 1984.
39. Chairman, Joint Chiefs Special Studies Group report to Secretary McNamara—*Pentagon Papers* Vol IV p. 291.
40. Kelly op. cit.
41. Ibid.
42. William Shawcross: *Sideshow—Kissinger, Nixon and the Destruction of Cambodia*—Andre Deutsch 1979.
43. Shelby L. Stanton: *Vietnam Order of Battle*—Stackpole Books 2003—Retrieved 10 September 2009.
44. Taylor Owen and Ben Kiernan: *Bombs Over Cambodia*—The Walrus ("Canada's Best Magazine") October 2006, retrieved 10 September 2009.
45. Abrams cable obtained under Freedom of Information Act, quoted by Shawcross op. cit.
46. John Morocco: *Operation Menu*—Boston: Boston Publishing Company, 1988.
47. Haig op. cit.
48. Kelly op. cit.
49. Ibid.

50. Ibid.
51. Weiner op. cit.
52. Sedgwick Tourison: *Secret Army, Secret War*—Naval Institute Press 1996.
53. Anon: *The Tet Offensive*—U.S. Library of Congress in countrystudies.us, retrieved 14 September 2009.
54. Ibid.
55. Ibid.
56. Frank R. Barnett, B. Hugh Tovar, Richard H. Schultz et al.: *Special Operations in US Strategy*—National Defense University Press in cooperation with National Strategy Information Center Inc. 1984.
57. Henry Kissinger, Secretary of State: *Lessons of Vietnam*—Memorandum 3173-X The White House 12 May 1975 declassified 24 November 1998, retrieved 14 September 2009.
58. Dr. Sam C. Sarkesian, Professor of Political Science, Loyola University: *Special Operations in US Strategy*, op. cit.
59. Major General Michael D. Healey USA (Retd): *Special Operations in US Strategy* op. cit.
60. See, for example: Susan Lynn Marquis: *Unconventional Warfare: Rebuilding US Special Operations Forces*—Brookings Institution Press.
61. Ben Macintyre: *Obama must face down the ghost of Vietnam*—*The Times* 28 October 2009.
62. Colonel Charlie A. Beckwith (Retd) and Donald Knox: *Delta Force—The Inside Story of America's Super-secret Counterterrorist Unit*—Arms & Armour Press UK 1984.
63. *Iran Hostage Rescue Mission Report*—Statement of Admiral J.L. Holloway III USN (Ret.) Chairman of Special Operations Review Group (Unclassified Version), August 1980.
64. Beckwith op. cit.
65. James Bamford: *Body of Secrets: Anatomy of the Ultra-Secret National Security Agency*—First Anchor Books 2002.
66. Heike Hasenauer: *A Special Kind of Hero*—Special Operations.com2000 retrieved 28 May 2009.
67. Beckwith op. cit.
68. Anon: *Eagle Claw*—www.specwarnet/miscinfo/eagleclaw.htm retrieved 28 May 2009.
69. Carney op. cit.
70. Michael Smith: *Killer Elite—America's Most Secret Soldiers*—St. Martin's Press 2007.
71. Lieutenant-General Philip C. Gast: *Memorandum . . . Intelligence Capability* 10 December 1980 quoted in The National Security Archive, *A National Security Archive Electronic Briefing Book* edited by Jeffrey T. Richelson 23 May 2001, retrieved 4 June 2005.
72. *ISA, Brief History of Unit, 1986* cited by Richelson in National Security Archive 2001.
73. Smith op. cit.

74. Bill Cowan interview, *Target America*, *PBS* late September 2001 retrieved 5 June 2009.

75. Ibid.

76. Ibid.

77. Ibid.

78. Congressional Committee investigating Iran Contra majority report issued November 1987.

79. Richelson: *ISA; United States Intelligence Support Activity 1987, Historical Report.*

80. Ibid.

81. Ibid.

82. Ibid.

83. Alfred W. McCoy and Cathleen B. Read: *The Politics of Heroin: CIA Complicity in the Global Drug Trade*—Harper & Row/HarperCollins/Lawrence Hill Books 2003.

84. Tim Weiner: *Legacy of Ashes: The History of the CIA*—Doubleday 2007.

85. *National Commission on Terrorist Attacks on the US (9/11 Commission Report)* chapter 4.

86. Alan Greenspan: *The Age of Turbulence: Adventures in a New World*—Penguin, 2007.

87. Colonel John T. Carney and Benjamin F. Schemmer: *No Room For Error—The Covert Operations of America's Special Tactics Units from Iran to Afghanistan*—Ballantine Books 2002.

88. James Paul and Martin Spirit: *The Desert Rats Return: The Gulf War 1991 Operation Granby*—http://www.britains-smallwars.com/gulf/sbs.htm.

89. Fred Kaplan—*Centcom's real secret weapon*—Slate: War Stories—posted online 20 May 2003; retrieved 25 October 2009.

90. Simon Jenkins: The rise of imperialism lite is prolonging the Iraqi horror—*The Sunday Times* 16 March 2008.

91. Joyce Battle and Thomas Blanton (eds): *Top Secret Polo Step: Iraq War Plan Assumed only 5,000 US Troops Still There by December 2006*—National Security Archive Electronic Briefing Book No. 214 (14 February 2007). Accessed 12 July 2009.

92. See Col. (Retd) Gregory Fontenot USA, Lieut.-Col. E.J. Degen USA, Lieut.-Col. David Thon USA: *On Point: The US Army in Operation Iraqi Freedom*—Center for Army Lessons Learned, 2004: "Conventional forces are traditionally the supported force and not the other way around."

93. Major Isaac J. Peltier: *Surrogate Warfare: The Role of US Army Special Forces*—monograph, School of Advanced Military Studies US Army Fort Leavenworth, Kansas, 2005.

94. *History of the 10th Special Forces Group (Airborne)*, online at www.soc.mil.

95. Fontenot et al. op. cit.

96. Ibid.

97. Spec. Adrian Schulte, SETAF Public Affairs: *Paratroopers remember the jump into Iraq*—USEUR Public Affairs 23 March 2004.

98. Fontenot et al. op. cit.

99. See Gerry J. Gilmore: *Special Operations Troops Recount Iraqi Missions*—American

Forces Press Service, 5 February 2004, accessed 17 June 2009; Sean D. Naylor: *Battle of Debecka Pass: How 31 Special Forces troops outgunned and outmanoeuvred an overwhelming enemy force*—Army Times 22 September 2003, accessed 17 June 2009.

100. Naylor op. cit.
101. John Simpson: *This Is Just a Scene from Hell*—BBC News online 6 April 2003.
102. Ilene R. Prusher: *Iraqis abandon pledge to resist—and Kirkuk falls*—Christian Science Monitor 11 April 2003.
103. Field Manual 3-05.20: *Special Forces Unconventional Operations.*
104. Fontenot et al. op. cit.
105. Smith op. cit.
106. Fontenot et al. op. cit.
107. Jon Swain, Marie Colvin, Christina Lamb, Mark Franchetti: *Focus: Battle for Iraq: Aftershock*—Sunday Times 23 March 2003.
108. James W. Crawley: *SEALs Give Glimpse of Missions in Iraq*—San Diego Union-Tribune 27 June 2003; Robert Winnett and Justin Sparks: *Saddam's sea of fire foiled by Polish SAS*—Sunday Times 29 February 2004.
109. Vice Admiral William Gortney: *Rescue of Captain Richard Phillips*—DoD News Briefing 12 April 2009.
110. Lieutenant-Colonel Terry Ferrell cited by Fontenot op. cit.
111. Steve Call: *Danger Close: Tactical Air Controllers in Afghanistan and Iraq*—Texas A&M University Press 2007.
112. Tim Dyhouse: *'Black Ops' Shine in Iraq War*—VFW Magazine 1 February 2004.
113. Anon: *Saddam bounty may go unclaimed*—CN 15 December 2003 retrieved 25 June 2009; Mary Leonard and Tatsha Robgertson: *For colonel, search mission was a perfect fit*—Boston Globe 16 December 2003; Anon: *How Saddam Hussein was captured*—BBC News 15 December 2003 accessed 25 June 2009; David Pratt: *Revealed: Who Really Found Saddam?*—Sunday Herald (Scotland) 21 December 2003.
114. David Leppard: *US says it has right to kidnap British citizens*—The Sunday Times 2 December 2007.
115. Richard Owen: *23 CIA agents are sentenced over 'extraordinary rendition' kidnap*—The Times 5 November 2009.
116. Smith op. cit.
117. Ann Scott-Tyson: *Anatomy of the raid on Hussein's sons*—Christian Science Monitor 24 July 2003.
118. Scott MacLeod: *Zarqawi's Last Dinner Party: We go inside the search for the ringleader of al-Qaida in Iraq*—Army Times 8 May 2006; Sean D. Naylor: *Spec ops' 'unblinking eye' leads to airstrike that kills terrorist leader*—Marine Corps Times 9 June 2006; Hala Jaber et al.: *How Iraq's ghost of death was cornered*—Sunday Times 11 June 2006.
119. Shane Bauer: *Iraq's New Death Squad*—The Nation 3 June 2009.
120. Richard Holbrook: *To End A War*—Random House 1999.
121. Jeff McKaughan: *Interview with Michael G. Vickers, Assistant Secretary of Defense for Special Operations*—Special Operations Technology 14 November 2007.

122. Isabel Oakeshott and Michael Smith: *SAS to expand in army shake-up—Sunday Times* 26 April 2009.

123. John D. Negroponte and Porter J. Goss: *Establishment of the National Clandestine Service—*CIA press release 13 October 2005.

124. Colonel Kathryn Stone: *"All Necessary Means": Employing CIA Operatives in a Warfighting Role Alongside Special Operations Forces—*U.S. Army War College Strategy Research Project Academic Research Paper.

125. Gary C. Schroen: *First In: An Insider's Account of How the CIA Spearheaded the War on Terror in Afghanistan—*Presidio Press 2005.

126. Robert Gates: *From The Shadows: The Ultimate Insider's Story of Five Presidents and How They Won the Cold War: 1997—*Simon & Schuster 1996.

127. See Geraghty: *Guns For Hire—*Pegasus 2009.

128. Ken Connor: *Ghost Force: The Secret History of the SAS—*Cassell 1998.

129. Schroen op. cit.

130. Dana Priest: *"Team 555" Shaped A New Way of War . . .—*Washington Post 3 April 2002.

131. Stone op. cit.

132. Ibid.

133. Colin Soloway: *"He's Got To Decide . . ."* —Newsweek Web Exclusive updated 6 December 2001, retrieved 12 May 2009.

134. Steve Coll: *Ghost Wars: The Secret History of the CIA, Afghanistan and Bin Laden From the Soviet Invasion to September 10, 2001—*Penguin Books 2005.

135. Professor Richard Schultz: *Preempting Terrorists was not an Option: The Non-Use of SOF CT Units in the 1990s* cited in *Rowan Scarborough: Rumsfeld's War: The Untold Story of America's Anti-terrorist commander;* see also Michael Smith, *Killer Elite* op. cit.

136. Bruce Anderson: *Is This How Bin Laden Escaped?—The Spectator* 12 February 2002.

137. Richard L. Kugler, Michael Baranick and Hans Bennendijk: *Operation Anaconda, Lessons for Joint Operations—*Center for Technology and National Security Policy, National Defense University, March 2009.

138. See Interview with Lt. Col. Rowan Tink, Australian SAS commander, in Defence Talk Forum online.

139. *Operation Enduring Freedom: The US Army in Afghanistan—*U.S. Army Center for Military History.

140. Ibid.

141. Anon: *Operation Anaconda—*Wikipedia, retrieved 14 May 2009.

142. Ibid.

143. *Operation Enduring Freedom* op. cit.

144. Ibid.

145. Seymour Hersh: *Chain of Command: The Road from 9/11 to Abu Ghraib—*Harper-Collins 2004.

146. *Operation Anaconda: Lessons for Joint Operations* op. cit.

147. Jonathan Wiseman: *CIA, Pentagon feuding complicates war effort—USA Today* 17 June 2002.

148. Professor Marc W. Herold: *The Problem With Predator*—Cursor.org posted 12 January 2003 retrieved 8 May 2009.
149. Olivier Roy: *The Lessons of the Soviet/Afghan War*—Adelphi Press 259, International Institute for Strategic Studies/Brassey's 1991.
150. Carney op. cit.
151. Douglas Waller: *How Rumsfeld Plans to Shake Up the Spy Game*—Time magazine 30 January 2005.
152. Schroen op. cit.
153. See *DOD Examines 'Pre-emptive' Intelligence Operations*—Secrecy News, from the Federation of American Scientists Project on Government Secrecy, Vol. 2002, Issue No. 107, 28 October 2002, retrieved 10 May 2009.
154. Marc Carlasco, with Michael Shaikh: *Troops In Contact: Airstrikes and Civilian Deaths in Afghanistan*—Human Rights Watch, September 2008, retrieved 13 May 2009.
155. Tom Coghlan and Michael Evans: *Troops put at greater risk in war on Taleban: Death a price worth paying, says Nato chief*—The Times 9 July 2009.
156. Jerome Starkey and Giles Whittell: *16 dead as bloody Monday turns up pressure on Obama*—The Times 27 October 2009.
157. Imre Karacs: *Opium barons at the top of 'kill or capture' list as US targets Taleban moneymen*—The Times 11 August 2009.
158. Senator John F. Kerry, chairman, Senate Committee on Foreign Relations: *Afghanistan's Narco War. Breaking the Link between Drug Traffickers and Insurgents*—U.S. Government Printing Office 2009; See Appendix 2.
159. Anthony Dworkin: *Israel's High Court on Targeted Killing: A Model for the War on Terror?*—Crimes of War Project 15 December 2006, retrieved 3 November 2009.
160. Kerry op. cit.
161. Tom Coghlan: *We thought Italian soldiers had betrayed us, says Taleban fighter: French demand answers over 'deal'*—The Times 16 October 2009.
162. Michael Evans: *Army tells its soldiers to 'bribe' the Taleban*—The Times 17 November 2009.
163. Kerry op. cit.
164. Stephen Grey: *'Lawrence of Afghanistan' and the lost chance to win over Taliban fighters*—Sunday Times 29 March 2009.
165. David Wise: *Why the Spooks Shouldn't Run Wars*—Time magazine 3 February 2003.
166. Tim Reid: *Security firm aided CIA assassination plan*—contractor ran training in hunt for al-Qaida—The Times 21 August 2009.
167. Robert Baer: *Blackwater Hit Squads: What Was the CIA Thinking?*—Time magazine 21 August 2009.
168. Tim Reid: *Former CIA agent's hunt for bin Laden in Pakistan's badlands*—The Times 9 September 2009.
169. Richard Tomlinson: *The Big Breach: From Top Secet to Maximum Security*—Cutting Edge Press 2001.
170. Johan Meiring BCR: *Major Andre Dennison MLM BCR*—quoted in *The War Diaries of Andre Dennison*—Ashanti Publishing Ltd Gibraltar 1989.

171. Lyman B. Kirkpatrick, CIA Inspector General: *Survey of the Cuban Operation and Associated Documents*—October 1961, declassified 1996, retrieved 8 October 2009.

172. Ibid.

173. Henry Hurt: *Reasonable Doubt: An Investigation Into The Assassination of John F. Kennedy*—Sidgwick & Jackson 1986.

174. HSCA p.129.

175. HSCA: Summary of Findings.

176. Anon: *CIA Activities in Chile*—Central Intelligence Agency Report 18 September 2000 retrieved from https://www.cia.gov/library/reports/general-reports-1/chile/index.html retrieved 22 November 2009.

177. Prime Minister's Office: Secret—Minutes of conversation between the President of the United States and Lord Home, Washington DC, 4 October 1963.

178. Johnny Cooper with Peter Kemp: *One Of The Originals*—Pan/Macmillan 1991.

179. Imperial War Museum/Neil McLean Papers, quoted in Clive Jones: *Britain and The Yemen Civil War 1962–1965: Ministers, Mercenaries and Mandarins: Foreign Policy and the Limits of Covert Action*—Sussex Academic Press 2004.

180. Jones op. cit.

181. CNN: *Good Guys, Bad Guys*—Cold War Special, Episode 18, 1988.

182. Jane Standley: *Cold War In A Hot Climate*—BBC Radio 3, 4 August 2006.

183. John Stockwell: *In Search of Enemies*—Replica Books 1997.

184. Weiner, *Legacy of Ashes* op. cit.

185. Stockwell op. cit.

186. Nina Burleigh: *Two Views of the Land: Some Israeli settlers think they are doing God's work. Palestinians think they are thieves*—Time 17 July 2009.

187. W.R. Inge, Dean of St Paul's, London, 1939, quoted by Robin Neillands in: *A Fighting Retreat: The British Empire 1947–97*—Hodder & Stoughton 1996.

188. *Bricha*—Adam Mickiewics Institute, Warsaw, online at http://www.diapozytyw.pl/site/slownik_terminow/bricha, retrieved 23 July 2009.

189. Ian Black & Benny Morris: *Israel's Secret Wars: The Untold Story of Israeli Intelligence*—Hamish Hamilton 1991.

190. Shlomo Sand: *The Invention of the Jewish People*—Verso 2009.

191. Max Hastings: *The land of imaginary exile*—The Sunday Times books pages, 15 November 2009.

192. Claire Hoy & Victor Ostrovsky: *By Way of Deception: An Insider's Devastating Expose of The Mossad*—Bloomsbury Publishing 1990.

193. Edwin Black, *Why is Jonathon Pollard still in prison?*—JewishJournal.com 2 July 2002, retrieved 22 July 2009.

194. Black & Morris op. cit.

195. Anon: *Terror—He Khazit* (The Front), Lehi underground newspaper, Issue 2, August 1943 retrieved online 26 July 2009.

196. Aviv Lavie: *Inside Israel's secret prison*—Ha'aretz 15 July 2009.

197. Yossi Melman: *Preventive measures*—Bergensavisen (The Bergen Newspaper) 17 February 2006—Retrieved 28 July 2009.

198. Yossi Melman op. cit.
199. Anon: *Obituary, Lieutenant-General Dan Shomron—Daily Telegraph* 29 February 2008.
200. Major Louis Williams: *Operation Thunderball: The Raid on Entebbe—Israeli Defence Forces Journal* May 1985, as abridged in *Israeli Paras*—Orbis 1986.
201. Guy Walters: *Hunting Evil*—Transworld 2009 and *The head Nazi-hunter's Trail of Lies—Sunday Times* 19 July 2009.
202. See, for example, Tim Weiner: pp. 42–43, *Legacy of Ashes: The History of the CIA*—Doubleday 2007.
203. Sunday Times: Insight: *From the archive: The secrets of Israel's nuclear arsenal, revealed—October 5 1986: Insight finds the warhead factory buried in the desert— Sunday Times* 21 September 2008.
204. Mark Willacy: *Israeli whistleblower due to be released from jail*—Australian Broadcasting Corporation 12 February 2004.
205. Ostrovsky op. cit.
206. Robin Wright and Ronald D. J. Ostrow—*Arab Hijackers's Trial to Pose Test of US Terrorism Policy—Los Angeles Times* 20 February 1989.
207. Anon—*Italian court says state secrets breached in CIA kidnap case*—AFP 11 March 2009.
208. Philippe Sands: *Lawless World: America and the Making and Breaking of Global Rules*—Allen Lane 2005.
209. Aviv Lavie op. cit.
210. Anon: *Israeli interrogators in Iraq: An exclusive report—Jane's Intelligence Review* 7 July 2004.
211. Julian Borger: *Israel trains U.S. assassination squads in Iraq—The Guardian* 9 December 2003.
212. Michael Paul Kennedy: *Soldier I SAS*—Bloomsbury 1990.
213. Ken Connor: *Ghost Force: The Secret History of the SAS*—Cassell, 1998.
214. Fred Holroyd with Nick Burbridge: *War Without Honour*—The Medium Publishing Co. 1989.
215. Colonel Michael Mates quoted by the author in *The Irish War:The Hidden Conflict Between the IRA and British Intelligence*—Johns Hopkins University Press, Baltimore, 2000.
216. David McKittrick: *Brian Nelson: Army Double Agent—The Independent* Obituaries 14 April 2003.
217. Anon: *Collusion, murder and cover-up: After 14 years, three inquiries and 144 arrests, Met [Police] chief finally delivers verdict on security forces—The Guardian* 16 April 2003: Edited text of Stevens Inquiry Report.
218. Martin Bright, Kamal Ahmed and Henry McDonald: *British Army ran second Ulster spy . . . The Observer* 20 April 2003.
219. Anon: *Rosemary Nelson inquiry begins work on final report—Belfast Telegraph* 25 June 2009.
220. Nuala O'Loan et al.: *Report Into a Complaint from Rita and John Restorick Regarding The Circumstances of the Murder of Their Son, Lance Bombardier Stephen Restorick on 12th February 1997*—Police Ombudsman For Northern Ireland.

221. General Sir Mike Jackson: *Operation Banner: An Analysis of Military Operations in Northern Ireland*—Ministry of Defence July 2006.

222. Chris Ryan: *The One That Got Away*—Arrow Books 2001.

223. Andy McNab: *Bravo Two Zero: The True Story of an SAS Patrol behind the lines in Iraq*—Bantam Press 1993.

224. Lord Hoffman et al.: *Privy Council Appeal No. 61 of 2002: "R" v. Her Majesty's Attorney-General for England & Wales from The Court of Appeal of New Zealand*—Judgment of the Lords of the Privy Council, Delivered the 17th of March 2003 (Hearing attended by the author).

225. UK Ministry of Defence: *Personal in Confidence: Not for Disclosure*—Letter to Members of the SAS Regimental Association dated 29 August 2002.

226. Alastair McQueen: *War of the Words: SAS Special*—*Punch* magazine, 1996.

227. Connor op. cit.

228. Bernard Gray et al.: *Wasted Billions Put Lives At Risk*—*Sunday Times* 23 August 2009.

229. Michael Evans: *A little Whitehall lie cost years, millions—and lives: Defence officials kept up a 15-year fiction about Chinook deal*—*The Times* 25 August 2009.

230. Michael Evans: *Afghanistan operation was crippled by spending limit, former commander tells MPs*—*The Times* 10 June 2009.

231. Thomas Harding: *Cheap bullets put lives of paratroopers at risk*—*Daily Telegraph* 23 November 2006.

232. John Kay: *Who Dares is Binned*—*The Sun* 17 July 2007.

233. Deborah Haynes—*General Petraeus hails SAS after Iraq success over al-Qaeda car bombers*—*The Times* 11 August 2008.

234. Danny Fortson: *Former SAS chief keeps tabs on workers in world's danger zones*—*Sunday Times* Business Section 5 April 2009.

235. Michael Evans, Deborah Haynes and Anthony Lloyd: *SAS take on Taliban in Afghanistan after defeating al-Qaeda in Iraq*—*The Times* 30 May 2009.

236. Sean D. Naylor: *US officer: Pakistan aided Taliban*—*Army Times* 21 September 2008.

237. Howard Hart interviewed by Brian Hanrahan, *The World This Weekend*—BBC Radio 4 13 September 2009.

238. Lieutenant-General Sir Graeme Lamb, BBC interview 17 September 2009.

239. General Stanley A. McChrystal, Commander, U.S. Forces Afghanistan International Security Assistance Force, Afghanistan: *COMISAF'S INITIAL ASSESSMENT 30 August 2009*.

240. Major-General Nick Carter, commander of ISAF Regional Command South, BBC interview 3 December 2009.

INDEX